NAIS

Journal of the NATIVE AMERICAN *and* INDIGENOUS STUDIES ASSOCIATION

VOLUME 13.1

Spring 2026

NAIS (ISSN 2332-1261) is published two times a year in spring and fall (Northern Hemisphere) by the University of Minnesota Press, 111 Third Avenue South, Suite 290, Minneapolis, MN 55401-2520. https://www.upress.umn.edu

Postmaster: Send address changes to *NAIS,* University of Minnesota Press, 111 Third Avenue South, Suite 290, Minneapolis, MN 55401-2520.

Information about manuscript submissions can be found at naisa.org, or inquiries can be sent to journal@naisa.org.

Books for review should be addressed to *NAIS* Journal, Centre for Indigenous Research and Community-Led Engagement, The University of Victoria, 3800 Finnerty Road, Saunders Annex 130C, Victoria, BC, V8P 5C2, Canada.

Address subscription orders, changes of address, and business correspondence (including requests for permission and advertising orders) to *NAIS,* University of Minnesota Press, 111 Third Avenue South, Suite 290, Minneapolis, MN 55401-2520.

SUBSCRIPTIONS

- **Individual subscriptions to *NAIS*** are a benefit of membership in the Native American and Indigenous Studies Association. NAISA's tiered membership ranges from $25 to $150 annually. To become a member, visit https://naisa.org/.
- For current **institutional subscriptions** and **back issue** prices, please visit: https://www.upress.umn.edu.
- **Digital subscriptions to *NAIS* for institutions** are now available online through Project MUSE at https://muse.jhu.edu.

NAIS

Journal of the NATIVE AMERICAN *and* INDIGENOUS STUDIES ASSOCIATION

CONTENTS

VOLUME 13 ● ISSUE 1

Spring 2026

Articles

Notes from the Field

Critical Review Essays

Reviews

COREY SNELGROVE

Reconciliation and Its Articulations: Crisis, Counter-Hegemony, and the Struggle over Indigenous Self-Determination

Abstract

In this essay, I turn to Stuart Hall's use of articulation—in the sense of both "connection" and "expression"—to examine the politics of reconciliation in Canada. I argue that articulation enables an appreciation of ideological struggle within the politics of reconciliation—the contestation over the meaning of reconciliation—while refusing to treat that struggle as exogenous to social structure and social forces—allowing us to understand what reconciliation is doing. This provides a framework to explain the belated take-up of reconciliation in 2015, as it was then that reconciliation was articulated to a resource-led accumulation strategy across the Canadian federation in an effort to suture crisis. As I argue, the articulation of reconciliation to a resource-led accumulation strategy de-economizes Indigenous self-determination, amplifies patriarchal settler colonialism, and garners consent for coercive action against those who refuse this new arrangement. The upshot of this counter-history of reconciliation is that it (1) foregrounds the role of capitalist property as a constraint on Indigenous self-determination and flourishing; (2) identifies the role and function of "the economy" as a conceptual abstraction in circumscribing Indigenous self-determination and suturing crisis; and (3) facilitates a more productive reinterpretation of the "resurgence-reconciliation" debate as one that revives the politics of counter-hegemony.

IN THE CONTEXT of Indigenous–non-Indigenous relations in Canada, the mid-1990s saw the use of reconciliation shift from sporadic references invoking its ordinary and everyday sense to an explicit ethical idea. As an ethical idea, reconciliation acknowledges historical injustice and signals an aspiration to transform a settler colonial relationship into a noncolonial one. Since 2015, reconciliation has undergone another transition, becoming what Neal Bradford refers to as a "governing idea": an "operational language and organizational framework for state officials"—and in our case, more than state officials—"in implementing and criticizing public policy" on a national scale (1999, 21). Faster than the transition from an ethical idea to a governing idea, reconciliation has since been announced dead. The occasion? In February 2020, Royal Canadian Mounted Police (RCMP) invaded the Unist'ot'en Camp in Wet'suwet'en territory in central British Columbia to ensure construction of a natural gas pipeline. Attentive to the political power of aesthetics, the Unist'ot'en Camp erected a blockade with reconciliation painted in black across a wooden plank connecting two pieces of plywood (Bracken 2020). The reconciliation plank was accompanied by numerous red dresses, a symbol for the ongoing crisis of Missing and Murdered Indigenous Women and Girls. To make their arrests, the RCMP had to break down the blockade, including of course the reconciliation plank, and proceed indifferently past the red dresses. Following the arrests, the Unist'ot'en Camp turned these powerful images into words: "We have had enough. Enough dialogue, discussion, negotiation at the barrel of a gun. Canada comes to colonize. Reconciliation is dead."

The claim—"reconciliation is dead"—spread throughout the country as a hashtag on social media, on placards in the streets, and as a topic of debate in the pages of Canada's national newspapers. This debate over reconciliation and its future has essentially mainstreamed debates that have been taking place across Indigenous and Canadian politics for over a decade. On one side of the debate, reconciliation is criticized as an ideology that obfuscates and depoliticizes ongoing settler colonialism by separating projects of healing from self-determination, manufacturing a break between a colonial past and a postcolonial present, and refusing to connect moments of settler colonialism to its systemic logic and to the capitalist totality of which it is part (Alfred 2009; Coulthard 2014 George 2017; Million 2014; Nichols et al. 2017; A. Simpson 2016a). On the other side of the debate, reconciliation is viewed as more ambivalent, its meaning subject to ideological struggle. On this view, we can and should distinguish between Indigenous and state conceptions of reconciliation (Lightfoot 2020), true from false reconciliation (Wilson-Raybould 2022), reconciliation with and without recollection (Nichols 2019), reconciliation-as-transformation versus reconciliation-as-resignation (Borrows and Tully 2018; Craft 2019). This has been called the "resurgence-reconciliation debate"—because many of the former advance a politics of "resurgence" that calls for the renewal of Indigenous forms of life while displacing "reconciliation" with the state.

This debate raises questions about the relationship between contingency and determination as well as the role of ideological struggle in social change. Resurgence theorists are critical of what reconciliation is *doing,* attentive to the political-economic determinations of settler colonialism that constrain reconciliation as an ethical idea. Defenders of reconciliation can be further distinguished between those who seek to justify the status quo and those who understand and so remain critical of the limits of reconciliation in its current iterations. Setting aside the former, the critical defenders of reconciliation are attentive to ideological struggle over what reconciliation *could* be. For them, the current meaning given to reconciliation is *contingent.* While the pragmatism of this position is grounded in the idea that no concept is immune to co-optation and misuse, critical defenders of reconciliation too often treat this ideological struggle as exogenous to social structure and social forces, while minimizing the countervailing forces and the political-strategic questions of solidarity and alliance it gives rise to.

I argue that Stuart Hall's conception of articulation enables a reinterpretation of the politics of reconciliation. Section 1 illustrates how Hall's conception of articulation provides one method to think of settler colonial society as a differentiated and contradictory totality that refuses all forms of reductionism—economic, political, and ideological. What's more, articulation enables us to incorporate a consideration of both contingency *and* determination as well as the central yet insufficient role of ideological struggle in social change. While Hall never theorized the politics of Indigeneity, let alone the contemporary politics of reconciliation—and remains a "minor" figure in the field of Indigenous studies more generally—it is my contention that his theorization of articulation provides a framework that can explain the belated take-up of reconciliation in 2015 despite its emergence as an ethical idea in the 1990s. Contra the critical defenders of reconciliation, this explanation reveals the necessity and insufficiency of ideological struggle. What's more, Hall's framework also enables a reinterpretation of the resurgence-reconciliation debate in a more productive direction.

Toward these ends, the second section presents a brief history of reconciliation's emergence. I show how the ethical idea of reconciliation emerges in response to Indigenous Peoples' long-standing and multidimensional challenges to existing practices of articulation. Underlying the point that ideological struggle is necessary yet insufficient, the ethical idea of reconciliation was not taken up as a governing idea across the federation until 2015. To be sure, the release of the Truth and Reconciliation Commission's Final Report and 94 Calls to Action was certainly a contributing factor to this. But it wasn't the only factor at play. Deploying Hall's conception of articulation in section 3, I offer a "counter-history" of reconciliation that describes how reconciliation became a governing idea precisely because the long-standing crisis—or in Hall's terminology, organic crisis—of Indigenous resistance to settler colonialism was connected to a conjunctural crisis: namely, the delegitimization of a resource-led accumulation strategy by, among others, Idle

No More, the Defenders of the Land Network, and environmental activists. When the conjunctural merges with the organic, mere defense is insufficient. The response must be formative, involving "a new balance of forces, the emergence of new elements, the attempt to put together a new 'historical bloc'" (Hall [1988] 2021, 43). In our current moment, reconciliation as a governing idea just is this attempt to put together a new "historic bloc," where some Indigenous individuals and governments are included if only as junior partners. This new "settlement" remains dependent on dispossession, though now legitimized through various schemes of distribution (resource revenue sharing, impact-and-benefit agreements, etc.), which amplify patriarchal settler colonialism. Under this settlement, the exercise of Indigenous self-determination remains dissociated from the "economic" where the power of capitalist property is left intact, backed up by the coercive apparatus of the state and insulated by an emerging discourse of eco-colonialism.

This counter-history of reconciliation and Hall's theoretical framework more generally matter for the study and practice of Indigenous politics, reconciliation, and decolonization in three ways. First, this counter-history of reconciliation's emergence foregrounds the structural constraints of capitalist property on Indigenous self-determination and flourishing. While scholars such as Mishuana Goeman (2015, 72) have criticized the limits of the property *form* in expressing Indigenous relationships to land, I foreground how capitalist property mediates the capacities of state-led redistribution and the practice of Indigenous self-determination.

Second, this counter-history identifies the role and function of "the economy" as a conceptual abstraction in both circumscribing Indigenous self-determination and as a vector that enables the formation of a new historic bloc that strives to suture crisis. Recalling Hall's argument about society as a differentiated totality, an articulation of the political, economic, and ideological through historically specific practices, I argue here that there is no such thing as "the economy" in general. However, the emergent discourse of economic reconciliation circulates through this very idea of "the economy" that Indigenous Peoples are now included in. Not only does this wrongly portray immiseration and the rhythms of dispossession as somehow outside "the economy," but it also effectively de-economizes Indigenous self-determination. Indigenous Peoples are included in a naturalized framework that is outside social control, subjecting Indigenous values, traditions, and ethical orientations to the contingencies of capital accumulation on a global scale.

Third, I argue that Hall's theoretical framework enables a reframing of the resurgence-reconciliation debate as one that revives the politics of counter-hegemony. In other words, the resurgence-reconciliation debate raises the question of how to construct an alternative politics of articulation *through* Indigenous self-determination. Whether we look to the contestation of reconciliation that opened this article or the resurgence of economic nationalism, I argue that the structural crisis that gave rise to the "take-up" of reconciliation has not been resolved. This continues to provide the grounds for a counter-hegemonic politics that moves *through* Indigenous self-determination.

Stuart Hall and the Concept of Articulation

Reading across Hall's impressive inventory of political interventions—from youth resistance to policing, from the politics of labor to theorizations of race, from Thatcherism to neoliberalism—one notices the demand to think at the level of the whole. Rather than an expressive totality where each moment reflects and so is subsumed under a single principle, Hall understands the whole as a complex, differentiated, and contradictory totality. Hall's reworking of the concept of totality rejects reductionism in all its varieties—political, economic, and ideological. Coupled with his emphasis on the conjunctural, Hall's analysis remains attentive to the plural sites of conflict and struggle. While he appreciates the politics of singularity, this is not an analysis where the part is elevated at the expense of the whole, nor does this involve conceding to a pluralism of causal explanations. Hall's theoretical and political interventions remain attuned to the "whole": it is about thinking a complex unity, not complexity instead of unity, nor for that matter unity at the expense of difference.

Crucial to this theoretically demanding endeavor is the concept of articulation—understood in the sense of both *connection* and *expression*. Following Louis Althusser, Hall insists that it is through historically specific practices of articulation that political, economic, and ideological levels are *connected* in a historically specific form. What determines the particular form of a complex social order are *practices* of articulation that connect these levels rather than one governing principle alone ([1977] 2021, 86). Antonio Gramsci's concept of hegemony represents one illustrative example of the practice of articulation while also refining the concept, allowing Hall to incorporate the *expressive* dimension of articulation (Hart 2023, 9; Levenson 2022, 187). Practices of articulation connect the economic and political through practices of meaning-making ("expression") that aspire to secure the rule of a historic bloc. These practices of articulation work on common sense to translate the particular political and economic interests of a historic bloc into the supposedly general interests of the masses ([1983] 2016, 162, 169–70).

There is both a methodological and a political upshot of articulation. *Methodologically,* historically specific practices of articulation do not leave the constituent parts untouched. As I'll return to in section 4 , this means that there is no such thing as "the economy" abstracted from its historically specific form. On this point, Hall ([1980] 2021) uses the concept of articulation to reject one-sided explanations of racial capitalism that reduce it to either class or race, which effectively treats these categories as externally related rather than reworked by the other. Instead, Hall insists that racism must be situated in—articulated to—a totality of historical and concrete social relations (235). From this position, Hall famously states that, in some contexts, "race is thus, also, the modality in which class is 'lived', the medium through which class relations are experienced, the form in which it is appropriated and 'fought through'" (239). The method of articulation insists on the development and use of determinate abstractions—*forms* of economy, *forms* of racism, both of which are understood in relation to the complex totality they are part of—rather than general, ahistorical abstractions—*the* economy and *the* practice of racism.

Politically, the concept of articulation is important because while complex social orders are given a particular determinate form through these historically concrete practices of articulation, as practices, the form these social orders take remains contingent rather than necessary (Hall [1983] 2021, 121). Forms of connection can be challenged or loosened (Hall [1983] 2016, 121–22). When these challenges are successful, crisis occurs. "Conjunctural" crises are the more immediate crises that regimes of rule face. Considering this kind of challenge, practices of articulation must be defended and maintained (Hall [1988] 2021, 43). "Organic" crises, on the other hand, are long-standing, and they can last for decades. When "organic" crises become "conjunctural," defense is insufficient (ibid.). New practices of articulation are required. These new practices can represent either *renewal*—where at least some segments of the existing historic bloc are maintained—or *transformation*—where a new form is inaugurated. While both take place through ideological struggle, ideological struggle is insufficient for this transformation (146). Transformation requires the activity of a new historic bloc: where, through ideological struggle, differences are articulated into a "collective will" and "the dispersed conditions of practice of different social groups can be effectively drawn together in ways which make those social forces not simply a class 'in itself,' positioned by some other relations over which it has no control, *but also* capable of intervening as a historical force, a class 'for itself', capable of establishing new collective projects" (125–26, emphasis original). The purposes to which the politics of articulation can be applied, then, are multiple: for stabilization and renewal, a slight modification, or a transformation of a social order (173; Massey and Hall 2010, 57).

The Emergence of Reconciliation

As a settler colony, Canada is a complex and differentiated totality. The political, economic, and ideological levels of the Canadian social formation have taken a particular form through practices of articulation. Practices of meaning-making have been crucial to this articulation. To give just two examples, the criminalization of Indigenous Peoples functions to obfuscate the criminality of settler colonialism (Stark 2016) while the discourse of Indigenous "savagery" and settler "civilization" has functioned to transform cross-racial solidarity against colonial-capitalist development into cross-class solidarity for settler colonial dispossession (Adams [1975] 1995, 73–75). Since the foundation of the Canadian state, Indigenous Peoples have been pressing on these practices of articulation, specifically the political, economic, and ideological contradictions that they attempt to suture. For example, over the twentieth century, Eurocentric justifications for sovereignty experienced a partial delegitimization through anticolonial and Indigenous resistance the world over. In so doing, Indigenous Peoples have loosened prior practices of articulation.

In response to this loosening, practices of articulation were revised from above in an effort to maintain settler colonial relations of rule. Some of these efforts at revision simply failed. Consider, for example, the 1969 White Paper in Canada, which attempted to resolve discrimination and inequality by eliminating Indigenous political difference. In resistance to this attempt, Indigenous political organizations such as the Indian Association of Alberta, Union of British Columbia Indian Chiefs, and Manitoba Indian Brotherhood proposed their own alternatives grounded in histories of treaty-making, negotiation, and political recognition. Faced with a crisis of legitimacy, settler colonial governments were forced into conceding a circumscribed form of legal and political recognition. The best example of this is the political and legal struggles of Indigenous Peoples for decolonization during the patriation process. This led to the inclusion of Section 35 of the *Canadian Constitution Act,* 1982. However, in a result predicted entirely by Indigenous political organizations who had pushed instead for an internationally supervised "imperial conference," the domesticated conferences of Section 37 failed to define the meaning of Section 35, given federal and provincial government recalcitrance (Feltes 2021, 143, 197, 218, 222). In its wake, provinces and the federal government continued to assume Crown sovereignty grounded in unilateral assertion, while Indigenous Peoples continued to refuse this understanding. In the absence of a resolution, the meaning of Section 35 shifts to the courts. After all, when Indigenous Peoples act in accordance with their own legal and political orders, they become criminalized from the view of Canadian law. As Indigenous Peoples defended themselves vis-à-vis the ambivalence of Section 35, reconciliation emerged first as a legal and then an ethical idea in Canada. Rather than rehearsing this history of reconciliation's emergence in extensive detail (for this, see Wylie 2023), I limit myself to just a few key moments and sites of its development. The choices here are governed by a dual purpose: to identify a gap between reconciliation's emergence as an ethical idea and its take-up as a governing idea while documenting the "changing same" of Canadian settler colonialism. This, in turn, allows us to appreciate the importance yet insufficiency of ideological struggle.

Reconciliation first appears in the post-Section 35 legal landscape in 1990 (Wylie 2023, 323). Justice Lamer deployed it in *R v. Sioui,* and then Chief Justice Dickson deployed it in *R v. Sparrow.* In both cases, reconciliation enters the Section 35 jurisprudence in its colloquial sense of rendering things consistent. However, this use had an "asymmetrical" result. In the case of *R v. Sioui,* which dealt with Wendat treaty rights, Wendat *uses* and *understandings* of land had to be rendered consistent with non-Indigenous uses and understandings (Wylie 2023, 323–24; Christie 2005, 48–50). In the case of *R v. Sparrow,* what had to be rendered consistent was the recognition of Aboriginal rights and title (Section 35) and the federal power over "Indians and lands reserved for Indians" (Section 91(24)). For the Court, justifications for infringement could reconcile Section 35 and Section 91(24). While the requirement for justification offers some protection for Indigenous rights (McCrossan 2013, 159–160), this too had an "asymmetrical result" as the power to infringe reproduced the unilateral assumption of sovereignty and legislative power that licenses the federal power to infringe (Nichols 2019, 45).

Around the same time as the emergence of reconciliation colloquially in the Supreme Court of Canada—and with express attention to the limits of the courts (Stanton 2017, 24)—reconciliation was first invoked as an ethical idea in the Royal Commission on Aboriginal Peoples (RCAP) that lasted from 1991 until the release of its final report in 1996. RCAP emerged in response to the failure of the constitutional resolution to Indigenous–non-Indigenous relations, and an uptick in Indigenous-led blockades and occupations—especially the 1990 Siege of Kanehsatà:ke—alongside publicization of socioeconomic disparities between Indigenous and non-Indigenous peoples (Coulthard 2014, 115–119). To resolve these issues, RCAP recommended a return to a treaty relationship—as a model of reconciliation (1996, 122, 658)—based on the inherent rights of Indigenous Peoples as the framework for relations, a public inquiry into residential schools, and an increase in expenditure of $1.5 to 2 billion *above* current spending levels per year for fifteen years (which excluded additional settlement claims).

While critiques have been made against RCAP's ethical vision (for example, Ladner 2001), all three recommendations were rejected. Instead, the 1995 Inherent Rights Policy limited Indigenous self-determination to matters "integral to Aboriginal cultures" or "internal to Aboriginal groups," where conflicts between federal, provincial, territorial, and Indigenous laws are to be resolved in favor of federal and provincial law (Government of Canada 1995, 6). Other areas such as international relations and foreign policy, international trade, and the management and regulation of the national economy are excluded from the exercise of self-determination as "there are no compelling reasons for Aboriginal self-government or institutions to exercise law-making authority" (7). This represents an explicit containment and de-economization of Indigenous self-determination that I'll return to below. Instead of a public inquiry, the government offered a *Statement of Reconciliation* in 1998, recognizing "the mistakes and injustices of the past." Finally, RCAP's call for a $1.5 to 2 billion annual increase above current spending was also rejected. Well short of the RCAP proposal, the government instead announced a $350 million fund to establish the Aboriginal Healing Foundation, and a $250 million fund for economic development, self-government, employment, and social services.

While *R. v. Sioui* and *R. v. Sparrow* mark the introduction of reconciliation in the colloquial sense in the post-Section 35 jurisprudence, *Haida Nation* (2004), the decision that outlined the Crown's Duty to Consult, marks the turn towards reconciliation as an ethical idea within the courts. Rather than reconciling the "pre-existence of Aboriginal societies with the sovereignty of the Crown"—a formulation from Van der Peet (1996) that historicized Indigenous sovereignty while presuming Crown sovereignty—the purpose of Section 35 becomes reconciling "pre-existing Aboriginal sovereignty with assumed Crown sovereignty" (524). Although this discursive shift suggests an understanding of the problem as one of competing sovereignties, the presumption of Crown sovereignty that informs the power to infringe remains. This has the effect of shoring up the position of federal and provincial governments, though now they must meet the procedural requirements under the Duty to Consult. While some see this as a move toward the sharing of power (Stacey 2018), for Robert Hamilton and Joshua Nichols, it circumscribes negotiations between Indigenous and settler political orders. This is because only one party's sovereignty and title are subject to debate, undermining any incentive on the part of provincial and federal governments to substantively negotiate the terms of co-existence (2020, 439).

On the heels of what Dian Million describes as an Indigenous feminist project of resignification—where what was previously seen as personal and private testimonies of residential school abuse are reinterpreted as a political critique of the intimacies of colonialism (2014, 56)—survivors of the residential school system mobilized, organized, and filed lawsuits beginning in the 1980s. Under the threat of a class action lawsuit, the government agreed to settle out of court in May 2005 for over $2 billion. On May 10, 2006, the Indian Residential Schools Settlement Agreement (IRSSA) was signed. The Canadian Truth and Reconciliation Commission (TRC) was funded through the IRSSA—by survivors—rather than the government. In 2008, former Prime Minister Stephen Harper delivered an apology to Indigenous survivors of the Indian Residential School System. Like the previous government's *Statement of Reconciliation,* the apology has been criticized for historicizing colonialism while presenting residential schools apart from the "much broader system of land dispossession, political domination, and cultural genocide" (Coulthard 2014, 125). In light of this, there was some skepticism with the TRC (Alfred 2009). How would the project of healing be connected to the practice of Indigenous self-determination? Would it consider residential schools as an important part of a wider project of settler colonialism, or would it be used to shore up national legitimacy?

To their credit, the TRC took a transformative rather than ameliorative route by "making Indigenous knowledge, perspectives, and practices central to its work, and by expanding the scope of reconciliation beyond residential schools to encompass the whole settler colonial project" (Regan 2018, 211). Rather than the vision of reconciliation offered by the SCC, the TRC understood reconciliation to be a process aimed at establishing and maintaining mutually respectful relationships. What's more, whereas the SCC presumed Crown sovereignty, the TRC did not, offering a vision of reconciliation through Indigenous treaty visions and the United Nations Declaration on the Rights of Indigenous Peoples rather than municipal self-government (see Truth and Reconciliation Commission 2015, 325–27). Where the SCC and RCAP tended to be directed toward federal and provincial governments, with implications for other actors, the TRC was unique in its attempt to connect directly with non-Indigenous individuals, civil society organizations, and corporations through public outreach and dissemination (Nagy 2013, 68; TRC 2015, 27). As former research director for the TRC, Paulette Regan notes that the TRC was meant to be "a catalyst for ongoing public education, dialogue, and action at national, regional, and local levels" (2018, 213). Key to the TRC's messaging was the moral obligation and responsibility of all Canadians—and all institutions and actors, for that matter—for reconciliation.

Following the release of the TRC's Final Report, reconciliation has become what Bradford refers to as a governing idea: "an operational language and organizational framework for state officials in implementing and criticizing public policy" (1999, 21). Reconciliation has been embraced by the prime minister as well as premiers across the country, as well as leaders of political parties. It has been appealed to in elections and included in cabinet mandate letters. The extent to which state officials—and nonstate officials—advance or obstruct reconciliation has been used to justify, evaluate, and criticize policies and political actors across the political spectrum, both within and without the formal political system. While not unanimously accepted, as the phenomenon of residential school denialism speaks to (Carleton 2021), the acknowledgment of historical injustices has catalyzed public consciousness raising and public education reform around the issues of not only residential schools but the ongoing settler colonial project they are a part of (see, e.g., Wilson-Raybould 2022, 3). We are also beginning to see important efforts toward what Naiomi Metallic refers to as "legislative reconciliation," where "governments in Canada [use] their legislative powers to recognize and protect the inherent rights of Indigenous peoples" as a supplement to negotiation and litigation (2023, 38). In the area of child welfare, for example, Bill C-92 *An Act Respecting First Nations, Youth and Families,* enables the federal government to use its legislative power to recognize Indigenous nations' jurisdiction over children and families as an aspect of the right to self-government.

Nevertheless, Eva Jewell and Ian Mosby (2023) have argued that 81 of the 94 TRC Calls to Action remain unfulfilled as of 2023. Even the aforementioned example of legislative reconciliation faces serious and concerning limitations. On the question of jurisdiction, Naiomi Metallic, Hadley Friedland, and Sarah Morales express concern that the act invokes a concurrent law model, which may cause confusion for workers and judges determining which standards and procedures apply, while also effectively making the inherent jurisdiction of Indigenous Peoples dependent upon coordination agreements (2019, 8). On the question of funding, concerns are raised about the lack of commitment to fund according to the standard of "substantive equality," especially given the history of neglect through "jurisdictional squabbling" (9). Returning to the relationship between healing and self-determination, Million (2014) sees the deployment of reconciliation as a co-optation of Indigenous feminism's "felt theory" that tied healing to self-determination. Now positioned as traumatized victims rather than citizens of self-determining nations, Indigenous Peoples are tasked with healing even as colonization remains ongoing (Million 2014, 20, 105–6; see also A. Simpson 2016a). As the arrests of Wet'suwet'en land defenders exemplify,

Indigenous women's more expansive critique of colonial gender violence is contained, and their healing strategies are depoliticized, severed from wider struggles for self-determination and reproducing the public/private divide as Indigenous women and their concerns are subordinated to the "domestic" (Million 2014, 6).

Reconciliation emerges then in response to the loosening of prior practices of articulation. However, as this history has recounted, this did not represent a fundamental transformation but a modification of the existing practices of rule. What's more, this history reveals a gap between the formulation of reconciliation as an ethical idea in 1996 and its take-up as a governing idea across the Canadian federation in 2015. In the next section, I argue that Hall's conception of articulation as both "connection" and "expression" is crucial to explaining this shift.

A Counter-History of Reconciliation

Comments from commissioners of the TRC like the late Murray Sinclair suggest that the gap between the emergence of reconciliation as an ethical idea in 1996 and its take up as a governing idea in 2015 is due to the *audience* of the TRC report—that is, civil society and not simply the state. Here I want to draw attention to another explanation—one that picks up on the insufficiency of ideological struggle. Recall that the RCAP report's vision of reconciliation called for a restructuring of the political relationship between Indigenous Peoples and the Canadian state and redistribution to the tune of $22.5 to $30 billion over fifteen years (excluding settlement claims) in order to achieve substantive equality. However, these demands were presented in the context of the worst economic crisis in Canada since the Great Depression. As others observed, at this moment there was no politically capable citizens' movement able to "defend collective services by forcing the state to raise taxes, particularly on the owners of productive assets, which meant that the fiscal crisis [was] met by calls for restraint and 'market efficiency' in public spending" (Albo 1993, 18). Underscoring Hall's point regarding the necessity yet insufficiency of ideological struggle absent the formation of a collective will, implementing RCAP would have had to involve the formation of a "politically capable' citizens" movement. This movement would have had to be able to both *defend* collective services by forcing the state to raise taxes on owners of productive assets—to block fiscal restraint—but also go on an *offensive strategy* in a settler colonial society primed to see Indigenous Peoples as undeserving of equality in terms of self-determination and public services. This would have entailed the development of a counter-hegemonic politics against austerity that moved through

Indigenous self-determination. In the absence of such a movement, we get a turn to multilevel governance through "sector-specific governance agreements" oriented toward participation in the marketplace rather than substantive self-determination as third-order governments or coexisting sovereignties supported by substantive redistribution policies (Papillon 2014, 125; see also Altamirano-Jimenez 2004 and Kuokkanen 2011). If the failure of RCAP reflected a mismatch between a vision of self-determination and substantive redistribution in an era of fiscal restraint and austerity, this turn to "market citizenship" (Altamirano-Jimenez 2004) was reflective of an overlap between the neoliberal crisis of fiscal restraint, austerity, and self-determination redefined as devolution (Angus 1991; Slowey 2008).

Turning from the failure of RCAP's vision of reconciliation to become a governing idea in the context of fiscal restraint and austerity to the emergence of reconciliation as a governing idea in 2015, it is important to recall a shift to a national resource-led accumulation strategy in the mid-2000s. This is marked most obviously by the election of the Stephen Harper–led Conservatives in 2006. The shift was expressed in both *rhetoric*—Harper announcing the goal of Canada becoming an "energy superpower" in his first speech abroad as prime minister—and *policies* that sought to streamline, if not eliminate, barriers to new projects. This included attempts to liberalize foreign investment flows into resource industries, reduce business taxes, replace Canada's *Environmental Assessment Act* to accelerate the review process, reduce the number of projects that required review, withdraw from the Kyoto protocol, and alter labor legislation to enable temporary foreign workers for resource extraction projects (Stanford 2019, 80; Mills and Tufts 2019, 123). Arguably, the greatest symbol of this shift has been the effort to build new export pipelines to global markets because Canada's traditional export partner—the United States—became a "net exporter" thanks to fracking (Gordon and McCormack 2020).

The embrace of a resource-led accumulation strategy occurred alongside the work of the TRC (2008–2015). It also provided impetus for and political efficacy to the Defenders of the Land Network and the Idle No More Movement. The Defenders of the Land Network emerged as an attempt to develop coordination on a national scale of Indigenous land defense struggles such as blockades and occupations at contested sites of circulation and extraction (Lukacs 2020). The Idle No More movement, which subsequently linked up with the Defenders of the Land network, emerged in reaction to ongoing colonization in the form of omnibus bills passed by the Conservative government that sought environmental deregulation that would erode treaty rights and violate the treaty relationship in order to facilitate economic development in the form of resource extraction.

In an attempt to suture emerging cracks, industry, the Harper government, and the media labeled opponents as "foreign funded radicals" threatening jobs and government revenues, omitting of course corporate profits, low royalty rates, climate concerns, and the emergent yet constrained multinational reality (Neubauer and Gunster 2019, 2). This "symbolic nationalization" of resource extraction represented an attempt to maintain and defend the existing practices of articulation by suturing "the interests of oil sands firms and investors to the 'average Canadian worker' or 'taxpayer'" (ibid.). Opponents challenged this legitimation strategy by invoking the "illegitimacy of extra-regional elites" pushing the pipeline in contrast to their own "popular legitimacy", drawing attention to regional unity as well as Indigenous self-determination (9).

Meanwhile, an alternative practice of articulation was emerging through the 2013 Conservative government-commissioned report, *Forging Partnerships, Building Relationships: Aboriginal Canadians and Energy Development,* authored by Douglas Eyford. This report explicitly called on the government to connect extraction and resource-revenue sharing from such projects to reconciliation. Importantly, the report emerged out of consultation with Indigenous Peoples, industry representatives, as well as local and provincial governments (2013, 3). Essentially, this alternative practice of articulation was more in line with the emergent multinational reality. It was able to speak to both aspects of the crisis—the long-standing organic crisis of settler colonialism and the conjunctural crisis facing a resource-led accumulation strategy. While they commissioned this report, and perhaps blinded by the idea of becoming an "energy superpower," the Conservative government's indifference to this emergent multinational reality expressed in its "symbolic nationalization" strategy meant it was too late to reform their image and heed this advice. By claiming to be the face of change—rolling back extractivism, responding to climate change, and pursuing reconciliation (Neubauer and Gunster 2019, 11)—the Trudeau Liberals were able to return to government.

While some read this resource-led accumulation strategy as an effect primarily of domestic politics (Stanford 2008), it is important to note that this (re)turn to resource extraction is conditioned by the effects of limited alternatives within a capitalist world system, heightened competition in manufacturing sectors, and the absence of an alternative growth engine (Benanev 2020). It is precisely because of these more systemic constraints that, even as they claimed to be the face of change, the Trudeau Liberals have not departed from a resource-led accumulation strategy either (McCormack and Gordon 2020; see also Alook et al. 2023). Importantly, however, they have departed from the Conservatives' legitimation strategy. Picking up on the strategy proposed in the Eyford Report, the Trudeau Liberals have embraced the idea of reconciliation through its articulation to this resource-led accumulation strategy. Across the federation, Conservatives and New Democrats have followed suit.

While available as an idea since the early 1990s, it was not until 2015 that reconciliation appeared to offer an answer across the federation and across the political spectrum to the delegitimization of a resource-led accumulation strategy. Through the practices of articulation that connect reconciliation to resource extraction, the resource-led accumulation strategy can be legitimized as an example of "economic reconciliation" that apparently corrects for colonial exclusion from economic development while it politically disarticulates Indigenous struggles for self-determination from ecological and ontological concerns partly through a discourse of "responsible resource development." While positioning capitalist development as an answer to colonially imposed immiseration is certainly long-standing—it formed the premise of early welfare policies, as Hugh Shewell has argued (2004), and more recent attempts by neoliberals to privatize reserve lands as Shiri Pasternak illustrates (2015)—the publicity and speed of this development is remarkable though explicable. The attempt to shore up legitimacy for resource extraction explains why corporate thinktanks are attached to reconciliation and participate in this ideological struggle in their own right (Yonker 2019), while the increasing dependence on resource extraction for direct revenues as well as investment in light of a crisis of accumulation explains why governments across the federation and party lines have also embraced the concept (McCormack and Gordon 2020). But there is also an attachment to this vision of reconciliation from below because the crisis of accumulation is experienced as austerity, precarity, and immiseration. As others have argued through the concept of petro-populism, resource extraction is presented as a solution to this (Neubauer and Gunster 2019). This resource-led accumulation strategy is crucial then for the more conventional legitimation functions of liberal democracy as well: of winning and maintaining broad political power. What's more, because agreements with resource extraction and circulation companies are justified in terms of jobs and revenue, this same dependence can account for the embrace of this strategy by Indigenous Peoples as well—at the scale of the individual or the band. Indeed, the Indian Resource Council explicitly framed participation in resource extraction as an example of Indigenous self-determination (Quesnel 2019). Similarly, Crystal Smith—chief councillor of Haisla First Nation—justified a benefit agreement with Coastal Gas Link's liquified natural gas pipeline by referencing histories of economic exclusion as well as exhaustion with managing poverty, suicide, and low employment and educational opportunities (J. Ivison 2020; Stephen Buffalo quoted in Alberta Native News 2019). Returning to the failure to implement RCAP in a period of fiscal crisis, this is all "primed" by a colonially imposed, austerity-amplified experience of immiseration (Scott 2022).

Attending to accumulation should not be misread as a return to economic reductionism, as if reconciliation were simply an epiphenomenon of underlying economic changes. The connection of reconciliation to a resource-led accumulation strategy does not occur automatically but by virtue of political and ideological struggle, including struggle from above that works on prior interventions from below that have done much to put reconciliation on the agenda. What's more, this work of articulation from above—connecting reconciliation to resource extraction—is embraced from below precisely through reconciliation's expressive aspects. Colonially imposed, austerity-amplified experience of capitalist immiseration gets 'constructed' as colonial exclusion from economic development. Coupled with an absence of economic vision beyond extraction, reconciliation articulated to resource extraction becomes an expression, then, of Indigenous self-determination through the market (Kuokkanen 2011). In other words, the way in which capitalist property excludes one from meeting their needs encourages an embrace of reconciliation through resource extraction. Here, the owners of capitalist property that, as a class, exclude people from meeting their needs become, as individual representatives of that class, saviors under reconciliation.

When the organic collides with the conjunctural, the structure with the event, Hall tells us that defense is insufficient; a formative response is necessary. The bet of the Trudeau Liberals—and for that matter, former British Columbia Premier John Horgan's New Democratic Party, as well as former Alberta Premier Jason Kenney's United Conservative Party—is that reconciliation could and must become part of their accumulation strategy that included a cross-class and cross-nation coalition. The particular type of accumulation is important here too because one reason behind the possibility of this cross-class and nation coalition, and why reconciliation could be the responsibility of all, is that distribution through resource rents "do not require income redistribution, let alone [capitalist] expropriation", nor does it require productivity increases—two important limits to the RCAP strategy. This is because "commodity-export-led growth is a positive-sum game: governments can boost the incomes of the poor without reducing the wealth of the rich, thus ensuring the political support of the former without provoking the reaction of the latter" (Riofrancos 2019). In Hall's words, this represents "a new balance of forces, the emergence of new elements, the attempt to put together a new 'historic bloc'" ([1979] 2019, 378).

Understanding reconciliation as articulation not only explains its belated take-up in 2015 and the various sources of attachment, but more importantly, it draws out what reconciliation is doing. Reconciliation aims to garner consent for this accumulation strategy as a response to an overdetermined crisis. Crucial to this is the depoliticization of this strategy through a paradoxical politicization of redistribution—in the form of direct Impact and Benefit agreements between corporations and Indigenous nations or in resource revenue sharing between governments that can be used for community-defined purposes—while naturalizing the economy and thus capitalist production—where needs are subordinated to profit and where land remains a resource rather than a relation. The effect of this is the de-economization of Indigenous self-determination; the exercise of self-determination is circumscribed by the market. As Rauna Kuokkanen importantly points out, Indigenous self-determination through the market represents not the elimination of dependence but another form of it (2011, 279). Indeed, at the same time as resource extraction is presented as an exercise of self-determination, it is also surrounded by the language of its opposite: fate (e.g., Quesnel 2019).

While redistribution through resource rents is a positive-sum game providing traction for the "Eden" of reconciliation, in practice, resource extraction amplifies patriarchal settler colonialism. Not only are the purported redistributive benefits of resource extraction gendered (Kuokkanen 2019), but negotiation too often continues the political disenfranchisement of Indigenous women (Yellowhead Institute 2019, 26–27). The final report of the Missing and Murdered Indigenous Women and Girls Inquiry—*Reclaiming Power and Place*—has drawn attention to how resource extraction can increase the burden of reproductive labor on Indigenous women and their exposure to physical and sexual violence (584–94). As Million argued, reconciliation also contains Indigenous women's more expansive critique of colonial gender violence, domesticating it to a private rather than public—and political economic—vision. By placing red dresses along the route of their eventual arrest, the Unist'ot'en Camp used aesthetics to powerfully map these connections.

Finally, if this consent wavers, reconciliation's articulation to resource extraction cultivates consent for coercive action against those who refuse this response. This is one function of the eco-colonialism charge, which is levelled not only against environmentalists, those standing in solidarity with Indigenous land defenders (Ivison 2020), but now those land defenders themselves. Indeed, industry and lobbyists have embarked on a targeted social media ad campaign defending resource extraction as reconciliation and their opponents as eco-colonialists (McCool and Lewton

2022). Moreover, these ad campaigns were directly correlated to the arrest of hereditary chiefs and land defenders protesting the Coastal Gas Link pipeline and the solidarity protests that emerged in response (ibid.). The de-economization of Indigenous self-determination, the amplification of patriarchal settler colonialism, and the cultivation of consent for those who refuse this vision of reconciliation through resource extraction represent key "limits" of the new settlement.

Three Insights of Articulation

Besides explaining the emergence of reconciliation in 2015 and what reconciliation is doing, Hall's conception of articulation has both methodological and political ramifications for the study and politics of Indigenous self-determination, reconciliation, and decolonization. The first insight concerns the role of capitalist property as a constraint on both state capacities and Indigenous self-determination, and so as an object of decolonization struggles. As the failure of RCAP suggests, the capacity of the state to embark on a redistributive program as part of a broader project of decolonization is conditioned by the power of capitalist property. While the state could raise taxes to finance an expansionary redistributive program to address long-standing material inequalities related to public services and historical obligations rooted in treaty, this is conditioned on something to be taxed. The power of capitalist property, including simply the threat of capital flight, can significantly constrain state capacities to redistribute via taxation on owners of productive assets. While an expansionary—and exclusionary—welfare state was financed through an accommodation between the state, capital, and labor, this too was conditioned on the growing profitability of the manufacturing sector after the Second World War. As economies in Western Europe and Japan rebuilt, soon joined by other East Asian countries, competition in the manufacturing sector squeezed profitability, undermining the accommodations that enabled the welfare state in the first place, giving rise to a fiscal crisis. Rather than go on the offensive against the owners of productive assets through increasing taxation, the state pursued cuts to the social wage and increased the share of the tax burden of the middle class. This crisis of profitability continues, undermining the historical conditions for a reemergence of a substantive redistributive policy while also pushing states to pursue resource-led accumulation strategies.

As the justifications for embracing a resource-led accumulation strategy on the part of Indigenous Peoples suggest too, Indigenous self-determination is also constrained by the power of capitalist property. One of the disastrous structuring effects of the settler colonial transition to capitalism—the simultaneous dispossession of Indigenous Peoples and consolidation of capitalist property—is that individuals and nations are excluded from meeting their needs *except* through entering the circuits of capitalism. While the welfare state historically offered some reprieve, it did so by reinforcing paternalistic relations between service-users and government agencies (see for example, Cardinal [1969] 1999, 81–82). In any case, the pursuit of fiscal restraint and austerity in light of the fiscal crisis has only amplified the immiseration that Indigenous Peoples often experience in the form of unpotable water, housing insecurity, and so forth. This is surely one reason why the de-economization of Indigenous self-determination in the 1995 Inherent Rights Policy, the exclusion of Indigenous Peoples from having a say over fiscal policy, for example, must be contested. More fundamentally, though, absent a challenge to the way in which capitalist property appropriates decision-making power over social reproduction while excluding people from meeting their needs, there is little option but to enter the circuits of capitalist accumulation. Given the aforementioned crisis of profitability, and the geographical location of many Indigenous communities across Canada, this often requires an ontological transformation—where land, once seen as a relation, becomes a resource to be extracted to meet one's needs. Rather than a form of repressive authenticity or attributing false consciousness to Indigenous leaders stuck between immiseration and capitalist extraction, the point is to diagnose capitalist property as a constraint on Indigenous self-determination, and so a set of social relations to struggle over. Indeed, if we listen to the words of Indigenous land defenders, including the Wet'suwet'en that opened this article, we can hear this as well. In response to internal and external defenses of the Coastal GasLink project on the basis of its redistributive possibilities—employment and revenue sharing—hereditary chief Na'Moks (John Ridsdale) of the Tsayu Clan challenged the choice of extraction or immiseration, returning politics to the economy: "Yes, they [referring to members who support CGL] need a paycheque, but I think there's better ways to get a paycheque that will look after the environment, that will look after the water, the salmon, our culture" (quoted in Little 2020). What Na'Moks is pointing to here is the way in which capitalist property excludes Indigenous Peoples from meeting their needs except through circuits of capital accumulation, which may very well require the violation of Indigenous values, laws, and ethics (see also Coulthard 2014, 171).

Related to this point, the second insight concerns the political role and function of general, transhistorical abstractions in contrast to historical, determinate abstractions (on this distinction, see Murray 1988, chap. 10). Recall Hall's argument about society as a differentiated totality, an articulation of the political, economic, and ideological through historically specific practices that do not leave the constituent parts untouched. As I argued in the second section, the method of articulation insists then on the development and use of determinate abstractions—in this case, *forms* of economy understood in relation to the complex totality they are part of—rather than general, ahistorical abstractions—such as *the* economy. As this counter-history of reconciliation shows, this methodological principle is also political. The conceptual abstraction of "the economy" not only circumscribes Indigenous self-determination, but it also works as a vector for the formation of a new historic bloc that strives to suture crisis. The emergent discourse of economic reconciliation and the historic bloc that it brings into being circulates through this very idea of "the economy" that Indigenous Peoples are now included in. Rather than asking the question of how one should produce and reproduce life, economic reconciliation assumes capitalist social relations, where profit takes priority over need, and then treats these social relations as a naturalized, transhistorical framework of social reproduction once interrupted by the state whose task now is to correct this departure from the norm through inclusion.[1] On this view, there is no accounting for the ways capitalism undermines social control, as Indigenous values, traditions, and ethical orientations, not to mention the very satisfaction of needs, are subject to and dependent on the contingencies of capital accumulation on a global scale.

The third lesson returns us to the resurgence-reconciliation debate that I opened with. One way to read the so-called resurgence-reconciliation debate is that it is a debate over how to make sense of the politics of reconciliation. Resurgence critics are attentive to what reconciliation is doing and the political-economic determinations that give rise to that project. For some critical defenders of reconciliation, resurgent critics are right in their diagnosis and critique of the existing project of reconciliation. But they insist that this project is contingent, and so it is possible to construct another project of reconciliation. Another way to put this is that the resurgence critics are attentive to the structure of settler colonialism, while the critical defenders are attentive to the event of reconciliation. Attending to the event of reconciliation—the emphasis on what reconciliation could be—helpfully grasps the fact that we're in an organic-conjunctural crisis where defense and stabilization remain insufficient. We're in a moment of "formation" and we can struggle, ideologically, to shape what that new settlement should look like.

The problem, though, is that in reacting against the structural analysis of their opponents (Lightfoot 2020, 168), the critical defenders of reconciliation have presented this ideological struggle as one that is exogenous to the determining force of social structure and, because of this, they are rather agnostic on the question of social forces. This represents an example of what Susan Marks (2009) elsewhere describes as "false contingency," inattentive to necessity. As Marks put it, "Things can be, and quite frequently are, contingent without being random, accidental or arbitrary" and that "there is a kind of necessity which must be reckoned into, rather than always contrasted with, our sense of what it is to be an artefact of history" (2). In contrast to critical defenders of reconciliation, resurgence critics are more attentive to the side of necessity, the determining force of social structure. Indeed, they offer a theory of the settler colonial capitalist state to explain the gap between the promise of reconciliation and the ongoing reality of patriarchal settler colonialism (Coulthard 2014, 7, 35; L. Simpson 2017, 41–2, 45–6, 72; A. Simpson 2016b: 11). This does not lead to "resignation" or "pessimism" as some critical defenders of reconciliation falsely claim (Lightfoot 2020). Nor does it suggest an ontological commitment to "independence" and "separation" (Borrows and Tully 2018, 5–8). Rather, it has led to a more explicit consideration of what social forces one can align with toward the goal of decolonization since access to Indigenous lands and resources is "the foundation of colonial state-formation, settlement, and capitalist development" (Coulthard 2014, 7; see also L. Simpson 2013).

For instance, Leanne Simpson calls for a "radical resurgence," which involves the "re-creat[ion] and regenerat[tion] of [Indigenous] political systems, education systems, and systems of life from within our own intelligence" (2017, 236). Radical resurgence "must respond to the basic social needs of our communities," which includes poverty, clean drinking water, recognition of youth, harm reduction, accountability for gender violence, and care (226–27). For Simpson, this is not something the state "can do for us." This is because of the structural dependence of the state and capital on access to Indigenous lands and resources, and because responding to these needs *is* the work of self-determination. For Simpson, deploying individual and national Indigenous intelligence toward solving practical problems builds "more connection, more engagement with Indigenous thought" and "stronger relationships between our peoples and our lands" (227). What's more, "coming to state power with working alternatives in place, with strong nations, is coming to the state with grounded, authentic Indigenous power" (ibid.). Similarly, for Coulthard, this "turn away" from the state enables some critical distance from the present: This is strategically necessary because it forces the other side to alter its positions in negotiations but also critical for emancipation because it enables an examination into which strategies hold the most promise for liberation and which seek to have the colonized identify with colonially imposed practices and values (2014, 47).

Importantly, this displacement of the state does not lead to a politics of separation and independence but an examination into the cracks of a contradictory society for possibilities of solidarity and co-resistance. As Simpson puts it,

> If we recognize settler colonialism to be dispossession, capitalism, white supremacy, and heteropatriarchy, that recognition points us to our allies: not liberal white Canadians who uphold all four of these pillars but Black and brown individuals and communities on Turtle Island and beyond that are struggling in their own localities against these same forces, building movements that contain the alternatives. (2017, 228–29)

For Coulthard, citing bell hooks, turning away from the assimilative lure of the state is accompanied by "recognizing ourselves and [then seeking to] make contact with all who would engage us in a constructive manner" (quoted in 2014, 48). As he puts it more directly later,

> We also have to acknowledge that the significant political leverage required to simultaneously block the economic exploitation of our people and homelands while constructing alternatives to capitalism will not be generated through our direct actions and resurgent economies alone. Settler colonialization has rendered our populations too small to affect this magnitude of change. This reality demands that we continue to remain open to, if not actively seek out and establish, relations of solidarity and networks of trade and mutual aid with national and transnational communities and organizations that are also struggling against the imposed effects of globalized capital, including other Indigenous nations and national confederacies; urban Indigenous people and organization; the labor, women's GBLTQ2S (gay, bisexual, lesbian, trans, queer, and two-spirit), and environmental movements; and, of course, those racial and ethnic communities that find themselves subject to their own distinct forms of economic, social, and cultural marginalization. (2014, 173)

While the critics of resurgence overstate their critique by misrepresenting the resurgence school as resigned pessimists, ontologically committed to independence and separation, I suggest reframing their critique more productively as a challenge to the resurgence school's muted politics of counter-hegemony. To be sure, there is a politics of counter-hegemony within the work of resurgent critics. We can notice this in the aforementioned discussion of solidarity and alliance but also in the explication of grounded normativity as a form of place-based ethics that not only critiques settler colonial capitalism's treatment of one another and the earth but suggests that Indigenous forms of life have something to teach us about what it means to ensure our forms of interdependence between and beyond human communities become free (Coulthard 2014, 63–4; Klein 2013).

This, then, is less a point of discovery than one of redescribing and underscoring the continued importance of these tendencies at work in Indigenous studies and Indigenous struggles for self-determination more generally. Nevertheless, the counter-hegemonic dimensions of the resurgent politics remain muted. And so, the defenders of reconciliation's insistence on ideological struggle over the meaning of reconciliation alongside their concern over "separation" can be read as pointing to the need for a more explicit counter-hegemonic politics to not only resist the latest wave of settler colonialism under the veneer of reconciliation but to construct a decolonial alternative. The key difference from the critical defenders of reconciliation is that, as Hall teaches, this ideological struggle must be attentive to the social structure that, at present, sets determinate limits to what can be done as well as those social forces that can render those limits contingent through political action. In other words, it must be a politics of articulation: where differences are articulated into a "collective will" and "the dispersed conditions of practice of different social groups can be effectively drawn together in ways which make those social forces not simply a class 'in itself,' positioned by some other relations over which it has no control, but also capable of intervening as a historical force, a class 'for itself', capable of establishing new collective projects" (Hall [1983] 2016, 125–26). As I argued above, ideology is necessary but insufficient for this task. Indeed, as the very history of reconciliation shows—from RCAP's conception of reconciliation to the emergent discourse of "economic reconciliation"—the force of an ideology "depends on the social groups that can be articulated to and by it" ([1983] 2016, 146). What that history also shows is that this will necessarily require an articulation of how such a historic bloc will produce and reproduce life.

To be sure, the concept and practice of hegemony is contentious in the field of Indigenous studies. This is so for at least four reasons. The first is the "unifying" dimension of hegemony. As noted above, hegemonic approaches to social transformation require the articulation of differences into a "collective will." This movement risks the subordination of differences in the name of a fictional unity, as the last forty years of contemporary theorizing have warned.

Picking up on this point about fictional unity, any counter-hegemonic politics will be formulated through deliberation and debate, the latter of which may expose differences not only between parties but within parties—between Indigenous Peoples and within particular nations and communities. As the Palestinian political theorist Raef Zreik acknowledges in a different context, this division among Indigenous Peoples about the future can undermine resistance to settler colonialism (2016, 354–55). Nevertheless, since it involves an attempt to generalize interests, the advantage of a counter-hegemonic politics is that the division that remains inescapable in politics will have to be worked through rather than relying on discourses that naturalize capitalist social relations and so depoliticize the economy on one hand and discourses of repressive authenticity or accusations of false consciousness on the other. Not only do these discourses end debate and deliberation, but they also miss understanding the conditions that enable an attachment to, say, reconciliation as resource extraction. At worst, individuals rather than conditions become the problem. Related to this point, a counter-hegemonic politics will require some articulation of an ethical vision that extends, in this case, to those who currently occupy the role of the colonizer. Hegemony then may fall into one of those "moves to innocence" that Eve Tuck and K. Wayne Yang have cautioned against because it appears to be a move to rescue settler futures (2012, 35). This is a fair concern; Hall himself admitted there are moments when refusal more than hegemony is called for (see Colpani 2022, 238–240). Indeed, Indigenous theorists of resurgence recognize the importance of refusal. Nevertheless, Zriek has cautioned against minimizing the political importance of ethical claims and visions in "influencing peoples attitudes, fears, and conceptions of self and Other" (2016, 356). On this view, the turn to ethics may loosen prior practices of articulation between the state, capital, and settler citizens, while opening new forms of articulation towards different ends. This does not overcome or eliminate the danger identified by Tuck and Yang but shifts it from the realm of absolutes to a consideration informed by an analysis of the conjuncture.

The third reason is that, for Hall, the articulation of differences into a "collective will" necessarily occurs through the state. Given the role of the state in subordinating and dispossessing Indigenous Peoples, this will clearly give some pause for pursuing a politics of counter-hegemony. Is the state simply an instrument that can be wielded for a diversity of ends? If not, must the state be abolished or transformed? How? Is the state the only institutional form capable of articulating differences into a "collective will," or is there another mode of organization that could do so while avoiding the baggage of the state? Since this would require its own sustained analysis, this problem cannot be explicitly addressed here. I only note that the role of the state in the process of decolonization is itself a subject of robust debate within the field of Indigenous studies (see, for example, Bruyneel 2007, xv, xvii), including the resurgence-reconciliation debate and within the work of resurgence critics,[2] and so this alone should not jettison the concept of hegemony.

The final reason why the concept of hegemony is contentious in the field of Indigenous studies is the close relationship of hegemony to "normativity."

This is because hegemony proceeds through the generalization of a new common sense that carries the inherent risk of disciplining and subordinating some social practices over others. Writing at the intersections of queer theory and Indigenous studies, Jodi Byrd (2020) problematizes the role of normativity in resurgence theory on these very grounds. Hegemony, then, may illicit a similar cautionary note. However, Byrd doesn't seem to give up on coalitional politics, and so perhaps there is a role for counter-hegemony in their theory of change. For Hall, hegemony is not about the suppression of difference but an articulation of differences. Giovanna Colpani (2022) tentatively calls this Hall's "queer" theory of hegemony, one that remains open to the eruption of difference requiring its reconstitution (240). Returning to Byrd's queer theoretical critique of the role of normativity in the work of resurgence theorists, perhaps one way to characterize Hall's theorizing of hegemony across his work is that it strives to keep the normative and the anomalous in view, enabling the latter to reconstitute the former.[3]

Conclusion

In this article, I've deployed Stuart Hall's conception of articulation in order to explain the emergence of reconciliation as a governing idea in 2015 and to reinterpret the resurgence-reconciliation debate as one that invites a return to a politics of counter-hegemony. Reading the resurgence-reconciliation debate through Hall and in light of reconciliation's emergence reminds us that ideological struggle is a necessary but insufficient task, as the very power of ideology is dependent on material conditions and the social groups that can be articulated to and by it.

As Hall might have said, there are no guarantees to the success of reconciliation articulated through a resource-led accumulation strategy. As proof of this, one can point to strains from within the more autonomist elements of the Indigenous political movement, as the "reconciliation is dead" slogan signals and the resurgence critics attest to. Between submitting this article and writing these revisions, we have also witnessed the resurgence of economic nationalism across North America—another symptom of the long crisis of profitability that gave rise to the resource-led accumulation strategy (Merchant 2024). The limits of reconciliation can be observed in this moment too, not only through the return of the Canadian flag as a symbol of pride but through the denial of Indigenous Peoples as partners rather than simply stakeholders in responding to this moment—a denial that is symptomatic of how the politics of reconciliation de-economized Indigenous self-determination over the preceding three decades. It is too early to know for certain what will come of this. Nationalism may or may not replace reconciliation as the legitimating discourse of resource extraction in the form of developing intercontinental resource infrastructure or expediting critical mineral development. A resurgence of Canadian nationalism may amplify the reactionary sources of strain to the ethical idea of reconciliation: the active and organizing group of settlers insistent on defending the myth of the settler colonial nation that they feel is robbed from them through the TRC and the historical reconsiderations it has triggered. Or perhaps the moment may disclose the need for a wholesale transformation in how we meet our needs. While this is a time of uncertainty across colonial borders, it may also be a conjuncture ripe for the articulation of a counter-hegemonic vision that refuses settler nationalism, centers Indigenous self-determination, and challenges the constraints of capitalist property, joining the Wet'suwet'en land defenders who opened this essay by asking the question: How should we produce and reproduce our lives together?

COREY SNELGROVE (settler) is an assistant professor in the Department of Political Science at the University of Alberta. His recent publications examine conceptualizations of settler colonialism and the politics of treaty interpretation. These essays can be found in *Theory & Event*, *Legal Form*, *Polity*, and *Philosophy and Social Criticism*.

References

Adams, Howard. [1975] 1995. *Prison of Grass: Canada from a Native Point of View.* Fifth House Books.

Alberta Native News. 2019. "Indigenous Misrepresentation: Indian Resource Council Chiefs Respond To Edmonton Climate Strike." October 18. https://www.albertanativenews.com/indigenous-misrepresentation-indian-resource-council-chiefs-respond-to-edmonton-climate-strike/.

Albo, Greg. 1993. "Democratic Citizenship and the Future of Public Management." In *A Different Kind of State? Popular Power and Democratic Administration,* edited by Gregory Albo, David Langille, and Leo Panitch. Oxford University Press.

———. 2009. "The Limits of Eco-Localism: Scale, Strategy, Socialism." *Socialist Register* 43: 337–63.

Alfred, Taiaiake. 2009. "Restitution is the Real Pathway to Justice for Indigenous Peoples." In *Response, Responsibility, and Renewal,* edited by Jonathan Dewar, Gregory Younging and Mike Degagne. Aboriginal Healing Foundation.

Altamirano-Jimenez, Isabel. 2004. "North American First Peoples: Slipping Up into Market Citizenship?" *Citizenship Studies* 8, no. 4: 349–65.

Alook, Angele, Emily Eaton, David Gray-Donald, Joël Laforest, Crystal Lameman, and Bronwen Tucker. 2023. *The End of This World: Climate Justice in So-Called Canada.* Between the Lines.

Angus, Murray. 1991. *'And the Last Shall Be First': Native Policy in an Era of Cutbacks.* NC Press.

Benanav, Aaron. 2020. *Automation and the Future of Work.* New York: Verso.

Borrows, John and James Tully. 2018. "Introduction." In *Resurgence and Reconciliation: Indigenous-Settler Relations and Earth Teachings,* edited by Michael Asch, John Borrows, and James Tully. University of Toronto Press.

Bradford, Neal. 1999. "The Policy Influence of Economic Ideas: Interests, Institutions and Innovation in Canada." *Studies in Political Economy* 59, no. 1: 17–60.

Bracken, Amber. 2020. "In Photos: Wet'suwet'en Matriarchs Arrested as RCMP Enforce Coastal GasLink Pipeline Injunction." *The Narwhal,* February 10. https://thenarwhal.ca/in-photos-wetsuweten-matriarchs-arrested-as-rcmp-enforce-coastal-gaslink-pipeline-injunction/.

Bruyneel, Kevin. 2007. *The Third Space of Sovereignty: The Postcolonial Politics of U.S.-Indigenous Relations.* University of Minnesota Press.

Byrd, Jodi. 2020. "What's Normative Got to Do with It? Toward Indigenous Queer Relationality." *Social Text* 38, no. 4: 105–23.

Cardinal, Harold. [1969] 1999. *The Unjust Society.* Vancouver and Toronto: Douglas & MacIntyre.

Carleton, Sean. 2021. "'I Don't Need Any More Education': Senator Lynn Beyak, Residential School Denialism, and Attacks on Truth and Reconciliation." *Settler Colonial Studies* 11, no. 4: 466–86.

Christie, Gordon. 2005. "A Colonial Reading of Recent Jurisprudence: *Sparrow, Delgamuukw and Haida Nation.*" *Windsor Yearbook of Access to Justice* 23, no. 1: 17–53.

Colpani, Gianmaria. 2022. "Two Theories of Hegemony: Stuart Hall and Ernesto Laclau in Conversation." *Political Theory* 50, no. 2: 221–46.

Constitution Act, 1982.

Coulthard, Glen. 2014. *Red Skin, White Masks: Rejecting the Colonial Politics of Recognition.* University of Minnesota Press.

Craft, Aimée. 2019. "Neither Infringement nor Justification—the SCC's Mistaken Approach to Reconciliation". In *Renewing Relationships: Indigenous People and Canada,* edited by Brenda Gunn and Karen Drake. Saskatoon: University of Saskatchewan Law Centre.

Eyford, Douglas. 2013. *Forging Partnerships, Building Relationships: Aboriginal Canadians and Energy Development.* Government of Canada. https://www.nrcan.gc.ca/sites/www.nrcan.gc.ca/files/www/pdf/publications/ForgPartOnline-e.pdf.

Feltes, Emma. 2021. *'We Don't Need Your Constitution': Patriation and Indigenous Self-Determination in British Columbia.* PhD diss., University of British Columbia.

Government of Canada. 1995. *Aboriginal Self-Government: The Government of Canada's Approach to Implementation of the Inherent Right and Negotiation of Aboriginal Self-Government.* Ottawa.

George, Rachel YacaaʔaŁ. 2017. "Inclusion is Just the Canadian Word for Assimilation: Self-Determination and the Reconciliation Paradigm in Canada."

In *Surviving Canada: Indigenous Peoples Celebrate 150 Years of Betrayal,* edited by Kiera Ladner and Myra Tait. Arbeiter Ring Publishing.

Goeman, Mishuana. 2015. "Land as Life: Unsettling the Logics of Containment." In *Native Studies Keywords,* edited by Stephanie Nohelani Teves, Andrea Smith, and Michelle Raheja. University of Arizona Press.

Gordon, Todd, and Geoffrey McCormack. 2020. "Canadian Capitalism in Crisis." *Briarpatch Magazine,* February 25. https://briarpatchmagazine.com/articles/view/canada-and-the-crisis-of-capitalism.

Haida Nation v. B.C. (Minister of Forests), [2004] 3 Supreme Court Reports 511.

Hamilton, Robert and Joshua Nichols. 2020. "Reconciliation and the Straitjacket: A Comparative Analysis of the *Secession Reference* and *R v Sparrow.*" *Ottawa Law Review* 52 (2): 403–53.

Hall, Stuart. [1977] 2021. "Rethinking the 'Base and Superstructure' Metaphor." In *Selected Writings on Marxism,* edited by Gregor McLennan. Duke University Press.

———. [1980] 2021. "Race, Articulation and Societies Structured in Dominance". In *Selected Writings on Race and Difference,* edited by Paul Gilroy and Ruth Wilson Gilmore. Duke University Press.

———. [1983] 2016. *Cultural Studies 1983: A Theoretical History,* edited by Jennifer Daryl Slack and Lawrence Grossberg. Duke University Press.

———. [1988] 2021. *The Hard Road to Renewal: Thatcherism and the Crisis of the Left.* Verso.

Hall, Stuart, and Doreen Massey. 2010. "Interpreting the Crisis." *Soundings* 44: 57–71.

Ivison, John. 2020. "The Millennial Eco-activists Stopping Trains Are the New Colonialists." *National Post,* February 17. https://nationalpost.com/opinion/john-ivison-the-millennial-eco-activists-stopping-trains-are-the-new-colonialists.

Jewell, Eve, and Ian Mosby. 2023. *Calls to Action Accountability: A 2023 Status Update on Reconciliation.* Yellowhead Institute https://yellowheadinstitute.org/wp-content/uploads/2023/12/YI-TRC-C2A-2023-Special-Report-compressed.pdf.

Justice, Daniel Heath. 2010. "Notes Toward a Theory of Anomaly." *A Journal of Lesbian and Gay Studies* 16, no. 1–2: 207–42.

Klein, Naomi. 2013. "Dancing the World into Being: A Conversation with Idle No More's Leanne Simpson." *Yes! Magazine,* March 6. https://www.yesmagazine.org/social-justice/2013/03/06/dancing-the-world-into-being-a-conversation-with-idle-no-more-leanne-simpson.

Kuokkanen, Rauna. 2011. "From Indigenous Economies to Market-Based Self-Governance: A Feminist Political Economy Analysis." *Canadian Journal of Political Science* 44, no. 2: 275–97.

Kuokkanen, Rauna. 2019. *Restructuring Relations: Indigenous Self-Determination, Governance, and Gender.* New York: Oxford University Press.

Ladner, Kiera. 2001. "Negotiated Inferiority: The Royal Commission on Aboriginal People's Vision of a Renewed Relationship." *American Review of Canadian Studies* 31, no. 1–2: 241–64.

Lightfoot, Sheryl. 2020. "The Pessimism Traps of Indigenous Resurgence." In *Pessimism in International Relations,* edited by Tim Stevens and Nicholas Michelsen. New York: Springer.

Little, Simon. 2020. "Wet'suwet'en to Consider All-Clan Meetings Amid Solidarity Protests, Internal Division." *Global News,* February 12. https://globalnews.ca/news/6542571/wetsuweten-all-clan-meetings/

Lukacs, Martin. 2020. "The Long Road to This Winter of Protests." *The Tyee,* March 27. https://thetyee.ca/Analysis/2020/03/27/The-Long-Road-This-WinterProtests/.

Marks, Susan. 2009. "False Contingency." *Current Legal Problems* 62, no. 1: 1–21.

McCool, Alice, and Thomas Lewton. 2022. "Canadian Pipeline Groups Spend Big to Pose as Indigenous Champions." *The Guardian,* March 20. https://www.theguardian.com/environment/2022/mar/10/canadian-pipeline-groups-spend-big-to-pose-as-indigenous-champions.

McCrossan, Michael. 2013. "Shifting Judicial Conceptions of 'Reconciliation': Geographic Commitments Underpinning Aboriginal Rights Decisions." *The Windsor Yearbook of Access to Justice* 31, no. 2: 155–79.

Merchant, Jamie. 2024. *Endgame: Economic Nationalism and Global Decline.* Reaktion Books.

Metallic, Naiomi. 2023. "Aboriginal Rights, Legislative Reconciliation, and Constitutionalism." *Review of Constitutional Studies* 27, no. 2: 1–39.

Metallic, Naiomi, Hadley Friedland, and Sarah Morales. 2019. "The Promise and Pitfalls of C-92: An Act respecting First Nations, Inuit, and Métis Children, Youth, and Families." *Yellowhead Institute.* https://yellowheadinstitute.org/wp-content/uploads/2019/07/the-promise-and-pitfalls-of-c-92-report.pdf.

Million, Dian. 2014. *Therapeutic Nations: Healing in an Age of Indigenous Human Rights.* University of Arizona Press.

Mills, Suzanne, and Steven Tufts. 2019. "Innis's Ghost: Canada's Changing Resource Economy." In *Change and Continuity: Canadian Political Economy in the New Millenium,* edited by Mark P. Thomas, Leah F. Vosko, Carlo Fanelli, and Olena Lyubchenko. McGill-Queen's University Press.

Missing and Murdered Indigenous Women and Girls Inquiry. 2019. *Reclaiming Power and Place: The Final Report of the National Inquiry into Missing and Murdered Indigenous Women and Girls.* https://www.mmiwg-ffada.ca/wp-content/uploads/2019/06/Final_Report_Vol_1a-1.pdf.

Murray, Patrick. 1988. *Marx's Theory of Scientific Knowledge.* Humanities Press International, Inc.

Nagy, Rosemary L. 2013. "The Scope and Bounds of Transitional Justice and the Canadian Truth and Reconciliation Commission." *The International Journal of Transitional Justice* 7, no. 1: 52–73.

Neubauer, Robert, and Shane Gunster. 2019. "Enemies at the Gateway: Regional Populist Discourse and the Fight Against Oil Pipelines on Canada's West Coast." *Frontiers in Communication* 4, no. 61: 1–14.

Nichols, Joshua. 2019. *A Reconciliation without Recollection?: An Investigation of the Foundations of Aboriginal Law in Canada.* Toronto: University of Toronto Press.

Nichols, Robert, Audra Simpson, and Glen Coulthard. 2017. "What Comes Next? Reconciliation and Its Afterlives." University of Alberta. Moderated by Fiona Nicoll. October 4. *YouTube.* Posted March 18, 2019. https://www.youtube.com/watch?v=JUycRXCpetY&ab_channel=-ctltech.

Oduro, Franklin and Rosemary Nagy. "What's in an Idea?: Truth Commission Policy Transfer in Ghana and Canada." *Journal of Human Rights* 13, no. 1: 85–102.

Pasternak, Shiri. 2015. "How Capitalism Will Save Colonialism: The Privatization of Reserve Lands in Canada." *Antipode* 47, no. 1: 179–96.

Papillon, Martin. 2014. "The Rise (and Fall?) of Self-Government." In *Canadian Politics,* edited by James Bickerton and Alain-G. Gagnon. University of Toronto Press, 113–31.

Quesnel, Joseph. 2019. "Indigenous Participation in Energy Sector an Exercise in Indigenous Self-determination, Economic Development." *The Hill Times,* December 2. https://www.hilltimes.com/story/2019/12/02/226243/266495/.

R. v Sioui. 1990. 1 S.C.R. 1025.

R. v Sparrow. 1990. 1 S.C.R. 1075.

R. v. Van der Peet. 1996. 2 S.C.R. 507.

Regan, Paulette. 2018. "Reconciliation and Resurgence: Reflections on the TRC Final Report." In *Resurgence and Reconciliation: Indigenous-Settler Relations and Earth Teachings,* edited by Michael Asch, John Borrows, and James Tully. University of Toronto Press.

Riofrancos, Thea. 2019. "What Comes After Extractivism?" *Dissent.* Winter. https://www.dissentmagazine.org/article/what-comes-after-extractivism.

Royal Commission on Aboriginal Peoples. 1996. *Report of the Royal Commission on Aboriginal Peoples, Volume 1: Looking Back, Looking Forward.* Ottawa: Canada Communication Group.

Scott, Dayna Nadine. 2022. "How Does The Settler State Prime a New Extractive Frontier?" *Midnight Sun Magazine,* June 10. https://www.midnightsunmag.ca/how-does-the-settler-state-prime-a-new-extractive-frontier/.

Shewell, Hugh. 2004. *'Enough to Keep Them Alive': Indian Social Welfare in Canada, 1873–1965.* Toronto: University of Toronto Press.

Simpson, Audra. 2016a. "Reconciliation and Its Discontents: Settler Governance in an Age of Sorrow." University of Saskatchewan. YouTube. Posted March 22, 2016. https://www.youtube.com/watch?v=vGl9HkzQsGg&ab_channel=UniversityofSaskatchewan.

———. 2016b. "The State is a Man: Theresa Spence, Loretta Saunders and the Gender of Settler Sovereignty." *Theory & Event* 19, no. 4: n.p.

Simpson, Leanne. 2013. "Restoring Nationhood: Addressing Land Dispossession in the Canadian Reconciliation Discourse". Simon Fraser University. YouTube. Posted January 13, 2014. https://www.youtube.com/watch?v=fH1QZQIUJIo&ab_channel=SimonFraserUniversity.

———. 2017. *As We Have Always Done: Indigenous Freedom Through Radical Resistance.* Minneapolis: University of Minnesota Press.

Slowey, Gabrielle. 2008. *Navigating Neoliberalism: Self-Determination and the Mikisew Cree First Nation.* Vancouver: UBC Press.

Snelgrove, Corey. 2024. "Treaty as De-Fetishizing Critique: A Social Theory of Treaty Interpretation." *Polity* 56, no. 1: 65–90.

Stacey, Richard. 2018. "Honour in Sovereignty: Can Crown Consultation with Indigenous Peoples Erase Canada's Sovereignty Deficit?" *University of Toronto Law Journal* 68: 405–39.

Stanford, Jim. 2008. "Staples, Deindustrialization, and Foreign Investment: Canada's Economic Journey Back to the Future." *Studies in Political Economy* 82, no, 1: 7–34.

———. 2019. "Staples Dependence Renewed and Betrayed: Canada's Twenty-first Century Boom and Bust." In *Change and Continuity: Canadian Political Economy in the New Millennium,* edited by Mark P. Thomas, Leah F. Vosko, Carlo Fanelli, and Olena Lyubchenko. McGill-Queen's University Press.

Stanton, Kim. 2017. "Reconciling Reconciliation: Differing Conceptions of the Supreme Court of Canada and the Canadian Truth and Reconciliation Commission." *Journal of Law and Social Policy* 26: 21–42.

Truth and Reconciliation Commission. 2015. *Honouring the Truth, Reconciling for the Future: Summary of the Final Report of the Truth and Reconciliation Commission of Canada.* https://ehprnh2mwo3.exactdn.com/wp-content/uploads/2021/01/Executive_Summary_English_Web.pdf.

Tuck, Eve and K. Wayne Yang. 2012. "Decolonization Is Not a Metaphor." *Decolonization: Indigeneity, Education, and Society* 1, no. 1: 1–40.

Wilson-Raybould, Jody. 2022. *True Reconciliation: How To Be A Force For Change.* McClelland & Stewart.

Wylie, Hannah. 2023. *Recontextualizing Reconciliation: A Genealogy of Constitutional Discourses in Canada, 1980–2006.* Ph.D. diss., University of Ottawa.

Yellowhead Institute. 2019. *Land Back: A Yellowhead Institute Red Paper.* October. https://redpaper.yellowheadinstitute.org/wp-content/uploads/2019/10/red-paper-report-final.pdf.

Yonker, Zoë. 2019. "Dispossession Politics: Mapping the Contours of Reconciliatory Colonialism in Canada through Industry-Funded Think Tanks." MA thesis, University of Victoria.

Zreik, Raef. 2016. "When Does a Settler Become a Native? (With Apologies to Mamdani)." *Constellations* 23, no. 3: 351–64.

Notes

1. In an examination of legal interpretations of treaty, I've described this as a settler colonial function of capital fetishism (see Snelgrove 2024).

2. At least as I read and have presented Simpson and Coulthard's approach to resurgence here (see p. 21), there is an ambiguity on whether they are calling for a turn away from the state absolutely or temporarily. My own view is that Indigenous resurgence theory advances an approach to the state that is conjunctural rather than ontological.

3. This formulation is in reference to the work of Daniel Heath Justice (2010) discussed in Byrd (2020, 120).

MINDY MORGAN

Reading Indigeneity in *Indians at Work*, 1933–39

Abstract

During the 1930s and 1940s, the Office of Indian Affairs (OIA) used the periodical *Indians at Work* to forward reforms and policies of the New Deal era. Seen primarily as a vehicle to transmit the views of John Collier, Roosevelt's commissioner of Indian Affairs, the periodical has often been overlooked as a source for understanding the perspectives and concerns of tribal communities. But many Indigenous authors appear in the magazine, and highlighting these contributions adds to the significance of *Indians at Work*. Critically, Indigenous authors conveyed meaning through culturally specific forms of expression that were recognizable to various audiences. Authors employed these discursive strategies to assert their authority to both Indigenous and non-Indigenous readers and to counter dominant historical narratives. Seen in this way, *Indians at Work* is a vital primary resource that illuminates how Indigenous communities were positioning themselves in a moment of significant political, social, and economic change. Local authors demonstrated a keen awareness of documentary power and used this form to challenge existing ideas and tropes about what it meant to be Indigenous in the early twentieth century.

IN THE SPRING OF 1936, James L. Long, a member of the Nakoda community at Fort Peck Reservation and an owner of a small grocery in northern Montana, published a story in *Indians at Work,* a magazine produced by the Office of Indian Affairs (OIA) to chronicle the activities of the Civilian Conservation Corps-Indian Division (CCC-ID).[1] In the simply titled "A Hunting Story" (1936), Long narrates a humorous tale of how he finds himself stalking a deer, only to discover that a bear, who is also stalking the deer, is stalking him. Soon, Long is uncomfortably positioned between the two and seeks safety by climbing a tree; but in haste, he leaves his gun at the base of the tree. The bear picks up the gun, curiously investigates it, cocks the hammer, and aims at Long not once but twice. The story ends with the bear smashing the gun in frustration and ambling away.

At first, the inclusion of this story in a magazine dedicated to documenting federal work projects and advocating for legislative reforms seems unusual. It appears as an interlude between a report by a forestry supervisor lauding the advantages of a tribally-run sawmill on the Warm Springs Reservation and the superintendent's account of the Red Cliff Band of Lake Superior Chippewa's acceptance of a tribal constitution and bylaws. But this slight story is not a diversion. While Commissioner of Indian Affairs John Collier used *Indians at Work* to promote his office's agenda, this was not the magazine's sole purpose nor impact. Published as a bi-weekly, and later monthly, periodical from 1933 to 1945, *Indians at Work* was meant to circulate among reservation communities as well as a general reading public. Editors, looking for anything with broad appeal, actively sought engaging news items, photographs, and stories to supplement supervisory reports and administrative directives. Many tribal members responded to this call and took advantage of the opportunity to contribute to the national discourse regarding Indigenous affairs.

Rather than an anomaly, Long's story reflects the creative and inventive submissions from Indigenous authors who used print journalism as a means to document their communities and to amplify their voices. At the time of publication, Long was forty-eight years old with experience as a clerk, a rancher, and a businessman. He had served on Fort Peck's Tribal Council Executive Board, among other leadership roles. Roosevelt's New Deal programs provided him with new and creative outlets from which to share his views regarding contemporary Nakoda culture. His story is funny, but it has a larger point about the commensurability of Indigenous and non-Indigenous stories. He begins by asserting, "The whites can have their fish stories, but let us listen to this Indian tell his hunting experience" (1936, 44). Rather than relying on a common trope that located the difference between the two in a modern versus premodern dichotomy, he positions his "tall tale" entirely in the present, comparable and equal to stories of white anglers. This submission was not Long's only foray into creative writing. Beginning in 1938, Long also worked for the Montana Writers' Project, conducting interviews and compiling stories for *Land of Nakoda,* one of the only tribal monographs to be published by the project (Morgan 2013; Morgan 2020). He used these projects to actively shape contemporary Indigenous representation and to engage directly with those who were determining state and federal policies.

This article provides a more comprehensive assessment of the impact of *Indians at Work* than existing scholarship by focusing on Indigenous authors and local stories that appear in the magazine. Scholars have effectively used *Indians at Work* to explore various New Deal programs and policies because of its breadth of coverage of political, economic, and educational programs

(Hosmer 2010; Laukaitis 2006; McLerran 2012; Zimmer 2015); however, these readings, even when critical of the federal reforms, center the Office of Indian Affairs and overlook the contributions of Indigenous authors. In this article, I deemphasize the contributions of politicians and policymakers and reconsider the magazine's usefulness by demonstrating how Indigenous authors utilized the magazine as a means of interacting with the larger U.S. polity and carving out a space within it. By carefully examining a representative sample of these contributions, I maintain that *Indians at Work* is a key site for constructing Indigeneity in the early twentieth century.

Critical to this argument are the ways in which Indigenous authors framed their contributions by employing rhetorical styles that often reflected or gestured to traditional storytelling and oratorical practices. Variations in form, tone, and imagery comprise culturally-specific communicative registers and provide the necessary context for understanding the contributor's purpose and intentions (Agha 2005; Davis 2020). By using these registers, the authors were able to convey meaning that was immediately recognizable to tribal members and that might not have been obvious to non-Indigenous readers. Form, as well as content, mattered in these submissions. The contributors, aware of their subjectivity and positionality, employed ways of speaking and writing to comment on the economic and political changes surrounding them.

In analyzing the selections from *Indians at Work,* I am ever mindful that Indigenous contributors wrote from their own experiences, which included participation in specific tribal networks as well as a familiarity with, and even consumption of, popularized representations of "American Indians" found throughout U.S. media at the time (Strong 2012). Similar to Indigenous athletes, artists, and performers in the early twentieth century, these writers were aware that to have a recognizable Indigenous voice, they had to conform to certain expectations of the non-Native readership; however, they were also aware that an Indigenous readership existed, and that this audience both expected and hoped for something beyond common stereotypes (Deloria 2004). Ultimately, these local authors demonstrated a keen awareness of the documentary power of the magazine and used it to challenge existing ideas and tropes about what it meant to be Indigenous in the early twentieth century.

The CCC-ID and a Newsletter for "Ourselves"

In August of 1933, the first issue of *Indians at Work* appeared with the subtitle, "A news sheet for ourselves." It was primarily intended to document the projects and the progress of the enrollees who served in the Indian

Emergency Conservation Work (IECW) program, later known as the Civilian Conservation Corps—Indian Division (CCC-ID).[2] This program, part of the larger Civilian Conservation Corps (CCC), came into existence during Franklin Delano Roosevelt's first hundred days, and was part of his vision to create a "forest army" intended to serve two primary purposes: to restore depleted land and provide jobs (Merrill 1981; Maher 2008; Alexander 2018). While the law that created the CCC did not necessarily stipulate inclusion of tribal communities, Charles Rhoads, then Commissioner of Indian Affairs, advocated for the funds to be used within reservation communities that were suffering greatly because of the depression. John Collier, who replaced Rhoads in April 1933, quickly saw that the CCC-ID would be crucial to realizing his vision for tribal land management and conservation efforts.

Although Robert Fechner, the director of the CCC, initially had oversight of the CCC-ID, Harold Ickes, the Secretary of the Interior, advocated that it be moved administratively under the OIA. This separation enabled the administration to develop conservation projects tailored to the specific needs of reservation land and to ensure that tribal members were employed within their communities (Gower 1972; Parman 1967, 1971). While still adhering to the rules and regulations of the CCC, the CCC-ID had significant organizational differences. Rather than being limited to single men between the ages of 18 and 25, enrollees in the CCC-ID could be married and did not have an upper age limit, provided they were in good health and able to do the work. They also did not have to adhere to the same requirements to live away from families or to sign up for a standard six-month term (Gower 1972, 6–7). There were a few barrack-style camps constructed for CCC-ID use, but most enrollees were able to live at home or with their families at encampments close to the work sites. Tribal councils worked with superintendents and forestry agents to determine the specific needs of the reservation and to develop projects that would aid in the restoration of land, as well as provide jobs for residents. Over the course of its nine years, the CCC-ID enrolled 85,000 workers on 70 different reservations located across the country. These workers were ultimately responsible for, among other accomplishments, building 10,000 miles of truck trails, controlling pine beetles and blister rust over 700,000 acres of land, and reseeding 70,000 acres of forest (Parman 1967, 241). *Indians at Work* served to document all these efforts.

While Collier viewed *Indians at Work* as an effective way of publicizing the accomplishments of the CCC-ID, the idea of a magazine that would chronicle the efforts of the program was not novel. In fact, a hallmark of the CCC was the creation of company newsletters that served to provide enrollees with experience in journalism, promote the projects, and inform friends and families about camp activities. Over the course of the CCC, there were approximately 5,000 camp papers published by about 3,000 CCC companies (Cornebise 2004, 25). Included in this number were papers published by CCC-ID camps such as *The Tattler* from the Wind River Reservation, Wyoming and *Tom Tom Echoes* from Blackfeet, Montana (White 2016). Often run by a journalism class sponsored by the education department, these pop-up newsrooms created biweekly and monthly papers that included a wealth of content, including descriptions of camp life, cultural commentaries, and creative writing. Participants served as writers, illustrators, and editors of the papers, acquiring journalistic skills while providing information and entertainment for the entire company. Enrollees often sent copies of the papers to families and friends and exchanged them with other camps, libraries, and institutions.

But the most well-known and widely distributed publication during this time was *Happy Days,* the weekly publication of the CCC that covered the projects nationally from 1933 until 1942. Importantly, the government did not publish the paper; rather, it was a private venture financed through subscriptions and advertisements. Melvin Ryder, the editor of the paper, had been on the staff of *Stars and Stripes* during World War I, and sensed an opportunity to create a paper that would not only appeal to CCC enrollees but keep families at home apprised of their doings. While remaining independent in terms of finances and editorial decisions, the government officially recognized *Happy Days* as the "voice" of the CCC (Cornebise 2004, 65—67). It had a small editorial staff and depended on contributions from the various camps for its reports and information. *Happy Days* also served as an arbiter of the camp papers, developing a system of stars that were awarded to papers that showed distinction. Staff earning five stars, the highest allowed, often touted this recognition in their papers (Cornebise 2004, 49). The CCC publications were not static documents but were in constant circulation, moving between various audiences and readerships and continually referencing each other.

Indians at Work emerged within this dynamic intertextual space, and while there were significant differences between these papers, the periodical needs to be understood within this network of documentary production. As previously mentioned, the magazine began as a biweekly publication but was reduced to a monthly in November 1937. Each issue was approximately fifty-five to sixty pages long and contained photographs and illustrations as well as articles (see figure 1). While the CCC-ID officially ended in 1942, the administration continued to publish *Indians at Work* for three more years and employed these issues to highlight the contributions of tribal communities to the war effort. Ultimately, there were 138 issues

FIGURE 1. *IAW* January 1, 1937, pg. 32, Smithsonian Institution, National Museum of the American Indian Collection.

published throughout its twelve-year run. Collier used *Indians at Work* to promote legislative reforms and advance his agenda, and this overt political stance makes the magazine distinct from other CCC publications and camp newsletters. While publications such as *Happy Days* were meant to serve as boosters for New Deal programs, they operated without direct oversight from the Roosevelt administration and were intended to be apolitical (Cornebise 2004). This was not the case with *Indians at Work,* as the OIA used it to chronicle the development, passage, and acceptance of the Indian Reorganization Act, oftentimes publishing the vote counts from different tribal communities. The March 15, 1934 issue provides specific details about the Wheeler-Howard Act and covers the various congresses held among tribes (Stewart 1934, 4–7). Vote counts continued to appear throughout various issues over the years. The issue from January 1939 has a rather late reporting of tribal votes on charters and constitutions (Office of Indian Affairs 1939, 4). Administrators such as John Herrick, assistant to the commissioner; Willard Beatty, Collier's director of education; and René d'Harnoncourt, director of the Indian Arts and Crafts Board, were frequent contributors to the magazine, detailing the reforms and programs Collier was championing. But these submissions were counterbalanced by contributions about local happenings and daily life within the CCC-ID projects that often meant the magazine, while national in scope, operated like a large camp newsletter. It is this quality that allowed for unofficial voices to appear and challenge the assumptions of the administration.

Form and Content

Issues of *Indians at Work* were organized in a manner that emphasized how the Office of Indian Affairs expected the magazine to be read and by whom. Collier began each issue with an editorial that reflected his vision of contemporary Indigenous life and used the periodical to promote and explain the changes initiated by his office. These were often overtly political and designed to gain support among the reading audience. In the copy from January 15, 1934, six months before the passage of the Wheeler-Howard bill, Collier used his prefatory editorial to discuss a report on the prospective legislative reforms that, in his estimation, was "the most vital news in this issue of *Indians at Work*" (1934, 1). Later, commenting on the passage of laws to extend the reach of the Wheeler-Howard Act, he writes, "These legislative victories are merely a beginning. They are a charter for action. They are a license to work" (1936, 1).

Other editorials were more philosophical, and Collier used them to forward what he perceived to be an Indigenous approach to federal Indian policy. His vision of Indigeneity was shaped by his disillusionment with the preoccupation on the individual within dominant American culture (Collier 1963; Kunitz 1971; Philp 1981). In a lengthy editorial for a special issue ("Indians at Play"), Collier mused on the importance of recreation and leisure to humankind and criticized the U.S. for its puritanical focus on work and the commodification of leisure in contemporary U.S. society. In contrast, he argued, tribes created robust practices of leisure and recreation that contributed to the building of community life. But Collier worried that these, too, were under threat. He wrote, "Whether these undestroyed ancient values can hold their own against the levelling, dismembering influence of the modern world, remains to be seen. An issue vital for the human spirit here waits unanswered" (1935, 4). He often employed romanticizing and essentializing views toward tribal communities within his editorials that not only framed the contents of the magazine but also dictated how the reader should approach the remaining articles.

The early issues mostly comprised contributions either from administrators reporting on the work of the OIA or from superintendents and supervisors detailing the progress on projects within the communities. In a lengthy contribution, Willard Beatty wrote about Collier's initiative to establish community day schools as an alternative and corrective to boarding schools.

These schools, he argued, served multiple community purposes, including educating adults about New Deal reforms (1936, 29). Other critical legislation, such as the Indian Arts and Crafts Bill, was also thoroughly discussed within the pages of the periodical, accompanied by testimonials about how this could positively affect tribal communities (Indian Arts and Crafts Board 1937; Office of Indian Affairs 1936). But to gain the social and political capital he needed to fully implement his reforms, Collier needed to educate lawmakers and the public about tribal communities and convince them that he had the solutions to the issues that they were facing. As a result, he solicited other submissions for *Indians at Work* that were intended to educate the larger U.S. populace about Indigenous communities, both contemporary and historical. Scholars, Indian Service employees, and long-term missionaries shared stories based on their own experiences to supplement the magazine.

Various editors guided the selection of material and contributed to the perspective of *Indians at Work*. For example, Mary Heaton Vorse, the well-known writer and labor journalist, served as editor from 1935 until 1937. She shared Collier's romantic view of Indigenous communities and the idea that many of the ills of contemporary U.S. society could be remedied if Indigenous practices and worldviews could be incorporated into dominant U.S. culture (Garrison 1989). As part of her duties, Vorse made multiple trips to various reservations in the Northern Plains and the Southwest that provided her with material for articles. Recounting a trip to Rosebud and Pine Ridge, she describes the people she encountered in a florid and nostalgic tone. A young girl is "shy as a fawn" and lives in a home where "daylight showed through the chinks." After praising the ECW family camps for being "in accordance with Indian ways," she is left with the "sense that the way people were living, the way they were working, was natural to them" (Vorse 1935, 11). In an appeal to non-Native readers who are likely Collier's political allies, Vorse employs the common trope of Indigenous communities as the innocent "other" throughout her articles. This essentializing often places tribal communities outside of contemporary times, separating them from the demands of the modern world.

Other prominent voices helped to shape and define the periodical. The author and activist Oliver LaFarge authored many stories about issues facing tribes in the early twentieth century, including the plight of returned World War I veterans and preparations for involvement in World War II. Anthropologists working for Collier under the Applied Anthropology Unit (AAU) as well as others working for the Bureau of American Ethnology submitted numerous original articles, excerpts, and reprints to *Indians at Work* (Morgan 2017). Contributions regarding Mexico and South America provided comparative examples to U.S. tribes while also arguing for a hemispheric approach to Indigenous policy (Head and Holloway 1937; Cook 1936). Missionaries and teachers at tribal schools also offered descriptions of historical and contemporary reservation communities from their vantage point.

Many submissions were not original to *Indians at Work* but rather were reprints from other publications, including popular magazines and scholarly sources.[3] Using reprints was also a strategy shared by other CCC publications. Many of the papers relied heavily on republished materials from local newspapers and national publications such as *Parade* magazine. *The Trojan,* an acclaimed camp newsletter published by the 2694 Company from Harrison, Michigan, which comprised solely of Black enrollees, regularly republished articles from notable Black newspapers such as *The Chicago Defender* and the *Pittsburgh Courier.* Similarly, *Indians at Work* reprinted columns from local papers that featured cultural activities and stories of interest. The issue from October 1, 1937, has several short reprints, including one that shares the apocryphal naming of an Oklahoma county. The county was supposed to be named "Oologah" but Clem Vann Rogers, the editor of the local paper and father of Will Rogers, complained "there aren't enough O's in my type box to be using Oologah in my paper all the time," and so the decision was made to call the county "Rogers" (Wilson 1937, 34). These curated reprints were a way of allowing readers access to other publications without additional subscription costs. They also enhanced the quality of publications and connected readers to different locales.

In addition to this reliance on reprints, *Indians at Work* bore a similarity to other Civilian Conservation Corps newsletters and camp papers in the way that it relied on local talent to provide reporting and commentary on camp happenings. The magazine did not just publish pieces from administration officials or outside "experts," but also encouraged submissions from reservation communities. Tribal Council members, elders, and CCC-ID enrollees were frequent contributors to the magazine: offering descriptions of relief work, authoring poems and fictional stories, and providing commentary on contemporary social and cultural practices. These submissions stand in stark contrast to and present valuable counter-narratives to the ones emanating from the OIA—even within contributions that support the basic New Deal reforms.

These submissions appear in various places within the magazine. Generally, letters and articles from tribal leaders would be published toward the beginning of the magazine, especially if Collier wanted to highlight a particular issue or concern. A lengthy letter from Adelbert Thunder Hawk, secretary of the Rosebud Tribal Council, was published on page 7 of the October 15, 1936, issue, which contained concerns regarding the creation of charters as part of the Indian Reorganization Act and expressed distrust of the Office of Indian Affairs. Collier's response appears immediately after, in which he assuages these concerns and again promotes the benefits of the legislation (1936, 9). Other contributions were interspersed with other stories. While officials would generally get a byline and acknowledgment in the table of contents, Indigenous contributors were more haphazardly acknowledged (see figure 2). Some contributors would have their name in the table of contents and were clearly identified in the stories themselves; others were not listed and only had the title of their contribution appear. This was not systematic, but in general, solicited pieces and contributions from tribal leaders would receive acknowledgment, while pieces that were reprinted or reports written for other purposes would not have an author indicated. Poems and other creative pieces oftentimes do not appear in the table of contents at all and are left for readers to discover as they flip through the pages of the magazine.

But the most regular submissions from enrollees were always found at the end of each issue. These were small accounts coming from participants themselves and chronicled the daily life of the camps. Initially called "IECW Reports" and later "Reports from the Field," these submissions documented work projects while also providing glimpses into the daily workings of the camps. The majority of the submissions are brief updates on the work in which enrollees were engaged. Descriptions of building roads and fences, controlling pests, and planting trees populate the column. Additionally, there is a strong focus on recreation within the camps, including social dances and sports teams. Foremen and supervisors, who were tribal members, authored most of the descriptions, and are identified by name and role at the end of each of the submissions. Because of the monthly coverage of the magazine, these snapshots provide a view of the seasonal cycle of the camps and how this dictated both work and leisure. During the winter, the companies completed tasks such as dam building and forest clearing as weather permitted, as well as hauling firewood. The January 1939 issue discusses how enrollees in Oregon were preparing for the holidays by "making doll beds out of knocked down apple boxes and stick horses for the kiddies to ride" (Shawver 1939, 44). Spring reports are populated by discussions of insect control and creating truck trails. Summer is the time of planting, clearing, and controlling fires. These reports detail how local companies responded to specific needs, in terms of the type of work needed and the social life created. In so doing, they reminded readers of the geographic and tribal diversity that the CCC-ID represented. At the same time, these reports also demonstrate shared experiences of Indigenous communities and illustrate a growing intertribal awareness. For example, baseball dominates the reports from late spring to autumn, and there are multiple entries about teams besting their intercamp

I N D I A N S A T W O R K

CONTENTS OF THE ISSUE OF OCTOBER 15, 1936

Volume IV Number 5

FIGURE 2. *IAW* October 15, 1936, Table of Contents, Smithsonian Institution, National Museum of the American Indian Collection.

rivals, thus, extending an athletic practice that had roots in the mid-1800s (Deloria 2004, 116). In this way, *Indians at Work* served to connect reservation communities and help spur pan-Indigenous consciousness.

While most reports are short and simply describe the work, several entries contain humor and poke fun at the enrollees. Titled "A Lonely Project at Cheyenne River," Leon Poitras writes about a remote job that had an enrollee cutting and tying willows to use as riprap for a reservoir retaining wall. Poitras observes, "The man working on this project seems to be getting wilder and shyer than ever before. In fact, we have a difficult time locating him at work as he has been working so far from anyone and anywhere. We generally stand on a hill and watch for a wave in the willows to locate him at work" (1936, 50). In another report from the Consolidated Chippewa camp, P. Grey describes how a bear visited a remote camp where a crew had been building a watch tower. The bear left after rummaging through food and tools, and "there was no damage done, except feelings" (1936, 51). Taken as a composite, these short descriptions reveal the range of projects while also giving insight into camp morale and culture. The submissions were not static, but part of the circulation of information and dialogue between the central administration and the enrolled workers. Willie Pinto, a contributor from the Navajo reservation, even voiced his frustration at the seeming lack of response from the Bureau when, at the end of report regarding fire suppression, he wrote, "We had been writing these ECW reports every week and never had heard any reply and we like to hear an answer regarding these reports" (1937, 49). These pieces most resemble the contributions to other CCC magazines and are what connect *Indians at Work* to this larger network of publications, which regularly featured discussions of camp happenings. They are condensed reports, but they document the same details of daily living and provide a glimpse of the perspective of the enrollees themselves.

Reading the magazine from back to front and inverting the perceived priorities of the central office highlight the contributions of Indigenous authors. Aware of the dominant tropes and stereotypes that depicted tribal communities as unable to engage with the modern world, the authors wrote pieces that invoked and unsettled these established registers (Deloria 2004; Usner 2009). Fundamentally, Indigenous submissions located tribes in the present and fully engaged in the betterment of their communities. These articles ultimately illuminate the various strategies contributors employed to claim Indigeneity and the ability to set their definitional terms. The authors used their articles to map the changes happening in their communities, thereby producing a documentary record that contested the federal government's oftentimes anachronistic and romanticized view of tribal communities.

Voicing Registers of Resistance

By closely analyzing articles submitted to *Indians at Work* by a range of Indigenous authors, we can see the divergent ways in which tribal members constructed authoritative voices that both supported and played with contemporary conceptions of Indigeneity in full view of a diverse reading audience. The authors were geographically, culturally, and socially diverse; however, they shared challenges and concerns that resulted from the historical relationship between tribes and the federal government and the standardizing effect of national policies. While not monolithic, Indigenous authors were all engaged in social and economic programs resulting from New Deal reforms. Many were actively involved in tribal politics and had previously engaged with the Office of Indian Affairs regarding economic development and treaty obligations. Some were federal employees hired to oversee program implementation. Notably, D'Arcy McNickle, who served as Collier's assistant commissioner as well as director of information for a brief time, contributed many original articles for the magazine. Throughout the twelve-year run, hundreds of tribal members contributed to *Indians at Work* in the form of reports, articles, letters, poems, and illustrations. Because of this breadth, my discussion below is limited and focuses on examples from issues published from 1934 to 1938, as these were the years of the greatest variety and productivity.[4] In selecting contributions, I concentrated on authors living within reservation communities who represent a range of ages, tribal affiliations, and experiences.

Despite tribal differences, editorial selection ensured that there was a certain degree of conformity among both the content and the format of submissions that were recognizable as "Indigenous" to the non-Native administrators. While there is a certain repetition in the types of stories that were selected for publication, this does not mean that Indigenous authors accepted dominant representations of Indigenous communities. In particular, the authors took issue with characterizations of Indigenous communities as dependent, unable or unwilling to work, or as anachronistic societies opposed to modernity. These tropes, which circulated widely throughout U.S. society in the ninenteeth and twentieth centuries, were often employed by politicians, educators, and reformers as justifications for policies that restricted tribal sovereignty and autonomy (Fear-Segal 2007, 31–47; Usner 2009, 69–92). Indigenous writers, artists, and activists were aware of the potency of these images and often structured their work to either directly or indirectly counter these views (Vigil 2015). The same could be said for many of the contributors to *Indians at Work* who described how they engaged in distinct types of labor. While in some cases these stories seem to reinforce prevalent stereotypes about tribal communities and interlocutors, other contributions problematize the ideas of Indigeneity produced by the Office of Indian Affairs. This paradox—being "Indian" enough to be identified as such yet challenging the limits of these stereotypes—confronted many Indigenous people at this time (Bruchac 2018; Deloria 2004). Examining these contributions closely provides an opportunity to see how Indigenous authors used their voices to operate in a highly mediated space and how and to whom they become recognizable. This view allows for the stories to be seen as polyvalent texts that change meaning according to the reader of the story. This makes seemingly straightforward articles that attest to the benefits of the New Deal more complicated and nuanced.

Many Indigenous contributors offered content that was presented for the edification of the non-Native readers of the periodical, whom Collier needed for political support. These pieces often detailed how OIA reforms were aiding their communities. Irving Pabanale, a leader within the Hopi tribe during the early twentieth century, is illustrative of this type of voice within the magazine. Pabanale was born in 1881 and grew up within the Arizona Tewa community at First Mesa. After time spent at school, including the Phoenix Indian School, and off the reservation working as a police officer, Pabanale returned home. In 1936, he was selected to be a delegate from First Mesa to assist with the drafting of the Hopi constitution and later served as a judge for the Hopi Tribal court. From 1966–1972, Pabanale collaborated with the anthropologist Robert Black to record his life story, which was eventually published as *Standing Flower: The Life of Irving Pabanale, an Arizona Tewa Indian* in 2001. His contributions to *Indians at Work* reflect his commitment to Collier's reforms; however, there is no mention within his pieces about his active engagement with Hopi tribal politics, nor his acquaintance with people such as Oliver LaFarge, who frequently visited the region in the 1930s to garner support for Collier's reforms.

Pabanale's earliest contribution demonstrates his understanding of the simultaneous ability of the magazine to reach other Indigenous communities and to serve as a direct conduit to Collier's office. In an article that describes the various improvements on the Hopi reservation as a result of CCC-ID, he observes, "Ever since the copies of INDIANS AT WORK have been sent out to us Indians, I have been reading them through . . . Yet I never found a word in it that would let other Indians know what good has been done on our Hopi Reservation" (Pabanale 1934, 25). In this piece, he acknowledges that the purpose of the magazine is to inform and connect Indigenous readers from different communities; however, he knows that the ability to select information resides with the editors at the central office and that they are responsible for the relative lack of content regarding the Hopi community.

It is this absence Pabanale seeks to fill. Finding his voice, he writes directly to non-Indigenous readers by appointing himself as a spokesperson for the Hopi tribe in his later contributions. In a brief discussion of pottery, he describes the decorating and firing process. Pabanale is not an artist, but he asserts his authority to speak by stating, "My home is here where this pottery is made by the women on this mesa, and I keep some on hand right along." The real purpose of the piece is to critique white traders who profit off local artists and to warn against inauthentic replications. He writes, "This type of work is very slow, but we Hopis would rather make it by hand than to have anyone make it by a machine" (1935, 21). Finally, Pabanale personifies the entire Hopi nation in a short contribution that reminds readers that the Hopi inhabited their lands long before the government designated them as reservation land. He writes, "I am the Hopi Tribe. My home is in the desert land; however, I love my land just the same. I have been living on this reservation for at least six hundred years and it is my home" (1936, 45). These three articles comprise an arc: from realizing the potential reach of the magazine to using it to intentionally advocate for the community among its various audiences. Pabanale's articles exemplify contributions by Indigenous authors who write for non-Native readers who may be sympathetic but ignorant of the contemporary situation of tribal communities.

James L. Long, referenced at the beginning of this article, also used the platform of *Indians at Work* to disrupt popular tropes about the lack of a work ethic among tribal communities. In a contribution dissimilar to the hunting story previously discussed, he imagines a dialogue between a local shopkeeper and a visiting salesperson who is observing a group of tribal members working for the CCC-ID. After the salesman expresses surprise that the men are productively engaged, the merchant responds, "Indians are the same as anybody" (Long 1935, 28). He goes on to talk about the dedication the men have for work and the benefits of WPA programs. The shopkeeper ends with a discussion of self-sufficiency; tribal members do work and will work if jobs are available. The title of the piece is "The Indian Trader Speaks," which is ambiguous; the reader could assume that the narrator is Indigenous or a non-Indigenous person with experience working with tribal communities. Despite basing the exchange on his own experience at his grocery, Long employs nothing in his story to dispel this vagueness and identify the shopkeeper as part of the Fort Peck tribal community (Morgan 2013). Rather, he authenticates his knowledge through his position as a businessman, a voice that he felt necessary to be taken seriously by non-Indigenous subscribers. The idea of an unskilled or unwilling Indigenous worker ignored the history of tribal members successfully engaging in wage labor, yet it remained a common trope in U.S. popular culture (Littlefield and Knack

1996; Raibmon 2005; Usner 2009). Long's story reflects his keen awareness of the needs among the diverse readership of the magazine; tribal members did not need to be schooled against stereotyping, but a white readership did. He willfully and skillfully modified his voice to the one that best delivered that message.

Other contributors voiced their Indigeneity in ways that were less obvious to a largely white readership, but certainly recognizable to an Indigenous one. Often, these selections argued for less governmental reliance and more self-sufficiency and directly addressed tribal audiences. While not countering Collier directly, they argued for tribal autonomy beyond the reforms initiated by the Office of Indian Affairs. Some contributions by tribal members reinforced, in similar ways, the dramatic changes that they experienced in their own lives and how the Indian New Deal brought a sense of renewal to reservation communities. Many of these took the form of letters and testimonials, and commented on improvements in contemporary reservation conditions from previous administrative eras. They are written by a range of authors from various communities; however, they share some striking characteristics. For example, several employ a protocol for speaking that mentions places and dates of birth, lineages, and authority to tell stories—a framing device that is common among many tribal communities (Archibald et al. 2022; Morgan 2005). In a letter from Fort Hall, Frank Randall writes, "I have been here on this reservation all my life. I was raised here—my mother used to be the interpreter. I am one of the oldest men among the grown men today [who] is trying to do the right thing to help the people on this reservation" (1937, 37). In addition to his authority as an elder, it is important that Randall makes the claim about his mother's position as interpreter. In this statement, he simultaneously invokes Indigenous language knowledge as well as the ability to serve as an intermediary between tribal and non-tribal communities. This is an illustration of what Jenny Davis has termed an "epistemic stance" in relation to contemporary Chickasaw speakers (2020, 66–67). It is a discursive form that makes claims to Indigenous oratory as well as awareness about the proper dissemination of knowledge while discussing contemporary politics and programs. These voices are largely masculine and generally serve in leadership positions within the community. Tribal chairpersons and elders often used *Indians at Work* in this way to assert authority among the reading audience.

Other contributors resisted this authoritative voice but chose to write in a way that simultaneously evoked established tropes associated with Indigeneity while creating novel ways of addressing contemporary concerns within tribal communities. Carl Gorman, renowned Navajo artist, code talker, and professor at UC Davis, contributed poems to *Indians at Work* when he was a young man. Both "Arrowhead" and "Rain on my Reservation" are thoughtful ruminations on the observable changes resulting from settler colonialism. In "Rain on My Reservation," Gorman contrasts earlier times, "when it rained it purred," to contemporary times when in drought-stricken lands, "it pours after it rains—down into washes and gullies." While not explicitly pointing to agricultural practices that stripped fertile lands, leading to runoffs, this shift is alluded to in his references to earlier times when rain used to fall, "feeling its way amongst the high grass." The criticism is more explicit in his second poem, where he directly addresses a found arrowhead: "Once you had power. Prized and praised with pride by great hunters. But now white brother says: 'A pen is mightier" (1936, 42). The metadiscursive moment with Gorman using this "pen" to criticize dominant U.S. society is not lost on the reader. Importantly, this critique is oblique and reminiscent of the use of storytelling to correct listeners without directly addressing them and risking social embarrassment (Basso 1996). These examples of voice resist established categories of "the Indian" yet are distinct and thoughtful expressions of Indigeneity.

Not surprisingly, many of these contributions question, if not contest, the role of the federal government in Indian affairs. Martin Mitchell, a police officer on the Fort Peck Reservation in Montana, was another contributor who provided a few pieces to *Indians at Work* that focused primarily on an Indigenous reading audience. Born in 1870, Mitchell was a well-established member of the Fort Peck community who had served in various capacities as a translator, a police officer, and a rancher. He lived in Wolf Point and was in his late sixties when he wrote for the magazine. Actively engaged in the political life of the reservation, he provided testimonies for Congress regarding reservation conditions throughout the 1920s and 1930s. In 1929, he provided testimony to the subcommittee on Indian Affairs, where he detailed how the Fort Peck community engaged in various forms of stock raising, only to be undermined repeatedly by the federal government's intervention through leasing practices and stock selloffs. He writes, "So we do not know what to do now if the Indian Bureau does things against our will and keeps us broke all the time. The way it looks to me, we could be better off a hundred times without the Indian Bureau" (United States Congress 1929, 12407). Mitchell's observation that the OIA was hindering rather than helping tribal communities was a common refrain through congressional testimony in the early twentieth century.

Well versed in talking directly to the federal government, Mitchell took a different approach in *Indians at Work* and tailored his appeal to tribal citizens and an Indigenous readership. In an article published in January 1938, he discusses the dependent relationship between tribal communities and the federal government with an analogy regarding horses to chastise his fellow tribal members. He writes, "The way some of the Indians are—reminds me of an old horse I had. He had been an awfully good horse, but he was raised in a barn. When he got to be 20 years old, I retired him . . . Do you think he quit the barn and went out and ate grass? No. . . . Now we don't want to be like that old horse" (Mitchell 1938, 22). He finishes his piece with a list of five "programs" that tribal members should employ. The last of these is "Let's stay at home and tend to our own business. Sometimes I wish that this office [of Indian Affairs] would burn to the ground so that you would have to do more for yourselves." Consistent with his congressional testimony, Mitchell views federal interventions as detrimental to the community. For Mitchell, the federal government will never be in full support of Indigenous autonomy and sovereignty. In the article for *Indians at Work,* he articulates this by directly addressing Indigenous readers, imploring them to demonstrate their agency and work against failed reforms.

Mitchell's contributions resist stereotypes of taciturn individuals brimming with nostalgia and place the voice of the activist within the artful play of the trickster. In an issue from 1937, Mitchell submitted a hunting story reminiscent of the one submitted by James L. Long. In this case, a young hunter foolishly spends precious ammunition shooting at random objects. Frustrated, he sits beneath a cherry tree, and as he eats his fill, a deer surprises him. Out of shells, he loads his gun with cherry pits and aims at the deer's head. The deer—unsurprisingly—survives, but the hunter encounters the same deer a year later, only to find it has cherry trees growing from its head (Mitchell 1937, 44). Along with Long's piece about his run-in with the bear, the story's primary purpose is humor; however, it also unsettles the reader's expectations of what these "hunting" stories should be. Humor plays a vital role in these examples of Indigenous voicing, providing early examples of what others have noted regarding the prominence of joking behaviors as a way of reinforcing tribal values and dispositions (Basso 1979, 1996; Spielmann 1998). Like the opening hunting story, Mitchell's contribution, while funny, is not trifling. The author intentionally identifies the hunter as a "young lad," and the story reinforces values of patience and persistence. Tribal membership in these stories is about behaviors, not about claims to authenticity or authority. Mitchell's story rejects the image of Indigenous stoicism and disrupts dominant stereotypes of Indigenous storytelling as set in a mythic past and as primarily concerned with disappearing lifeways. These contributions from tribal members are simultaneously Indigenous and located entirely within the present conditions of reservation life. They utilize subtle puns and insider comments that reflect the specific audience to whom these authors were attempting to connect. They seem less concerned with making their Indigeneity recognizable to non-Natives and more interested in engaging directly with the Indigenous readership of the periodical.

Andrew Knife, a member of the Oglala Lakota community at Pine Ridge, provides another type of storytelling that is focused primarily on an Indigenous listening audience. His contribution is not authored directly by him, but rather a transcription of stories he told to an assembled classroom of fifth graders at Oglala Community School. Knife was born in 1872, making him sixty-four at the time of publication. He was employed as a building custodian when he told a selection of stories that largely concerned his own traumatic experiences while attending government schools. He recounts evading the authorities sent to deliver him to school, the embarrassment of having his hair cut, and the forced daily regimen. In the selection "On Learning to Speak English," he details his frustration in trying to learn the colonial language. When he's unable to understand the words of his teacher, he asks his father for advice: Knife was told to "listen to what the teacher say[s] and say everything she say." This then leads to an exchange where the "Next day teacher say 'Sit still' so we say 'sit still.' Pretty soon she say 'Stand up' so we say 'Stand up.' Teacher get mad and she holler 'Shut up' and we holler 'Shut up.' That evening teacher take us home and tell father children won't behave" (1936, 44). The story is masterful in not only capturing the difficulties of learning a foreign language but also demonstrating the power of social difference inherent in types of speech. The children's transgression is not repeating English words, but rather using the imperative form that presumes one has the authority to issue commands. Other sections, such as "Naming a Boy," similarly discuss misunderstandings that arise through the forced imposition of Euro-American norms on Indigenous communities. The events are troubling and reflect the forms of structural violence that students like Knife encountered in the boarding and day schools in the late nineteenth and early twentieth centuries (Adams 1995; Child 2000; Rose and Fear-Segal 2016; Lajimodiere 2019); however, Knife chooses to recount the events to the listening audience in a manner where children are the primary actors and non-Indigenous adults are presented as silly and unthinking. These stories are told with humor but with a serious underlying message. Like Mitchell's story of the horse, the criticism of settler colonial practices is explicit and intended for Indigenous listeners to understand that authority is fallible and that they control their own futures.

There is little contextual information about the event—what preceded it, and who organized it. An unnamed teacher, identified only as an "Indian girl" who "knows shorthand," writes down the stories (Knife 1936, 43). This information is regrettably sparse; it does not even clarify if the stories were told in English or Lakota. But it does suggest that Knife told the story with the intention that it was primarily for the children's benefit and not necessarily for a non-Native readership. At the same time, one can assume that he knew the stories would end up in the magazine and was perhaps asked for permission for their inclusion. This presents an intriguing situation where Knife possibly used the storytelling opportunity to offer an explicit critique of the U.S. government, while softening the bluntness of the stories by framing them as a presentation to the students.

As with Mitchell, Knife had experience in representing his community to outsiders. Andrew Knife was the son of the well-known Oglala warrior, Knife Chief, and as such, was well-positioned to discuss the social and political upheavals of the late nineteenth century and document reservation life in the early twentieth.[5] Knife was one of the primary sources for John Neihardt's collection of interviews that became the basis for the book, *When the Tree Flowered* (Neihardt and DeMallie 1991). A few years after his contributions to *Indians at Work,* Knife appeared as a subject in photographs by Helen Post who was working as a photographer for the OIA, including the role of "Grandfather" in her photographs for Ann Nolan Clark's book *Brave Against the Enemy,* which was a fictitious account of generations of Lakota through the perspective of a Lakota youth (Nolan and Afraid of Hawk, 1944). The introduction of Knife as simply an "employee of the school" contradicts his deep cultural knowledge and community engagement. In these varied contributions, Knife proves himself to be acutely aware of how outsiders read him and uses this knowledge as a means of shaping his own representation. In claiming his grandfather status among the school children, he emphasizes his relationship to them while also establishing his role to outsiders as a knowledgeable elder.

While most Indigenous contributors to *Indians at Work* were men, they were not exclusively so. Since the CCC-ID did employ women, they sometimes provided descriptions of their engagement with work within the camps and on reservations more generally. They did not comment on political or legislative happenings, nor did they provide more creative content, but their reporting allowed for glimpses into the educational programs sponsored by the CCC-ID and the ways in which women were using the programs to create new social and economic opportunities. Mylie Lawyer was one such contributor. Born on the Pine Ridge reservation among her mother's family, she grew up in Lapwai, Idaho, with her father's family within the Nez Perce community.[6] She was educated at Chemawa and Lapwai High School and earned a degree in home economics from Willamette University.[7] Later, she taught home economics at Warm Springs Indian School, where she eventually became principal. She followed this appointment with a position at Stewart Indian School in Carson City, Nevada.

At the time of her submission to *Indians at Work,* Lawyer was twenty-one years old, working for the CCC-ID, and was charged with helping with education programs in the Two Medicine Family camp on the Blackfeet Reservation. Her report to *Indians at Work* in the October 15, 1933 issue details experiences working with women and youth on a variety of projects, including food preparation, sewing, and baking. Her descriptions highlight the innovative ways in which the women adapted traditional practices to contemporary skills such as embroidering "old Blackfeet designs on table runners and luncheon cloths" (Lawyer 1933, 17). Throughout, she emphasizes the creative ways women have been adapting, from adding pectin to their chokecherry jelly to improvising high-altitude recipes, to crafting novel quilt designs (Lawyer 1933, 17). Since it is a report, it is not directly obvious who her intended audience is, but Lawyer writes in a way that depicts the women she works with as fully engaged members of the family camps who bring proven skills to new tasks. In so doing, she keeps with submissions from other Indigenous women who resist tropes that depict Indigenous women as passive, either trapped in a premodern lifeway or having abandoned or forgotten their cultural heritage (Morgan 2017, 444).

Lawyer's interests in the maintenance of Indigenous knowledge went beyond the requirements of her job. At the same time as she was working for the OIA, Lawyer collaborated with J. F. Santee on an article regarding her great-grandfather, Chief Lawyer, and received an acknowledgment from him when the article was published in 1934 (Santee 1934, 37). Importantly, after retiring from her government job, Mylie directed her efforts to maintain her family and tribal stories, contributing to the maintenance of Nez Perce cultural life. When Lawyer died at the age of ninety-two, she was a respected elder within the Lapwai community and a keeper of both tangible and intangible Nez Perce heritage and history.

Lawyer's voice, as well as those of other women, make *Indians at Work* unique among CCC publications that male enrollees solely authored, and their inclusion provides a fuller perspective on daily experiences. A brief mention of the dedicated work of Mrs. Myron Sippi, a supervisor of work in the family camp at San Carlos Reservation, in an early issue of *Indians at Work* resulted in a published report from her a few issues later that detailed the activities and daily happenings within the camp. Aged fifty-nine at the time of her report, Sippi provides a bookend to Lawyer's experiences. Born Naomi Kohtin, she was raised within the Tskokanende band of Chiricahua Apache. At twelve, she was one of the children taken prisoner and sent to Fort Sill and Fort Marion, and later transferred to Carlisle Indian School.[8]

After being widowed, she returned to Arizona, married Myron Sippi, a member of the San Carlos Apache tribe, and worked as both a laundress and housekeeper for the agency school. These experiences provide the necessary context for her authoritative commentary on the benefits and limitations of the family camps. In her report, she praises the women at the camp for their industriousness and handiwork. After complaining that women were not given their own space within the camp to make their quilts, Sippi writes, "Who ever takes [a] quilt gives me a dollar. So I take this dollar and buy some more goods with it. In that way we can carry on work. All I asked for was cotton at [the] Office. All these women seem to think it fair." (1933, 16) In her estimation, the government inhibits women's productivity rather than enables it, an argument that aligns with contributions of other Indigenous authors within the magazine. While not a considerable number, women's inclusion in the CCC-ID meant that they had occasion to submit to *Indians at Work.* The magazine thereby provides a more nuanced view of how all people were participating in New Deal economic and social programs than the gender-restricted CCC newsletters, as well as taking advantage of opportunities to voice their own perspectives on the transformations.

Drawings and Defiance

In addition to reports, speeches, and stories, tribal members contributed various drawings and other forms of artwork to the magazine, thereby providing another means of demonstrating Indigenous knowledge and authority beyond written works. *Indians at Work* was not comprised solely of text but contained a substantial number of photos and illustrations. While most of the photographs were by non-Indigenous photographers hired by the Bureau, the sketches are almost all from enrollees, tribal members, and school-aged children (see figure 3). This abundant use of artwork creates another connection between the Civilian Conservation Corps camp papers and *Indians at Work.* CCC papers have abundant examples of pen-and-ink drawings created to enhance stories and to draw attention to regular columns. Additionally, these papers frequently incorporated cartoons both as single illustrations and as featured comics. For example, *The Trojan* maintained three to five artists on staff to provide a range of drawings from illustrations for sports reports and headers for regular columns. *The Chieftain,* the CCC-ID paper from Fort Cobb, Kiowa Agency, also featured illustrations, particularly cartoons that made fun of the daily work of the camp. The drawings within *Indians at Work* fall within related categories and serve a similar purpose: to offer a perspective on the work of the projects that could not be captured in simple prose.

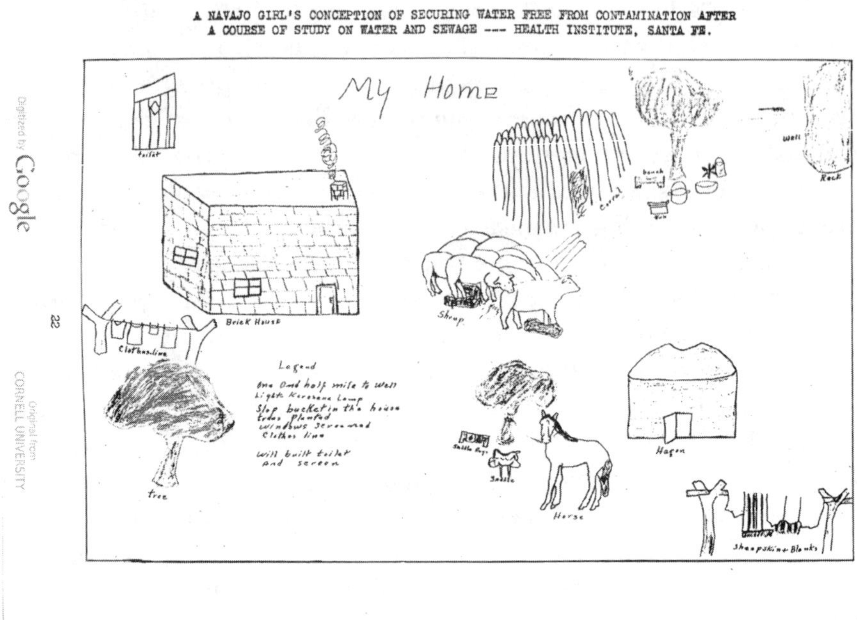

FIGURE 3. *IAW* October 1, 1935, pg. 22, HathiTrust, Cornell University Collection.

Cover designs provided a means for artists to articulate a tribal identity and to challenge popular ideas of what constituted "Indian" design. While there are a few photographs of work projects, most of the early issues of *Indians at Work* are abstracted black and white designs primarily, but not exclusively, created by students enrolled in the School of Art and Design in Santa Fe, New Mexico. Some of these covers were patterns found in local artistic traditions such as pottery, while others were contemporary designs based on tribal motifs. The covers provided an opportunity for artists to honor traditional design while being creative at the same time. The issue from June 15, 1936, has a cover reminiscent of the previous issues with a stylized black and white circular design, but has "IECW" incorporated in the design and a small illustration of a field with the words, "Save the Soil" (see figure 4). Created by Madwahqua Tuft, who was employed as a typist at Shawnee Agency, the cover melds Indigenous elements with the aims of the CCC-ID. But as with the written contributions, the cover artists often had fun, turning mundane issues into creative spaces. The cover of the issue from October 1, 1935, which was dedicated to Indian health, shows a stylized and "Indigenized" illustration of a mosquito with the ominous directive "Kill him. He brings disease." Illustrated by an unnamed participant in the Indian Health Congress, it reflects the contents but also plays with ideas of what is "typical" Indigenous design (see figure 5). What connects the two covers

FIGURE 4. *IAW* June 15, 1936, Cover Page, Smithsonian Institution, National Museum of the American Indian Collection.

is the incorporation of issues that were dominant throughout the United States at the time, health and soil conservation, into a distinctly Indigenous sphere. The covers, therefore, linked the experiences of Indigenous and non-Indigenous communities, erasing an imagined difference between them.

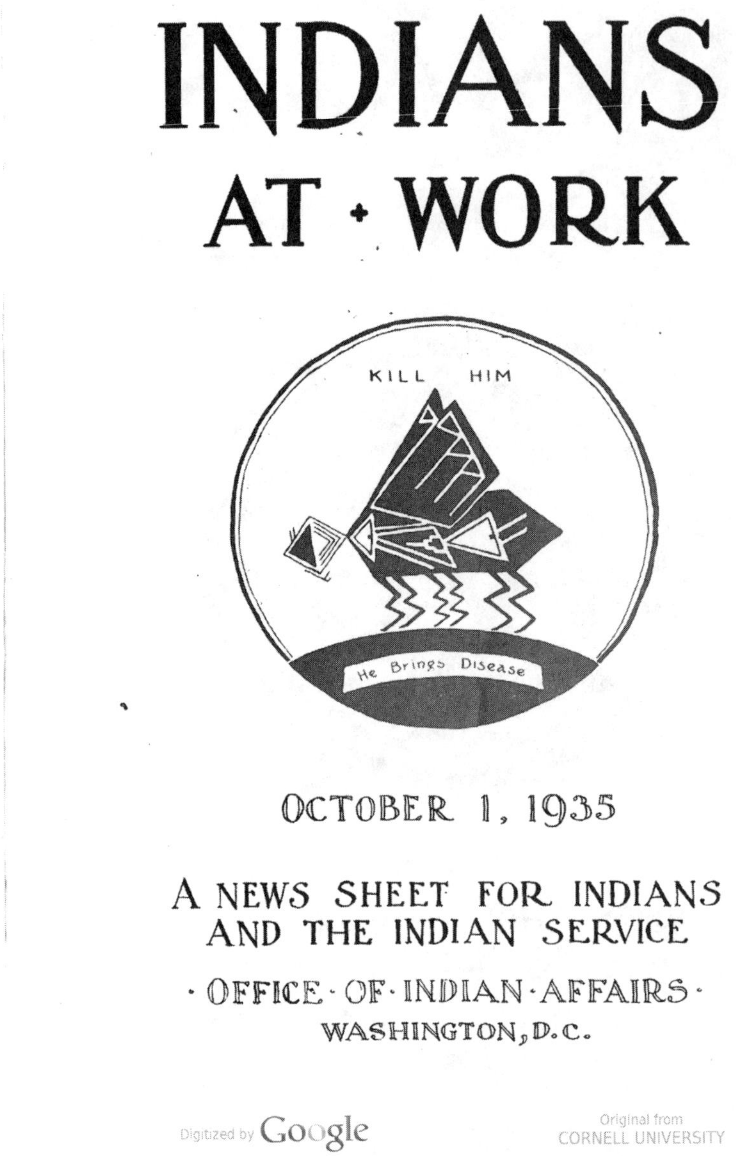

FIGURE 5. *IAW* October 1, 1935, Cover Page, HathiTrust, Cornell University Collection.

Other illustrations were instructive and offered artists a way of demonstrating their skill as a means of asserting authority. In the issue from April 15, 1936, Wilford Jones, a Navajo silversmith, submitted an account of how he made a ring. Only a page long, he intersperses short descriptions with detailed illustrations of the process. Jones also annotates the illustrations, providing further information to the reader (1936, 31). The use of the drawings provides a visual shorthand for the reader to appreciate Jones's skill and knowledge as a practicing artist. The reader can easily view what Jones describes in brief language as he describes the dynamic process of jewelry making. This focus on silverwork and material production is itself an expressive form that communicates complex intra-and intertribal relationships (Tone-Pah-Hote 2019, 99). In this case, *Indians at Work*, rather than being a mouthpiece for the OIA, provides a space for Jones to rescue the discussion of Indigenous art from bureaucrats and actively participate in conversations with a large and diverse reading audience. The use of illustrations throughout the magazine, including the many pictures from schoolchildren who chose to document their experiences through images rather than words, liberates both the artist and the reader from the limits of descriptive prose, allowing them to find additional messages and meanings.

Conclusion

There are over eight thousand pages of *Indians at Work*, with substantial contributions by Indigenous authors and illustrators. While this article has highlighted a few exemplary pieces, many more contributions within the magazine can aid in our collective understanding of the experiences of Indigenous communities in the early twentieth century. These contributions have not been noticed mainly because of the sheer scope of the magazine and the lack of a comprehensive indexing of its contents. But the voices are there. Tribal members working in the projects used *Indians at Work* as an opening and an opportunity to reshape representations of Indigenous life within the United States at the time.

Indigenous creators meant for their contributions to be read and shared among a varied audience. While they viewed *Indians at Work* as a conduit for messages to the Office of Indian Affairs, the contributors knew the reach of the periodical, and they used this to connect with the wide readership. They were writing for themselves, for their communities, and for the larger U.S. polity. These authors also played with the forms and styles that reflected the social and cultural tropes of the time. They tested limits and questioned premises explicitly through critique, and implicitly through lived experience. These alterations and creative subversions allowed them to be heard by those who were listening.

Authors seized the chance to contribute to this periodical, imperfect and problematic as it was, to directly engage in a public space about the current situation within tribal communities. To ensure that they were heard in the ways they intended, they relied on Indigenous speech registers and framing that marked their contributions as authoritative to a knowing audience. These authors referenced specific tribal practices to disrupt visions of an essentialized and romanticized Indigeneity, and they used humor to provoke and unsettle stereotypes of dependency. These contributions also disassembled the idea that Indigenous cultures were incongruous with modern life. This trope was not just prevalent in the U.S. at the time but also found within the editorials and articles written by others in *Indians at Work*. Ultimately, these contributions are a form of "storywork" where the authors use established discursive practices to claim knowledge and use it for social commentary and cultural instruction (Archibald et al. 2022). The administration, always looking for more material to supplement the magazine, provided Indigenous authors an opening in which they could articulate a complex and nuanced tribal identity. The periodical itself was a highly mediated space. Still, because of its breadth and access, it was in some ways less restrictive than other arts, language, and cultural programming associated with New Deal programs. The authors disrupted images and ideas fully located within established parameters of modernity and Indigeneity and created a space for something new.

MINDY MORGAN is an associate professor of anthropology and an affiliated faculty member of the American Indian and Indigenous Studies Program at Michigan State University. Her research concerns issues such as Indigenous language use and transmission, literacy practices, and knowledge construction within Indigenous communities in the United States.

Bibliography

Adams, David Wallace. 1995. *Education for Extinction: American Indians and the Boarding-School Experience, 1875–1928*. University of Kansas Press.

Agha, Asif. 2005. "Voice, Footing, Enregisterment." *Journal of Linguistic Anthropology* 15, no. 1: 38–59. https://doi.org/10.1525/jlin.2005.15.1.38.

Alexander, Benjamin F. 2018. *The New Deal's Forest Army: How the Civilian Conservation Corps Worked*. Johns Hopkins University Press.

Archibald, Jo-ann, Jenny Lee-Morgan, and Jason De Santolo, eds. 2022. *Decolonizing Research: Indigenous Storywork as Methodology*.Bloomsbury Academic.

Basso, Keith H. 1979. *Portraits of "the Whiteman": Linguistic Play and Cultural Symbols among Western Apache*. Cambridge University Press.

———. 1996. *Wisdom Sits in Places: Landscape and Language among the Western Apache*. University of New Mexico Press.

Beatty, Willard. 1936. "Education for the Whole Community." *Indians at Work* 3, no. 21: 28–30.

Benedict, Ruth. 1936. "The Broken Cup." *Indians at Work* 4, no. 5: 13.

Bruchac, Margaret M. 2018. *Savage Kin: Indigenous Informants and American Anthropologists.* University of Arizona Press.

Child, Brenda J. 2000. *Boarding School Seasons: American Indian Families, 1900–1940.* University of Nebraska Press.

Collier, John. 1934. "Editorial." *Indians at Work* 1, no. 11: 1–2.

———. 1935. "Editorial." *Indians at Work* 2, no. 24: 1–4.

———. 1936. "Editorial." *Indians at Work* 3, no. 23: 1–4.

———. 1963. *From Every Zenith: A Memoir; and Some Essays on Life and Thought.* Sage Books.

Cook, O.F. 1936. "Terrace Gardens and Other Agricultural Attainments of Indians of Ancient Peru." *Indians at Work* 3, no. 24: 6–9.

Cornebise, Alfred E. 2004. *The CCC Chronicles: Camp Newspapers of the Civilian Conservation Corps, 1933–1942.* McFarland & Co.

Davis, Jenny L. 2020. *Talking Indian: Identity and Language Revitalization in the Chickasaw Renaissance.* University of Arizona Press.

Deloria, Philip Joseph. 2004. *Indians in Unexpected Places.* 1st ed. University Press of Kansas.

Fear-Segal, Jacqueline. 2007. *White Man's Club: Schools, Race and the Struggle of Indian Acculturation.* University of Nebraska Press.

Garrison, Dee. 1989. *Mary Heaton Vorse: The Life of an American Insurgent.* Temple University Press.

Gorman, Carl. 1936. "Poems." *Indians at Work* 4, no. 7: 42.

Gower, Calvin W. 1972. "The CCC Indian Division: Aid for Depressed Americans, 1933–1942." *Minnesota History* 43, no. 1: 3–13.

Grey, P. 1936. "From IECW Reports." *Indians at Work* 4, no. 7: 51.

Head, Phil, and L. E. Holloway. 1937. "We Went to Mexico to See the Bolsas." *Indians at Work* 4, no. 20: 10–15.

Hosmer, Brian C. 2010. "'Dollar a Day and Glad to Have It': Work Relief of the Wind River Indian Reservation as Memory." In *Native Pathways: American Indian Culture and Economic Development in the Twentieth Century,* 97–105. University of Colorado Press.

Indian Arts and Craft Board. 1937. "Indian Silver Work Standards Announced." *Indians at Work* 4, no. 15: 45–46.

Jones, Wilford. 1936. "How I Make a Silver Navajo Ring." *Indians at Work* 3, no. 17: 31.

Knife, Andrew. 1936. "Indian Stories." *Indians at Work* 3, no. 17: 43–45.

Kunitz, Stephen J. 1971. "The Social Philosophy of John Collier." *Ethnohistory* 18, no. 3: 213–29. https://doi.org/10.2307/481531.

Lajimodiere, Denise K. 2019. *Stringing Rosaries: The History, the Unforgivable, and the Healing of Northern Plains American Indian Boarding School Survivors.* 1st ed. Contemporary Voices of Indigenous Peoples Series, Vol. 2. North Dakota State University Press.

Laukaitis, John J. 2006. "Indians at Work and John Collier's Campaign for Progressive Educational Reform, 1933–1945." *American Educational History Journal* 33, no. 2: 97–105.

Lawyer, Mylie. 1933. "Family Work in Two Medicine Camp, Blackfeet Reservation." *Indians at Work* 1, no. 5: 17.

Littlefield, Alice, and Martha C. Knack, eds. 1996. *Native Americans and Wage Labor: Ethnohistorical Perspectives.* University of Oklahoma Press.

Long, James L. 1935. "The Indian Trader Speaks." *Indians at Work* 3, no. 3: 28.

———. 1936. "Indian Hunting Story." *Indians at Work* 3, no. 19: 44.

Maher, Neil M. 2008. *Nature's New Deal: The Civilian Conservation Corps and the Roots of the American Environmental Movement.* Oxford University Press.

McLerran, Jennifer. 2012. *A New Deal for Native Art: Indian Arts and Federal Policy, 1933–1943.* University of Arizona Press.

Merrill, Perry Henry. 1981. *Roosevelt's Forest Army: A History of the Civilian Conservation Corps, 1933–1942.* P.H. Merrill.

Mitchell, Martin. 1937. "Hunting for Deer." *Indians at Work* 4, no. 20: 44.

———. 1938. "A Message from Fort Peck, Montana." *Indians at Work* 5, no. 5: 22.

Morgan, Mindy J. 2005. "Constructions and Contestations of the Authoritative Voice: Native American Communities and the Federal Writers' Project, 1935–41." *American Indian Quarterly* 29, no. 1/2: 56–83.

———. 2013. "Acts of Inscription: Dialogism in the Archives." In *Transforming Ethnohistories: Narrative, Meaning, and Community,* edited by Sebastian Braun. University of Oklahoma Press.

———. 2017. "Anthropologists in Unexpected Places: Tracing Anthropological Theory, Practice, and Policy in *Indians at Work*." *American Anthropologist* 119, no. 3: 435–47. https://doi.org/10.1111/aman.12892.

———. 2020. "'Through Word and Picture': Land of Nakoda and the Montana Writers' Project." In *New Deal Art in the Northwest: The WPA and Beyond,* edited by Margaret E.

Bullock. Tacoma Art Museum.

National Park Service. n.d. "Mylie Lawyer and Her Collection." Department of Interior. https://npshistory.com/publications/nepe/brochures/mylie-lawyer.pdf.

Neihardt, John Gneisenau, and Raymond J. DeMallie. 1991. *When the Tree Flowered: The Story of Eagle Voice, a Sioux Indian.* University of Nebraska Press.

Nolan, Ann, and Afraid of Hawk, Emil. 1944. *Brave Against the Enemy.* United States Indian Service, Education Division. https://digital.library.cornell.edu/catalog/hunt0111.

Office of Indian Affairs. 1936. "Appointment of Rene D'Harnoncourt." *Indians at Work* 4, no. 6: 12.

———. 1939. "Reorganization News." *Indians at Work* 6, no. 5: 4.

Pabanale, Irving. 1934. "A Hopi Appreciation." *Indians at Work* 1, no. 20: 25.

———. 1935. "Hopi Pottery." *Indians at Work* 2, no. 24: 21.

———. 1936. "A Hopi Loves His Desert Land." *Indians at Work* 3, no. 23: 45.

Pabanale, Irving, and Robert A. Black. 2001. *Standing Flower: The Life of Irving Pabanale, an Arizona Tewa Indian.* University of Utah Press.

Parman, Donald L. 1967. "The Indian Civilian Conservation Corps." PhD diss., University of Oklahoma.

———. 1971. "The Indian and the Civilian Conservation Corps." *Pacific Historical Review* 40, no. 1: 39–56.

Philp, Kenneth Roy. 1981. *John Collier's Crusade for Indian Reform: 1920—1954*. University of Arizona Press.

Pinto, Willie. 1937. "From IECW Reports." *Indians at Work* 4, no. 15: 49.

Poitras, Leon. 1936. "From IECW Reports." *Indians at Work* 3, no.17: 50.

Raibmon, Paige Sylvia. 2005. *Authentic Indians: Episodes of Encounter from the Late-Nineteenth-Century Northwest Coast*. Duke University Press.

Randall, Frank. 1937. "A Message from Fort Hall." *Indians at Work* 5, no.4: 37.

Santee, J. F. 1934. "Lawyer of the Nez Perces." *The Washington Historical Quarterly* 25, no. 1: 37–48.

Rose, Susan D., and Jacqueline Fear-Segal, eds. 2016. *Carlisle Indian Industrial School: Indigenous Histories, Memories, and Reclamations*. University of Nebraska Press.

Shawver, James. 1939. "From CCC-ID Reports." *Indians at Work* 6, no. 5: 44.

Sippi, Naomi (Myron). 1933. "Work in the Family Camps at San Carlos." *Indians at Work* 1, no. 6: 15.

Smith, Dama Margaret. 1936. "Hopi Pottery." *Indians at Work* 4, no. 5: 12.

Spielmann, Roger Willson. 1998. *"You're so Fat!": Exploring Ojibwe Discourse*. University of Toronto Press.

Stewart, James. 1934. "Plains Indian Congress." *Indians at Work* 1, no. 15: 4–7.

Strong, Pauline Turner. 2012. *American Indians and the American Imaginary: Cultural Representation across the Centuries*. Paradigm Publishers.

Thunder Hawk, Adelbert. 1936. "Rosebud Weighs the Future." *Indians at Work* 4, no. 5: 7–10.

United States Congress. 1929. *Survey of Conditions of the Indians in the United States. Hearings before a Subcommittee of the Committee on Indian Affairs, United States Senate, Seventieth Congress, Second Session*. U.S. Government Printing Office. https://catalog.hathitrust.org/Record/000622054.

Tone-Pah-Hote, Jenny. 2019. *Crafting an Indigenous Nation: Kiowa Expressive Culture in the Progressive Era*. The University of North Carolina Press.

Usner, Daniel H. 2009. *Indian Work: Language and Livelihood in Native American History*. Harvard University Press.

Vigil, Kiara M. 2015. *Indigenous Intellectuals: Sovereignty, Citizenship, and the American Imagination, 1880–1930*. Studies in North American Indian History. Cambridge University Press.

Vorse, Mary Heaton. 1935. "There Is Hope in South Dakota." *Indians at Work* 3, no. 2: 11.

White, Cody. 2016. "The CCC Indian Division." *Prologue* 48, no. 2: 53–59.

Wilson, Thomas. 1937. "How an Oklahoma County Was Named." *Indians at Work* 5, no. 1: 34.

Zimmer, Eric Steven. 2015. "Building the Red Earth Nation: The Civilian Conservation Corps—Indian Division on the Meskwaki Settlement." *Native American and Indigenous Studies* 2 (2): 106–33. https://doi.org/10.5749/natiindistudj.2.2.0106.

Notes

1. The Office of Indian Affairs (OIA) was the title of the department for Indian Affairs within the Department of the Interior. It became the Bureau of Indian Affairs (BIA) in 1947. I have used OIA for this article as that was the name during the time under discussion.

2. The IECW formally became the CCC-ID in 1937. For clarity, I use CCC-ID throughout the article to reference the program.

3. For example, the issue from October 15, 1936, includes a reprint of author Dama Margaret Smith's article "Hopi Pottery" which originally was published in *Southwest Tourist News* (Smith 1936). Anthropologist Ruth Benedict submitted several articles, including "The Broken Cup," which was excerpted from her book, *Patterns of Culture* (1936).

4. These dates include most issues since they cover the transition from a bi-weekly to a monthly publication. Later issues of the magazine were more highly curated, and the contributions were narrower in range due to the influence of Floyd LaRouche, a former labor journalist and investigative reporter, who became the Director of Information for the Office of Indian Affairs and the primary editor for *Indians at Work* in 1939.

5. Knife Chief participated in the Battle of the Little Bighorn, was with Crazy Horse at the surrender at Red Cloud and escaped to Canada with Sitting Bull. He and his family were ultimately transferred back to Pine Ridge in the early 1880s.

6. Mylie Lawyer's paternal great-grandfather was the well-known Chief Lawyer who led the Nez Perce in treaty negotiations during the mid-nineteenth century. Her great-great-grandfather was Twisted Hair, who was one of the Nez Perce leaders who met the Lewis and Clark expedition.

7. While the introduction to her 1933 submission states that she was a graduate of Willamette University, she earned her degree in home economics in 1934 (National Park Service, n. d.).

8. Early boarding schools, such as Carlisle, were directly tied to the displacement and incarceration of Indigenous families (Fear-Segal 2007; Rose and Fear-Segal 2016).

ALLYSON LAFORGE

"We Are Building for Our Children": Crafting Intertribal Activism in Southern New England

Abstract

Intertribal organizing has long been a feature of resistance to settler colonialism in southern New England. In the eighteenth and nineteenth centuries, shared material culture practices facilitated ongoing intertribal connections and activism. The emergence of the Rhode Island–based organization the Sons and Daughters of the First Americans (SDFA) in 1937 illuminates how twentieth-century intertribalism in the Native Northeast constituted a continuation of these practices and responded to uniquely unfolding local settler colonial policies and narratives. The SDFA worked to recover and disseminate Native histories to assert the active presence of Native peoples in Rhode Island after the state's attempt to detribalize the Narragansett Indian Tribe in the late nineteenth century. The SDFA's focus on the creation of material culture, with members crafting, displaying, and selling their handicraft, communicated their continued existence and ensured the transmission of cultural knowledge to the next generation of Native children. For the SDFA, material culture practices did not only encompass handicraft, but the continuation of their relationships with historical landscapes, gathering places, and architectures. The study of these material culture practices reveals how twentieth-century intertribal activism in southern New England maintained Indigenous knowledge away from colonial sites of meaning-making while also intervening in false narratives of Native disappearance.

ON A WARM JUNE DAY in 1937, a group of Native people from southern New England met at the Kenyon, Rhode Island home of Ruth Brown for the first formal meeting of the Sons and Daughters of the First Americans (SDFA). A club for people of Native descent, the SDFA brought together Narragansetts, Wampanoags, Pequots, and other members of tribal nations in order to, in their words, maintain the "true spirit of Indianhood in New England."[1] Based in Narragansett homelands, the SDFA's intertribal membership was also heavily informed by Narragansett political and intellectual genealogies. At their first meeting, the members resolved to compile what they called a "true to life history of the red race and its tradition" through "detailed research work."[2] Compiling this "true to life history" contested the histories written and disseminated by Euro-American settlers to assemble a body of Native-led knowledge that would be stewarded into the future.

The SDFA was established in the decades-long aftermath of Narragansett detribalization, which the state of Rhode Island implemented in 1880 in an attempt to dissolve Narragansett tribal governance and sell tribal lands into private hands. In 1934, when the federal government passed the Indian Reorganization Act (IRA), or Wheeler-Howard Act, Narragansetts pursued reorganization as a strategy for reversing detribalization and its assimilative policies. Detribalization had also imposed United States citizenship on Narragansett tribal members, preceding the 1924 Indian Citizenship Act by nearly fifty years.[3] While Narragansetts resisted these acts, the IRA was the first piece of legislation that provided a pathway for reinstatement of tribal lands as well as federal recognition of tribal status. Upon receiving a new tribal charter from the state of Rhode Island, the Narragansett established several new clubs to provide opportunities for tribal involvement, including the Narragansett Historic Club. The SDFA, which evolved from the Narragansett Historic Club, decided to open its membership to members of all southern New England tribes in 1937, when this first meeting took place.[4]

The SDFA's emphasis on historical recovery emerged from both tribal reorganization and intertribal activism, including a long history of resistance to settler colonial policies and narratives of Indigeneity in the Northeast. During this meeting, Narragansett member Christopher Noka proposed the name the "Sons and Daughters of the First Americans," which challenged settler claims of belonging to New England. As Noka announced, eligibility for membership would be reserved only for those who were descendants of the true first Americans, which the club described as the "Aborigines" of New England.[5] Settler-run organizations, such as the Daughters of the American Revolution and the General Society of Mayflower Descendants, drew upon their members' lineage-based connection to early American history to proclaim their belonging to the United States. The SDFA challenged these processes of settler identity-crafting, which also took shape in town histories and other forms of historical narrativization. As Jean O'Brien has shown in *Firsting and Lasting: Writing Indians out of Existence in New England,* throughout the nineteenth century, white town historians wrote "replacement narratives" that "appropriate[d] the category 'indigenous' away from Indians and for themselves."[6] The intertribal alliance of people involved in the SDFA protested these replacement narratives by vowing to "save all that is fine in our history" and proclaim their active presence and future as Native people, the *true* descendants of the first Americans.[7]

The SDFA joined a network of intertribal organizations in southern New England dedicated to the preservation of Native lifeways in the early twentieth century. Central to their advocacy was the creation of material culture, which they not only shared at ceremonies and exhibits but also used to facilitate collaboration and organizing across these intertribal Native groups.[8] The organization drew from long-standing histories of material culture activism in southern New England, which grew from intertribal connections and relationships that preceded the establishment of twentieth-century intertribal organizations like the SDFA, National Algonquin Indian Council (NAIC), and American Indian Federation (AIF). While both the NAIC and AIF incorporated handicraft into their programming, such as pageants, the SDFA was unique in its focus on crafting and exhibiting material culture from southern New England to intervene into Western collecting and displaying practices and the appropriation of Native art by non-Native organizations and institutions.

SDFA members referred to many of their original works as "handicraft," which included baskets, bows, arrows, regalia, and more. For millennia, Native people created the material culture they needed for their lives in the Dawnland.[9] After colonization, members of Algonquian nations adapted certain items, like baskets, for sale to settlers to ensure their cultural and economic survival. They worked within and across their tribal nations and continued long-standing mobility practices to organize and craft these Belongings.[10] In the twentieth century, the concept of handicraft reflected the desires of Western consumers for handmade, non-industrialized items, particularly those made by Native makers whose works settlers considered exotic or as "curiosities."[11] Both in their name and mission, the SDFA recognized that playing on these settler desires for Indianness and wielding their handicraft internally and externally could help advance their organizational goals.

This article argues the SDFA's collective creation, use, and display of handicraft facilitated an intertribal movement for Native sovereignty that continued in the tradition of material culture activism and communicated the ongoing presence of tribal nations in New England after centuries of settler colonial erasure. From the lead-up to their founding in 1937 through their disbanding in 1970, the SDFA resolved to craft and display "Indian handicraft" in multiple settings. The organization's bylaws explained the goals of the organization were to "study, portray and preserve, the history, art, rituals, language, handicraft and music of the New England Indians."[12] As these bylaws show, written history was not the only, nor even the most important, mode of understanding Native history.[13] The SDFA's collective activities were not limited to stories about the past, but included the transmission of multiple knowledges. For the SDFA and other Native-led organizations in the twentieth century, the transmission of knowledge about the creation of material culture at all stages—gathering, preparing, crafting, and using—was foundational to ensure the continuity of these practices in future generations.

The SDFA also maintained relationships with homelands that contained the resources for gathering materials, building physical places, and crafting and disseminating Native-made items. The ability to carry on these material culture practices was contingent on this access to land, which was critical to the process of securing Indigenous futures. For the SDFA, the land provided resources for the creation of handicraft while also serving as a source of social and place-based gathering. Material culture did not only consist of the handicraft that SDFA members created, like baskets, wampum, and pottery, but included Indigenous architectures like long houses, wetuash, and other dwellings that hosted gatherings and communicated to outsiders that Native lifeways and modes of existence persisted in southern New England.[14] The materiality of the SDFA encompassed the entire embodied set of physical and political relations with these Belongings, architectures, and places. These places had been Indigenous since time immemorial and continued to be so, despite years of colonial incursions that attempted to delegitimize tribal relationships to their lands and each other. These relations show another dimension of material culture, in which many "artifacts" are *not* objects, but rather are agential and alive.[15] While much of the handicraft of the SDFA is no longer either extant or identifiable, recognizing the agency of the material Belongings that members created requires a method of reading that engages them as powerful political tools.

The records of the SDFA are currently held in the Tomaquag Museum, an Indigenous-led museum presently located in Narragansett homelands in Exeter, RI, with a planned move to a new campus adjacent to the University of Rhode Island.[16] Begun in 1958 by non-Native anthropologist Eva Butler and Narragansett and Wampanoag SDFA co-founder Princess Red Wing, the Tomaquag Museum emerged in part from the intertribal networks within which the SDFA was situated.[17] Like the SDFA, the Tomaquag Museum is based within Narragansett homelands and aims to educate the public about tribal relations across the Dawnland, with a focus on southern New England.[18] I have been embedded in the work of the Tomaquag Museum since 2019, when I began a long-term project inventorying the museum's vast collection of more than twelve thousand Native-made cultural "Belongings," the term that Narragansett and Niantic Executive Director Lorén Spears uses today to describe the Native-made items in the museum's collections. The museum's current collections policy describes Belongings as a concept that "recognizes that they are interconnected to the cultural contexts of their creation and maintain connections to people, both historical and contemporary."[19] These Belongings include not only handicraft, but also the documentary records within the museum's archival collections. My research on the SDFA has taken place within the context of my ongoing collaboration with the Tomaquag Museum, which has led me to ask questions about how Narragansett, Niantic, Wampanoag, and other tribal peoples from southern New England have stewarded their own histories through the present day.

The notebooks of the SDFA include dozens of examples of poetry and other creative works alongside meticulous meeting minutes, evincing exactly how the organization worked to transmit Indigenous knowledge to future generations. Like the handicraft of the SDFA, these records are agential material Belongings that can be used to build community within the intertribal networks that continue to structure the Native Northeast. A handwritten poem in an SDFA notebook from 1947 by L. Weeden powerfully illustrates how the SDFA juxtaposed the traditional language of history-making alongside the language of Indigenous sovereignty, drawing from both physical and metaphorical architectures.[20] In "We Are Building for our Children," Weeden wrote,

> Our children will hear of Marco Polo
> The Venetian traveler and author of history.
> Of Socrates, the Athenian philosopher,
> Of which sayings have come down from B.C. to A.D.
> Of the Chinese philosophers with one of the
> Oldest histories in this world.
> Yes, we could go on and on endlessly,
> But WHY continue this?
> Our children have a heritage
> That goes back before the beginning of America
> Their Platos are the Sun, the Moon, the Sky and the Earth.
> Yes, we are building for our children
> Not just a house, but an era
> That will stand and remain
> Down thru the ages to come![21]

Situating Native histories and philosophies as both equal in stature to European and Asian philosophies and embedded in the natural world, Weeden made clear the primary goal of these intertribal movements of the mid-twentieth century: to ensure that Native history and sovereignty endured into the future. The act of building "not just a house, but an era" materialized these goals as a long-term practice.

This essay situates the emergence of the SDFA in the 1930s within a broader history of intertribal material culture activism that sustained relationships with Indigenous homelands in the face of destructive settler colonial incursions and policies. It also analyzes two preceding projects—the publication of the periodical *The Narragansett Dawn* between 1935 and 1936 and the Tercentenary Events of 1936—that led to the founding of the SDFA. These projects included many of the SDFA's future members as participants and reflected intertribal commitments to material culture activism. SDFA projects to create and exhibit handicraft, build long houses and wetuash, and teach their children how to craft material culture drew from these intertribal knowledge bases that maintained histories away from colonial sites. As Weeden's poem argues, the SDFA drew from these histories to create a temporal and ideological shift in the present and future of New England. The maintenance of these histories depended on ongoing tribal and intertribal relationships that continued despite destructive settler colonial policies and ideologies, including documentary genocide, land seizures, and the state of Rhode Island's attempt to forcibly detribalize the Narragansett nation in 1880.[22] In the midst of these onslaughts, tribal members of Narragansett, Niantic, Nipmuc, Wampanoag, Pequot, and other nations wielded material culture to affirm their ongoing relationships to the land and each other. These nations continued to exist *as nations* throughout this nineteenth- and early twentieth-century period, despite colonial narratives of Indigenous decline. As a deliberate counterpoint to these colonial frameworks, this essay draws from multiple Native-authored and colonial sources to narrate the historical contexts of the SDFA's activism and community building to emphasize the organization as a continuation of these intertribal traditions in southern New England.

Twentieth-century intertribalism in the Native Northeast was a means of protecting tribal sovereignty through coalition-building that honored the distinctiveness of individual tribal nations while also being attentive to their shared histories and goals. The intertribalism of the SDFA was distinct from the pan-Indian movements of the early twentieth century, which developed from Assimilation Era policies that sought to eradicate tribal sovereignty and racialize Native peoples as subjects of the American nation-state. As Beth Piatote has described, "Assimilation-era policies . . . were driven by the notion that the tribal-national polity, as a competing national sovereignty, must be destroyed."[23] Kent Blansett has further elucidated how the concept of pan-Indianism grew from this era toward the racialization of American Indians as a collective group. In contrast to Pan-Indianism, Blansett offers the term "Intertribalism," which "centers on the power of place and Native Nationalist definitions of shared culture."[24] Blansett's analysis of intertribalism is rooted in the Red Power movement of the 1960s and 70s, but this article argues for an earlier political movement of intertribalism that took place in the Native Northeast during the first half of the twentieth century, which also did not subscribe to the logics or goals of pan-Indianism. While SDFA members incorporated elements of pan-Indianism into their public-facing advocacy, such as wearing Plains-style headdresses, their organizational goals focused specifically on preserving the histories and cultures of the "New England Indians."[25] The SDFA wielded its intertribalism to assert the sovereignty and survival of Native peoples in the Northeast. The roots of this resistance in the Native Northeast trace back to intertribal movements against English incursions beginning in the seventeenth century, and continue through the present day.[26]

Survival Strategies on Native Land

The SDFA's mission to steward their histories beyond the purview of colonial meaning-making derived from centuries of survival strategies that affirmed ongoing relationships with Indigenous homelands outside the bounds of settler colonial property ownership. Throughout the eighteenth and nineteenth centuries, Native people in southern New England gathered natural materials from their homelands to create and sell items like baskets, chairs, and brooms, traveling across these homelands and often staying with other Indigenous people as they peddled their wares.[27] The maintenance of material culture practices connected Native people to each other, their homelands, and Native histories, establishing the foundations of intertribal material culture activism. Weaving woodsplints, bark, sweetgrass, and other locally sourced materials into baskets for sale to colonial households came to represent Native ingenuity and craft, while also providing vital sources of income for basket-makers who depended on these sales to feed and clothe their families amidst land loss and the imposition of capitalism on their communities. While distinct, Algonquian nations had similar processes of harvesting and crafting material culture from interconnected homelands. The creation of items like twined bags, mishoonash (dugout canoes), burl bowls, woodsplint baskets, and more spanned across these nations and enabled continuous intertribal connections in the eighteenth and nineteenth centuries. These material culture practices persisted into the twentieth century to become an element of New England intertribal organizing, while also challenging the vanishing Indian myth, which claimed that Native people had disappeared from New England.[28]

These colonial mythologies also connected Indigenous material culture to settler constructs of Native vagrancy and poverty. As Ella Wilcox Sekatu and Ruth Wallis Herndon have demonstrated, an oppositional relationship existed between Native people and Rhode Island town officials during the Revolutionary Era, in which town leaders designated Narragansetts and other Native people as "'the poor,' in need of official oversight." Town officials also designated Native people as no longer "Indian," instead racializing them as "Negro," "black," or "mustee," a term that reflected the mixture of "Indian" and "Negro."[29] These processes of documentary genocide, in which colonial officials wrote Narragansett and other Native people from southern New England out of town records, paralleled processes of marginalization and colonial "management" of Native people who continued to live within and beyond their homelands.[30] Attempts to shift the political identity of Indian to these racialized categories was a settler colonial strategy, which, as Patrick Wolfe argues, "destroys to replace" Native peoples as Native.[31] In the case of Rhode Island, the racialization of Native people as Black not only aimed to erase the possibility of Natives who held both Black ancestry and kinship relations but also created an oppositional relationship between Blackness and Indigeneity, in which the former evolved to eliminate the latter.[32] Despite these processes, both continuous Native identities and Native-Black kinship persisted.

Throughout the nineteenth century, instances of ongoing Indigenous material culture practices appeared in colonial histories, in which authors frequently subscribed to similar settler colonial logics of marginalization and elimination that town officials did in their classifications of Native people. Many colonial authors of town histories and local studies viewed Native people as impoverished and dying out. These authors often failed to see how practices like weaving basket or creating other material Belongings maintained both tribal and intertribal relationships on Native lands. For example, Esther Bernon Carpenter included a scene about a Native woman in her 1887 book *South-county Neighbors,* which consisted of her oft-exaggerated character studies from "forty or fifty years ago." Carpenter described a Native woman, presumably Narragansett, from Charlestown, RI, who was "laden with baskets, her handiwork and stock in trade." This Narragansett woman was the "boon companion" of Lettice Jetsam, a "more commonplace vagrant," who "was searching the swamp on the Waterside shore always known as the 'Indian Garden,' whither, as traditionary story relates, Miantonomi resorted for the potent herbs used in his wigwam, pitched a few miles inland, at 'Miantonomi's Rock.'" With the Narragansett woman's help, Jetsam "pursued her hunt after simples."[33] Carpenter associated the Narragansett woman with "vagrancy," ignoring the ways that existing beyond the borders of towns enabled cultural survival and the continuance of Indigenous mobility practices. This garden had existed since at least the

FIGURE 1. Stamped woodsplint basket from the collections of the Tomaquag Museum. This basket was likely crafted by a Native artist from southern New England in the nineteenth century. Photograph courtesy of the Tomaquag Museum.

seventeenth century, when the Narragansett sachem Miantonomi traveled there with his kin to gather the cattails, bulrushes, and other plants to be woven into mats for his wetu, or home.[34]

Although Carpenter recounted how Miantonomi and his relations had gathered plants in this place, she did not acknowledge the connection between the Narragansett woman's baskets and the swamp where she found her. Carpenter missed the connection between ongoing environmental acumen and place-based knowledge, as the Narragansett woman frequented a well-known swamp where plants such as cedar, sweetgrass, bulrushes, cattails, and many herbs and "simples" grew. These plants, such as the cattails and bulrushes woven into mats for Miantonomi's "wigwam," had multiple purposes. While colonial accounts framed Native access to and use of land as acts that did not respect property rights, these gathering practices allowed Native people to return to places imbued with history and memory. Christine DeLucia has described how swamps "provided critical shelter during times of conflict," offering specific places where, into the nineteenth century, Narragansett people could find refuge. Swamps and wetlands were also an environment that generated plant-sustaining nutrients, which produced the "simples" that the Narragansett woman gathered.[35] The plants from this swamp not only facilitated Narragansett medicine and recipes but also provided materials for the Narragansett woman to craft baskets and other handicrafts she carried, used, and sold. She repeatedly returned to this swamp, gathering these known plants to create baskets and medicines that had sustained her community's sovereignty for centuries.

The ongoing use of Native lands to gather plants to craft baskets and other items also constituted acts of resistance to settler colonial private property ownership. Henry Reed Stiles wrote mockingly of these practices in his 1859 history of the town of Windsor, CT, reflecting in a footnote on how a "prevalent notion among the people of New England, that the Indians, of the present day, have still a claim or *right* to certain privileges within the domains once owned by their ancestors" still persisted.[36] Per Stiles, the Indians took advantage of this notion to "steal from the forest with perfect impunity the materials for the manufacture of their basket, willow, and fancy wares."[37] These practices represented the continuation of Native rights to hunt, fish, and gather within their homelands, which Stiles correctly identified as a "hereditary right" commonly understood by both settlers and Native people as deriving from "many Indian deeds." Yet he refused the legitimacy of this hereditary right, recognizing only the property rights of the new "owners" of these lands.[38] This "privilege" was also recorded in the proceedings of the Commission of Investigation on the Affairs of the Narragansett Indians to the General Assembly of Rhode Island, the body that in multiple instances, ultimately determined detribalization.[39] Even as some property owners, town officials, and writers like Stiles refused the notion that Native people had an ongoing right to gather materials from their homelands, the practice persisted, as did the common knowledge of these rights. Crafting material culture was entwined with access to land, and the ongoing use of the land to continue basketry and other crafting practices became a mode of refusal of settler constructs like private property. "English fixity sought to replace Indian mobility," as William Cronon wrote of early New England colonization, but did not succeed in doing so.[40]

Resisting Illegal Detribalization in Rhode Island

In the late nineteenth century, the state of Rhode Island made moves to detribalize the Narragansett Tribe as a whole and dissolve tribal lands, which were not only sites with deep historical meaning but communal sources of wood, basket sticks, beach barks, and other plants and herbs.[41] Detribalization targeted the survival strategies that Narragansett and other Native people in Rhode Island pursued throughout the eighteenth and nineteenth centuries. In 1880, the Rhode Island State Assembly passed "An Act to Abolish the Tribal Authority and Tribal Relations of the Narragansett Tribe of

Indians." As described a century later, when the United States Department of the Interior finally reversed this decision and granted the Narragansett Indian Tribe federal recognition in 1983, this 1880 act "purported to abolish tribal authority and tribal relations, declared tribal members citizens, ended the state's relationship with the tribe, and . . . authorized the sale of all land held in common."[42] Just two acres of land surrounding the Narragansett Church in Charleston, RI, were saved for the tribe. From this dissolving of tribal lands, Narragansetts received $5,000, divided among eligible tribal members. The Assembly determined the number of eligible tribal members, including children, to be 334, meaning each member received the paltry sum of $15.43.[43]

The officials who decided on detribalization based their decision on specious evidence of Narragansett decline, including the notion that "there is not a person of pure Indian blood in the tribe," with colors ranging from "Caucasian to the Black race."[44] A result of the processes of documentary genocide in the eighteenth century—as well as Reconstruction-era race policies in New England that deemed Indians as "non-white" as a tool for assimilation—this decision followed the settler colonial logic that Native identity was exclusively racial, rather than political and relational.[45] Yet even in the 1880 proceedings of the Commission, this logic contradicted itself. One of the major pieces of the evidence that the Commission reported in their recommendation to dissolve the Narragansett Tribe was that "morally, the tribal relation exercises a pernicious influence, and encourages pauperism and vagabondism."[46] *The tribal relation.* While no "pure Indians" existed in their narrative, the Commission recognized that the Narragansett Tribe continued as a relational body, whose members were bound to each other, the Tribe, and other tribal nations. The reference to "pauperism and vagabondism" concerned not only economic oppression but the ongoing Indigenous place-based mobility and material culture practices that the Commission also acknowledged in its discussions of wood cutting, basket stick gathering, and other modes of gathering and existing in relationship with Narragansett land.[47]

Detribalization successfully privatized the majority of Narragansett tribal lands, but the law did not dissolve tribal relationships, nor did it prevent the ongoing use of land for gathering and mobility practices. Throughout the late nineteenth and early twentieth centuries, Narragansetts continued to hold August Meetings at the Narragansett Church every year, which was just one means of visible gathering.[48] Narragansetts also carried on in relation to each other beyond the church, maintaining old relationships and creating new ones within and beyond the tribe. These continuous relationships formed the basis of a new movement of twentieth-century intertribal organizing in southern New England.

Public-Facing Advocacy: The Narragansett Dawn *and Rhode Island Indian Day*

The creation of the tribal periodical *The Narragansett Dawn* in 1935 was a landmark moment within the history of Native activism in Rhode Island, offering a print forum that put into writing the web of relationships that survived the years after detribalization. The newspaper, while focused primarily on Narragansett issues, reflected the intertribal organizing that led to the SDFA's founding, incorporating articles, stories, poetry, and more from multiple members of the Narragansett and other New England tribal nations. Two founding members of the SDFA, Ernest Hazard and Red Wing, also founded the periodical, serving as editors and writers during its two-year run. In the first issue, Red Wing described the nearly sixty years between detribalization and the publication of *The Narragansett Dawn* as a "long night," in which "the Narragansett Spirit has lain dormant," with the August meetings at the Indian Church as "the only star that has twinkled in and out, during this time." The framing of these years as a "long night" of political dormancy was a useful metaphor, as it made clear that detribalization was a temporary state. Red Wing refused the implications of the act of detribalization, writing that even though this act had "recorded the tribe as extinguished, . . . all the recording in the country can not change the blood or wipe it out."[49] While detribalization created an era of political dormancy, it did not destroy the Narragansett Tribe as it intended to. The fact that the Assembly had sold off Narragansett land as private property did not transform it from ancestral territory; the land itself remained Narragansett, even as its "owners" changed.

The Narragansett Dawn made these continuous relationships legible and operated not only as a community forum, but as a political tool that disseminated both Narragansett and intertribal topics in southern Rhode Island. Published in the two years following the 1934 Indian Reorganization Act, Red Wing and Hazard included relevant political letters of support in the first issue of the periodical. Eleanor Roosevelt, writing from the White House, stated her support of what Red Wing was "trying to do for the Narragansett Tribe of Indians" and offering her "best wishes for success."[50] Another note of support came from the Rhode Island State Federation of Women's Clubs, who offered "encouragement" that "the movement may grow, and through the issues of the 'Narragansett Dawn' many friends will help make practical the visions of a few sincere Narragansett Indians who pray a new deal and a dawn for their people."[51] The periodical's keeper of records, Marion Brown, also reported that Mohegan medicine woman and anthropologist Gladys Tantaquidgeon traveled from Washington, D.C. to attend the first

Narragansett tribal meeting in fifty-three years as a representative from the Indian Bureau of the Department of the Interior.[52]

Red Wing was committed to finding support for the Narragansett cause at multiple levels and from multiple significant people and organizations as an activist strategy. For her, the Indian New Deal offered one possibility for support, but as her writing in *The Narragansett Dawn* made clear, Narragansett people did not consider their validity as stemming from governmental recognition. Just as state detribalization did not destroy the Narragansett Tribe, federal acknowledgment would not legitimize it. Rather, the work to publicize and organize around Narragansett and other Native histories, particularly through teaching and sharing histories and crafting and displaying material culture, communicated Native sovereignty within intertribal spaces and to the general public through multiple forums. Tantaquidgeon's presence at the Narragansett Tribal Meeting demonstrated how these interrelationships structured political life; while her role at the Indian Bureau was significant for Narragansetts, she also attended as a member of these intertribal networks, including as the former Secretary of the National Algonquin Indian Council.

The editors of *The Narragansett Dawn* also worked to recover early Indigenous histories, narrating how Native people adapted to colonization and publishing accounts from tribal members who shared their family histories. The creation and sale of material culture had often maintained both mobility practices and relationships between extended kinship networks, connecting people across southern New England. In the August 1935 issue, Red Wing focused her editorial on narratives of "home," considering the ways that Narragansetts and other Native people "changed their conception of homes" after the arrival of English colonists. Even though Native people had lost much of their freedom of movement after King Philip's War, Red Wing noted that many would still "move to the woods in summer" where they would "gather herbs, berries, roots and barks; make baskets and matts." When the season turned to fall and winter, "they traveled, selling their wares."[53] As Nipmuc knowledge-keeper Sarah Cisco Sullivan recalled, "Coming through Grafton, this seemed to be the stopping place. I was a little girl then, but I remembered how grandma used to have the attic floor filled with mattresses, some times for men to sleep on. The ladies and girls slept downstairs."[54] These intertribal networks sheltered relatives and extended kin, ensuring that those engaged in the seasonal trade of baskets and other wares had a place to stay.

The continuation of these mobility and material culture practices depended on these ongoing relationships, which also maintained Indigenous histories away from colonial accounts and town histories. These accounts in

The Narragansett Dawn demonstrate how Native people in the early twentieth century deliberately worked to record and publish these histories from the early period, listing activities like gathering and basket-making that had survived since deep time. The periodical also advertised and reported on Native handicraft for sale or display in multiple issues, evidencing how these practices had an unbroken lineage, despite detribalization's effects on land stewardship.[55] Unlike Carpenter and other colonial narrators, the Native people who worked on this tribal periodical understood that these relationships between place-based knowledge and tribal and intertribal networks had existed since time immemorial and continued through the present day. Their histories served not only to challenge these colonial accounts but the entire myth of Native disappearance. Listing multiple specific places and homesteads that had sheltered Native families for centuries, Red Wing concluded her editorial with a specific aim: "We tell you these family relations to show you our tribal blood has married tribal blood and therefore cannot possibly be lost. If some of these old roofs could talk,—they would laugh at some theories of the 'Vanishing American.'"[56]

In addition to the publication of *The Narragansett Dawn,* Red Wing and other Native organizers pursued strategies for Native recognition in Rhode Island. Nineteen thirty-six was the Tercentenary Year of Rhode Island, a key moment for Native people to proclaim their ongoing presence in the state. That year, Red Wing proposed the first annual Rhode Island Indian Day, an intertribal celebration that intervened in the state's lack of acknowledgment of Narragansett and other Native nations' existence since detribalization. Red Wing petitioned for this day in the Rhode Island House of Representatives, which formed a branch of the General Assembly—the same body that voted to detribalize the Narragansett fifty-six years prior.[57] On April 24, the bill to "annually issue a proclamation setting apart a day as Indian Day and recommending that it be observed by the people of this State with appropriate exercises in the public schools and otherwise commemorative of the Indian Tribes of Rhode Island, including the Narragansetts, Wampanoags, Nipmucs, Aquednecks, and Niantics" became law.

Red Wing attended the ceremony alongside Chief Nighthawk (Philip Peckham), Chief Pine Tree (William Wilcox), Princess Minnetonka (Marion Brown), and twenty-one other members of the Narragansett Tribe "dressed in full Indian regalia."[58] The bill signing also included the exchange of gifts. Chief Nighthawk presented a peace pipe to the governor, Theodore Francis Green, who gave him the pen with which he signed the bill. Chief Pine Tree and Princess Minnetonka also gave the governor an arrow and a "string of beads," presumably wampum or a wampum reproduction.[59] Historically, wampum functioned as a form of record-keeping to affirm treaties and as a mnemonic device to record communal histories. This exchange of gifts demonstrates the power of material culture to bind words to deeds and actions.[60] Tribal members at the ceremony referenced these processes to conduct diplomacy with the state, negotiating stereotypical ideas about Indianness while referencing intertribal histories of exchange and diplomacy.

The organizers drew from these histories to inform and plan their activism. As the central activity of Rhode Island Indian Day, organizers planned a reproduction "Indian village at Goddard Park" in Potowomut, or Warwick, RI, where "Narragansetts will hold ceremonies during the summer and fall."[61] The Indian village would showcase aspects of Native life and seasonal practices using material culture. The reproduction village offered tribal members from across southern New England the opportunity to both educate the public and craft a space for themselves to gather and exist as Native people. The construction of the village was sponsored by the Works Progress Administration, which funded their labor, allowing for multiple Native people to participate in the project. Strategically aligning themselves with a federally funded project under the New Deal, participants saw an opportunity to regain access to Algonquian lifeways and skills at a critical moment in state and national history.

This project reflected how Native people drew from and honored their histories as part of their movements for resurgence and recognition in the twentieth century.[62] As Red Wing reported in *The Narragansett Dawn,* the village was "representative of an Indian village of the period 300 years ago, near a field for planting, a forest for hunting and water for fishing." It contained multiple structures, including a winter long house and summer wetu. One "long house" contained "an Indian fireplace, bough couches and native utensils, while in the blockade was a genuine dugout canoe." The process of creating and opening this village involved the skill and handiwork of multiple Narragansetts and "many friendly tribes residing in Rhode Island, Connecticut and Massachusetts."[63] While organizers credited the village's "historical accuracy" to the research of Charles C. Willoughby of Harvard University's Peabody Museum and Douglas S. Byres of Philips Academy's Department of American Archaeology, the Native people involved with planning and building the village also drew from their own work. Knowledge about crafting Native Belongings and building Native architectures had been stewarded from generation to generation prior to the twentieth century, which is evinced by oral histories, the material culture record, and internal record-keeping.

Red Wing in particular maintained practices of knowledge-keeping through research projects as well as activities that enabled ongoing material culture practice. As a camp mother, knowledge-keeper, and founding

FIGURE 2. Sketch of bark berry basket and covered box by Red Wing. Photograph by Allyson LaForge. Courtesy of the Tomaquag Museum.

member of the SDFA, Red Wing frequently documented histories of basketry and other handicraft, painstakingly drawing and recording different types of wood splints, barks, vines, berries, clay, shells, and other natural materials to make baskets, wampum, clay pots, bark houses, and other items. In a hand-assembled photo journal that depicted a series of events that likely took place in the 1930s or 1940s, participants fired clay products, engaged in activities around the fire, ate succotash and shellfish, worked on a wampum belt, thatched a bark hut, gathered reeds and cattails, used baskets and mortars made from wood and vines, dressed a deer skin, and participated in ceremonies and dancing. The group gathered most of their materials locally, drawing from their collective knowledge of Native lands and the plants necessary for crafting these items. Red Wing brought this knowledge to her work with the SDFA, which worked to ensure that Native people kept these material culture practices alive, even after colonists documented their supposed decline throughout the eighteenth and nineteenth centuries.

On one page, Red Wing sketched images of a dipper, a bark berry basket, a covered box, and bark rattles underneath descriptions of "Materials Found in the Woods," which included "bark" for "Baskets of various shapes." Below, a photo depicts participants thatching a bark wetu, just as various Native people did for the Indian Village. A list above that photo, "Materials Found Along the Shore," described the beach grass that could be gathered for "basket making & burden straps." Even after detribalization attempted to cut off Narragansetts' ties to the land, including gathering beach grass, bark, and other plants, these practices continued to hold a central place within the recovery of Native identity. The archives of the SDFA also reflected commitments to the continuation of these practices, demonstrating the interrelationship between intertribal organizing and ongoing material culture activism.

Networks of Intertribal Organizing in Southern New England

The opening of the Indian Village and celebration of the Tercentenary Events were the results of networks of intertribal organizing. While the first official meeting of the SDFA took place in 1937, members of the Narragansett Historic Club worked with members of other tribes to organize the Tercentenary Events of 1936, building from a legacy of intertribalism in New England. In March 1936, Red Wing wrote to the National Alqonquin Indian Council, or NAIC, on behalf of these organizers. The NAIC was another Rhode Island–based intertribal group, founded in the 1920s to assert Indigenous political continuance in southern New England. Red Wing invited members of the NAIC to participate in "a pageant for Indian history for R.I." she had been working on for the Tercentenary, which would be performed at her farm over two days in July. In addition to a clam bake and other "Indian dishes" for food, Red Wing "invite[d] all to exhibit their handiwork and Indian relics."[64] The NAIC read this letter from Red Wing at their March meeting and considered her proposal, but resolved to turn down her request to participate in the pageant to instead focus their time on their own play.[65] Responding, Annie Farrow, the secretary of the NAIC, wrote in encouragement of Red Wing's work, reassuring her that "it isn't that they don't want to co-operate but they feel they haven't time" due to their deep interest in and need to devote time to their drama, "The Law of Tribe."[66] In the twentieth century, Native groups staged pageants and public displays as a means of devising community and representing contemporary Native people as still Native.[67] The NAIC and SDFA held shared and interconnected goals, even as they worked separately on projects like their pageants and performances.

A key connection between these groups was their collective commitment to the preservation and dissemination of material culture. When Farrow wrote back to Red Wing to share that the NAIC elected not to participate in the Tercentenary pageant, she added, "I think perhaps you will hear from some of them that would like to exhibit some of their work or sell some of their baskets etc."[68] Exhibiting and selling baskets and other work connected Native people to each other and their shared histories. This exchange between Farrow and Red Wing reflects how Indigenous material culture played a central role in processes of historical recovery and contestation of settler rhetoric about Indigeneity. These processes were foundational goals of the intertribal political organizing that the SDFA and NAIC led in the early twentieth century.

When the SDFA first met in June 1937, they built from these pre-existing intertribal relationships and dynamics. While the group responded to the political issues that Native people faced in this region in the early twentieth century, it was also a space of Indigenous gathering embedded in preexisting networks of communication and collaboration across the Native Northeast. In this way, the SDFA paralleled the goals of the NAIC.[69] The NAIC limited its membership to members of Algonquin tribes of the Northeast, just as the SDFA restricted its membership to those it determined to have "Indian blood."[70] While these categories were not tied to specific blood quantum measures, which is how some tribal nations have established membership requirements, they reflected processes of genealogical and historical research that Algonquian nations in the Northeast conducted in the twentieth century to assert sovereignty following years of documentary genocide and after illegal detribalization.[71]

The SDFA and NAIC focused on these processes of historical recovery and research in order to reclaim Indigenous identity amidst twentieth century stereotypes. The groups were both based in Rhode Island—the NAIC in Providence and the SDFA in Kenyon—which was a hub of intertribal organizing at that time, also hosting the American Indian Federation, another intertribal organization based in Westerly. Before a change in leadership in the 1930s, the American Indian Federation made more of an effort to include Native people with African American ancestry in its membership, welcome non-Native spouses and relatives into the group, and expand non-Native participation in public events.[72] After this leadership change, many local Natives felt excluded by the new Federation leaders, who were mostly non-locals. In the September 1936 issue of the *Narragansett Dawn,* Theodore Dennis Brown critiqued the Federation for "discrimination" after not being allowed to dance at their powwow, which likely led to several Narragansett and other Native members to leave the group and join the newly formed SDFA in 1937.[73] Both the SDFA and NAIC provided spaces of social gathering to advocate for cultural survival and preservation of traditional practices like basket-making, as the exchange between Red Wing and Farrow in March of 1936 reflected. Another member of the NAIC, LeRoy Perry, had worked as an educator at the newly established King Philip Museum in Bristol, RI, between 1930 and 1933, where he collaborated with non-Native collector Rudolph Haffenreffer to interpret his Native collections.[74] Yet the *Narragansett Dawn,* Tercentenary Events, and founding of the SDFA provide evidence of an alternative process of preserving and presenting material culture histories beginning in the 1930s, with Native people as both makers and interpreters of new material Belongings.

The Sons and Daughters of the First Americans

The work of the SDFA continued the goals that the intertribal group of people organizing the Tercentenary Events had begun. As noted in its first set of bylaws, the "basic theory" of the SDFA was to "study, portray and preserve,

FIGURE 3. The cover page of first SDFA meeting minutes, designed by Red Wing. Red Wing's design would become the basis for the Narragansett Indian Tribe's tribal seal. Image courtesy of the Tomaquag Museum.

the history, art, rituals, language, handicraft and music of the New England Indians."[75] These bylaws went into effect after the group's first official meeting, held in June 1937. While Red Wing had deemed the first Indian Day a success in articulating Narragansett tribal existence to the state of Rhode Island, the Indian Village faced threats after the conclusion of this celebration. In the September 1937 meeting, SDFA members discussed "ways and means of preserving the Narragansett Indian Village at Goddard Park from sightseers . . . tearing it to pieces," concluding that "the state should appropriate a sum for its maintenance."[76] The destructiveness of the public threatened the goal of the organizers to use the Indian Village to host continuing ceremonies for Native people in Rhode Island.

In addition to the preservation of the village, the SDFA also maintained connections with other Native people and intertribal organizations. Christopher Noka spoke at the October 1937 meeting on "the benefit that could be derived from these meetings and the necessity of visiting and conversations with other Indians so that we may get a good clear understanding of the true character of the Indian in a true light from his descended SONS and DAUGHTERS, not as the white historians and novelists had pictured our ancestors."[77] While the events that took place in the Indian Village had partially accomplished this goal, the SDFA prioritized the work of Native descendants to facilitate new processes of historical recovery. In order to do so, the SDFA needed to contend with the replacement narratives of settler colonialism, which depended on narratives of Indigenous disappearance.[78] White fraternal organizations like the Improved Order of Red Men, established in 1834, misappropriated Native American imagery, regalia, and rituals to claim belonging to the United States, erasing enduring Indigeneity in the process. By the twentieth century, the myth of the vanishing Indian permeated school curricula, children's camps and programs, museums, and the public imaginary.[79]

Material culture as well as ceremonies and written histories, which the SDFA often connected to specific Indigenous landscapes in Rhode Island, played a central role in these processes of historical recovery. Members of the SDFA gathered together to create, sell, and display "Indian handicrafts," which they framed as an explicitly political process. The group criticized "white people commercializing on the Indians," suggesting "we should study some way to protect the Indians' rights and do away with imposters."[80] While they did not come to any definitive conclusions on how to do so, they did decide during that meeting to devote one additional night per month to getting together to "work and show each other . . . plans . . . for making beadwork, and other handicraft articles of Indian nature."[81] This resulted in an exhibit of items made by members, which "showed that natural instinct for Indian handicraft still exists in New England Indians."[82] These crafts

FIGURE 4. Chief White Oak That Bends (Mohegan/Pequot), or Daniel Francis Congdon, Red Wing's husband who was a founding member of the SDFA, holds a Narragansett birchbark canoe as Red Wing looks on, ca. 1939. Photograph courtesy of the Tomaquag Museum.

FIGURE 5. A nearly identical Narragansett birchbark canoe passed down since the 1840s or 50s through the Dove family hangs from the ceiling of the Tomaquag Museum. The canoe was crafted by the great uncle of the Narragansett Chief Roaring Bull, or Ferris Dove (Narragansett/Niantic). Photograph by Allyson LaForge. Courtesy of the Tomaquag Museum.

included bows, arrows, turtle shell rattles, deer bone rings, and root clubs, with multiple members of the SDFA taking part.

After this internal exhibit, Noka gave an "inspirational" talk to SDFA members on handicraft, exhorting "each knowing how to do any basketry, bead work or wood work" to "teach it to the younger group of Indians and keep the children interested."[83] The president of the SDFA, Elias Brown, a "Pequoit descendant," "sanctioned these remarks" and added that beyond ensuring the intergenerational transmission of these practices, SDFA members should "make Indian articles for sale, since so many white people were doing it," noting that these articles "would at least be original Indian in their handicraft, either present day or imitation of the old arts."[84] Again resisting settler appropriations of Indigeneity, the SDFA resolved to continue to plan for the dissemination of these Native-made items as an activist practice.

One year later, SDFA members and members of other Rhode Island Indian organizations presented their "handicraft" along with "a few R.I. relics" at an exhibit sponsored by the Rhode Island State Federation of Women's Clubs. At the meeting following the exhibit, the SDFA declared the event a "great success and best we had ever put up before the public collectively." Viewed by thousands of visitors, the exhibit received reports that "some said they had learned more of Indian history in one week than all their years at school." The exhibition corrected narratives about Native peoples and showed that the "efforts of the Sons and Daughters of the First Americans have not been in vain." The SDFA concluded that "from this little beginning we hope to go further in maintaining our tribal arts and handicrafts."[85] Exhibits of handicraft offered an opportunity to present Native histories that challenged public views. The SDFA's methods of creating decolonizing displays about Native people preceded recent conversations about decolonizing museum practices, which have called for Native people's involvement and authority in developing exhibitions about their cultures and histories. These conversations have largely emerged from critiques of museums, which have long been colonial sites of control over Native histories and material culture.[86] The SDFA collaborated with non-Native-run Rhode Island–based organizations to host their exhibits, but did not seek out a traditional museum to share their histories with the public, instead preferring settings where they could reclaim their own historical narratives.

SDFA members also sold their handicraft to fundraise for the organization, which in turn funded further research, crafting, and community events. After the exhibit with the State Federation of Women's Clubs, the SDFA created an "Indian gift shop" with "handmade articles made by members" who donated their time making items.[87] Just as the crafting and sale of material culture facilitated Native survivance in the eighteenth and nineteenth centuries, the revitalization of handicraft practices by the SDFA helped support the resurgence of Native community in the twentieth century.[88] Crafting, displaying, and selling material culture constituted processes that were both economic and political. In the first half of the twentieth century, Native people in southern New England often worked long hours doing wage labor. As Lorén Spears has recalled, her great-great-grandmother Mabel Nichols Cordwell worked as a milliner during the 1940s.[89] Native people also played key roles in stone masonry, maritime industries, and the service industries.[90] Wage labor (and unemployment) could coexist with seasonal trade economies, often within the same families.[91] Participating in the SDFA and the making and selling of handicraft similarly coexisted with members' jobs and lives, offering an alternative way of spending time with a community of people while still earning needed funds to support these activities.

Another fundraising project documented ongoing place-based knowledge of Native histories within Rhode Island. Beginning in 1938, the SDFA assembled a souvenir book, which included photographs taken by Narragansett member Theodore Brown. Published in 1940, the "What Cheer! 'Netop' What Cheer! Historical Picture Book" included ten landscapes. SDFA members narrated each landscape's significance within Native history, which often stretched back to the early period. In Charlestown, "Cup and Saucer Rock" was a drumming rock, which they described as a large rock placed on another rock "in such a position and location, that it could be rocked by two or more men and the sound thus produced could be heard from miles around" in order to "summon their people to council." Another "Indian Drumming Rock" in Apponaug was a "signal between the Cowesett Indians and the Narragansetts" and could be "heard and understood twenty miles away." In addition to these drumming rocks, "The Coronation Rock" on the "old King Tom Place" in Charlestown was the site where, in the eighteenth century, "Esther, last of the line of the ruling family of Ninigrets was crowned Queen of the Narragansetts in a very imposing ceremony."[92] Rocks were sites that could communicate across intertribal networks as well as mark places of memory within Narragansett history. These memory practices included large geologic formations as well as "memory heaps," which were piles of stones or brush that Algonquian people placed and maintained at locales where significant events had taken place.[93] Settler colonialism had disrupted these memory practices, but the Historical Picture Book offered an alternative form of marking these sites through text and photography.

The Historical Picture Book also documented continuous Narragansett presence in Rhode Island after King Philip's War. Indeed, the book included "King Philip's Monument," the stone obelisk monument built by settlers in 1906 within the Great Swamp to commemorate the 1675 massacre of Native noncombatants during the war.[94] The description by the SDFA was a retelling of this history that departed from the settler narratives that the colonial monument represented. Rather than framing colonists as the protagonists, the SDFA noted that the obelisk marked "the graves of hundreds of Indian men, women and children, who fell in their last great stand for home, loved ones and freedom against the white settlers."[95] The outcome of King Philip's War in southern New England resulted in continuous colonial violence and attempted containment of the intertribal networks of people who fought against the English, but the SDFA emphasized the resilience of their ancestors.[96] Another location documented by the Historical Picture Book, "The Old Anthony Place," was the home of SDFA member Nettie Davis, whose parents retained the house after detribalization in 1880. As Davis noted, "This is the only home never owned by white people in the State." Like the history of "The Narragansett Indian Church," another location in the book, which had been continuously stewarded by Narragansetts since they constructed the first version of the building in the seventeenth century, these sites continued to be embedded in Indigenous homelands.[97] Ongoing Native caretaking and memorializing practices had maintained them across time. With their Historic Picture Book, the SDFA strategized new modes of preservation to challenge colonial meaning-making that had attempted to overwrite these Native practices of knowledge-keeping. The Historic Picture Book operated in conjunction with the sale of other handicraft, highlighting the relationship between place-making, material culture, and the documentation of Indigenous history.[98]

Conclusion: Refusing Colonial Appropriation and Building Indigenous Futures

After years of marginalization by settlers and the state of Rhode Island, the SDFA offered tribal members a means of reclamation of cultural sovereignty. While one of the SDFA's goals was public education, they also rejected requests by non-Native organizations that Native material culture knowledge be taught to the general public on demand. In March 1941, the club received a request from the 4H Club of Stonington to teach basket making to their members. When Red Wing, the secretary of the SDFA, announced this request for a basket maker, members refused. "Although some can make baskets," Red Wing explained in the meeting minutes, "none feel to teach basketry to white students."[99] Knowledge about basket making had survived centuries of land loss and marginalization of tribal members who harvested wood splints, bark, sweet grass, and other plant materials from their homelands. Denying the 4H Club request was an act of refusal as tribal members focused on their own resurgence as a people, connected to each other and their homelands. Audra Simpson writes that such refusals can be deployed "as a political and ethical stance that stands in stark contrast to the desire to have one's distinctiveness as a culture, as a people, recognized." As she further elaborates, "Refusal comes with the requirement of having one's *political* sovereignty acknowledged and upheld."[100] While the SDFA could not afford to refuse the politics of recognition by the settler state in the aftermath of detribalization, they still found ways to express their sovereignty on their own terms as Native people committed to the recovery and resurgence of Native lifeways.

Despite this refusal, education of white children and the general public remained a central goal of the SDFA. Red Wing and other members responded to community requests for educational programming and presentations frequently, and the organization prioritized outreach in multiple settings. Yet resisting settler appropriations of Indigenous practices and identity remained a challenge to negotiate. What was the line between education and appropriation? How could members communicate their continued existence without allowing for non-Native people and children to "play Indian," in the words of Philip Deloria, as they so often did in the early twentieth century?[101] How could cultural sovereignty be affirmed in educational programming? One way the SDFA prioritized cultural sovereignty was by teaching each other and their own children their histories and practices, even as they presented programs and exhibits to the public. In 1942, Red Wing noted in a report on the "Activities of R.I. Indians" that the "most active group this last year, was the Sons and Daughters of the First Americans" whose members met each month "for the bringing in of hand made original articles." She continued, "In this way they have encouraged many to use hidden talents and promoted Indian handicrafts."[102]

In 1945, the SDFA bought land from Hannah and Charles Hazard in Charlestown, RI, to build a gathering location, which they referred to as the club's "long house." The long house would provide a central spot for the organization to meet and hold events.[103] This moment marked a shift in the organization. The acquisition of land for a long house was a critical step for the SDFA, which had traditionally met in the homes of members. Detribalization meant that much of the land that formerly belonged to the Narragansett Tribe was no longer available either as a community space or an environment from which to gather resources for material culture. Land was central to their projects, and while the SDFA had achieved the continuity and revitalization of many material culture practices in spite of these limitations, a place to host a community building was sorely needed. Planning and strategizing for the long house constituted a significant part of SDFA meetings after 1951, with fundraising a central goal. As fundraising continued, club members began the construction of the long house, but encountered challenges doing the work themselves, rather than hiring contractors and taking out a mortgage to help finance the building.[104]

In 1955, Red Wing suggested club members make and sell "articles of Indian motifs" to help fundraise for SDFA causes, including the long house, mobilizing the creation and sale of material culture to help secure the building and provide funding for other community events.[105] Members completed work in April 1957, and the first meeting recorded at the SDFA long house was held on May 6, 1957.[106] While the long house was not weatherized for winter use, the SDFA met there each month until September. The long house provided a community building to host the events and meetings that the SDFA focused on as an organization until it disbanded in 1970, when other community spaces had grown in the SDFA's place.

FIGURE 6. Finger woven twined bag made by Dawn Dove (Narragansett/Niantic) during a class taught by Diosa Summers (Choctaw) at the Tomaquag Museum. Photograph by Allyson LaForge. Courtesy of the Tomaquag Museum.

Yet even after the disbanding of the SDFA, the group's organizing through material culture persisted through other venues, such as the Tomaquag Valley Indian Memorial Museum. Red Wing collaborated with non-Native anthropologist Eva Butler to found the museum in 1958, which provided a space for the creation and display of material culture to continue. At the Tomaquag Museum, the interplay between handicraft and living Indigenous practices connected the past to the present, continuing the work of the SDFA. Material culture created in the early years of the Tomaquag Museum by Red Wing as well as the Mashantucket Pequot, Narragansett, and Wampanoag activist Tall Oak Weeden and Narragansett educator Princess Pine Needles built on the resurgence work of the early twentieth century to sustain Indigenous presence and sovereignty in Rhode Island.[107] The legacy of the SDFA and other twentieth-century intertribal organizations also continues at contemporary powwows, festivals, and celebrations across southern New England, where dancers don regalia and artisans exhibit and sell their works.[108]

FIGURE 7. Drum made by Tall Oak Weeden for the National Day of Mourning in 1970. Photograph by Allyson LaForge. Courtesy of Toni Weeden.

The national activism of the 1960s and 70s also took root in New England. On Thanksgiving Day in 1970, an intertribal group of Native people from New England organized the first National Day of Mourning, which is now held every year on Thanksgiving to remember Native resilience and protest ongoing oppression.[109] Tall Oak Weeden, one of the primary organizers, crafted a drum for the day's events in Plymouth, Massachusetts, which included a full slate of programs.[110] On Cole's Hill, next to a statue of Wampanoag sachem Massasoit and facing Plymouth Rock, Aquinnah Wampanoag educator and activist Frank James, or Wamsutta, delivered a speech that organizers of an event celebrating the 350th anniversary of the arrival of the Pilgrims had censored. In his speech, Wamsutta declared, "You the white man are celebrating an anniversary. We the Wampanoags will help you celebrate in the concept of a beginning. It was the beginning of a new life for the Pilgrims. Now, 350 years later, it is a beginning of a new determination for the original American: the American Indian."[111] These sites and protests built upon a legacy of intertribal activism in southern New England, which firmly rejected settler discourses and projects that placed Native peoples as absent from modernity to instead craft Native futures through the recovery of Indigenous lands, materialities, and histories.

ALLYSON LAFORGE is the Abbott Lowell Cummings Postdoctoral Fellow in American Material Culture at Boston University. She received her Ph.D. in American studies from Brown University. Her book project, "Materializing Futurity: Networks of Native Women's Organizing in the Northeast," examines the role of Indigenous women as leaders and knowledge-keepers who employed and stewarded material culture to hold their communities together and maintain their homelands across the nineteenth and twentieth centuries.

Bibliography

Act of June 2, 1924, Public Law 68–175, 43 STAT 253, which authorized the Secretary of the Interior to issue certificates of citizenship to Indians. Enrolled Acts and Resolutions of Congress, 1789–2011. General Records of the United States Government, Record Group 11. National Archives Building, Washington, D.C. https://www.docsteach.org/documents/document/indian-citizenship-act. Accessed October 2023.

Annie Farrow to Princess Red Wing, March 4, 1936. Box 1, Folder 7, National Algonquin Indian Council Records, Beinecke Library, Yale University, New Haven, Connecticut.

Baron, Donna Keith, J. Edward Hood, and Holly V. Izard. "They Were Here All Along: The Native American Presence in Lower-Central New England in the

Eighteenth and Nineteenth Centuries." *William and Mary Quarterly* 53, no. 3 (1996): 561–86.

Belz, Anthony M. "From the Archives: Dovecrest Restaurant and Thanksgiving." *Belongings Blog*. Tomaquag Museum. November 22, 2020. https://www.tomaquagmuseum.org/belongingsblog/2020/11/2/dovecrest-restaurant-and-thanksgiving.

Blansett, Kent. *A Journey to Freedom: Richard Oakes, Alcatraz, and the Red Power Movement*. Yale University Press, 2020.

Brooks, Lisa. *The Common Pot: The Recovery of Native Space in the Northeast*. University of Minnesota Press, 2008.

———. *Our Beloved Kin: A New History of King Philip's War*. Yale University Press, 2018.

Brown, Marion. "Keeper of Records: Narragansetts Hold First Tribal Meeting in 53 Years." *Narragansett Dawn* 1, no. 1 (May 1935).

———. "Sunrise News." *Narragansett Dawn* 1, no. 12 (April 1936).

———. "Sunrise News." *Narragansett Dawn* 2, no. 4 (August 1936).

———. "Sunrise News." *Narragansett Dawn* 2, no. 2 (June 1936).

———. "Sunrise News." *Narragansett Dawn* 2, no. 3 (July 1936).

Brown, Theodore. "Editorial." *Narragansett Dawn* 2, no. 6 (September 1936).

Butler, Eva. "The Brush or Stone Memorial Heaps of Southern New England." *Bulletin of the Archaeological Society of Connecticut* 19 (April 1946): 2–12.

Calloway, Colin G., ed. *After King Philip's War: Presence and Persistence in Indian New England*. University Press of New England, 1997.

Carpenter, Adria. "'Playing Indian': A Retrospective on the YMCA's Indian Guides Program." University of Minnesota Library News. October 13, 2023. https://libnews.umn.edu/2023/10/playing-indian-a-retrospective-on-the-ymcas-indian-guides-program/.

Carpenter, Esther Bernon. *South-County Neighbors*. Roberts Brothers, 1887.

Child, Brenda. *My Grandfather's Knocking Sticks: Ojibwe Life and Labor on the Reservation*. Minnesota Historical Society Press, 2014.

Cronon, William. *Changes in the Land: Indians, Colonists, and the Ecology of New England*. Rev. ed. Hill and Wang, 2003.

"Daisy Elena Fairchild Sherman Application for Associate Membership." National Algonquin Indian Council Records. Box 1, Folder 4. Beinecke Library, Yale University, New Haven, Connecticut.

Deed to Parcel of Land in Charlestown, RI from Hannah M. Hazard and Charles F. Hazard to the Sons and Daughters of the First Americans. June 27, 1945. SDFA Box 2. Tomaquag Museum Archives.

Deloria, Philip J. *Playing Indian*. Yale University Press, 1998.

DeLucia, Christine M. "Locating Kickemuit: Springs, Stone Memorials, and Contested Placemaking in the Northeastern Borderlands." *Early American Studies: An Interdisciplinary Journal* 13, no. 2 (Spring 2015): 467–502. https://doi.org/10.1353/eam.2015.0011.

———. *Memory Lands: King Philip's War and the Place of Violence in the Northeast*. Yale University Press, 2018.

Frank, Caroline, Kevin P. Smith, and Kirsten Hammerstrom, eds. *Customes, Manners, and Worships: Rhode Island Begins.* Rhode Island Historical Society and Haffenreffer Museum of Anthropology, 2011. Exhibition catalog.

Fisher, Linford D. *The Indian Great Awakening: Religion and the Shaping of Native Cultures in Early America.* Oxford University Press, 2012.

"Governor Signs Bill for Indians, Gives Narragansetts the Right to Fix Day for Special Observance." *Westerly Sun.* April 24, 1936. Westerly Library Digitized Newspapers.

Hart, Siobhan M. *Colonialism, Community, and Heritage in Native New England.* University Press of Florida, 2018.

Herndon, Ruth Wallis, and Ella Wilcox Sekatu. "The Right to a Name: The Narragansett People and Rhode Island Officials in the Revolutionary Era." *Ethnohistory* 44, no. 3 (Summer 1997): 433–462. https://doi.org/10.2307/483031.

Igloliorte, Heather. "'Hooked Forever on Primitive Peoples': James Houston and the Transformation of 'Eskimo Handicrafts' to Inuit Art." In *Mapping Modernisms: Art, Indigeneity, Colonialism,* edited by Elizabeth Harney and Ruth B. Phillips. Duke University Press, 2018.

Indian Committee. "Council & Pow-Wow of Native Indians of The New England Tribes of The Algonquin Nation at Providence." December 13, 1923. Rhode Island College Digital Commons. https://digitalcommons.ric.edu/cgi/viewcontent.cgi?filename=57&article=1003&context=crgross_papers&type=additional.

Introduction to "National Day of Mourning." In *Dawnland Voices: An Anthology of Indigenous Writing from New England,* edited by Siobhan Senier. University of Nebraska Press, 2014.

James, Frank (Wamsutta). "National Day of Mourning." November 26, 1970. In *Dawnland Voices: An Anthology of Indigenous Writing from New England,* edited by Siobhan Senier. University of Nebraska Press, 2014.

Kauanui, J. Kēhaulani. "A Structure, Not an Event": Settler Colonialism and Enduring Indigeneity." *Lateral* 5, no. 1 (2016).

LaRose, Silvermoon Mars. Personal conversation with author. March 18, 2025.

Lonetree, Amy. *Decolonizing Museums: Representing Native America in National and Tribal Museums.* University of North Carolina Press, 2012.

Mancini, Jason. "Beyond Reservation: Indian Survivance in Southern New England and Eastern Long Island, 1713–1861." Ph.D. diss., University of Connecticut, 2009.

Mandell, Daniel R. *Tribe, Race, History: Native Americans in Southern New England, 1780–1880.* Baltimore: The Johns Hopkins University Press, 2008.

McMullen, Ann. "'The Heart Interest': Native Americans at Mount Hope and the King Philip Museum." In *Passionate Hobby: Rudolph Frederick Haffenreffer and the King Philip Museum,* edited by Shephard Krech III, 167–86. University of Washington Press, 1994.

"Milestones." *The Narragansett Dawn* 1, no. 2 (June 1935).

Miller, G. Wayne. "Tomaquag Museum to Build Spacious New Home Near URI." *The Providence Journal,* February 12, 2021. https://www.providencejournal.com/story/news/local/2021/02/12/tomaquag-museum-build-spacious-new-home-central-location/4433886001/.

Narragansett Historian. "Report for the Year." *The Narragansett Dawn* 1, no. 12 (April 1936).

National Algonquin Indian Council. Report of March 1936 meeting. National Algonquin Indian Council Records. Box 1, Folder 15. Beinecke Library, Yale University, New Haven, Connecticut.

O'Brien, Jean M. *Firsting and Lasting: Writing Indians out of Existence in New England.* University of Minnesota Press, 2010.

Pezzarossi, Heather Law. "Native Basketry and the Dynamics of Social Landscapes in Southern New England." In *Things in Motion: Object Itineraries in Anthropological Practice,* edited by Rosemary A. Joyce and Susan D. Gillespie, 179–99. School for Advanced Research Press, 2015.

Phillips, Ruth B. *Trading Identities: The Souvenir in Native North American Art, 1700–1900.* University of Washington Press, 1998.

Piatote, Beth H. *Domestic Subjects: Gender, Citizenship, and Law in Native American Literature.* Yale University Press, 2013.

Plane, Anne Marie and Gregory Button. "The Massachusetts Indian Enfranchisement Act: Ethnic Contest in Historical Context, 1849–1869." *Ethnohistory* 40, no. 4 (Autumn 1993): 587–618. https://doi.org/10.2307/482589.

"Plans for Tercentenary Celebration." *The Narragansett Dawn* 2, no. 1 (May 1936).

Princess Red Wing. "Activities of the R.I. Indians in 1942." Activities of RI Indians in 1942 Folder. Unprocessed Red Wing Files. Rfi.F669. Tomaquag Museum Archives.

———. "Editorial." *The Narragansett Dawn* 1, no. 4 (August 1935).

———. "Editorial." *The Narragansett Dawn* 1, no. 1 (May 1935).

———. "First R.I. Indian Day." *The Narragansett Dawn* 2, no. 5 (September 1936).

———. "Narragansett Tribal Reorganization." In Miya, ed. *The Memoirs of Princess Red Wing: A New England Native Woman's Journey through the 20th Century.* Audenreed Press, 1999.

———. Photo Journal. Unprocessed Files. Tomaquag Museum Archives.

———. "The Sons and Daughters of the First Americans." In Miya, ed. *The Memoirs of Princess Red Wing: A New England Native Woman's Journey through the 20th Century.* Audenreed Press, 1999.

Princess Red Wing to National Algonquin Indian Council, March 4, 1936. National Algonquin Indian Council Records. Box 1, Folder 7. Beinecke Library, Yale University, New Haven, Connecticut.

Reiser, Christine N. "Materializing Community: The Intersections of Pageantry, Material Culture and Indigeneity in Early 20th-Century New England." *Material Culture Review* 69 (January 2009). https://journals.lib.unb.ca/index.php/MCR/article/view/18146.

Rhode Island State Federation of Women's Clubs. "Greetings from Friends of the Tribe." *The Narragansett Dawn* 1, no. 1 (May 1935).

Roosevelt, Eleanor. "Greetings from Friends of the Tribe." *The Narragansett Dawn* 1, no. 1 (May 1935).

Rubertone, Patricia E. "Memorializing the Narragansett: Placemaking and Memory Keeping in the Aftermath of Detribalization." In *Archaeologies of Placemaking: Monuments, Memories, and Engagement in Native North America,* edited by Patricia Rubertone, 195–216. Left Coast Press, 2008.

———. *Native Providence: Memory, Community, and Survivance.* Lincoln: University of Nebraska Press, 2020.

Salisbury University. "HIST 384: Native American History: Improved Order of Red Men." April 28, 2025. https://libraryguides.salisbury.edu/c.php?g=1070744&p=7843346.

Simpson, Audra. *Mohawk Interruptus: Political Life Across the Borders of Settler States.* Durham: Duke University Press, 2014.

State of Rhode Island and Providence Plantations. *Report of the Committee of Investigation; A Historical Sketch, and Evidence Taken, Made to the House of Representatives, at its January Session, A.D. 1880.* E. L. Freeman & Co., 1880.

———. *Report of Commission on the Affairs of the Narragansett Indians made to the General Assembly at its January Session, 1881.* E.L. Freeman & Co., 1881.

Sons and Daughters of the First Americans. "By-Laws." June 4, 1937. SDFA Box 1. Tomaquag Museum Archives.

———. "What Cheer! 'Netop' What Cheer: Historical Picture Book." 1940. Tomaquag Museum Archives.

Sons and Daughters of the First Americans Meeting Minutes, 1937—1970. SDFA Box 1. Tomaquag Museum Archives.

Spears, Lorén, and Amanda Thompson. "As We Have Always Done': Decolonizing the Tomaquag Museum's Collections Management Policy." *Collections* 18, no. 1 (March 2022): 31–41. https://doi.org/10.1177/15501906211072912.

Spears, Lorén. Personal conversation with author. November 18, 2022.

———. Personal conversation with author. September 16, 2024.

Stiles, Henry Reed. *The history of ancient Windsor, Connecticut, including East Windsor, South Windsor, and Ellington, prior to 1768, the date of their separation from the old town, and Windsor, Bloomfield and Windsor Locks, to the present time.* New York: Charles B. Norton, 1859.

Todd, Zoe. "An Indigenous Feminist's Take on the Ontological Turn: 'Ontology' Is just Another Word for Colonialism." *Journal of Historical Sociology* 29, no. 1 (2016): 4–22. https://doi.org/10.1111/johs.12124.

Tomaquag Museum. "History." https://www.tomaquagmuseum.org/history. Accessed May 20, 2024.

Tomaquag Museum Scrapbook. 1958–1968. Tomaquag Museum Archives, Exeter, RI.

United American Indians of New England (UAINE). "National Day of Mourning." http://www.uaine.org/. Accessed September 2023.

United States Department of the Interior, Bureau of Indian Affairs. *Recommendation and Summary of Evidence for Proposed Finding for Federal Acknowledgement of the Narragansett Indian Tribe of Rhode Island Pursuant to 25 CFR 83.* Washington, D.C.: 1982. https://www.bia.gov/sites/default/files/dup/assets/as-ia/ofa/petition/059_nargst_RI/059_pf.pdf.

Vizenor, Gerald. *Fugitive Poses: Native American Indian Scenes of Absence and Presence.* Lincoln: University of Nebraska Press, 1998.

Wampanoag Tribe of Gay Head (Aquinnah). "Ancient Ways." https://wampanoagtribe-nsn.gov/ancientways. Accessed August 13, 2025.

Weeden, L. "We Are Building for Our Children." ca. 1947. SDFA Box 2. Tomaquag Museum Archives.

Weeden, Tall Oak. National Day of Mourning Flyer. 1970. Tall Oak Weeden Collection (unprocessed). John Hay Library, Brown University.

Wickman, Thomas. "Our Best Places: Gender, Food Sovereignty, and Miantonomi's Kin on the Connecticut River." *Early American Studies: An Interdisciplinary Journal* 19, no. 2 (Spring 2021): 215–263. https://doi.org/10.1353/eam.2021.0008.

Wolfe, Patrick. "Settler Colonialism and the Elimination of the Native." *Journal of Genocide Research* 8, no. 4 (2006): 387–409. https://doi.org/10.1080/14623520601056240.

Wolverton, Nan. "'A Precarious Living': Basket Making and Related Crafts Among New England Indians." In *Reinterpreting New England Indians and the Colonial Experience,* ed. Colin G. Galloway and Neal Salisbury. Boston: The Colonial Society of Massachusetts, 2003.

Zobel, Melissa Tantaquidgeon. "Foreword." In *Savage Kin: Indigenous Informants and American Anthropologists,* edited by Margaret Bruchac. Tucson: University of Arizona Press, 2018.

Notes

1. Princess Red Wing, Sons and Daughters of the First Americans Meeting Minutes, June 4, 1937.

2. Princess Red Wing, SDFA Meeting Minutes, June 4, 1937.

3. Act of June 2, 1924, Public Law 68–175, 43 STAT 253; United States Department of the Interior, Bureau of Indian Affairs, *Recommendation and Summary of Evidence for Proposed Finding for Federal Acknowledgement of the Narragansett Indian Tribe of Rhode Island.*

4. Princess Red Wing, "Narragansett Tribal Reorganization" and "The Sons and Daughters of the First Americans," in Miya, ed., *The Memoirs of Princess Red Wing,* 72–23; 86.

5. Princess Red Wing, SDFA Meeting Minutes, June 4, 1937.

6. O'Brien, *Firsting and Lasting,* 6.

7. Princess Red Wing, SDFA Meeting Minutes, June 4, 1937. For more on survivance and the concept of active presence, see Vizenor, *Fugitive Poses,* 15.

8. The SDFA began many of the thanksgiving ceremonies hosted at Dovecrest in the 1970s, where the Tomaquag Museum moved shortly after Eva Butler's death in 1969. These included Maple Sugar (March), Strawberry (June), Green Bean (July), Cranberry (September), Hunter (November) and Nikkomo 'Winter Moon' (December). Belz, "From the Archives: Dovecrest Restaurant and Thanksgiving," November 22, 2020.

9. The Dawnland refers to the expanse of the Native Northeast and derives from the names the peoples of the Dawnland call themselves; for example, Wampanoag means "People of the First Light" and Wabanaki means "People of the Dawnland."

10. Wolverton, "A Precarious Living,'" 342 and Baron, Hood, and Izard, "They Were Here All Along," 564.

11. For more on handicraft, see Phillips, *Trading Identities,* 7 and Igloliorte, "'Hooked Forever on Primitive Peoples,'" 63–90.

12. SDFA, "By-Laws," June 4, 1937.

13. Brooks, *Our Beloved Kin,* 5.

14. Wetuash is the plural of wetu, which is an Algonquian term for traditional dwellings. Wampanoag Tribe of Gay Head (Aquinnah), "Ancient Ways."

15. For more on these other-than-human relationships, see Zobel, "Foreword," ix–iii and Todd, "An Indigenous Feminist's Take on the Ontological Turn," 4–22.

16. Miller, "Tomaquag Museum to build spacious new home near Exeter, RI."

17. Red Wing was born Mary Ella Glasko, and also went by her married names, Mary Ella Peek and Mary Ella Congdon.

18. Tomaquag Museum, "History."

19. Lorén Spears and Amanda Thompson, "'As We Have Always Done'," 37.

20. L. Weeden may be Lillian Weeden. Lorén Spears, personal conversation with author, September 16, 2024.

21. L. Weeden, "We Are Building for our Children."

22. For more on documentary genocide, see Herndon and Sekatu, "Right to a Name," 433–62. For more on Narragansett detribalization, see DeLucia, *Memory Lands,* 164–200.

23. Piatote, *Domestic Subjects,* 5.

24. Blansett, *Journey to Freedom,* 8.

25. SDFA, "By-Laws," June 4, 1937.

26. For example, Weetamoo, the Pocasset Wampanoag saunskwa, and King Philip, a Pokanoket Wampanoag sachem, forged critical intertribal alliances during King Philip's War, a multifaceted resistance movement to English settler colonialism that took place between 1675 and 1678 in New England. See Brooks, *Our Beloved Kin,* 1–9.

27. Wolverton, "'A Precarious Living,'" 342 and Princess Red Wing, "Editorial," August 1935.

28. Hart, *Colonialism, Community, and Heritage in Native New England,* 2 and O'Brien, *Firsting and Lasting,* 139–43.

29. Herndon and Sekatu, "Right to a Name," 447.

30. Herndon and Sekatu, "Right to a Name," 447.

31. Wolfe, "Settler Colonialism and the Elimination of the Native," 388.

32. Herndon and Sekatu, "Right to a Name," 447–448.

33. Carpenter, *South-County Neighbors,* 35–36.

34. For more on Miantonomi's kin and freshwater sites, see Wickman, "Our Best Places," 215–263.

35. DeLucia, "Locating Kickemuit," 475. See also Mandell, *Tribe, Race, History,* 32.

36. Stiles, *History of Ancient Windsor, Connecticut,* 113.

37. Stiles, *History of Ancient Windsor, Connecticut,* 114.

38. Stiles, *History of Ancient Windsor, Connecticut,* 114.

39. State of Rhode Island and Providence Plantations, *Report of Commission on the Affairs of the Narragansett Indians made to the General Assembly at its January Session, 1881,* 117.

40. Cronon, *Changes in the Land,* 53.

41. State of Rhode Island and Providence Plantations, *Report of Commission,* 117. The states of Connecticut, Rhode Island, and Massachusetts each pursued detribalization during the second half of the nineteenth century, leading to the detribalization of multiple Native nations. This essay focuses on the Narragansett case study not only to emphasize the tribal relationships to land, mobility practices, and gathering for crafting found within this document, but also to frame the work of the SDFA as a Rhode Island-based organization whose members responded directly to Narragansett detribalization.

42. United States Department of the Interior, Bureau of Indian Affairs, *Recommendation and Summary of Evidence for Proposed Finding for Federal Acknowledgement of the Narragansett Indian Tribe of Rhode Island.*

43. DeLucia, *Memory Lands,* 159.

44. State of Rhode Island and Providence Plantations, *Report of the Committee of Investigation; A Historical Sketch, and Evidence Taken, Made to the House of Representatives, at its January Session, A.D. 1880,* 6.

45. Plane and Button, "Massachusetts Indian Enfranchisement Act," 588.

46. State of Rhode Island and Providence Plantations, *Report of the Committee of Investigation,* 3–4. White characterizations of pauperism and vagabondism derived from misunderstandings or attacks on Native lifeways that did not value the accumulation of property or possessions.

47. State of Rhode Island and Providence Plantations, *Report of the Committee of Investigation,* 3–4; State of Rhode Island and Providence Plantations, *Report of Commission,* 117.

48. Princess Red Wing, "Editorial," May 1935.

49. Princess Red Wing, "Editorial," May 1935.

50. Roosevelt, "Greetings from Friends of the Tribe."

51. Rhode Island State Federation of Women's Clubs, "Greetings from Friends of the Tribe."

52. Brown, "Keeper of Records: Narragansetts Hold First Tribal Meeting in 53 Years."

53. Princess Red Wing, "Editorial," August 1935.

54. Sarah Cisco Sullivan, quoted in Princess Red Wing, "Editorial," August 1935.

55. See "Milestones," June 1935; "Report for the Year," April 1936; "Plans for Tercentenary Celebration," May 1936; "Sunrise News," June 1936; "Sunrise News," July 1936.

56. Princess Red Wing, "Editorial," August 1935.

57. Princess Red Wing to National Algonquin Indian Council, March 4, 1936.

58. This regalia included elements from both Algonquian cultures and nonlocal Native cultures, such as Plains-style headdresses. While scholars like Ann McMullen have argued for the NAIC and AIF as "pan-Indian organizations" that "included members of diverse groups and produced a synthetic 'Indian' culture by drawing on traditions from across the country," this essay argues for these nonlocal traditions as a strategic way of presenting their "Indianness" while maintaining both internal and external local material culture practices that retained their specific Algonquian histories. See McMullen, "'The Heart Interest'," 167.

59. "Governor Signs Bill for Indians, Gives Narragansetts the Right to Fix Day for Special Observance."

60. Brooks, *Common Pot,* 13; 220.

61. Brown, "Sunrise News," April 1936.

62. After the opening of the Indian Village at Goddard Park on June 16, Red Wing also hosted a series of Tercentenary Events at Camp Ki-Yi, located on her farm in Oakland, RI, on July 4 and 5, at which "Indians of forty-three different tribes were represented from the Micmac of Canada to the Seminoles of Florida and the Sioux of South Dakota and Cherokee of Oklahoma." Multiple groups of people sold and exhibited their handicraft at these events. Brown, "Sunrise News," August 1936.

63. Princess Red Wing, "First R.I. Indian Day."

64. Princess Red Wing to National Algonquin Indian Council, March 4, 1936.

65. National Algonquin Indian Council, Report of March 1936 meeting.

66. Annie Farrow to Princess Red Wing, March 4, 1936.

67. Reiser, "Materializing Community," 48.

68. Annie Farrow to Red Wing, March 4, 1936.

69. Indian Committee, "Council & Pow-Wow of Native Indians of The New England Tribes of The Algonquin Nation at Providence." The NAIC was originally known as the Indian Council of New England when it was founded in 1923 by an "Indian Committee" convened by non-Native historian Thomas Bicknell, and became the NAIC in 1926 under Narragansett Chief Alfred A. Perry, among other founders.

70. "Daisy Elena Fairchild Sherman Application for Associate Membership," National Algonquin Indian Council Records.

71. Rubertone, *Native Providence,* 171.

72. Rubertone, *Native Providence,* 222.

73. Brown, "Editorial," and McMullen, "'The Heart Interest'," 185nn49–50.

74. McMullen, "'The Heart Interest'," 173.

75. SDFA, "By-Laws," June 4, 1937.

76. Princess Red Wing, SDFA Meeting Minutes, September 6, 1937.

77. Princess Red Wing, SDFA Meeting Minutes, October 2, 1937.

78. O'Brien, *Firsting and Lasting,* 6.

79. Salisbury University, "HIST 384: Native American History: Improved Order of Red Men." For more on enduring Indigeneity, see J. Kēhaulani Kauanui, "'A structure, not an event': Settler Colonialism and Enduring Indigeneity." The YMCA Indian Guides, established in 1926, was another example of predominantly white children and parents using Native stereotypes. Adria Carpenter, "'Playing Indian': A retrospective on the YMCA's Indian Guides program."

80. Princess Red Wing, SDFA Meeting Minutes, February 7, 1938. This particular critique was a shared sentiment across Indian country that eventually led to the passage of the Indian Arts and Crafts Act of 1990.

81. Princess Red Wing, SDFA Meeting Minutes, February 7, 1938.

82. Princess Red Wing, SDFA Meeting Minutes, March 4, 1938.

83. Princess Red Wing, SDFA Meeting Minutes, April 1, 1938.

84. Princess Red Wing, SDFA Meeting Minutes, April 1, 1938.

85. Princess Red Wing, SDFA Meeting Minutes, May 5, 1939.

86. Lonetree, *Decolonizing Museums,* 1–2.

87. Princess Red Wing, SDFA Meeting Minutes, February 7, 1941.

88. For more on survivance, see Vizenor, *Fugitive Poses,* 15.

89. Lorén Spears, personal conversation with author, November 18, 2022.

90. Fisher, *Indian Great Awakening,* 191; and Mancini, "Beyond Reservation," 72. In 2011, Narragansett stonemason Robin Spears Sr. constructed a stone wall in front of the Haffenreffer Museum on Brown University's campus for the exhibit *Rhode Island Begins,* which still stands today. See Frank, Smith, and Hammerstrom, *Customes, Manners, and Worships: Rhode Island Begins,* 11.

91. Child, *My Grandfather's Knocking Sticks,* 3–13.

92. SDFA, "What Cheer! 'Netop' What Cheer: Historical Picture Book."

93. DeLucia, "Locating Kickemuit," 485–488; Butler, "The Brush or Stone Memorial Heaps of Southern New England," 2–12.

94. Christine DeLucia, *Memory Lands,* 123.

95. SDFA, "What Cheer! 'Netop' What Cheer! Historical Picture Book." Red Wing also began the Great Swamp Memorial Pilgrimage in the 1940s, which brought Native people back to this site for ceremony and commemoration. See DeLucia, *Memory Lands,* 174. Following detribalization, Narragansett people engaged with multiple Rhode Island monuments that Euro-Americans raised in their memory at various junctures. See Rubertone, "Memorializing the Narragansett."

96. See, for example, Brooks, *Our Beloved Kin* and Calloway, *After King Philip's War.*

97. SDFA, "What Cheer! 'Netop' What Cheer! Historical Picture Book."

98. For more on the role of baskets in the practice of place-making in New England throughout the nineteenth century, see Pezzarossi, "Native Basketry and the Dynamics of Social Landscapes in Southern New England."

99. Princess Red Wing, SDFA Meeting Minutes, March 1941.

100. Simpson, *Mohawk Interruptus,* 11.

101. Deloria, *Playing Indian.*

102. Princess Red Wing. "Activities of the R.I. Indians in 1942."

103. Deed to Parcel of Land in Charlestown, RI from Hannah M. Hazard and Charles F. Hazard to the Sons and Daughters of the First Americans, June 27, 1945.

104. Ferris Dove, SDFA Meeting Minutes, January 3, 1955.

105. Princess Red Wing, SDFA Meeting Minutes, February 7, 1955.

106. Princess Red Wing, SDFA Meeting Minutes, May 6, 1957.

107. Tomaquag Museum Scrapbook.

108. The term "powwow" is Narragansett in origin; it also described the August Meetings that took place across the eighteenth and nineteenth centuries on the Narragansett Reservation, which continued through today. Silvermoon Mars LaRose, personal conversation with author, March 18, 2025.

109. "Introduction to National Day of Mourning," in Senier, *Dawnland Voices,* 455; United American Indians of New England (UAINE), "National Day of Mourning."

110. Weeden, National Day of Mourning Flyer, 1970.

111. James, "National Day of Mourning," in Senier, *Dawnland Voices,* 458.

ANGEL M. HINZO

Not Your "Queen," Not Your "Sq**w": Reclaiming Ho-Chunk Histories of Hąpoguwį̨ga and Challenging Settler Memory

Abstract

Ho-Chunk leader Hąpoguwį̨ga (Glory of the Morning) led her village in Wisconsin during a pivotal era of Ho-Chunk history. However, narratives crafted by settlers decenter her legacy, working to legitimize settler colonial occupation and identity. These narratives participate in and inspire settler affect—physical and emotional attachment to place identities—and further settler myths of Indigenous consent regarding land occupation. Jonathan Carver's *Travels through the Interior parts of North America, in the Years 1766, 1767, and 1768,* illustrates the formation of Eurocentric nation-building narratives that dismiss Native American governance and relationships to land. Within the text, Carver describes Hąpoguwį̨ga as the "queen" of her village yet diminishes her role as a sovereign leader. This colonial imaginary strengthens settler attachment to place and erases Ho-Chunk presence. The twentieth-century play *Glory of the Morning* (1914) by William Ellery Leonard, serves a similar function by focusing on her consensual relationship with a French trader to reinforce a myth of settler belonging. This play describes Hąpoguwį̨ga as her husband's "sq**w," erasing her role as a Ho-Chunk leader and autonomous woman. As a historical figure, Hąpoguwį̨ga embodies Ho-Chunk presence amidst settler encroachment. In contrast, Carver's travel writing and Leonard's play reveal how settler affect shapes her presence in settler memory to sustain the myth of Indigenous consent to land occupation.

IN 2022, I visited the Winnebago Tribe of Nebraska's Angel De Cora Museum & Research Center. As I was looking through the exhibits, I noticed a portrait painted by a Sioux City artist, Cassie Gillette. The picture depicted a middle-aged Ho-Chunk woman standing near a stream and looking out over the water. The description for the portrait noted:

> Hąpoguwį̨ga
> Born: early 1700s Died: early-mid 1800's
> Hąpoguwį̨ga, also known as Coming of the Day or Glory of the Morning is the first recorded woman in Wisconsin history and the only known female Ho-Chunk Chief. The daughter of a Chief, she spent most of her life on Doty Island. As a young woman she would marry a French fur trader named Sabrevoir Descaris, (also referred to as Joseph Descaris). The family name De Cora comes directly from Descaris. Sabrevoir and Hąpoguwį̨ga's male children and many of her descendants would become leaders of the Tribe. Eventually the couple separated and Hąpoguwį̨ga continued to lead her people. She would play a major role in international diplomacy, selecting which European power to ally her people with.

I was ecstatic when I saw the portrait; it was a new addition since I last visited the center years earlier. The portrait's description and presence affirmed the research I had conducted on Hąpoguwį̨ga and offered insight into how community members remember this Ho-Chunk leader. I am one of many Decora descendants, and I am named after my great-grandma, whose maiden name was Decora.[1] Growing up, my mom mentioned that French ancestry was mixed with our Winnebago (Ho-Chunk) background from the fur trade period. However, it wasn't until I engaged in historical research that I learned that Decora ancestors were the signatories on treaties, and many Decoras served as civil chiefs for the Winnebago people. As I grew older, I learned from family that my great-great grandfather, William Decora, was the last traditional civil chief of the Winnebago Tribe in Nebraska. The combination of this family history and the way ancestors emerged from the archive has shaped my academic trajectory and my work documenting Ho-Chunk tribal history.[2]

While engaging with this work, I have come to realize that Native American communities understand their histories in substantially different ways than non-Native perspectives of history. Historically, non-Native narratives have centered the male European experience, functioning to obscure Indigenous understandings of place. When confronted with the reality of Native American women occupying leadership and central roles in Native communities, European settlers often worked to erase or belittle the contributions of these women. Additionally, various efforts continue to be made to undermine the philosophical foundations held by Native American communities that support the roles of women in their social and political structures.

Hąpoguwį̨ga (Glory of the Morning) remains one of the few Native American women leaders recorded by settlers in the 1700s. Her experience offers a glimpse into the roles of women within the Ho-Chunk community before the rise of settler states. Whether it is through her encounter with Jonathan Carver in the eighteenth century or the theatrical imaginings of her relationship with her husband, French trader Sabrevoir Descaris, in the 1900s, Hąpoguwįga is cast in the Euro-American archive in relation to her associations with settler men. The archive centers the experiences of these settler men, rather than the contributions Hąpoguwįga and her children made to their community's longevity. The shifting settler portrayal of Hąpoguwįga from Carver's description of a "queen" in the 1760s to her representation as a "sq**w" in the play *Glory of the Morning* offers important insight into the role of historical representation in settler memory. As a historical figure, Hąpoguwįga has been portrayed in settler histories as a cultural mediator, purportedly supporting settler presence, rather than through her role preserving the traditions of her community during a period of sociopolitical change.

Settler narratives place Hąpoguwįga within acceptable Western gender roles to legitimize settler occupation. Settler affect toward land and Indigenous women is informed by and reinforces these Western gender roles. Settler affect is a framework theorized as "an exaggerated attachment to place identities grafted onto colonized places."[3] These settler place-identities contribute to logics of white nativism in the United States by supporting the idea that European-descent settlers are the only inhabitants in the colonized lands who are worthy of belonging.[4] My intervention in this framework considers how the shifting portrayal of Hąpoguwįga reflects settler desire for belonging while redefining Indigenous women within acceptable Euro-American gender roles and erasing the historical realities of gender violence inflicted on Native American communities.

In the first section of this article, I give an overview of the political climate during Hąpoguwįga's lifetime and introduce how she is represented by British-American travel writer Jonathan Carver. Next, I discuss Carver's *Travels through the Interior parts of North America, in the Years 1766, 1767, and 1768* and argue his imagining of Ho-Chunk land emphasizes settler attachment to place while erasing Ho-Chunk people and practices. The following section focuses on *Glory of the Morning* and how Hąpoguwįga's relationship with French trader Sabrevoir Descaris becomes the center of settler narratives, strengthening settler place-based identities. This representation of Hąpoguwįga joins the life stories of other Indigenous women who have been co-opted to serve settler nation-building narratives. In the final section, I argue that these settler histories create a myth of consent regarding settler occupation of Indigenous lands and erase histories of gendered violence.

Carver Meets the Winnebago "Queen"

Hąpoguwįga's position as the Ho-Chunk leader of Doty Island, in present-day Wisconsin, challenged European conceptions of leadership and women's social roles. Within Ho-Chunk communities, Ho-Chunk women held property such as home goods, were the stewards of mines and forested areas, and had roles that differed considerably from settler women within Euro-American society. When describing Native American women generally, Kahnawake Mohawk scholar Audra Simpson states, "They were the inverse of the settler colonial woman, they had legally mandated authority and power."[5] Within traditional Ho-Chunk practices, women were responsible for determining access to areas for harvest and for their family's gardens and agriculture. [6] Ho-Chunk communities worked to maintain the land rights of women throughout the twentieth century despite U.S. policies limiting women's property rights.

Hąpoguwįga was the first elected woman chief of the Ho-Chunk people and remained in this position throughout her life after her father passed away.[7] Traditional Ho-Chunk leadership included civil chiefs, known as "peace chiefs," and military leaders, described as "war chiefs" by anthropologists.[8] These positions were determined by clan membership and family relations. Additionally, the community had to consent to their leaders, and those who did not consent could leave. This reportedly happened when Hąpoguwįga was elected to succeed her father. According to tribal historian David Lee Smith, clan chiefs withdrew from the Ho-Chunk Grand Council when Hąpoguwįga was elected chief.[9] Hąpoguwįga inherited a volatile state, as New France soldiers led by Constant Le Marchand de Lignery and their Indigenous allies moved to invade Ho-Chunk lands. The Ho-Chunk had previously allied with the Mesquakie Alliance against New France, and Hąpoguwįga had to determine how to protect her people from invasion. Hąpoguwįga and her people left their village and moved northward to escape the advancing army. Lignery burned and destroyed the emptied village and fields before leaving the region. After Lignery's attack, Hąpoguwįga and other Ho-Chunk leaders had to decide how to navigate this turbulent political landscape. Hąpoguwįga led her people to the French outpost at Michilimackinac to negotiate peace. Part of this peace was promising that her people would disengage from the Mesquakie Alliance.[10] All of the people who remained in her village consented to Hąpoguwįga's decision-making and her service as their representative. The Doty Island village was a prominent Ho-Chunk village, and the continuation of her leadership illustrates that she was found to be a suitable leader during this dire political moment. Hąpoguwįga's actions would not be included within mainstream histories, as this era is remembered mainly from the colonial perspective as the Sac and Fox wars and the struggle between New France and the might of the Mesquakie Alliance.

Colonial powers shifted to the British in the Great Lakes region, but the Doty Island Ho-Chunk village remained under the leadership of Hąpoguwį̨ga. British American military captain Jonathan Carver describes meeting Hąpoguwį̨ga in his travel writings. By the time Carver had traveled across Wisconsin and Minnesota in the eighteenth century, Hąpoguwį̨ga was an elder. Carver's *Travels Through the Interior Parts of North America, in the years 1766, 1767, and 1768,* was the first English-language account of the physical territory. Carver's writings became popular internationally, being translated into German, French, and Dutch before 1800.[11] Carver's travel writings comprise a multifaceted narrative that reveals how colonizing forces utilized mapping of the lands as a tool of settler colonialism. As a passive observer, Carver claims a degree of innocence in his travel writing, although he is participating in imperial imagining.[12] This imagining is even more prominent as the authenticity of Carver's travel descriptions has been questioned. Carver has been accused of plagiarizing previous settler narratives, including La Hontan's *New Voyages to North-America* (1735) and Pierre-François-Xavier de Charlevoix's *Journals* (1744).[13] One critic noted in 1823 that Carver did travel in the region of Ho-Chunk villages, but possibly did not take appropriate notes, resulting in copied descriptions from previous narratives.[14] Despite this plagiarism, Carver's recorded information reinforced British claims over Indigenous lands, orienting these locations as possessions of the Crown within the settler imaginary.[15] Carver's documentation of meeting Hąpoguwį̨ga places her firmly within the settler narrative of imagined expansion and settler cartography. His travel narrative enabled settlers to reinvent Ho-Chunk lands as heteropatriarchal spaces.[16] Additionally, Carver's writings and his assertion of self within his narratives illustrate the early use of settler affect to support European expansion, devalue the role of Ho-Chunk women, and dismiss Indigenous land rights.

When Carver reportedly arrives at the Ho-Chunk village on Doty Island, he is received by Hąpoguwį̨ga, whom he refers to as the queen of the tribe. Carver describes, "On the 25th I arrived at the great town of the Winnebagoes, situated on a small island just as you enter the east end of Lake Winnebago. Here the queen who presided over this tribe instead of a Sachem, received me with great civility, and entertained me in a very distinguished manner, during the four days I continued with her."[17] Carver describes Hąpoguwį̨ga as "a very ancient woman, small in stature, and not much distinguished by her dress from several young women that attended her." [18] Carver's description of Hąpoguwį̨ga's clothing illustrates Ho-Chunk sociocultural views regarding wealth and class. Within Ho-Chunk communities, civil chiefs were expected to give away their belongings in service to the people, resulting in a humble appearance.[19] This practice reflects values regarding social class that are markedly different from European nations. Carver briefly describes his interactions with Hąpoguwį̨ga and notes, "When I saluted her, which I frequently did to acquire her favor. On these occasions the good old lady endeavored to assume a juvenile gaiety, and by her smiles showed she was equally pleased with the attention I paid her."[20] These physical demonstrations of respect emphasize Carver's performative recognition of Hąpoguwį̨ga's role, but his phrasing infantilizes the leader. Carver's description of Hąpoguwį̨ga's reactions portrays Ho-Chunk women as desiring flattery and "attention" from settler men, mapping a racialized and gendered affect within the settler imaginary.

When Carver describes attending a council of Ho-Chunk village leaders to receive permission to pass through their territory, he notes that the queen was present, "but only asked a few questions, or gave some trifling directions in matters relative to the state."[21] Carver's brief and dismissive description of Hąpoguwį̨ga's role in the Ho-Chunk council may reflect his cultural views toward women. Carver notes that it is uncommon for a woman to be in a leadership position for the Ho-Chunk and that even within this position, she generally does not speak or participate in councils as much as her male counterparts. He also offers an additional account from another tribe that describes how a woman of that community came to be in a leadership position. Carver's account operates as a primary source for British settlers to learn about the territory and the Indigenous people of the area, proliferating a narrative that imposes a settler lens of governance and women's roles in communities without an in-depth understanding of Native American communities. From Carver's description, the council is considered the central power, rather than the people, and women do not contribute to this political structure. Hąpoguwį̨ga stands more as a figurehead to be impressed and entertained rather than a representative who has participated in diplomacy with the previous French power. Additionally, Ho-Chunk sovereignty is further eroded in Carver's writing as he trivializes the need for the council's permission to pass through Ho-Chunk territory.

Settler Mapping of Ho-Chunk Land

Carver's travel writing enabled settlers and the settler state to experience exoticized territories and Indigenous people. Through the depictions offered in his text, readers could imagine the land empty of Native people and available for white settlement. Settlers used these imaginings to establish place-based identities and develop affect for Indigenous lands. These feelings incorporate entitlement over land and possession over the bodies of Indigenous people. Goeman notes settler writings such as Carver's were and continue to be "instrumental in mapping the often violent fantasies of American masculinities, frontiers, and borders."[22] This is evident explicitly as Carver states, "There is no doubt but that at some future period, mighty kingdoms will emerge from these wildernesses and stately palaces and solemn temples, with gilded spires reaching the skies, supplant the Indian huts, whose only decorations are the barbarous trophies of their vanquished enemies."[23] Carver actively imagines Native communities replaced by the symbols of European civility, including places of worship and monarchal structures. Carver's assertion attempts to make Native American livelihoods irrelevant, actively erasing their presence, an act of violent settler imagination. Settlers increase their spatial attachments to Indigenous lands through these imaginings and further support their rights to the area.[24] I argue that Carver's imaginings extend beyond geographic spaces; for his settler affect to exist, there must be a denial of Ho-Chunk governing structures and social roles.

Carver's travel writings include descriptions of how the environment may be used to fit the settler economy, specifically British nation-building in the Americas, connecting settler affect to economic growth and capitalism. Carver describes, "The waters of this as well as the other great Lakes are clear and wholesome, and of sufficient depth for the navigation of large ships . . . The country adjacent either to the east or west side of this lake is composed out of an indifferent soil, except where small brooks or rivers empty themselves into it; on the banks of these it is extremely fertile." [25] Carver's description of the land is rooted in imagining how these features could facilitate white settlement and position the land as a resource to be exploited. In his assessment of the land, Carver ignores the use and cultivation already taking place by the Ho-Chunk and other Native American people of the area.[26] He goes on to describe the sand cherries, berries, and wild rice growing in significant quantities in the area without noting the Ho-Chunk's land stewardship practices furthering their cultivation. Rather, as Carver continues his travels, he notes grapes, plums, and fruits "grow spontaneously," actively denying Indigenous land use.

Contrary to Carver's imaginings of an empty landscape, Ho-Chunk people actively participated in gardening and harvesting practices that supported the area's wildlife. Hąpoguwįga's village had been stewards of the area for generations. The political and social organizing required to steward this area, and the established relationships with surrounding Indigenous communities, demonstrate what would be termed as *sovereignty* within

Western conceptions of governance. Ho-Chunk people were organized on Doty Island under a governing structure, whose autonomy and rights were understood by the surrounding Indigenous communities and settler traders. Hąpoguwįga was a key person within this Ho-Chunk community's trade and political mechanisms. Despite Carver's denial of Ho-Chunk spatial and political sovereignty, evidence of sustainable land management practices is apparent in his narrative.

> Winnebagoes raise on it [land adjacent to Winnebago Lake] a great quantity of Indian corn, beans, pumpkins, squash, and water melons [*sic*], with some tobacco. The Lake itself abounds with fish, and in the fall of the year, with geese, ducks, and teal. The latter, which resort to it in great numbers, are remarkably good and extremely fat, and are much better flavoured than those that are found near the sea, as they acquire their excessive fatness by feeding on the wild rice, which grow so plentifully in these parts.[27]

Carver's descriptions of the land's fertility overlook the gendered land management styles of Native American people of the area. Additionally, the Ho-Chunk's seasonal agricultural methods encouraged the continued growth of wild rice along the lake, which in turn enabled the surrounding fauna to thrive. Seasonal harvesting practices reserved rice for animals to consume, and overfishing of the lake was prevented by adhering to sustainable harvesting practices.[28] These methods of land management are possible through centuries of close monitoring and establishing relationships with environmental systems.[29] Carver, like many settlers, did not recognize the ingenuity and technology necessary to achieve the balance and abundance that was being recorded. He writes a flattering description of the region, imagining settler possession, and advancing the trope of Indigenous Peoples' primitivity. Carver's description of unused fertile land and the imagining of settler structures strengthen settler affect, erase the land stewardship practices of Indigenous peoples, and legitimize the future encroachment and resource exploitation that would occur in the next century.[30]

In Carver's journals, Ho-Chunk people are viewed as occupants, and their ecological knowledge and political workings are indiscernible to the settler gaze. Traditional Ho-Chunk sociopolitical systems rely on a clan system that is rooted in relationships to the land. Settler dismissal of Ho-Chunk people's relationship with the land also denies recognition of Ho-Chunk political structures and sovereignty. Carver's devaluing of the role of Ho-Chunk people and Ho-Chunk women's participation in land management decisions demonstrates the foundational Eurocentric ideals that would be used to validate settler encroachment and Native American land dispossession. Carver's narrative mirrors the settler colonial concept of discovery that would be adopted within the United States government.[31] The Doctrine of Discovery relies on ideas of white supremacy to assert that Indigenous peoples did not use land, blatantly ignoring the importance of land to Indigenous epistemology, philosophy, and daily life.[32] Carver's narrative furthers the proliferation of these ideologies by implementing the language of passive Indigenous occupation and land as wilderness, inviting colonists to imagine themselves replacing the Ho-Chunk people in the region. Carver's readers are then able to develop feelings of belonging and longing for lands they have never seen.

Within Indigenous philosophies, there are significant interconnections between land systems and women's bodies. These philosophies inform social and spiritual practices for many Native American communities. Erasing and devaluing the gendered social responsibilities of Ho-Chunk women empowers settlers to excuse violences inflicted on Indigenous women in their attempts to gain access to land and further settler economic development.[33] Within the framework of settler affect, Native American women are valued for the access they may provide to the possession of lands, erasing their sociopolitical contributions within their communities. These attempts at devaluing Indigenous sovereignty and land stewardship further settler colonialism and participate in the active disavowal of Indigenous histories while strengthening settler affect and settler place-based identities.[34] While Carver discusses many interactions with Native American people throughout his travels, his writing continuously repeats Western centrist and Eurocentric perspectives regarding land and culture. Carver maintained these perspectives in his journals, even while his experiences within Native American communities challenged his views. British readers of the day were expected to be titillated by the possibilities of gaining access to Indigenous lands and confident that the British could grow their power in the region.

*From Queen to "the Chevalier's Winnebago Sq**w"*

Before the arrival of white settlers, Ho-Chunk and other Native American communities utilized marriage to strengthen community bonds, negotiate political alliances, and extend kinship networks with other Indigenous Peoples.[35] Within many Native American communities, marriages to settlers operated in the same manner, offering an opportunity to connect communities and strengthen alliances. Susan Sleeper-Smith emphasizes the importance of Native women in creating these alliances noting, "Native women who married fur traders successfully incorporated their French husbands into their communities. These women were important links in the exchange process."[36] Sleeper-Smith describes that marriages between Native women and French traders were "not always permanent, were neither casual nor promiscuous."[37] As described in her community portrait in the introduction of this article, Hąpoguwįga was one of the Native women who shaped "international diplomacy" through marriage.

Hąpoguwįga married the French officer Sabrevoir Descaris in 1728. By the time of their marriage, the Ho-Chunk people had already attended a treaty summit with New France and experienced the breakdown of political and economic trust. Hąpoguwįga entered her marriage shortly after making peace with the French at Michilimackinac. Her union with French trader Decaris strengthened Ho-Chunk and French alliances during a politically tense era.[38] Tensions were heightened by shifting colonial and Indigenous powers competing for land and trade in the region. Descaris left his wife and children to participate in the Seven Years' War (French and Indian War) against the British and reportedly died in the 1760 Battle of Sainte-Foye near Quebec. Hąpoguwįga and Descaris's relationship illustrates how marriage with the French continued the Ho-Chunk practice of strengthening political alliances through the building of kinship networks and trade relationships.[39]

Hąpoguwįga's union with Decaris resulted in the birth of three children: two sons and a daughter.[40] Hąpoguwįga and Descaris's sons followed their mother's leadership role in the community. Their descendants negotiated treaty-making and survived removal from their homelands in the following century. According to Wisconsin Historical Society sources, Hąpoguwįga's daughter returned to New France, now Canada, with her father, and eventually married a trader in Montreal. The marriage of Hąpoguwįga to Descaris, the separation of Hąpoguwįga from her daughter, and her daughter's marriage to another French trader reflect broadly on the sociopolitical relationships between Ho-Chunk and settler populations in the 1700s. It also demonstrates the formation of a Native diaspora that Native American people began to face with increasing contact with settlers.

Considering the prominence of Hąpoguwįga's family and her social standing as a "queen," as described by Carver, it is unsurprising that her marriage to Descaris inspired white settlers to formulate their own historical narratives regarding her life. Carver's description of Hąpoguwįga in his travel writings cemented her social standing within settler memory as regal enough to marry a white settler and become part of settler nation-building. In the early 1900s, Wisconsinite William Ellery Leonard wrote the play *Glory of the Morning,* centered on Hąpoguwįga and Decaris's relationship. Leonard's retelling depicts Hąpoguwįga and Decaris's relationship as a tragic love story, pulled apart by insurmountable cultural differences. Rather than portraying Hąpoguwįga as a political leader and cultural intermediary,

Leonard's play frames her as a tragic figure. This play also includes fictionalized aspects to further the plot. Hąpoguwį̨ga's character is named "Glory of the Morning" and Descaris is named "the Chevalier." Although the play is titled *Glory of the Morning* the plot relies on the movements of her settler husband, the Chevalier. The audience is introduced to Glory of the Morning, waiting for her husband's return, and the play concludes with his departure. This centering of the settler perspective reaffirms settler belonging and the destined erasure of Ho-Chunk people.

Glory of the Morning was part of the Wisconsin Dramatic Society's repertory and was performed regularly in Madison, Milwaukee, and other Midwestern venues located on Ho-Chunk homelands.[41] An article written by Louise Phelps Kellogg in preparation for the play's 1912 performance describes the imagined meeting of the two main characters. It connects the character of Glory of the Morning to the historical figure, Hąpoguwį̨ga.

> To her [Glory of the Morning's] village came a young Frenchman of good colonial family who had been an officer in the French-Canadian army . . . either enamored with her bright eyes, or charmed with the life of the woods, he resigned his commission in the army, and buying some blankets and beads, he embraced the profession of Indian trader. His marriage with Ho-po-ckaw [*sic*] was an excellent stroke of policy as well as romance for by this means he secured the trade of her tribe and their warmth and enduring good will.[42]

Glory of the Morning and Descaris's marriage is described primarily from the settler perspective in this review, noting the socioeconomic benefits gained from their union. Kellogg's framing eroticizes settler encroachment of Native lands by equating the Chevalier/Descaris's attraction to Glory of the Morning to his affinity for living in the area. These romantic descriptions detract from the settler militarization occurring within the region, and Descaris's role in the settler occupation is absolved due to his attachments. As mentioned previously, relation-building through marriage was part of Ho-Chunk practice before the arrival of white colonizers. However, as evident in this narrative, imagining these relationships through the central figure of a white man further justifies settler economic and territorial expansion while disregarding Indigenous land possession and sovereignty.

Within Leonard's *Glory of the Morning,* the audience witnesses the night the Chevalier returns to Glory of the Morning's village to inform her that he is leaving the country. The scene is tragic as Glory of the Morning and her daughter plead to go with him. However, the Chevalier states, "Your mother would not be very happy, I think, over there in the big stone lodge, the Chevalier's chateau, with its high towers and its wide rooms and its long halls."[43]

Similar to Carver's imaginings of Western towers in Ho-Chunk lands, the Chevalier remarks, "it's longer than the longhouses [*sic*] of the Winnebago."[44] This Western exceptionalism becomes central to the Chevalier's dialogue as he tries to convince his children to join him. At the conclusion of the play, their daughter joins him, but his son refuses and stays with his mother. Although Leonard attempts to humanize the character Glory of the Morning through dialogue and stage directions, she is reduced to being described as "The Chevalier's Winnebago sq**w" in the character description for the play. This depiction presses Hąpoguwįga and Ho-Chunk livelihood to the periphery of settler memory.

The settler fixation on Hąpoguwįga's relationship with Descaris parallels settler narratives of Sacagawea, Pocahontas, and Malinalli (La Malinche). Sacagawea guided the Lewis and Clark expedition, Pocahontas has been mythologized as the savior of John Smith and cultural broker for the British and Powhatan Alliance, and Malinalli, also known as Malintzín Tenépal, was the Nahua interpreter and strategist for Hernán Cortés's invasion of Mexico. These Indigenous women are represented within settler histories as furthering "foundation myths" and advancing the image of Native American women as complicit and supportive of the founding of settler states.[45] Additionally, their love stories with settler men offer a romanticized perspective of colonial history. Glory of the Morning's narrative mirrors that of Pocahontas and Malinalli, considering her historical account, as preserved by non—Native sources, is reliant upon the life of a white settler male. Paula Gunn Allen notes, "In the narrative of the Indo-European peoples, a woman's adventure story is inevitably about love . . . Because of this narrative convention, books and articles about Pocahontas have largely fallen into the romance genre."[46] The transformation of settler narratives describing Hąpoguwįga as an elderly woman leader to a young, bright-eyed love object demonstrates this convention. These settler narratives weaponize love and romantic unions to diminish the centrality of Indigenous women and further the stories of white men to advance Indigenous land dispossession. Additionally, settler affect remains at the center of this construction as settler care for Indigenous women justifies land occupation and validates a settler place-based identity.

Sacagawea as a historical figure has been mythologized to serve the frontier myth and doctrine of manifest destiny. Donna J. Kessler traces the shifts of literary and artistic production regarding Sacagawea's role in the Lewis and Clark expedition through U.S. history and notes the growth of reinterpretations that depict Sacagawea as an Indian Princess during the Progressive Era.[47] Leonard's *Glory of the Morning* is also a Progressive Era settler imagining that depicts Glory of the Morning as a tragic figure, whose identity hinges on her connection to her husband. In the play, Glory of the Morning and her husband argue to keep their children, insinuating that a mixed cultural heritage is not possible. This ideology is reflective of early twentieth century U.S. assimilation policies targeting Native American peoples. These features contribute to the vanishing Indian trope and favor the white imagining of the inevitability of westward expansion.

Although Sacagawea is primarily known for her role as the guide for the Lewis and Clark expedition, narratives reframing her as a love interest appeared in the 1940s.[48] These modes of cultural production highlight the settler desire to construct narratives that center Indigenous women as primarily settler love interests, rather than as autonomous Indigenous knowledge-keepers, to maintain Western supremacy and legitimate settler nation-building. In Leonard's play, Hąpoguwį̨ga's fictionalized character, Glory of the Morning, is not a "queen" or leader. Rather, Descaris's character experiences a sociopolitical promotion as "the Chevalier, called Half Moon, a nobleman, now an adventurer in the French fur-trade."[49] The Chevalier is called "Half Moon" by the Ho-Chunk characters in the play, participating in tropes of Indian naming and settler fantasies of becoming Native American people. The playwright's diminishment of Glory of the Morning's leadership role to better fit Euroamerican misogyny and racial imaginings illustrates the assertion of heteropatriarchal roles and the disempowerment of Indigenous women within settler memory. This portrayal objectifies Glory of the Morning, simplifying her existence as only the love interest of her settler husband. However, unlike this settler's imagining, Hąpoguwį̨ga's life story did not end with Descaris's return to New France; she lived on and continued to serve as the leader in her village.

Consensual relationships between Native and non-Native people further the myth of consensual European settlement on Indigenous lands. Hąpoguwį̨ga's depiction as a woman in love and married to a Frenchman contrast with the notoriety of Malinalli, who is depicted as betraying her people to the Spanish. Yet both narratives focus on Indigenous women entering deliberate relationships with non-Native men. Narratives of Malinalli depict her as a hypersexual opportunist, ignoring the power dynamics she was subject to within her own community and in relation to the Spanish. Malinalli was a captive of the Spanish and had a contentious relationship with her community, which drove her decision-making.[50] Malinalli's autonomy and complex personhood are discounted in favor of the misogynistic Madonna-whore dichotomy.[51] In *Glory of the Morning,* Hąpoguwį̨ga is not sexualized like Malinalli and is portrayed as proud, yet naïve and subordinate to her husband. The play explicitly acknowledges that Glory of the Morning and the Chevalier had a Christian marriage ceremony, which contrasts with Malinalli's depiction as Cortés's concubine. Despite this portrayal, the play's cast of characters describes Glory of the Morning as "the Chevalier's Winnebago sq**w," an objectifying and sexist slur for Native American women. Although Glory of the Morning is the wife of the Chevalier and mother to their children, the term signals the sexualization and reduction of her role within this version of her life story.

Settler colonialism relies on the denial of Indigenous sovereignty to bodies and land, and the shifts seen in the portrayal of Indigenous women's histories illustrate settler acceptance of this manufactured dependence.[52] Sacagawea, Pocahontas, Malinalli, and Hąpoguwįga's life stories are separated geographically, temporally, and culturally, yet their histories have been co-opted to further settler colonial expansion. As settlers attempted to gain access to Ho-Chunk lands in the nineteenth century, gendered violence and extractive industry escalated. Although Hąpoguwįga served as the last woman chief, Ho-Chunk women continued the work of mothers, sisters, and community members, enabling Ho-Chunk people to survive a litany of violences in their homeland over the next century.

The Myth of Consent

Settler romanticization of Hąpoguwįga and Sabrevoir Descaris's relationship and the emphasis on its consensual nature work to effectively erase histories of exploitation and violence in the Great Lakes region. Settler narratives choose to promote and commemorate this tale of a Native woman and settler officer rather than historical narratives of violence and settler encroachment. The formation of this romantic narrative contributes to the framing of settler memory and the rejection of Indigenous histories. Collective memory works to reproduce settler colonialism and to "reaffirm the settler claim of belonging . . . on the one hand, and the disavowal of genocide, dispossession, and alienation of Indigenous peoples, on the other hand."[53] Therefore, settler memory works to reaffirm settler affect and vice versa to justify settler connection to place. The collective historical memory surrounding Indigenous women informs and is reinforced through this mythologizing process. The active disavowal of Indigenous histories is the crux of settler memory, contributing to the prevalence of inequity and the denial of Native American sovereignty today.

The Wisconsin play *Glory of the Morning* illustrates settler processes of romanticizing and creating a palatable nation-building narrative. Counter narratives, like those maintained by Ho-Chunk communities and this article, enable a greater understanding of historical legacies and offer an opportunity to move toward a decolonial future. Reclaiming these histories creates the opportunity to challenge heteropatriarchal white nation-building narratives that fuel settler collective memory of place.[54] These histories also participate in (re)mapping the areas that Carver and other settlers worked to imagine as devoid of Indigenous Peoples, creating space to question what Rifkin calls "settler commonsense" and disrupt settler-state nation-building narratives.[55] Settler histories that further colonial structures and contribute to continued violence must be actively questioned to dismantle colonialism.[56] In the field of U.S. history, the written archive is mainly in the control of the settler state. Community memory, intergenerational histories, and firsthand accounts made by individuals passing through these historical moments are often decentered in favor of romanticized narratives. These romantic representations become vehicles to further settler collective memory rather than serving the needs of existing Indigenous communities. Critical analysis of these representations and contextualizing them within the broader historical moment enables a fuller view of the complexities of Indigenous histories and the lives of Indigenous women.

The lack of information regarding Hąpoguwį̨ga's daughter and her absorption into settler society is disturbing when placed in the larger context of the epidemic of missing and murdered Indigenous women that continues into the present. The continuation of Hąpoguwį̨ga's familial legacy is a threat to settler colonial futures as it demonstrates the perseverance of Ho-Chunk people. The disappearance of Hąpoguwį̨ga's daughter may demonstrate to settlers the successful assimilation of Ho-Chunk people into settler society, as made clear in the play *Glory of the Morning.* In Leonard's play, before leaving with her father, Glory of the Morning's daughter continuously asks for settler trade goods and presents while denouncing Ho-Chunk customs. This representation advances the settler myth that Indigenous people are bound to disappear and that Native American women prefer Western culture. Hąpoguwį̨ga's daughter's absence from the settler archive and historical narratives is distressing when so many other descendants are documented. Did Hąpoguwį̨ga's daughter leave her village by choice as illustrated in Leonard's play? Why did her brothers remain in the Ho-Chunk village, able to become leaders in the community? Was she able to return home, and did she ever want to return? Hąpoguwį̨ga and her daughter's disappearance from the historical record and settler memory speaks to the physical and papered disappearance that Indigenous women continue to experience today. Gendered violence and the disappearance of Indigenous relatives have been issues since the first European settlers arrived in the Americas.[57] Even the "Indian princesses" who have been mythologized within the settler collective memory are not able to escape colonial gendered violence.

Through the journals of Lewis and Clark, it is documented that Sacagawea's husband, Toussaint Charbonneau, physically assaulted her on at least two different occasions. Kessler notes, "Reiterations of his [Charbonneau's] behaviours [*sic*] not only legitimate Sacagawea's vulnerability to another man's attentions but also demonstrate the injustices of native existence and bolster arguments of civilization's rightful conquest of the wilderness."[58] As a French-Canadian trader and interpreter with multiple wives, Charbonneau is considered part of the wilderness and is contrasted with Lewis and Clark in terms of civility. Charbonneau's abuse of Sacagawea is portrayed as savage behavior counter to the values of the emerging United States. Similarly, in *Glory of the Morning,* the Chevalier states, "Glory of the Morning, I've been good to you—I never beat you, as Big Canoe used to beat your mother—" to create a defining contrast between settler civility, domesticity, and Indigenous primitivity.[59] However, counter to imagined narratives of white American exceptionalism, Indigenous women experienced violence throughout the founding of the United States.

Settlers have centered the consensual relationship between Hąpoguwįga and Sabrevoir Descaris to create a narrative that justifies settler expansion and romanticizes settler militarized violence, while denying the lasting impacts of gendered violence in Indigenous communities. This narrative enables settlers to imagine themselves as inheriting Ho-Chunk lands through Hąpoguwįga and Descaris's relationship. Expanding the romantic narrative of settler love for an Indigenous woman and the lands she's responsible for furthers settler belonging and erases the injustices faced by Ho-Chunk communities. Additionally, settler erasure of succeeding generations of Indigenous Peoples dismisses the realities of Ho-Chunk communities working to maintain traditional life ways in defiance of settler presence.[60] Settlers are left to confront the historic fact of land theft, settler encroachment, and violence when the myth of consensual land occupation and their affect for land is upended.

Less than a century after Hąpoguwįga led the Ho-Chunk village on Doty Island, settlers increasingly encroached on treaty lands, and Ho-Chunk women were at risk of sexual and physical violence. These violent acts are largely glossed over within the written record. Thomas Forsyth, the Indian Agent of the region wrote in 1828, "[S]ome of the white people are insulting to the Indians and take liberties with their women, which the Indians do not like."[61] This sexual violence was common across the Americas and characterized settler encroachment on Native land. For the Ho-Chunk, these acts of gender violence paralleled their removal and dispossession, further unbalancing their cultural world.[62] Ho-Chunk people worked to maintain their traditional laws and preserve their treaty lands from encroachment by settlers.[63] These defensive actions against settler invasion included the use of intimidation by the Ho-Chunk war chief and his soldiers and the escorting of settlers from treaty lands. Settlers would categorize these actions as hostile activity to justify the removal of Ho-Chunk people.

By the 1820s, the British had lost control of the region and Wisconsin lands were considered part of Michigan Territory. During this time, Ho-Chunk were labeled "hostile Indians" due to their continued presence on homelands and increasing tensions with settler towns. The encroachment of settler miners on Ho-Chunk land and the violence perpetuated on Native American women were significant factors in the 1827 Winnebago Uprising, also known as the Winnebago War. The tensions with American settlers experienced by Ho-Chunk and their Native American allies would eventually erupt into the Black Hawk War.[64] Settler violence perpetrated on Native women in towns and rural areas grew with the increase in the mining population. In 1827, an Indian agent witnessed a woman who had been knocked to the ground by a white miner and grossly assaulted in the mining town of Galena, Illinois. The miner reportedly "stamped on her head, killing her." She was dying in the street when the Indian agent came across her.[65] The settler authorities did not prosecute the miner who murdered this Native woman. This case illustrates the tensions and violence present within mining towns and the risks of violence Native women were subject to in relation to these communities.

In describing the tensions between the Ho-Chunk and the encroaching miners, Governor Cass of the territory wrote to the Secretary of War in 1827, stating:

> Messages have been sent by the Winnebago chiefs to the miners, warning them to quit the country, and explicitly stating their intention to drive them from it by force. A series of insults and aggressions, such as mark the approach of Indian hostilities, have been sometime in progress. Travellers have been stopped, insulted, and plundered, and houses have been entered, and the inhabitants frightened.[66]

These acts of intimidation recorded by settlers are evidence of the Ho-Chunk attempting to police their territory and land by warning miners and intruders to leave the area. The incident that occurred above took place after settlers continued to trespass on Ho-Chunk land that had been negotiated by treaty. The settlers' feelings of entitlement to land, in pursuing economic gains, is reflective of the land policy being exercised by the growing United States as a whole. Settlers maintained a sense of privilege and disregarded treaty boundaries for the purposes of land exploitation. These acts of entitlement demonstrate the actualization of Jonathan Carver's settler imagining (of developing Ho-Chunk land). Throughout this settler encroachment, Ho-Chunk communities were clearly saying "no" through efforts to remove settlers from their territories and through the continuation of traditional practices. Settler refusal to adhere to treaties violated Ho-Chunk rights to land and life and constituted legal disregard for Ho-Chunk sovereignty.

As part of the 1827 Winnebago Uprising, a group of sixty Ho-Chunk and Dakota men attacked two keel boats bound for Fort Snelling after the crew members had abducted six or seven Ho-Chunk women. [67] This attack resulted in the deaths of three Native people and two white crew members. The attacks on the boats by Ho-Chunk and Dakota allies were viewed as acts of hostility and terrorism, dismissing the gendered violence and abduction perpetrated by the keel boat crews that drove the attacks. The perceived hostility of the Ho-Chunk and Dakota would be utilized to justify removal policies and lead to Euro-American narratives that focused on the victimization of settlers and the erasure of Ho-Chunk laws and traditional practices. Although occurring a century before, Carver's dismissive perception of Hąpoguwįga and his claiming of Indigenous lands through colonial imaginings is interconnected with this gendered violence. The violent actions of the settler keel boats demonstrate the presumptive attitude that settlers had rights to Indigenous lands and to Native American women's bodies. This abduction of Ho-Chunk women and the protests of Ho-Chunk and Dakota community members regarding settler actions further demonstrates the lack of Indigenous consent taking place regarding settler presence.

The attempts made by Ho-Chunk people to assert their physical and judicial presence on their lands were viewed as threats to the colonial project but were also viewed as mitigable by U.S. officials. Reportedly two thousand laborers fled the mining area near Galena due to the actions of the 1827 Winnebago Uprising. However, the population of that area remained at nearly fifteen hundred settlers.[68] U.S. officials sought to relieve tensions by urging the governmental purchase of land being illegally mined by settlers. While this solution would compensate Ho-Chunk people and legalize miners' encroachment, it did not consider that the Ho-Chunk may not want to sell their lands or that their ties to the lands superseded any claims made by the settler government. Following these events, Ho-Chunk people were forcibly removed from their homeland and subject to settler state-sanctioned violence. Some bands of Ho-Chunk managed to escape removal attempts, but all Ho-Chunk were severely affected by the imposition of settler boundaries and law in their ancestral territories.

The correlation between extractive industries and gendered violence continues to impact Indigenous communities today. The sexual violence that comes with resource extraction is a global occurrence that has been brought to the forefront by numerous Indigenous leaders and activists. Extractive industries have worked in tandem with settler colonialism to grow the political and economic power of the settler state. Additionally, the growth and continuation of the state hinges on the dismissal of Indigenous rights to steward their land base and exercise authority over their own bodies and space. Indigenous communities have been working to maintain their sovereignty and rights to lands while challenging settler resource extraction and land abuse for generations. For instance, the "Violence on the Land, Violence on our Bodies" (2016) toolkit released by the Women's Earth Alliance and Native Youth Sexual Health Network expands on the connections between gendered violence and extractive industries that result in environmental violence in Indigenous communities.[69]

The interconnected histories of Ho-Chunk women and lands endure from the imaginaries of Jonathan Carver's travel narratives to the forced removal of Ho-Chunk communities in the nineteenth century. These trespasses represent encroachment on land and disregard for the sovereign rights and traditional powers of Ho-Chunk women to determine and give consent for mining and land use. Without the consent of Ho-Chunk women and community members at large, the intrusion of settler miners was a violation of Ho-Chunk laws. Historical narratives that center settler belonging perpetuate settler affect and justify violence toward the land and toward Indigenous communities. For many settler communities, such complex realities have been replaced by imaginaries of rightful occupation and belonging to reinforce settler affect and sense of connection to place. Because Hąpoguwįga and her familial legacy do not align with settler memory, she is either transformed to fit settler frameworks or disremembered entirely.

Conclusion

Remembering Hąpoguwįga as a Ho-Chunk leader and refusing the distillation of her memory through her relationship to Sabrevoir Descaris enables a recentering of Ho-Chunk agency, values, and philosophies. When considering how to transform society and dismantle gender inequities, it is important to remember Indigenous ways and practices that demonstrate social and political possibilities beyond the settler imaginary. As many scholars have discussed, Indigenous resurgence is a method to counter settler affect and the histories that have supported settler colonial thought.[70] Questioning settler narratives and reclaiming Hąpoguwįga's narrative is important when considering the environmental and gendered crises impacting Indigenous communities today. The epidemic of missing and murdered Indigenous relatives is part of a longer history of devaluing Indigenous women's lives under the settler state. Settler histories have weaponized narratives to center settler men and to create mythic pasts that rely on Indigenous people who not only accept settler presence but also actively work to aid settler occupation of Indigenous lands. Indigenous women are often included within historical narratives when they can be portrayed as giving consent for settler occupation. This acquiescence to white settlement is part of a mythic past, contributing to the formation of settler memory that aids the continuation of the settler state. The objectification of Indigenous women to suit the needs of settler memory is visible in the varied characterizations of Hąpoguwį̨ga.

Jonathan Carver's expedition and his publication created a narrative and understanding of Ho-Chunk lifeways framed by the heteropatriarchal settler gaze. Carver highlights an active imagining of land where Native American communities are replaced by symbols of European civility and the goals of resource extraction. This Eurocentric narrative is dismissive of Hąpoguwį̨ga and of the Ho-Chunk communities' careful stewardship of the region. The assumption of settler rights to possess the region is expanded in the twentieth century and is visible in the representation of Hąpoguwį̨ga as the titular character in the play, *Glory of the Morning.* Leonard's play turns Hąpoguwį̨ga from Carver's "queen" into "the Chevalier's Winnebago sq**w." I argue that settler narratives construct a romanticized history of the region into the twentieth century by focusing on the relationship between Hąpoguwį̨ga and Descaris. This romanticization contributes to settler affect for the region and furthers the myth of consent regarding settler occupation while erasing the realities of gendered violence. Complicating these narratives enables a greater understanding of the nuances of Indigenous communities and offers more understanding of the varied experiences of Indigenous women in their communities. Native American women today continue to navigate systems of precarity as their bodies have been marked for violence due to the continuation of colonizing ideologies and the dehumanization of Native American people.

The continuation of nation-building and settler narratives works to reaffirm the colonial agenda. Remembering Hąpoguwį̨ga and other Indigenous women leaders is a discursive act directly challenging heteropatriarchal narratives of the state that work to marginalize women's community roles. This action aligns with the work of Indigenous women leaders and scholars who center Native American traditions and counter the settler colonial project of erasure. Reclaiming the memory and legacy of resilient Native American women who survived settler violence and mythmaking is pivotal in the effort to move toward a decolonial future.

ANGEL M. HINZO (Ho-Chunk, Winnebago Tribe of Nebraska) is an assistant professor of history and the institute of ethnic studies at the University of Nebraska-Lincoln. Her research centers Ho-Chunk history, while incorporating feminist and Indigenous methodologies in analyzing primary and secondary sources.

Bibliography

Allen, Paula Gunn. *Pocahontas: Medicine Woman, Spy, Entrepreneur, Diplomat.* HarperCollins, 2003.

Anzaldúa, Gloria. *Borderlands/La Frontera: The New Mestiza.* Aunt Lute Books, 2012.

Arrizón, Alicia. "Women Gender, and Sexuality in Latina/o Culture." In *The Oxford Handbook of Latino Studies,* edited by Ilan Stavans. Oxford University Press, 2020.

Bourne, Edward Gaylord. "The Travels of Jonathan Carver." *The American Historical Review* 11, no. 2 (1905–1906): 287–302. HathiTrust.

Bruyneel, Kevin. *Settler Memory: the Disavowal of Indigeneity and the Politics of Race in the United States.* University of North Carolina Press, 2021.

Carver, Jonathon. *Travels Through the Interior Parts of North America, in the Years 1766, 1767, and 1768.* Printed C. Dilly; H. Payne; and J. Phillips, 1781. www.americanjourneys.org/aj-127/.

Casselman, Amy. *Injustice in Indian Country: Jurisdiction, American Law, and Sexual Violence against Native Women.* Peter Lang, 2016.

Coulthard, Glen. "Place Against Empire: Understanding Indigenous Anti-Colonialism," *Affinities: A Journal of Radical Theory, Culture, and Action* 4, no. 2 (2012): 79–83. https://ojs.library.queensu.ca/index.php/affinities/article/view/6141.

Daigle, Michelle. "Awawanenitakik: The Spatial Politics of Recognition and Relational Geographies of Indigenous Self-Determination." *The Canadian Geographer / Le Géographe canadien* 60, no. 2 (2016): 259–269. https://doi.org/10.1111/cag.12260.

———. "Tracing the Terrain of Indigenous Food Sovereignties." *The Journal of Peasant Studies* 46, no. 2 (2019): 297–315. https://doi.org/10.1080/03066150.2017.1324423.

Deer, Sarah. *The Beginning and End of Rape: Confronting Sexual Violence in Native America.* University of Minnesota Press, 2015.

Dickinson, Thomas H. "Foreward." In *Wisconsin Plays: Original One-Act Plays from the Repertory of the Wisconsin Dramatic Society,* edited by Thomas H. Dickinson. B.W. Huebsch, Inc., 1914. HathiTrust.

Echo-Hawk, Walter. *In the Courts of the Conqueror: The 10 Worst Indian Law Cases Ever Decided.* Fulcrum Publishing, 2012.

Extract of a letter from Governor Cass to the Secretary of War, dated St. Louis, July 10, 1827. 20th Congress, 1st Session [Doc. No. 277] "Letter from the Secretary of War, transmitting the Information required by a Resolution of the House of Representatives, of the 12 inst. in Relation to the Hostile Disposition of Indian Tribes on the Northwestern Frontier." In *House Documents, Otherwise Published as Executive Documents: 13th Congress, 2d Session-49th Congress, 1st Session,* Vol. 7, p. 8. Gales & Seaton, 1828.

Goeman, Mishuana. *Mark My Words: Native Women Mapping Our Nations.* University of Minnesota Press, 2013.

Hinzo, Angel Mae. "Voicing Across Space: Subverting Colonial Structures in Ho-Chunk/Winnebago Tribal History." PhD diss., University of California, Davis, 2016. ProQuest (10182874).

Kantrowitz, Stephen. *Citizens of a Stolen Land: A Ho-Chunk History of the Nineteenth-Century United States.* University of North Carolina Press, 2023.

Kellogg, Louise Phelps. "Glory of the Morning and the Decorah Family." *The Madison Democrat,* Feb. 2, 1912. http://www.wisconsinhistory.org.

Kermoal, Nathalie and Isabel Altamirano-Jiménez, eds. *Living on the Land: Indigenous Women's Understanding of Place.* Athabasca University Press, 2016.

Kessler, Donna Barbie. *The Making of Sacagawea: A Euro-American Legend.* University of Alabama Press, 1998.

Leeuw, Sarah, and Sarah Hunt. "Unsettling Decolonizing Geographies." *Geography Compass* 12, no. 7 (2018): 1–14. https://doi.org/10.1111/gec3.12376.

Leonard, William Ellery. "Glory of the Morning." In *Wisconsin Plays: Original one-act plays from the repertory of the Wisconsin Dramatic Society,* edited by Thomas H. Dickinson. B.W. Huebsch, Inc., 1914, HathiTrust.

Lonetree, Amy. "Visualizing Native Survivance." In *People of the Big Voice: Photographs of Ho-Chunk Families by Charles Van Schaick, 1989–1942,* by Tom Jones, Michael Schmudlack, Matthew Daniel Mason and George A. Greendeer. Wisconsin Historical Society Press, 2011.

Murphy, Lucy Eldersveld. *A Gathering of Rivers: Indians, Métis, and Mining in the Western Great Lakes, 1737–1832.* University of Nebraska Press, 2000.

Pratt, Mary Louise. *Imperial Eyes: Travel Writing and Transculturation.* Routledge, 1992.

Radin, Paul. *The Winnebago Tribe.* University of Nebraska Press, 1970.

Rifkin, Mark. "Settler Common Sense." *Settler Colonial Studies* 3, no. 3–4 (2013): 322–40.

Romero, Rolando, and Amanda Nolacea Harris, eds. *Feminism, Nation and Myth: La Malinche.* Arte Público Press, 2005. ProQuest Ebook Central.

Shields, Rob. "Lifelong Sorrow: Settler Affect, State and Trauma at *Anne of Green Gables.*" *Settler Colonial Studies* 8, no. 4 (2017): 518–536. https://doi.org/10.1080/2201473X.2017.1388467.

Simpson, Audra. "The State is a Man: Theresa Spence, Loretta Saunders and the Gender of Settler Sovereignty." *Theory & Event* 19, no. 4 (2016). ProQuest.

Simpson, Leanne Betasamosake, "Land as pedagogy: Nishnaabeg intelligence and rebellious transformation." *Decolonization: Indigeneity, Education & Society* 3, no. 3 (2014). https://jps.library.utoronto.ca/index.php/des/article/view/22170.

Sleeper-Smith, Susan. *Indian Women and French Men: Rethinking Cultural Encounter in the Western Great Lakes.* University of Massachusetts Press, 2001.

Smith, David Lee. "The Events Leading up to the Permanent Split Within the Winnebago Tribe, 1800–1816." MA thesis, University of California Los Angeles, 1986.

Winnebago Tribal History: The Early History of the Ho-Chunk People from Creation to 1816. Unpublished Manuscript, 2001.

Thomas L. McKenney to the Secretary of War. St. Louis, MO September 17, 1827. 20th Congress, 1st Session. [Doc. No. 277] "Letter from the Secretary of War, transmitting the Information required by a Resolution of the House of Representatives, of the 12th inst. in relation to the Hostile Disposition of Indian Tribes on the Northwestern Frontier." In *House Documents, Otherwise Published as Executive Documents: 13th Congress, 2d Session-49th Congress, 1st Session,* Vol 7., p. 9. Gales & Seaton, 1828.

Tronnes, Libby Rose. "Corn Moon Migrations: Ho-Chunk Belonging, Removal, and Return in the Early Nineteenth-Century Western Great Lakes," Ph.D. diss., University of Wisconsin–Madison, 2017. ProQuest (10690192).

Tuck, Eve and Yang, K. Wayne. "Decolonization is not a Metaphor." *Decolonization: Indigeneity, Education & Society* 1, no. 1 (2012): 1–40. https://jps.library.utoronto.ca/index.php/des/article/view/18630/15554

Vimalassery, M., J. H. Pegues, and A. Goldstein. "Introduction: On Colonial Unknowing." *Theory & Event* 19, no. 4 (2016). Project MUSE.

Voyles, Traci Brynne. *Wastelanding: Legacies of Uranium Mining in Navajo Country.* University of Minnesota Press, 2015.

White, Richard. *The Middle Ground: Indians, Empires, and Republics in the Great Lakes Region, 1650–1815.* Cambridge University Press, 1991.

Wisconsin Historical Society. "Ho-poe-kaw (Glory of the Morning): Last Known Female Ho-Chunk Chief." Historical Essay. Accessed February 15, 2025. Wisconsin Historical Society. https://www.wisconsinhistory.org/Records/Article/CS517.

Women's Earth Alliance and The Native Youth Sexual Health Network, "Violence on the Land, Violence on Our Bodies: Building an Indigenous Response to Environmental Violence." 2016, Landbodydefense.org.

Notes

1. Family members have told me that she was named after the relative Angel DeCora (1871–1919) who was an artist and instructor at the Carlisle Indian School.

2. Angel Mae Hinzo, "Voicing Across Space: Subverting Colonial Structures in Ho-Chunk/Winnebago Tribal History" (PhD diss., University of California, Davis, 2016), 20–26, ProQuest (10182874). I first wrote about Hąpoguwįga (Glory of the Morning) in my dissertation.

3. Rob Shields, "Lifelong Sorrow: Settler Affect, State, and Trauma at *Anne of Green Gables*," *Settler Colonial Studies* 8, no. 4 (2017): 518, https://doi.org/10.1080/2201473X.2017.1388467.

4. As a political ideology, white nativism results in restricting the rights of nonwhite communities, furthering racialization of ethnic communities, and anti-immigration policy.

5. Audra Simpson, "The State is a Man: Theresa Spence, Loretta Saunders and the Gender of Settler Sovereignty." *Theory & Event* 19, no. 4 (2016): 1, ProQuest.

6. Libby Rose Tronnes, "Corn Moon Migrations: Ho-Chunk Belonging, Removal, and Return in the Early Nineteenth-Century Western Great Lakes" (PhD diss., University of Wisconsin Madison, 2017), ProQuest (10690192). Discusses the role of Ho-Chunk women in keeping gardens, planting corn, and protecting their fields.

7. "Ho-poe-kaw (Glory of the Morning): Last Known Female Ho-Chunk Chief," Historical Essay, Wisconsin Historical Society, accessed February 15, 2025, https://www.wisconsinhistory.org/Records/Article/CS517.

8. Paul Radin, *The Winnebago Indians* (University of Nebraska Press, 1970), 161.

9. David Lee Smith, *Winnebago Tribal History: The Early History of the Ho-Chunk People from Creation to 1816.* (Unpublished Manuscript, 2001), 108.

10. Smith, *Winnebago Tribal History,* 108–109. Smith's account cites Publius V. Lawson, "The Outagamie Village at West Menasha," Wisconsin Historical Society Proceedings. Democrat Printing Company, State Printers, 1889–1902, 204–211; Publius V. Lawson, "The Winnebago Tribe," *Wisconsin Archeologist* 6, no. 3 (July 1907), 96; Zachary Gussow and Raleigh Barlave. *Sac, Fox, and Iowa Indians I* (Garland Publishing, 1974), 134–5.

11. Edward Gaylord Bourne, "The Travels of Jonathan Carver," *The American Historical Review* 11, no. 2 (1905–1906): 287, HathiTrust.

12. Mary Louise Pratt, *Imperial Eyes: Travel Writing and Transculturation* (Routledge, 1992), 7.

13. Bourne, "The Travels," 293.

14. Henry R. Schoolcraft, *Personal Memoirs of a Residence of Thirty Years with the Indian Tribes on the American Frontiers* (1851), 168–69 cited in Bourne, "The Travels," 293.

15. The connection between land, settler imagination, and Indigenous erasure (physical and epistemic) is discussed in Nathalie Kermoal and Isabel Altamirano-Jiménez, eds. *Living on the Land: Indigenous Women's Understanding of Place* (Athabasca University Press, 2016); Mishuana Goeman, *Mark My Words: Native Women Mapping Our Nations* (University of Minnesota Press, 2013); Sarah Leeuw and Sarah Hunt. "Unsettling Decolonizing Geographies," *Geography Compass* 12, no. 7 (2018): 1–14, https://doi.org/10.1111/gec3.12376.; Traci Brynne Voyles, *Wastelanding: Legacies of Uranium Mining in Navajo Country* (University of Minnesota Press, 2015).

16. See Goeman, *Mark My Words,* 17; Pratt, *Imperial Eyes,* 10.

17. Jonathon Carver, *Travels Through, Travels Through the Interior Parts of North America, in the Years 1766, 1767, and 1768* (C. Dilly; H. Payne; and J. Phillips, 1781), 32, www.americanjourneys.org/aj-127/.

18. Carver, *Travels Through,* 33.

19. Radin, *Winnebago Indians*, 161.

20. Carver, *Travels Through*, 33.

21. Carver, *Travels Through*, 33.

22. Goeman, *Mark My Words*, 157.

23. Carver, *Travels Through*, viii.

24. Shields, "Lifelong Sorrow," 522 notes that "This taking possession of a place, re-spatializing it according to one's own needs, is both colonizing and constructing,"

25. Carver, *Travels Through*, 29–30.

26. Carver, *Travels Through*, 30, 37.

27. Carver, *Travels Through*, 37–38.

28. Tronnes, "Corn Moon," 40–43. The traditional Ho-Chunk calendar is largely based on food availability, such as the movement of animals and corn growing seasons.

29. Various scholars have discussed the interdependence and connections between Indigenous Peoples and the land including Glen Coulthard, "Place Against Empire: Understanding Indigenous Anti-Colonialism," *Affinities: A Journal of Radical Theory, Culture, and Action* 4, no. 2, (2012): 81, https://ojs.library.queensu.ca/index.php/affinities/article/view/6141. Coulthard discusses the interrelated meanings of "land-as-resource; and land-as-relationship."

30. Walter Echo-Hawk, *In the Courts of the Conqueror: The 10 Worst Indian Law Cases Ever Decided* (Fulcrum Publishing, 2012), 44–45; Eve Tuck and K. Wayne Yang, "Decolonization is not a Metaphor," *Decolonization: Indigeneity, Education & Society* 1, no. 1 (2012): 10–13, https://jps.library.utoronto.ca/index.php/des/article/view/18630/15554; Voyles, *Wastelanding*, 7.

31. Echo-Hawk, *In the Courts of the Conqueror*, 76.

32. Leanne Betasamosake Simpson, "Land as Pedagogy: Nishnaabeg Intelligence and Rebellious Transformation," *Decolonization: Indigeneity, Education & Society* 3, no. 3 (2014), https://jps.library.utoronto.ca/index.php/des/article/view/22170.

33. See Kermoal and Altamirano-Jiménez, eds. *Living on the Land : Indigenous Women's Understanding of Place;* Women's Earth Alliance and The Native Youth Sexual Health Network, "Violence on the Land, Violence on our Bodies: Building and Indigenous Response to Environmental Violence," (2016): 4, Landbodydefense.org; Kevin Bruyneel, *Settler Memory: the Disavowal of Indigeneity and the Politics of Race in the United States* (The University of North Carolina Press, 2021), xiii.

34. See M. Vimalassery et al., "Introduction: On Colonial Unknowing," *Theory & Event* 19, no. 4 (2016). Project MUSE; and Bruyneel, *Settler Memory.*

35. See Richard White, *The Middle Ground: Indians, Empires, and Republics in the Great Lakes Region, 1650–1815* (Cambridge University Press, 1991, 2001), 14–15; David Lee Smith, "The Events Leading up to the Permanent Split Within the Winnebago Tribe, 1800–1816." (MA thesis, University of California Los Angeles, 1986).

36. Susan Sleeper-Smith, *Indian Women and French Men: Rethinking Cultural Encounter in the Western Great Lakes* (University of Massachusetts Press, 2001), 5.

37. Sleeper-Smith, *Indian Women*, 168.

38. Smith, *Winnebago Tribal History*, 109.

39. Lucy Eldersveld Murphy, *A Gathering of Rivers: Indians, Métis, and Mining in the Western Great Lakes, 1737–1832* (University of Nebraska Press, 2000), 32; See also Sleeper-Smith, *Indian Women*.

40. "Ho-poe-kaw (Glory of the Morning)."

41. Thomas H. Dickinson, "Foreward" in *Wisconsin Plays: Original One-Act Plays from the Repertory of the Wisconsin Dramatic Society*, ed. Thomas H. Dickinson (B.W. Huebsch, Inc., 1914), HathiTrust.

42. Louise Phelps Kellogg, "Glory of the Morning and the Decorah Family," *The Madison Democrat*, February 2, 1912, http://www.wisconsinhistory.org.

43. William Ellery Leonard. "Glory of the Morning." in *Wisconsin Plays: Original One-Act Plays from the Repertory of the Wisconsin Dramatic Society*, ed. Thomas H. Dickinson (B.W. Huebsch, Inc., 1914), 162, HathiTrust.

44. Leonard, "Glory of the Morning," 162.

45. Donna Barbie Kessler, *The Making of Sacagawea: A Euro-American Legend*. (University of Alabama Press, 1998), 2; Bruyneel, *Settler Memory*, 154.

46. Paula Gunn Allen, *Pocahontas: Medicine Woman, Spy, Entrepreneur, Diplomat* (HarperCollins, 2003), 12.

47. Kessler, *Making of Sacagawea*, 99. Kessler references Rayna Green's description of the Indian Princess and describes that, "she occupies an ambiguous position between savagery and civilization, both physically and mentally . . . when the Indian princess acts, she does so to aid a white man or men, out of loyalty to his/their sacred mission into the wilderness" (23).

48. Kessler, *Making of Sacagawea*, 102.

49. Leonard, "Glory of the Morning," 115.

50. Malinalli, or la Malinche, is a well discussed figure in Chicano and Latina feminism. For further discussion of Malinalli and Indigenous Chicana and Mexican womanhood *see:* Rolando Romero and Amanda Nolacea Harris, eds. *Feminism, Nation and Myth La Malinche* (Arte Público Press, 2005), ProQuest Ebook Central.

51. Alicia Arrizón, "Women Gender, and Sexuality in Latina/o Culture," in *The Oxford Handbook of Latino Studies*, edited by Ilan Stavans, (Oxford University Press, 2020), 152 and Gloria Anzaldúa, *Borderlands/La Frontera: The New Mestiza* (Aunt Lute Books, 2012), 31.

52. See Women's Earth Alliance, "Violence on the Land."

53. Bruyneel, *Settler Memory*, 14.

54. Goeman, *Mark My Words*, 36; Bruyneel, *Settler Memory*, 16.

55. Mark Rifkin, "Settler Common Sense," *settler colonial studies* 3, no. 3–4 (2013): 330.

56. See Vimalassery et al., "Introduction."

57. Goeman, *Mark My Words*, 33; Bruyneel, *Settler Memory*, 154.

58. Kessler, *Making of Sacagawea*, 103.

59. Leonard, "Glory of the Morning," 177.

60. See Stephen Kantrowitz, *Citizens of a Stolen Land: A Ho-Chunk History of the Nineteenth-Century United States* (University of North Carolina Press, 2023).

61. Amy Lonetree, "Visualizing Native Survivance," in *People of the Big Voice: Photographs of Ho-Chunk Families by Charles Van Schaick, 1989–1942*, edited by Tom Jones, et al. (Wisconsin Historical Society Press, 2011), 16. Lonetree states, "These early 'settlers' and 'miners' of Wisconsin committed depredations against Ho-Chunk people including theft and rape."

62. Amy Casselman, *Injustice in Indian Country, American Law, and Sexual Violence against Native Women* (Peter Lang, 2016), 4. Casselman notes the legal frameworks justifying violences of removal and supporting the construction of gendered violence targeting Native American women.

63. See Sarah Deer, *The Beginning and End of Rape: Confronting Sexual Violence in Native America* (University of Minnesota Press, 2015), 16–30, for further discussion of gender and traditional legal practices.

64. For a more detailed discussion of the Black Hawk War see Tronnes, *Corn Moon Migrations* and Kantrowitz, *Citizens of a Stolen Land.*

65. Murphy, *Gathering of Rivers*, 125.

66. *Extract of a letter from Governor Cass to the Secretary of War, dated St. Louis, July 10, 1827* [Doc. No. 277] "Letter from the Secretary of War, transmitting the Information required by a Resolution of the House of Representatives, of the 12 inst. in Relation to the Hostile Disposition of Indian Tribes on the Northwestern Frontier," in *House Documents, Otherwise Published as Executive Documents: 13th Congress, 2d Session-49th Congress, 1st Session*, Vol 7. (Gales & Seaton, 1828), 8.

67. Murphy, *Gathering of Rivers*, 125.

68. *Thomas L. McKenney to the Secretary of War.* St. Louis, MO September 17, 1827. 20th Congress, 1st Session. [Doc. No. 277] Letter from the Secretary of War, transmitting the Information required by a Resolution of the House of Representatives, of the 12th inst. In relation to the Hostile Disposition of Indian Tribes on the Northwestern Frontier, May 21, 1828.

69. Women's Earth Alliance, "Violence on the Land," 13. Environmental violence is used in reference to the "horrendous amount of unspecified violence directed at a person, group of people, or land."

70. Leeuw, "Unsettling Decolonizing Geographies," 8; Michelle Daigle, "Awawanenitakik: The Spatial Politics of Recognition and Relational Geographies of Indigenous Self-determination," *The Canadian Geographer / Le Géographe canadien* 60, no 2 (2016): 3, https://doi.org/10.1111/cag.12260; Michelle Daigle, "Tracing the Terrain of Indigenous Food Sovereignties," *The Journal of Peasant Studies* 46, no2 (2019): 303. https://doi.org/10.1080/03066150.2017.1324423; Bruyneel, *Settler Memory*, 16.

NOZOMI NAKAGANEKU SAITO

Between Ruin and Rebellion: A Yuntaku Reading of Everyday Sovereignties in Okinawa's "Black District"

Abstract

During the U.S. Occupation, Teruya was designated the Black District of Okinawa because of U.S. racial prejudice. The prevailing literary and scholarly representations of the Black District portray it as a place of ecological, social, and moral ruination—yet ruin is not all there is to see. In this essay, I propose a "yuntaku reading method" as an Indigenous feminist methodology to read against and beyond ruination, putting literary analysis in dialogue with the Okinawan cultural and social form of yuntaku (Uchinaaguchi: chit-chat, gossip, conversation). Drawing on a close reading of Jun Kishaba's short story "Dark Flowers" (1955) and yuntaku with Teruya residents, I argue that even as tropes of ruination allowed Okinawans to critique the transpacific coloniality and racial logics underpinning the U.S.-Japanese settler militarist structure, they demonstrated a refusal to allow ruination to be the sole condition of their social and psychic lives. By reading against ruination, a yuntaku reading method reveals the complexities of living with/in occupation. Ultimately, by conceptualizing the literary and the everyday, I suggest that Okinawans, through their everyday actions, transformed Black-Okinawan relationalities into fertile ground for articulating other possible futures, enacting everyday sovereignties between ruin and rebellion in Okinawa's Black District.

> *K was the main business district in the middle part of Okinawa Island. It had the shabby postwar look of a town born and grown up along the military highway that ran through it from north to south. Its streets were lined with a jumble of souvenir shops, movie theaters, foreign import-export companies, bars, game centers, vendors' stalls, and brothels—all fronted with signs written in English. . . . Standing next to a bench in front of a restaurant, a boy with a G.I. haircut chewed sticks of gum one after another, spitting out the leftover wads. He was clapping his hands as he peered into a barbershop where a woman, whose low-cut blouse didn't quite cover her breasts, could be seen reflected in the mirror as she sat in the barber chair.*
>
> —KISHABA JUN, "DARK FLOWERS"[1]

THE DRIVE TO TERUYA from Highway 58 takes seven minutes from the toll gate. Gate Street starts (or ends, depending on your viewpoint) at Gate 2 of Kadena Air Force Base in Okinawa. You can't miss the guarded entry, the barbed wire fences, the wide streets leading onto base, the buildings spaced far apart, the neatly mown lawns. *You can tell it's a military base,* my uncle once said, *by how everything is so spread out. Okinawans don't build like that.* Gate Street was lined with tattoo parlors, strip clubs, bars, tailors, record stores, and restaurants advertising Indian, Peruvian, and Jamaican cuisine. Most of the signs were in English with a few in Japanese and Spanish. It was the summer of 2022, but as I drove toward Teruya, the area struck me as strangely familiar, as if little had changed since Kishaba Jun's "Kurai hana" ("Dark Flowers").[2] Published in 1955, the story describes the "shabby postwar look of a town born and grown up along the military highway," its streets "lined with a jumble of souvenir shops, movie theaters, foreign import-export companies, bars, game centers, vendors' stalls, and brothels—all fronted with signs written in English" (Kishaba 2000, 103). Set during the time of the U.S. Occupation, the story portrays the intimacy between the story's protagonist, Nobuko, a military prostitute, and her Black GI boyfriend, Joe.

I was heading to the Teruya neighborhood, which under the United States Civil Administration of the Ryūkyū Islands (USCAR), was designated the "Black District" in 1953 due to American racial segregation. Bars, tailors, and barbershops all catered to Black soldiers. As with many military towns, the area gained a reputation for sleaze and moral ruination due to the sex economy. At the height of the American War in Vietnam, the U.S. military presence brought an influx of American soldiers, and Old Koza became a hotbed of "transpacific anti-racisms" with anticolonial coalitions between Okinawans and Black soldiers culminating in the Koza Uprising of 1970 (Onishi 2013; Ueunten 2010). A history of anti-Black segregation under the U.S. Occupation, that was followed by a burgeoning Black cultural life, and the anticolonial uprising, gave the place new significance in ways that influence how many view the former "Black District" today.

Little of that rebellious past was visible when I visited Teruya. After the U.S. withdrawal from Vietnam and the reduction of troops in Koza City, followed by the 1972 Reversion to Japanese governance, the area experienced an economic downturn. By the time I arrived, the pandemic had shuttered many of the storefronts along the once-famous "Gate Street." In the heart of Teruya, I noticed empty buildings, dimly lit paths, and signs of dilapidation. A local resident, who had grown up there during the Occupation and returned to the area as an adult, later described the neighborhood as "*sabi-machi*" (run-down town). From its heyday as a military camp town to the economic downturn and the global recession caused by the pandemic, ruination had characterized much of the life of the place.

Yet ruin was not all there was to see.

Themes of ruin and ruination are prevalent tropes in a great deal of postwar literary and scholarly representations of Teruya and Okinawa more generally, largely as a result of its history of dual colonialism. Prior to 1879, Okinawa was an independent kingdom known as the Ryūkyū Islands. The Satsuma invasion from Japan in 1609 forced a tribute system that lasted for over two centuries and was the precursor to the official annexation of Ryūkyū into Okinawa.[3] This settler history, coupled with Japanese supremacist ideology, resulted in the sacrifice of Okinawa during the devastating Battle of Okinawa, which killed 150,000 Okinawan civilians. As former Okinawan governor Masahide Ōta notes, Japan's military strategists "sacrificed Okinawa to free more resources for the defense of the Japanese mainland. Okinawans were dragged into a losing battle, which reduced almost the whole Ryukyu chain to ruins" (1988, 10). After the war, the Ryūkyū Islands experienced another kind of ruination as the U.S. Occupation led to land seizures and the rapid development of military bases throughout the prefecture. While the 1972 Reversion ended the era of U.S. military governance and restored Japanese sovereignty over Okinawa, it did not lead to the closure of the military bases. Indeed, the U.S. militarization of Okinawa has continued unabated, resulting in various modes of social, economic, and ecological ruination throughout Okinawa.

How do you read a place, a landscape, as an archive of all the violence and loss without letting ruin become its singular story? As a growing body of scholarship has shown, an overemphasis on ruination and disappearance may also have the unintended effect of feeding into the settler project by promoting narratives of erasure, disappearance, and inevitable tragedy (Day 2021; Powell 2024; Tuck 2009). In this essay, I draw on a "yuntaku reading method" as a way to amplify community stories that show the richness and complexities of lives unfolding beyond narratives of ruin and ruination that too often foreclose understandings of the complex modes of place-making and self-determination practiced by Okinawans in their everyday lives. Drawing on what Shalini Puri (2015) elsewhere describes as "literary fieldwork" that highlights "the relationship between the literary, the historical, and the everyday," I put conventional literary analysis in conversation with community stories shared with me during yuntaku (40). Yuntaku, an Uchinaaguchi term, translates to "chit chat" or "talk story."[4] As Teruya-born Okinawan performance artist, scholar, and founder of the Koza MiXtopia Research Center and Archive, Ariko Ikehara describes, yuntaku as method combines "the local everyday chat and formal interview," resulting in what she conceptualizes as "yuntakuview" (2016, 19). Okinawan American scholar Mitzi Uehara Carter elaborates that "much like 'talk story' in Hawai'i," yuntaku is an Okinawan communal practice that "requires active forms of listening, the development of trust, and open exchange," out of which emerges the "co-creation of cultural forms" (2013, 19). While a traditional interview establishes a unidirectional and hierarchical relationship between the interviewer and interviewee, yuntaku as a dialogic exchange of information implicates the interviewer's own positionality and connections to the place and its people in the cocreation of knowledge.[5] Through these cocreations, the complexities of desire and life under occupation emerge, unsettling narratives of ruin and ruination.

The yuntaku I draw on here is based on my conversations with residents in Teruya, where I conducted research during the summer and fall of 2022 under the mentorship of Ariko Ikehara and the Koza MiXtopia Research Center and Archive. Through this relationship, I was able to meet and yuntaku with interlocutors who opened up to me because they trusted that Dr. Ikehara had vetted the interviewers. Dr. Ikehara's long-standing and respected position in the community facilitated my own interactions with community members, allowing me to build on her established connections rather than inserting myself into a community where I was an outsider despite being Okinawan (a discussion of positionality that I return to later in this essay). During our conversations, Dr. Ikehara and I discussed the ethics of community-based research projects and various ways of ensuring reciprocity when interacting with Okinawan community members. It was as important to me as it was to Dr. Ikehara that my methods did not reify a colonial model of extracting stories and research from Okinawa. My initial research trip was instead just the beginning of building relations with residents of Teruya. Over time, my associations with the research center, Dr. Ikehara, and the Teruya residents developed into forms of deeper engagement. I have come to view my involvement with the center, including social visits when I return for research and family trips, as well as assistance with community events, as just some of the ways that I continue to nurture reciprocity with the Teruyans who so generously gave of their time and memories. I share some of the stories from yuntaku here in an effort to shift the discourse about Teruya and pursue ongoing forms of reciprocal engagement.

Through yuntaku, I came to understand the relationship between the literary, the historical, and the everyday in ways that fundamentally changed my perception of the place beyond ruin. I begin the essay by first historicizing ruin and ruination in Okinawa to examine the impacts of Japanese settler colonialism and U.S. militarism that have jointly shaped Okinawa's dual colonial status today. Next, I conceptualize a yuntaku reading method that builds on Indigenous feminist methodologies to provide a framework for place-based interpretations that go beyond ruin and highlight stories of survivance. Throughout the rest of the essay, I perform this yuntaku reading method in the analysis of Kishaba's story, with a focus on three central themes: how militarized intimacies create estranged and gendered relations to land under U.S.-Japanese settler militarism, the articulation of everyday sovereignties through Black-Indigenous relationality in Okinawa's former Black District, and the resurgent practices of Okinawans in the protracted aftermaths of militarization. In each section, I place the literary analysis in dialogue with yuntaku from the local residents of Teruya. This method of "read[ing] telescopically," to borrow the term from Katerina Martina Teaiwa (2015), connects the literature to forms of communal knowledge production and shows how individual experiences and narratives are shaped by, but also exceed, narratives of ruin and ruination in conditions of militarization and settler colonialism.

I am indebted to the work of Indigenous and Okinawan feminists in my analysis of both yuntaku and Kishaba's story, including Mishuana Goeman (2013); Maile Arvin, Eve Tuck, Angie Morrill (2013); Ayano Ginoza (2016); and Megumi Chibana (2020). As Mishuana Goeman writes, "Colonialism is not just about conquering Native lands through mapping new ownerships, but it is also about the conquest of bodies, particularly women's bodies through sexual violence, and about recreating gendered relationships" (2013, 33). Okinawan feminist scholar Ayano Ginoza writes that the U.S. military transformed Okinawa into "militarized, colonized, raced, and sexual landscapes" (2016, 590). These gendered relationships are reflected in stories of militarization through tropes of rape and romance. However, I wish to read beyond reductive metaphors of women as the invaded land to examine the gendered impact on both women and men that resulted from the occupation and dispossession of Okinawans. Centering land in this analysis also reveals the continuities between U.S. militarism and Japanese settler colonialism that jointly comprise the U.S.-Japanese settler militarist structure.

I arrived in Teruya expecting stories of ruin and despair, and while those histories of ruination persist in the landscape as archive, I witnessed, too, the inventiveness of Okinawans and the strength of their communities. In the process, I learned valuable lessons about self-determination and sovereignty at the everyday level. As Kevin Quashie (2012) writes in the context of Black life, although frameworks of loud, public protest highlight the most visible representations of Blackness, there are other ways of being that become perceptible when we attune ourselves to the sovereignty of quiet, ordinary moments. Quashie's theorization resounds with Mvskoke scholar and teacher Laura Harjo's concept of "radical sovereignties" that are rooted in "local community knowledge and practice" (2019, 50). As Indigenous Okinawan scholar Megumi Chibana describes, everyday sovereignties emerge out of "everyday dialogues and interactions instead of acting within the statist legal and political structures" (2020, 135). Okinawans live out self-determination in the here and now rather than wait for an always deferred future in which the terms of self-determination are governed by settler militarist powers. In Teruya, where the military sex economy and the history of Black-Okinawan coalitions have generated polarizing representations of the place in terms of either ruin or rebellion, Quashie, Harjo, and Chibana offer alternate interpretive frameworks that alert us to how small acts of reciprocity and everyday self-determination open up space to enact everyday sovereignties. On my first day, Keiko-san, the owner of the bar, brought us fried mozuku tempura. Down the street, at Noor Café, I observed that the café owner had created a space where neighborhood children felt safe waltzing in and out of the café and the kitchen, with a comfort that suggested this was their second home. In observing these ordinary moments of reciprocity and place-making, and in yuntaku with Teruya residents, I felt my eyes opened to more than the ruin and ruination I had expected to find; I instead saw everyday sovereignties cultivated by Okinawans between ruin and rebellion.

Reading Against Ruin: Articulating Yuntaku as an Indigenous Feminist Reading Practice

The U.S.-Japan Security Treaty (1951) signed in San Francisco codified the terms of Japan's surrender and established the legal framework that enabled the U.S. military occupation of Okinawa after World War II. At the time of signing the treaty, Emperor Hirohito requested General Douglas MacArthur maintain occupation in Okinawa, to which MacArthur agreed, noting that such a decision should raise "no Japanese opposition to the United States holding Okinawa since the Okinawans are not Japanese" (quoted in Shimabuku 2012, 132). As second-generation Uchinaanchu Annmaria Shimabuku notes, "The price of 'peace' in Japan after the 1951 San Francisco Peace Treaty was paid by exporting the violence of the U.S. military from Japan to Okinawa" (2012, 132). I would add that without going as far as acknowledging the former sovereignty of Ryūkyūans, MacArthur's comment signaled how ideas of Okinawan racial difference were integral to both the century of preceding colonization under Japan and the subsequent decades of U.S. militarization and occupation to follow.

It is against this backdrop of Japan's colonization of the Ryūkyū Kingdom and its annexation into Okinawa Prefecture that the era of U.S. militarism must be understood, as the entanglement of the two imperial powers forms the structure of U.S.-Japanese settler militarism.[6] Shimabuku (2012) explains the treaty between Japan and the United States as a form of “transpacific colonialism,” with both Japan and the United States benefiting mutually and being jointly responsible for the social, moral, and ecological ruination of the islands. Where Japanese settler colonialism laid the structural foundations for the U.S. military occupation of the Ryūkyū Islands, the U.S. military bases maintain settler militarism through their infrastructure and the ongoing dispossession of Okinawans. As Jodi Kim notes, the U.S. military bases constitute a “settler garrison” that is maintained via the “enduring spatial logic and architecture of military bases, camptowns, and facilities” (2022, 82). Today, the ongoing dispossession of Okinawans can be seen in the continual presence of the U.S. military bases. While Okinawa prefecture makes up just 0.6 percent of Japan’s total landmass, it hosts over 70 percent of the U.S. military bases in Japan (All Okinawa Council for Human Rights 2022). The U.S. military bases disproportionately take up the lands of Indigenous people within the Japanese settler nation-state.

Calling attention to the dispossession of Okinawans as an issue of Indigenous rights, Ayano Ginoza notes that feminist organizations have taken to “articulating Indigeneity” to disrupt Japan’s discourse of ethnic minorities and multiculturalism. The government of Japan treats the base and land issue in Okinawa as an issue on par with other inequalities faced by ethnic minorities in Japan, such as discrimination, rather than as an Indigenous issue that emerges from the dispossession of Okinawans of their land and the dismantling of Ryūkyūan sovereignty under the Meiji Restoration.[7] Particularly in the context of U.S. military bases, articulations of Indigeneity are not claims of racial identity as much as assertions and affirmations of political identity and rights to self-determination. These land-based issues are gendered as well. As Maile Arvin, Eve Tuck, and Angie Morrill write, “Within the context of land and settler colonialism, the issues facing Indigenous women, [are] as inseparable from the issues facing Indigenous people as a whole” (2013, 10). In Okinawa, the expansion of the U.S. military bases through land seizures and leasing agreements, and the creation of a sex economy on Okinawan lands have had gendered impacts as well. In the case of farming, for example, while not all farmers are men, Okinawan men experienced disenfranchisement during the land seizures of Okinawan farmlands in the construction of military bases. Meanwhile, the militourist sex economy depends on and exploits the gendered labor of Okinawan women and girls, while exposing them to higher rates of sexualized gender violence.

Okinawan demands for demilitarization and self-determination emerge out of these entangled histories of transpacific colonial ruination. Okinawans protesting the violence perpetrated by the U.S. military, particularly against Okinawan women and girls, also understand this as an Indigenous women's and human rights issue. A report by the All Okinawa Council for Human Rights (2022) notes that sexual violence by U.S. military personnel has occurred since 1945, the beginning of U.S. occupation, and has continued even after the 1972 Reversion. Between 1972 and 2020, crimes committed by U.S. military personnel have reached nearly 6,000, with 581 of those crimes including rape, robbery, and murder. Thus, Japan's sacrifice of Okinawa during the war, its postwar exporting of the U.S. military to Okinawa after the war, the high rates of sexual violence committed by U.S. military personnel, and the ongoing U.S. military occupation have turned Okinawa into what Ann Laura Stoler calls a site of "imperial ruin," where the material and psychic residues of empire persist in "what people are 'left with' . . . in the corroded hollows of landscapes, on the gutted infrastructures of segregated cityscapes and in the microecologies of matter and mind" (2008, 194). In the post–World War II era, the dual colonial situation has fueled an anticolonial discourse that draws on this rhetoric of ruination. Okinawan women's rights and feminist organizations have taken to describing Okinawa as the "sacrificial daughter" of Japan to articulate Okinawa's victimization, neglect, and sacrifice (Angst 2009, 118). This racial-gendered violence, along with the ecological and economic impact of the war articulated by Ōta earlier in the essay, compounds the sense of Okinawa as being subject to varying scales of moral, ecological, and social ruination.

Without denying the urgency of demands for demilitarization, it is also necessary to counter stories of ruin with stories of survivance and agency. As Eve Tuck (2009) writes, there are limits to a damage-centered framework, for "we can practice our sovereignty within a framework of desire but cannot within a damage framework" (423). In the case of Okinawa, the rhetoric of ruin must also include stories of Okinawans' ordinary lives and desires, how they persist even in extraordinary circumstances of historical violence. Stories and storytelling are crucial to this effort, for as Gerald Vizenor explains, "the knowledge of survivance is shared through stories" (2013, 108). Interpretive practices are crucial to this transmission of survivance and cultural and ancestral knowledge, too, with Klamath scholar Angie Morrill teaching us that a Native feminist reading method is an act of "reading against disappearance . . . reading futures yet in store for Native lives" (2017, 15). In her work with Okinawan farmers, Indigenous Okinawan scholar Megumi Chibana shows how "through the telling and retelling of stories, Indigenous connection to the land in this space is maintained, fortified, and cherished" (2020, 7). Through stories, storytelling, and the interpretation of stories, Okinawans can share their experiences of self-determination, what it means to be Okinawan, their connections to the land, and the grounds of their everyday sovereignties.

Yuntaku is one way of sharing these lived experiences that cherish and fortify Okinawan cultural practices. While other terms like munugatai refer to more formal genres of storytelling (e.g., folktales and legends), yuntaku as a dialogic mode centers the exchange between speaker and listener. Reciprocity is central to this methodology. As Carter explains, "Yuntaku expects participants to take the vulnerable risk of sharing their own stories" (2013, 20). On one of my first days in Teruya, Dr. Ikehara introduced me to some oji-sans (uncles or older men) in the neighborhood. One of the men pulled out some foldable chairs, and we sat in the street for yuntaku. I explained where I had come from, my connection to Okinawa, and then, at Dr. Ikehara's encouragement, I also mentioned my grandmother from Miyakojima had worked as a hostess in Koza City during the Occupation. She worked under a pseudonym because, by then, she was in her mid-thirties and was married with three children. Like many Okinawans faced with poverty and famine, she did what she had to for survival.

When I mentioned my grandmother, the older men recalled the Miyakojima women who lived and worked in the area: "Miyako women are beautiful. All the Miyako women lived by the river. They were tight-knit."[8] One man recalled a Miyako woman who lived for many years across the street and not once spoke to him. I didn't understand the subtext of this conversation until later, when Dr. Ikehara explained the history of discrimination against Miyako islanders. At one point, people from Okinawa Island invaded Miyakojima. Thus while Okinawans from islands throughout the prefecture moved to Koza City and Okinawa Island during the Occupation era, the women from Miyakojima lived separately in their own ethnic enclaves. The remark that the Miyako women were "tight-knit" was a reference to how the women were protecting themselves from discrimination.

Yuntaku may reveal complicated histories, showing that there is not really one singular Okinawan identity or understanding of Okinawanness. Different power dynamics emerge, including the stigma Okinawan women faced as hostesses, the hierarchy of age and gender, and the privilege of positionality. During my fieldwork in Teruya, I was often asked to share where I'm from and my connections to Okinawa. These questions taught me early on that while I am Okinawan on my mother's side, with my family residing in Urasoe, I was also an outsider to Teruya. I myself was raised in the United States and trained in the U.S. academy, and my positionality and perspective as an outsider to Teruya shaped how I initially related to the community members and what I expected to find in Teruya. Yet these complexities also illuminate why yuntaku is necessary. For scholars, it requires us to think about our positionality and how that shapes the dynamics in community-engaged research. The cocreation of knowledge with community members may show us the limits of our own scholarly endeavors. And for Okinawans, it is how we come to know each other. In this way, yuntaku draws on Okinawan customs and involves community members in the co-creation of knowledge that moves us closer to a desire-based framework, one that "necessarily complicates our understanding of human agency, complicity, and resistance" (Tuck 2009, 420). Through a yuntaku reading, we can attend to these differential relations of power and continue the struggle for demilitarization, even as we leave space for complex workings of desire, agency, and resistance that emerge from a "life beyond ruin" (Powell 2024).

K-Town and Y-Town: Imperial Intimacies and Estranged Relations to Land

Kishaba Jun's "Dark Flowers" ("Kurai Hana," 1955) first appeared in the University of the Ryūkyūs' radical student literary magazine, *Ryūdai Bungaku.* The literary magazine published various writings of note by Okinawan writers, including Arakawa Akira's "The Colored Race" ("Yūshoku jinshu," 1956). Writings of this period exemplify what Michael Molasky (1999) defines as "occupation literature," or works written during the occupation. Kishaba himself published various art criticism essays and poetry in *Ryūdai Bungaku,* including his poem "Miserable Map" ("Mijimena chizu"), which appeared in the eighth issue of *Ryūdai Bungaku* as a protest poem concerning the U.S. militarization of the islands. Kishaba himself witnessed the 1955 Ishama land struggle, when the U.S. military bulldozed farmlands and forced farmers off their land at the tip of the bayonet. In an interview with the Okinawan newspaper *Ryukyu Shimpo,* Kishaba stated, "I witnessed the beautiful rice fields being bulldozed, houses being burned. Anger swelled up at the horrific burnings that I couldn't stay silent" (as cited in *Ryukyu Shimpo* 2021, para. 1, translation mine). Writing became a way for Kishaba to protest the violence of militarization but as his writing gained increasingly vocal and antimilitary tones at a time of censorship by the U.S. occupation authorities, and Kishaba himself joined in student protests against the occupation, the University of the Ryūkyūs expelled him.

"Dark Flowers" appeared in the magazine's tenth issue. Sketches of guard towers and barbed wire fences create a visual frame for the story, which portrays the ecological and social transformations brought about by militarization. The Okinawan woman protagonist, Nobuko, is in a transactional relationship with a Black soldier named Joe. Through Nobuko's narration and her quotidian affairs, including going to a movie and returning home to give her family the money she receives from Joe, the story shows how the settler colonial structure of U.S. militarism has permeated her intimate and familial life, and with it, the very land itself.

The story begins in this site of intimacy, as Nobuko awakens in Joe's bedroom. Her thoughts immediately turn to worries over whether she will have enough money left over, after paying for food and rent, to send to her family. Although she works to support her family, Nobuko views her work as a military prostitute as "corrupt" (Kishaba 2000, 99). Any intimacy with Joe is fraught because she knows all "her relationship[s] with these men always degenerated into one between the strong and the weak" (99). Any affection Nobuko has for Joe is tainted by this asymmetry in power, which also affects her familial and social relationships. Despite the fact that she has turned to sex work to support her family amidst the economic ruins of postwar Okinawa, she receives "the silent treatment . . . from the villagers" at home, and her younger brother is bullied at school (Kishaba 2000, 106). Thus, the moral ruination that Nobuko feels at doing something "corrupt" is further exacerbated by a reputation of social and perceived moral ruination due to her status as a sex worker.

Representations of the relationships between Okinawan women and American soldiers often follow this trope of "rape and romance" (Nguyen and Hoskins 2014,16). Although General Douglas MacArthur had prohibited soldiers from fraternizing with local women as early as 1946, its practice was common throughout sites of U.S. military occupation and shaped the relationships between U.S. soldiers and Okinawan women. As Catherine Mauldin, a writer for the Black newspaper, the *Chicago Defender,* reported after her visit in 1949, "as will all of the occupied forces, Okinawa has its native female camp followers and prostitutes, some in the guise of house girls, wash women, waitresses and hostesses" (Mauldin 1949, 19). Mauldin observed that American racism further segregated these sex economies, for "the Negro GI is forbidden to intermingle and cohabit with the native women." In this "unnatural situation of not being able to woo or wed the woman of their choice," Mauldin found that some men were willing to "break all moral laws to appease their sexual desires . . . Assault and rape of native women is no new story and many fights and bloodshed have taken place among the men over women. Even murder has been committed in a few instances" (18—19). Mauldin was troubled by what she saw as the moral and social ruination not of the Okinawans but of the American GIs.

In Kishaba's story, the intimacy between Nobuko and Joe as a portrayal of this "unnatural situation" also functions as a metonym for the imperial intimacy between Japan and the United States, which jointly contribute to Okinawans' estranged relations to land. As Setsu Shigematsu (2015) notes, the very fact of the U.S. military presence is evidence of the "imperial intimacies" between Japan and the United States. "Dark Flowers" is set in the town "K"—likely shorthand for Koza City, the name for Okinawa City before the 1972 Reversion of Okinawa to Japanese administration—a military town where the economy of souvenir shops, bars, and brothels caters to the desires and tastes of the U.S. military:

> It made for a weird landscape. These houses, with their fancy roofs, stood in the marshes, paddies, and potato fields dotted with old tree stumps. They were owned by farmers who had moved here after being forced to give up their lands to 'protect freedom from its enemies.' . . . But by this time none of the farmers, who'd been relocated here in this forced migration, were living inside. Instead, they lived in tin-roof shacks that had been built onto the kitchens or put up in the backyards. The interiors of these 'fine houses' had been partitioned into eight-by-eight-foot private rooms where yellowed bras and dresses in many colors now hung outside the windows, fluttering in the wind. At night these 'fine houses' became bars and cabarets. (Kishaba 2000, 101)

This "weird" ("kimyō") or strange landscape reflects how militarization has estranged Okinawans from their land, transforming the landscape and the everyday lives of Okinawans. The newly built houses "with their fancy roofs," intended for the farmers whose lands were seized by the military, have become brothels, while the thrice-displaced farmers live in tin-roof shacks. Further, the architecture of the red-roof houses, with women's undergarments, again recalls what Ginoza describes as Okinawa's "militarized, colonized, raced, and sexual landscapes" (2016, 590). The brothels reveal a specific gendered estrangement from land under U.S. Occupation, with mostly male Okinawan farmers feeling the impact of the land seizures and multiple displacements, and the Okinawan women working in the militourist sex industry. The "weird landscape" of K-Town is thus a palimpsest of U.S. militarization that captures intensifying stages of dispossession of Okinawans.

The landscape of Kishaba's story reflects the lived realities of the people who inhabited the area that would become Koza City. Before the war, the area consisted of farming villages and rice paddies. Shortly after the invasion during the Battle of Okinawa, the U.S. military established incarceration camps and transported the first camp residents in three trucks full of mostly children, women, and elderly people. According to the Okinawa City General and Administrative Division (2007), the population of the camps was 3,700 people in April 1945; that number had swelled to 11,600 people at Camp Koza by July 1945.[9] The U.S. military built the Koza Crossroads military transport highway between four existing farm villages: Teruya (40 houses, 150 people), Goeku (169 houses, 805 people), Nishihara/Misato (244 houses, 162 people), and Miyazato (32 houses, 38 people). As the Battle of Okinawa pushed the battleground to the southern part of Okinawa Island, the U.S.

military sent refugees and prisoners of war northward to Camp Koza.[10] Following the war, the U.S. military began seizing land, with the view that "the level land that was best suited for farming was also ideally suited for airfields, munitions dumps, and other military installations" (Fisch 2005, 56).

In capturing the transformation of Okinawan lands into militarized landscapes, Kishaba links the land seizures and dispossession of Okinawans to the structure of settler colonialism and the dispossession of Native people in Turtle Island/the United States. Nobuko and Joe attend a showing of a Western featuring Gregory Peck, who leads a battalion of cowboys to invade the Native lands and almost single-handedly annihilate the Native people. The film's aesthetics exemplify what, elsewhere, Aimee Carrillo Rowe and Eve Tuck describe as the culture of settler colonialism, in which "cultural productions remain complicit with ongoing settlement" (2017, 6). The American Western film valorizes settler colonialism and, by screening the movie for Okinawan audiences, is meant to woo Okinawan audiences with the glory and heroics of their Occupiers. Instead, for Nobuko, the intended effect of the film backfires as the scene "filled her with anger to see them [the Native charactes] desperately defending their homeland as old Indian women died in terror, young Indian men tumbled to their deaths from cliffs, and camera closeups showed the faces of men tramped to death after falling from their horses" (Kishaba 2000, 105). Later, as Nobuko walks home, the unsettling movie reminds her of a memory of seeing Okinawans being similarly dehumanized and terrorized:

> She again recalled the faces of the Indian men in the movie. They brought back a horrible memory. It had been a sweltering dawn in mid-July when she witnessed this brutal scene. Just before sunrise, across the military highway from her room, she'd seen the faces of men and women huddled together, trembling with rage. They had just been dragged outside the barbed-wire fence that now surrounded their land, and the young men among them were being arrested . . . everything these people owned was being taken from them. (Kishaba 2000, 106)

This incident that Nobuko recalls is part of the collective memory of Okinawans, who remember the U.S. military's land seizures as the *Jyuuken to burudouzaa* (bayonets and bulldozers) campaign. In drawing parallels between the genocide of Native people portrayed in the movie and the incarceration and dispossession of Okinawans, the story articulates the Indigeneity of Okinawans while inviting a comparative critique of colonization and militarization as twin pillars of settler colonialism.

This scene in Kishaba's story raises important questions about Indigenous women's relations to land and how they are inseparable from the larger issue of land dispossession under settler colonialism. Nobuko's own disidentification with the Native people represented onscreen first, rather than Peck's white bar mistress and romantic interest, places the issue of land and dispossession at the foreground of Kishaba's critique. In Nobuko's memory, both men and women experience the violence of dispossession at the hands of the U.S. military. But while the young men are subject to criminalization and incarceration, the women like Nobuko are forced to turn to sex work. Thus, both men and women experience the prolonged effects of dispossession under settler colonialism, though in varying ways. In both situations, the issue of Indigenous people being dispossessed and estranged from their relations to land is central to understanding the various forms of ruination they experience under U.S. Occupation.

In Nobuko's journey southward from K-Town to Y-Town, Kishaba reveals a landscape of entangled Japanese and U.S. imperial intimacies. According to sansei Okinawan scholar Wesley Ueunten, the concept of "yu" (or "yo" in Japanese) refers both to world and way of being as well as a period: "Japan's use of force to integrate Okinawa into the Japanese world (yamata yu), the world of war (ikusa yu) in the form of the horrific Battle of Okinawa in 1945, and the American military occupation (amerika yu) from 1945 to 1972" (2010, 97). These are not linear periodizations of Okinawan history but instead speak to a historical and structural continuity as "yu's coexist, overlap, and interact" (Ueunten 2010, 97). In Kishaba's story, the southern part of Okinawa Island, where the majority of the Battle of Okinawa took place, still bears the memory of the ikusa yu in the landscape: "The war had once denuded this forest, shamelessly exposing the barren red soil. Gone for some time after that was the sharp smell of resin that drifts from the thick groves of red pines, which stay dark during the day. Nor was there any sign of the red-bellied water lizards that hide lazily in the grassy shade" (Kishaba 2000, 107). The exposed forest turned barren by war, and the absence of the red-bellied water lizards as sites of imperial ruin, expose how the violence of imperial wars persists, not as metaphor, but in material, ecological, and embodied ways.

Unlike the weird landscape and amerika yu of K-Town, where the camptown economy runs on women's gendered labor and militarized intimacies with U.S. soldiers, Y-Town is an agrarian village that recalls the yamata yu of Japan's imperial aggression and the extraction of labor from Okinawan men. Nobuko's home is in the south, where the lands smell of mud and are planted with fields of "satokibi," or sugar cane (Kishaba 1955, 30). When Nobuko returns home, she asks after her family's well-being and their sugarcane crop. Her mother, Uto, replies, "A 'bumper crop?' Hah! On this teeny-weeny plot? Then we have to pay all that money to the farm co-op for fertilizer"

(Kishaba 2000, 108). The family's financial hardship in the postwar economy contrasts sharply with K-Town, where the economic boom has been driven largely by the extraction of sexualized labor from Okinawan women. The agrarian economy in ruins is further symbolized by the ruination of the Okinawan household, as Uto gripes, "Well, you know, this house is getting eaten up by termites. And old man Maeda says we have to replace the beams 'cause they won't last through the next typhoon. Of course, he wants the money up front" (108).

The name of the landlord "Maeda" (前田) is suggestive here, especially in the context of a lengthier conversation about the sugarcane (Kishaba 1955, 31). Following Japan's annexation of the Ryūkyū Kingdom in 1879, companies from mainland Japan transformed Okinawa into a cash crop economy with the sole purpose of producing cane sugar. Mainland Japanese sugar capital companies purchased large plots of land and leased the plots at low rent costs for farmers willing to produce sugar cane, while simultaneously introducing a system of satō maedai (sugar advance), which supplied producers with loans at high interest rates. Brown sugar production became a fundamental part of Japan's modernization program and national policy, with the satō maedai system promoting commodity culture in both "management and everyday life" (Shibuya 2008, 10). More than a cash crop, however, Okinawan American historian Wendy Matsumura notes that brown sugar production was tied to the production of Okinawan racial difference. Whereas agricultural producers in mainland Japan focused on rice, Okinawa "became intensely focused on the cultivation and manufacture of brown sugar" (2015, 48). The rapid industrialization of Okinawa "transformed the relationships that many small peasantry had to their lands" (Matsumura 2015, 131). These changes wrought by Japanese settlers occurred throughout Okinawa Island, including in central areas like Nishihara and Kadena (villages that would eventually be militarized in the development of Koza Crossroads and Kadena Air Base), and southern areas like Yonabaru, which became a center of sugar production during World War I.

Nobuko's Y-Town mirrors many of the transformations wrought by Japanese settlers in turning Okinawa's brown sugar into a cash crop economy. Given the history of Japanese sugar extraction and the establishment of the debt servitude through the establishment of the satō maedai system, the landlord's name "Maeda" could function as a near phonetic homonym for "satō maedai" (砂糖前代). In bringing forth this history of sugarcane and the biopolitical system of debt servitude that transformed Okinawan farmers' relations to land, the story therefore suggests that the structures of Japanese settler power have remained intact, even at a time when Japan maintained residual sovereignty over Okinawa. That these settler structures reflect the transpacific colonialism of Japan and the United States becomes further apparent when examining the gendered relations of labor and land in the two towns. Whereas the "fine houses" in K-Town appear to contrast with the poverty and termite-ridden homes of Y-Town, K-Town, and Y-Town are mirrors of each other: in both places, the yu's of U.S. militarism and Japanese settler colonialism extract labor, whether from Okinawan women in the form of sexual labor, or from Okinawan men in the form of agrarian labor. Thus, the apparent contrasts between K-Town and Y-Town are superficial, as the systematic exploitation, dispossession, and extraction of Okinawans under Japanese and U.S. transpacific colonialism has produced estranged relations to land.

In Teruya, one of my first interlocutors just so happened to be a sugarcane farmer. Shiroma-san came from Nanjo (formerly Oshiro), which is in a southern part of Okinawa Island where they grew sugarcane, much like Nobuko's Y-Town in Kishaba's story. The owner of Sanko Deli, he moved to Teruya in 1967 to work with his brother at a soba noodle shop. During our yuntaku, I asked Shiroma-san how Okinawa's landscape had changed over the years. He described the changes using the plant he knew best: sugarcane. *In the past,* he spoke, *farmers made hundreds of cuts in the sugarcane. From the small cuts, hundreds of smaller shoots sprouted out of the stalk.* He gestured with his hands to indicate the abundance of these stalks. *But later, farming practices changed. They began using a single, clean cut to harvest the cane. After that, the shots were shorter, stunted.*[11]

Shiroma-san's explanation contains a layered history about the successive stages of Japanese settler colonialism and U.S. militarism. (Even his name, "Shiroma," as he explained to me, is the Japanese word for "castle" but would have been "gusuku" in Uchinaaguchi.) His family's history as sugarcane producers reflected the material and linguistic transformations introduced by Japanese settler colonialism that long predated his birth and stretched back over a century to Japan's annexation of the Ryūkyū Kingdom. By the time Shiroma-san's family began cultivating sugarcane, mainland Japanese sugar companies had already industrialized Oshiro and other areas, including the farm villages of Misato and Kadena that would be re-industrialized by the U.S. military to create Koza City. While immediately after the war, the U.S. military government initially discouraged sugarcane production because it lacked nutritional value, the military government began actively encouraging sugarcane production as a "key export item" as demand in Japan (Fisch 2005, 131). Sugarcane production did not abate after Reversion, a fact that can be seen by the prevalence of Okinawan brown sugar sold in tourist areas today and exported for Japanese consumers, as a growing tourist economy has transformed Okinawa into the so-called Hawai'i of Japan.

Listening to Shiroma-san, I could not help but wonder how many more decades of militarization and Japanese industrial development Okinawa would survive. His story about sugarcane was a lesson about militarization, about what happens when the violence of dispossession and militarization has been rendered ordinary, and how in the militourist economy, life becomes stunted when it is mown down for efficiency or profit rather than tended to with care.

Everyday Sovereignties in the "Black District"

> *If ruin was my sole inheritance and the only certainty the impossibility of recovering the stories of the enslaved, did this make my history tantamount to mourning?*
>
> —SAIDIYA HARTMAN, *LOSE YOUR MOTHER* (2007)

From the beginning of the Occupation, Okinawans understood that anti-Blackness was a constitutive element of U.S. governance and viewed their own racialization in relation to the experiences of Black soldiers. Not only did Okinawans recognize their racialization within the white supremacist structure of Japanese settler colonialism, but they also understood the white supremacy of U.S. settler militarism that extracted labor and discriminated against Black soldiers as the racial logics underpinning the U.S.-Japan settler militarist structure. As Tiffany King writes, it is not only that "black labor literally tills, fences in and cultivates the settler's land," but that blackness functions as "the ultimate sign for expansion and unending space within the symbolic economy of settlement" (2014, 2). In Okinawa, Black soldiers were part of the expansion of the U.S. military, with job advertisements in *The Chicago Defender* recruiting Black soldiers "to Okinawa for construction work in the expansion of the army base . . . for bulldozer operations and . . . other constructional machinery" ("Vets Go Back to Okinawa" 1947, 8). Through recruitment and the instrumentalization of Black labor, the U.S. military was rapidly expanding its frontiers while transforming areas like Teruya into a "Black District."

Yet Okinawans recognized, too, that the racism experienced by Black soldiers differentiated them from the white soldiers. In a 1946 letter to the editor at *The Washington Post,* Amoz E. Gibson, from Naha, submitted a question posed to him by a local Okinawan: "How can the American authorities hold accountable the numerous Japanese leaders, civil and military, for crimes committed by their underlings when they (the American authorities) do not hold their own local leaders accountable for crimes which are committed by members of the locality directly responsible to the said local leaders?" Gibson described the Okinawan man's enumeration of various U.S. injustices, including "lynchings, of race riots, of religious intolerance, of economic inequity, of various unfair practices to keep impoverished certain minority groups, of such low standards of living in some areas as compared to those in other areas, and of laws which segregate and discriminate" (1946, 6). Whether the question came from an Okinawan man or Gibson himself, the question from Okinawa invites a closer examination of the anti-Blackness that undergirds the United States as a settler nation-state and contests the discourse of benevolence that touts the United States as a liberating power interested in freedom for all.

Kishaba's story draws parallels with the anti-Blackness that Black soldiers experienced within the settler structure of the U.S. military, and the racism that Okinawans experienced as the people sacrificed and sold by Japan to the U.S. military. The story makes several references to racial schematics, including Joe's "black skin, big, broad shoulders, and flattened nose [that] made him look like a prizefighter" (Kishaba 2000, 98). Kishaba makes a point to emphasize that Joe is a Black soldier, rather than just a U.S. soldier, as it is the relationality between Black and Okinawan people that becomes the driving force of critique within the story. Throughout, the narration also emphasizes Nobuko's physical appearance ("hers were the bony hands of a farm girl, hands that carried the smell of the soil"), and the other female prostitutes' Okinawanness ("Michikō, who also came from Y Village in the southern part of Okinawa"; "Saako's voice with its thick southern Ryukyus accent") (Kishaba 2000, 100, 99, 103). The associations with farming signify Okinawans' darker skin, which was seen as "a marker of the impurity and inferiority of Okinawans vis-à-vis Japanese from the main islands of Japan" (Ueunten 2010, 113). Through this emphasis on Okinawanness, at a time when Okinawans would have had a heightened awareness of how their racial differentiation from the Japanese was one of the justifications for the U.S. military bases, Kishaba's story gestures to how Okinawans understood themselves as racialized Others under the system of Japanese imperial racism, in ways that parallel the anti-Blackness that structures Euro-American settler colonialism and chattel slavery.

These parallels are further materialized when Nobuko sees a hedge of the dark flowers that give the story its title. "Kurai," meaning darkness or sorrow, in the story is associated with flowers of sadness.[12] According to the grandmother of Nobuko's childhood friend, the associations come from ancient times:

> Farmers were not only assessed heavy yearly tributes on their crops but were also drafted from districts far and near as forced labor to build the

> king's castle at Shuri. Day after day they marched in long columns, dragging logs and stones, and many died from starvation and sunstroke. There were horrible scenes of death. Under the relentless gaze of bailiffs, the farmers, nearly dead from exhaustion, collapsed in the shade of trees beside the road to give their bodies a brief rest. At such times they must have noticed these dark flowers blooming in the shrubbery. Perhaps these shabby dark flowers reminded the farmers of their suffering. Oppressed and impoverished, they might have felt toward these poor, dark flowers a kind of communion and, at the same time, a repulsion that came from their own self-loathing. (Kishaba 2000, 110–11)

Kishaba's comparative representation here recalls a similar parallel made by Iha Fuyu, known as the "father of Okinawan studies," in his essay, "A Story of Okinawan History" (1947) ("Okinawa reikishi monogatari"). In Iha's view, while Japan's annexation of the Ryūkyū Kingdom in 1879 brought the end of Ryūkyū sovereignty, it also heralded the end of the tribute system and brought emancipation from what he saw as a form of "slavery" (ix). As Katsunori Yamazato notes, Iha well understood the significance of the "parallel he was drawing with the history of slavery in America" (2011, ix). Writing two years into the U.S. Occupation, Iha, like many Okinawans, perceived that American democracy did not mean freedom and equality for all races. Iha's critique intended to lay the groundwork for liberation from all forms of imperialism, for only when imperialism came to an end would Okinawans be "liberated from the 'bitter world' [*nigayo*] and enjoy the 'sweet world' [*amayo*]" (as cited in Yamazato 2011, ix). Thus, while seeking the roadmap to Okinawa's future and liberation from occupation, Iha also looked to its past to articulate the need for a different kind of sovereignty.

Like Iha, Kishaba draws parallels between Joe's and Nobuko's histories as Black and Indigenous people subject to the racial extractions of U.S. and Japanese settler powers. Recalling Iha's characterization of the tribute system as a form of "slavery," this scene reveals how anti-Blackness and Indigenous dispossession have structured Japanese settler colonialism and U.S. militarism. Darkness signifies relationality for Nobuko: the dark flowers and their associations with sadness echo an earlier moment when she hears Joe humming songs that seem to express "the sadness of people who were resigned to hardship," and she wonders if "Joe had learned this song from his father while picking cotton in the fields or from his coworkers on the docks in Mississippi" (Kishaba 2000, 100). In seeing the dark flowers as symbols of histories of oppression, the story thus links the plight of the farmers forced to labor for the tribute system to that of enslaved Africans trafficked under chattel slavery. As Matsumura notes, the burden for the

Japanese tribute system forced upon the Ryūkyū Kingdom fell heavily on the farmers, who had to "sell themselves to those who were willing to take over their tax obligations in return for total control of their bodies" (2015, 32). The farmers' enslavement under the Japanese imperial tribute system parallels Nobuko's situation, as a daughter of a farming family and a woman forced into sex work with the U.S. military to help her family out of dire postwar poverty. This scene therefore draws historical parallels that show the entangled histories of Black and Indigenous people under the structure of settler colonialism.

Iha was critical of the oppressive Shuri regime and longed for a future free from imperialism, and Kishaba similarly depicts this scene at Shuri Castle to articulate a different vision of sovereignty, one that does not reproduce statist structures but is instead grounded in the everyday. After Nobuko sees the dark flowers that she associates with Joe's "sadness that refused to succumb to despair," she is reminded of her family and "the impoverished little farm village where Shinkichi was determined to start a vigorous new life" (Kishaba 2000, 100–111). Her brother, Shinkichi, has been organizing with other farmers from the union and reading from a book titled *The New Farm Village.* Like Joe, he carries a spirit of resolve and refusal to resign himself to despair. In the moment of relationality, Nobuko's own outlook changes as she determines to "fight what was hateful to her with everything she had, and, like Joe, to celebrate what made her happy with a joyful smile" (Kishaba 2000, 111). Although not an explicit or conspicuous gesture of rebellion, Nobuko's decision to live with joy in the face of ongoing occupation is a radical act of self-determination. Whereas formal sovereignties rely on recognition through recourse to the settler nation-state, everyday sovereignties emerge in these interstices of daily life, much like the "resurgents" in Chibana's work who transform the "understanding of Okinawan Indigeneity from an unyielding resistance to an envisioning self-determination of futures" (2020, 3). For Nobuko, living joyfully in spite of her circumstances is a refusal to succumb to ruin and despair, and an insistence on a different kind of future that she determines for herself. The critique of the Shuri king further suggests a new conceptualization of sovereignty is necessary, one that is not premised on hierarchical and individualized power and authority but on collective liberation. Shinkichi's vision of the New Farm Village, grounded in Indigenous Okinawan community-building, offers a blueprint for this different form of sovereignty, by reclaiming Indigenous relations to land and building a just future for Okinawans. In the face of settler colonialism's extractions, the everyday sovereignties of Nobuko, Shinkichi, and Joe shape a vision of the amayo (sweet world) of liberation from all forms of imperialism.

Aftermaths of the Black District

In the closing of his interview with *Ryukyu Shimpo,* Kishaba addressed "the young people of Okinawa: Today, Okinawa is facing increasing pressure to conform to conservatism, making the world a suffocating place. Young people, that is why I ask you to face the current situation head-on and hone your insight. To do so, I ask you to make an effort to find good friends, good teachers, and good books" (2021, translation mine). Like Shinkichi in "Dark Flowers" seeking another future in *The New Farming Village,* the younger generations who inhabit the protracted aftermaths of militarization are the ones who carry the hope for another possible future in spite of the long ruinations of Japanese and U.S. transpacific colonialisms.

The farmer selling his body to mainland sugar companies, the sharp edge of a bayonet, the rumbling terror of a bulldozer, the cold efficiency of the blade cutting down sugarcane to mass produce sugar for export—each successive stage of U.S. military base construction and Japanese industrial development seems to evidence the "ecological ruination deriving from settler colonialism, military imperialism, and neoliberal capitalist development" (Santa Ana, Amin-Hong, Chua, and Xiaojing 2022, 22). Yet in the aftermaths of these ruinations, there are other stories, too. The "aftermath" colloquially understood to articulate the loss and destruction that follows from a significant event, such as war, has its etymological roots in agriculture and once described a "second crop or new growth of grass. . . . after the first has been mown or harvested" ("Aftermath," *Oxford English Dictionary Online*). The aftermath attests to how the violence exists too, but it is not all.

In the aftermaths of militarization, the stories and memories shared, whether as literature or yuntaku, shape how communities cultivate their connections to the land "through the telling and retelling of stories, [so that] Indigenous connection to the land in this space is maintained, fortified, and cherished" (Chibana 2000, 7). At Shiroma-san's deli, I watched as neighborhood grandmothers and grandfathers stopped by to pick up fish tempura or saata-andagi, or sat down for a yuntaku on the foldout chairs in front. These small gestures and everyday actions extend the spirit of yuimāru, or Okinawan reciprocity. When I asked Shiroma-san about life in the Black District, he recalled with humor the Black soldiers who frequented Old Koza. "They loved oden!" he laughed. Neither activist nor victim, Shiroma-san adapted to the changing conditions precipitated by the aftermaths of war and militarization. He befriended soldiers and made a life for himself on his own terms. Others who lived in the area during Occupation expressed similar moments of relationality, friendship, and neighborly feeling. Another shopowner, Miyazato-san, moved to Teruya when she was sixteen to run a clothing store with her mother in 1955, the same year that Kishaba's story ran in *Ryūdai Bungaku.* She recalled the Black soldiers were "very stylish," often donning sharp suits and buying kimonos or Western clothing in the later years of the Occupation for their Okinawan girlfriends.[13] The stories shared during yuntaku with people in Teruya show that ruin is not, and never was, the endpoint of their lives. Stories of "ruin porn" perpetuate settler fantasies of Indigenous lands as sites of ruination, emptied of Indigenous presence (Day 2021). Instead, in Teruya, Okinawans and Black soldiers offered another way of being, proving the possibility of cultivating a "self-same ground" that pushes us "to supersede the conventions of settler colonialism and antiblackness toward another kind of futurity" (Tuck et al. 2014, 2).

The younger generation in Teruya is also part of the generation of Okinawan resurgence. Keiko-san, who runs a bar in Teruya, was born in Goeku, the neighborhood on the other side of Teruya across the Koza Crossroads military highway. Her son runs a successful YouTube channel that brings visitors from around the world into her bar. In the afternoons, Keiko-san volunteers her time cooking for an afterschool community program that gives meals to the children of single mothers while their mothers are at work. When I asked how she did it, she waved me off and said it was "everyone's collaboration."[14] In the aftermaths of militarization, Keiko-san and other Okinawans are redefining their relationship to the land and community without relying on statist structures. Instead, they are driven by the Okinawan ethos of yuimāru. Around the corner at Café Noor, Dai-san explained that while the area was run down when he opened his café, it also gave him a freedom to build the kind of space he wanted.[15] As a DJ and café owner, he has hosted events bringing together hip-hop and Okinawan style in a kind of champūrū street culture.[16] Here, in the former Black District, on the self-same ground, people like Shiroma-san, Miyazato-san, Keiko-san, and Dai-san act out their everyday sovereignties within and beyond the aftermaths of militarization.

The stories and interpretive methods we draw on to talk about places like Teruya influence how others apprehend a place as more than an archive of all the violence and loss. While as Tuck and Yang (2012) so aptly put it, "Decolonization is not a metaphor," the metaphors and narrative frames we use to talk about colonization and decolonization matter for envisioning liberatory futures. Metaphors of ruin and ruination may speak to the lived realities of violence stemming from militarization and settler colonialism, but they cannot come at the cost of preventing us from seeing other possibilities of survivance and resurgence. Stories impact not only what we read but how we read, and these interpretive frameworks shape our visions of what is possible in the longer struggle against imperialism, militarism, and settler colonialism.

At the same time, the conflicting desires that emerge in yuntaku can complicate how we conceptualize and articulate Okinawan Indigeneity as we build more just futures. Where I thought I would find stories of ruin, yuntaku with local residents helped me to read against these literary frames to understand the everyday as a crucial site of life-making beyond the ruinations of U.S. militarism and Japanese settler colonialism. Community food programs, innovative ideas to help with the area's economic revitalization, or simply sharing fruits and tea during yuntaku on metal foldout chairs in the alley—Teruya's residents taught me an important lesson about Okinawan peoples' determination in the face of histories of violence and dispossession. Their experiences call for us, as researchers, to see that even after loss, there is our survivance. In the quiet of the everyday, yuntaku with the people of Teruya reminded me that a place overwhelmingly inscribed by its military history was, and remains, first and foremost, Indigenous.

NOZOMI NAKAGANEKU SAITO (Uchinaanchu, Myaaku) is assistant professor at Amherst College in English and Asian American and Pacific Islander Studies and co-chair of the Five College Asian/Pacific/American working group. Her current book project, Under the Roots of the Gajumaru Tree: Seeding Dispossession in Okinawa's Transpacific, shows how representations of Okinawa's changing ecologies under US militarization reveal larger struggle for sovereignty between Indigenous Okinawans, Japanese settlers, and the United States military. Her research has received support from the Ford Foundation, the Mitsubishi Foundation, with articles published in *American Quarterly*, the *Journal of Asian American Studies*, and *Amerasia Journal*.

References

"Aftermath." *Oxford English Dictionary Online.* Oxford University Press.

All Okinawa Council for Human Rights. 2022. Report on Violence Against Indigenous Ryukyu/Okinawan Women and Girls, January 30. https://www.ohchr.org/sites/default/files/2022-03/AOCHR.pdf.

Angst, Linda Isako. 2009. "Loudmouth Feminists and Unchaste Prostitutes: 'Bad Girls' Misbehaving in Postwar Okinawa." *U.S.-Japan Women's Journal* 36: 117–41. https://www.jstor.org/stable/42771995.

Arvin, Maile, Eve Tuck, and Angie Morrill. 2013. "Decolonizing Feminism: Challening Connections between Settler Colonialism and Heteropatriarchy." *Feminist Formations* 25 1: 8–34.

Bhowmik, Davinder. 2008. *Writing Okinawa: Narrative Acts of Identity and Resistance.* Routledge.

Carter, Mitzi Uehara. 2013. "Nappy Routes and Tangled Tales: Critical Ethnography in a Militarised Okinawa." In *Under Occupation: Resistance and Struggle* in a Militarised Asia-Pacific, edited by Peter Simpson, Daniel Broudy, and Makoto Arakaki. Cambridge Scholars Publishing.

Chibana, Megumi. 2020. "Resurgents Create a Moral Landscape: Indigenous Resurgence and Everyday Practices of Farming in Okinawa," *Humanities* 9, no. 4: 135. https://doi.org/10.3390/h9040135.

Day, Iyko. 2021. "Ruin Porn and the Colonial Imaginary." *PMLA* 136, no. 1: 125–31. https://doi.org/10.1632/S0030812920000103.

Fisch, Arnold G. 2005. *Military Government in the Ryukyu Islands, 1945–1950.* US Government Printing Office, 1988. Reprint. University Press of the Pacific.

Gibson, Amoz E. 1946. "Question from Okinawa." Letters to the editor, *Washington Post,* January 5. ProQuest Historical Newspapers.

Ginoza, Ayano. 2015. "Dis/articulation of Ethnic Minority and Indigeneity in the Decolonial Feminist and Independence Movements in Okinawa." *Intersections: Gender and Sexuality in Asia and the Pacific* 37. http://intersections.anu.edu.au/issue37/ginoza.htm.

Ginoza, Ayano. 2016. "R&R at the Intersection of US and Japanese Dual Empire: Okinawan Women and Decolonizing Militarized Heterosexuality." *American Quarterly* 68, no. 3: 583–91.

Goeman, Mishuana. 2013. *Mark My Words: Native Women Mapping Our Nations.* University of Minnesota Press.

Hammine, Madoka. 2022. "Hear Our Voice: New Speakers of Ryukyuan Language—Negotiation, Construction, and Change of Identities." In *Discourses of Identity: Language Learning, Teaching and Reclamation Perspectives in Japan,* edited by Martin Mielick, Ryuko Kubota, and Luke Lawrence, 117–38. Palgrave Macmillan.

Harjo, Laura. 2019. *Spiral to the Stars: Mvskoke Tools of Futurity.* The University of Arizona Press.

Hartman, Saidiya. 2007. *Lose Your Mother: A Journey Along the Atlantic Slave Route.* Farrar, Straus, and Giroux.

Ikehara, Ariko. 2016. "A Theory of MiXtopia: Critical Performance Life/Art in Three MiXtopias: Teruya, Koza, Okinawa." PhD diss., University of California, Berkeley. ProQuest (10189824).

Kim, Jodi. 2022. *Settler Garrison: Debt Imperialism, Militarism, and Transpacific Imaginaries.* Duke University Press.

King, Tiffany. 2014. "Labor's Aphasia: Toward Antiblackness as Constitutive to Settler Colonialism," *Decolonization: Indigeneity, Education and Society,* https://decolonization.wordpress.com/2014/06/10/labors-aphasia-toward-antiblackness-as-constitutive-to-settler-colonialism/.

Kishaba, Jun. 1955. "Kurai Hana." *Ryūdai Bungaku 10:* 25–33. Ryukyu Daigaku Bungaku-bu.

Kishaba, Jun. 2000. "Dark Flowers." Translated by Steve Rabson. In *Southern Exposure: Modern Japanese Literature from Okinawa,* edited by Michael Molasky and Steve Rabson. University of Hawaiʻi Press.

Kishaba, Jun. 2021. "A Poem of Resistance Unyielding to US Censorship: 'Occupation Control' with the Strengthening of the Bases, Even Now, Kishaba Chojun's 'Cultural Activities Under Oppression,' interview, *Ryukyu Shimpo,*

April 27 [America kenetsu kussezu ni teiko no uta kichi kyōka de 'senryō shihai', ima mo Kishaba Chōjun 'asseika no bunka katsudō]. https://ryukyushimpo.jp/news/entry-1312243.html.

Okinawa City General and Administrative Division, ed. *Koza bunka box, 3.* Koubundo Printing Co., 2007.

Matsumura, Wendy. 2015. *The Limits of Okinawa: Japanese Capitalism, Living Labor, and Theorizations of Community.* Duke University Press.

Matsumura, Wendy. 2023. *Waiting for the Cool Moon: Anti-Imperialist Struggles in the Heart of Japan's Empire.* Duke University Press.

Mauldin, Catherine. 1949. "Okinawa 4 Years After." *The Chicago Defender,* September 10. ProQuest Historical Newspapers.

Molasky, Michael. 1999. *The American Occupation of Japan and Okinawa: Literature and Memory.* Routledge.

Morrill, Angie. 2017. "Time Traveling Dogs (and Other Native Feminist Ways to Defy Dislocations)." *Cultural Studies ↔ Critical Methodologies* 17, no. 1: 14–20.

Nebolon, Julie. 2024. *Settler Militarism: World War II in Hawai'i and the Making of US Empire.* Duke University Press.

Nguyen, Viet Thanh and Janet Hoskins, editors, 2014. "Introduction: Transpacific Studies: Criticial Perspectives on an Emerging Field." In *Transpacific Studies: Framing an Emerging Field.* University of Hawai'i Press.

Obermiller, David John. 2006. "The U.S. Military Occupation of Okinawa: Politicizing and Contesting Okinawan Identity 1945–1955." Ph.D. diss., University of Iowa. ProQuest (3225658).

Onishi, Yuichiro. 2013. *Transpacific Antiracism: Afro-Asian Solidarity in 20th Century Black America, Japan, and Okinawa.* New York University Press.

Ōta, Masahide. "War Memories Die Hard in Okinawa." *Japan Quarterly* (January–March 1988): 9–16.

Powell, Dana E. 2024. "Life Beyond Ruin: Diné Presence in the Anthropocene." *Native American and Indigenous Studies* 11, no.1: 71–113. https://dx.doi.org/10.1353/nai.2024.a924400.

Puri, Shalini. 2015. "Finding the Field: Notes on Caribbean Cultural Criticism, Area Studies, and the Forms of Engagement." In *Theorizing Fieldwork in the Humanities: Methods, Reflections, and Approaches to the Global South,* 29–50. Palgrave Macmillan, 2015.

Quashie, Kevin. 2012. *The Sovereignty of Quiet: Beyond Resistance in Black Culture.* Rutgers University Press,.

Rowe, Aimee Carrillo, and Eve Tuck. 2017. "Settler Colonialism and Cultural Studies: Ongoing Settlement, Cultural Production, and Resistance." *Cultural Studies ↔ Critical Methodologies* 17, no. 1: 3–13.

Santa Ana, Jeffrey, Heidi Amin-Hong, Rina Garcia Chua, and Zhou Xiaojing, editors. 2022. "Confronting Ecological Ruination in the Transpacific." Introduction to *Empire and Environment: Ecological Ruin in the Transpacific.* University of Michigan Press.

Shibuya, Yoshio. 2008. "The Control of Brown Sugar Distribution and Sugar Trading Capital in Modern Okinawa." *The Agricultural History Society of Japan* 42, no. 3: 3–13. http://doi.org/10.18966/joah.42.0_3. (Kindai Okinawa ni okeru tō-shō shihon ni yoru kokutō ryūtsū shihai ni tsuite)

Shigematsu, Setsu. 2015. "Intimacies of Imperialism and Japanese-Black Feminist Transgression: Militarised Occupations in Okinawa and Beyond." *Intersections: Gender and Sexuality in Asia and the Pacific* 37. http://intersections.anu.edu.au/issue37/shigematsu.htm.

Shimabuku, Annmaria. 2012. "Transpacific Colonialism: An Intimate View of Transnational Activism in Okinawa." *CR: The New Centennial Review* 12, no. 1: 131–58.

Stoler, Laura Ann. 2008. "Imperial Debris: Reflections on Ruins and Ruination." *Cultural Anthropology* 23, no. 2: 191–219.

Teaiwa, Katerina Martina. 2015. *Consuming Ocean Island: Stories of Phosphate and People from Banaba.* Indiana University Press.

Tuck, Eve. 2009. "Suspending Damage: Letter to Communities." *Harvard Educational Review* 79, no. 3: 409–27.

Tuck, Eve, Allison Guess, and Hannah Sultan. 2014. "Not Nowhere: Collaborating on Selfsame Land." *Decolonization: Indigeneity, Education and Society.* https://decolonization.wordpress.com/2014/06/26/not-nowhere-collaborating-on-selfsame-land/.

Tuck, Eve, and Kevin W. Yang. 2012. "Decolonization Is Not a Metaphor." *Decolonization: Indigeneity, Education & Society* 1, no.1: 1–40.

Ueunten, Wesley Iwao. 2010. "Rising Up from a Sea of Discontent: The 1970 Koza Uprising in U.S.-Occupied Okinawa." In *Militarized Currents: Toward a Decolonized Future in Asia and the Pacific,* edited by Setsu Shigematsu and Keith L. Camacho. University of Minnesota Press,.

United Nations. 2018. "State of the World's Indigenous Peoples: Indigenous Peoples' Access to Health Services." https://www.un.org/development/desa/indigenouspeoples/wp-content/uploads/sites/19/2018/03/The-State-of-The-Worlds-Indigenous-Peoples-WEB.pdf.

"Vets Go Back to Okinawa." 1947. *The Chicago Defender,* May 3. ProQuest Historical Newspapers.

Vizenor, Gerald, with Eve Tuck and K. Wayne Yang, eds. 2013. "Resistance in the Blood." In *Youth Resistance Research and Theories of Change.* Routledge.

Yamazato, Katsunori. 2011. "Editor's Note." In *Living Spirit: Literature and Resurgence in Okinawa,* edited by Frank Stewart and Katsunori Yamazato, vii–xiii. University of Hawai'i Press.

Yoneyama, Lisa. 1999. *Hiroshima Traces: Time, Space, and the Dialectics of Memory.* University of California Press.

Notes

1. I would like to thank the many people whose generous care, insights, and conversations allowed this essay to develop. First and foremost, my deepest gratitude to Dr. Ariko Ikehara, whose mentorship and modeling of ethically informed community-engaged research continues to shape my own methods. Her model of "yuntakuview" affirms the importance of Okinawan cultural forms. I am also indebted the community interlocutors—Miyazato-san, Dai-san, Keiko-san, and Shiroma-san—for their graciousness and willingness to collaborate with me. They are the ones whose sharing of memories and

knowledge lie at the heart of this yuntaku reading method. Many thanks to the research librarians at University of the Ryukyus and Okinawa Prefectural Library for their help in tracking down Kishaba's story in the original Japanese. A special thanks to my former dissertation advisors Shalini Puri, Shaun Myers, Piotr Gwiazda, and Mitzi Uehara Carter for their wisdom and patience in reading early drafts of this essay. And finally a note of thanks to the editors, Heidi Kiiwetinepinesiik Stark (Anishinaabekwe/Turtle Mountain Band of Chippewa descent), Gina Starblanket (Saulteaux/Cree, Star Blanket Cree Nation), Sabrina Lamanna (Mi'kmaq from Ktaqmkuk and Italian/Irish descent), and the reviewers for stewarding this essay. Ippee nifee deebiru for everyone involved and apologies for anyone I forgot to thank.

2. This essay looks to the faithful English translation of Kishaba's short story by S. Rabson (2000). However, where the Japanese character or material history of the source text may enrich this interpretation, I refer to the original (cited as Kishaba 1955, "Kurai Hana"). A copy of the issue of *Ryūdai Bungaku* in which Kishaba first published "Dark Flowers" ("Kurai Hana") is available at Okinawa Prefectural Library. See Jun Kishaba, "Dark Flowers," translated by Steve Rabson, *Southern Exposure: Modern Japanese Literature from Okinawa*, edited by Michael Molasky and Steve Rabson (2000, 98–111); Kishaba Jun, 1955, "Kurai Hana," *Ryūdai Bungaku* 10: 25–33.

3. There are various identifications when referring to the islands and people of Okinawa, which indicate different periods of sovereignty, including Lūchū, which refers to the Kingdom Period, also pronounced "Ryūkyū" in Japanese. The annexation by the Meiji Emperor in 1879 is when Lūchū/Ryūkyū Kingdom became Okinawa Prefecture. The prefecture was called the "Ryūkyū Islands" again during the official period of U.S. Occupation from 1945–1972, when the United States Civil Administration of the Ryūkyū Islands (USCAR) emphasized Ryūkyūans as a distinct people from the Japanese in order to minimize Japan's residual sovereignty. Another common term is "Uchinā," which refers specifically to present-day Okinawa Island but does not refer to other islands in Okinawa Prefecture such as Miyakojima. Most Okinawans refer to themselves as Okinawans or, when their ancestry is from Okinawa Island, as Uchinaanchu. For more on the distinctions of Ryūkyū/Okinawan identity in the postwar era, see David John Obermiller, "The U.S. Military Occupation of Okinawa: Politicizing and Contesting Okinawan Identity 1945–1955" (Ph.D. diss., University of Iowa, 2006).

4. Uchinaaguchi is one of several Indigenous languages in Okinawa, which include the languages spoken in Amami, Okinawa, Kunigami, Miyakojima, Yonaguni, and Yaeyama. As with most Okinawan writers of his generation, Kishaba does not use any Okinawan Indigenous languages in his text. Bhowmik (2008) notes this trend among many prewar and some postwar generations of Okinawan writers is the result of Japan's linguistic assimilation policies, starting in the 1880s and "intensifying as Japan's military gained power during the 1930s, culminated in humiliating punishments, both verbal and corporal" (69). For many prewar Okinawan writers, erasing Okinawan languages was a matter of necessity and survival. Despite the lack of Indigenous language in Kishaba's story, his story nonetheless gestures to Okinawan Indigeneity by connecting

the dispossession of Okinawans to the histories of imperial violence against Black and Indigenous people within the settler United States. My aim in drawing on yuntaku as an Okinawan epistemology and mode of sociality is therefore twofold: an insistence on Okinawan Indigeneity in the face of ongoing Japanese settler colonialism and U.S. militarism, and the centering of Okinawan voices driven by a desire, like Kishaba, to not stay silent or silence Okinawans. At the same time, I acknowledge that there are ways in which Uchinaaguchi also has become the hegemonic Indigenous language of Okinawa, particularly in more recent Indigenous language revitalization movements. As Yaeyama and Okinawan language scholar Madoka Hammine writes, even as Indigenous language revitalization is necessary to decolonization and reclaiming identities, "imposing the discourse of language revitalization on Indigenous language communities might not solve the complex issues on the ground" (117–18). As I show elsewhere in the essay, inter-island conflicts also can create resistance to claiming specific island ethnicities as "Okinawan" identities. See Hammine (2022).

5. Throughout this essay, I highlight when scholars are of Lūchūan/Ryūkyūan/Okinawan or Uchinaanchu ancestry, using the specific identifications by which the scholars or community members identify themselves as much as possible when this information is known to me. This is a common practice in Native American and Indigenous studies to mention the nation or affiliation of Indigenous scholars. However, marking positionality has yet to become standard practice in Okinawan studies. As with other fields that focus on studies of Native or Indigenous communities, Okinawan studies in the U.S. academy has been shaped by non-Okinawan scholars, those who either study Okinawa from the colonial perspective of Japan studies or the militarist lens of security studies. To be clear, I do believe that non-Okinawan scholars can produce—and indeed have produced—meaningful and ethical research about Okinawa. And being Okinawan does not exempt one from bad-faith scholarship. However, non-Okinawans have made harmful claims about our community or conducted research on Okinawan living community members and ancestors in ways that reify colonial paradigms about Okinawans, and I do not believe that these scholars could have made these claims if they were Okinawan. The appropriation of Okinawan identity by those who have lived in the prefecture and claim themselves "Okinawan at heart" is also an increasing trend. These false identifications allow non-Okinawans living in the islands to conceal their positionality as settlers and forgo their responsibilities to Okinawans. For this essay, in which positionality is part of the yuntaku methodology, I believe naming a scholar or community participant's Okinawan ancestry is crucial. Put simply, for those of us who are of Okinawan descent, we have skin in the game.

6. Juliet Nebolon (2024) defines "settler militarism" as "the dynamics through which settler colonialism and militarization simultaneously perpetuated, legitimated, and concealed one another during World War II" (5). While similar dynamics were used by the U.S. military in Okinawa during and after the war, including the land seizures and transformation of Indigenous lands into military bases, my use of the phrase "U.S.-Japanese settler militarism" is meant to highlight the specific and co-constitutive structure of both Japanese

settler colonialism and U.S. militarism. Other terms such as Jodi Kim's (2022) "settler garrison" also helpfully highlight the dynamics by which the U.S. military expanded its settler frontiers into Asia and Oceania in the postwar period.

7. Japan's ongoing disavowal of Okinawans' Indigenous status is especially egregious and conspicuous given the various reports by the United Nations (2018) confirming the status of Ryukyuan/Okinawans as Indigenous people, due to the distinct culture and languages. See United Nations (2018).

8. Personal communication with author, 2022.

9. It should be noted that the name "Koza" is itself a misnomer and product of militarization, as there was no corresponding village of that name prior to occupation. Michael Molasky's discussion of the name suggests a few possible sources for the appellation, including a mishearing of the town "Kujaa" or a mispronunciation of "Goya." Molasky writes, regardless of its precise origin, "in Okinawa's historical memory the town is intimately linked to the American occupiers" (1999, 53).

10. Reports from this time indicate that as some of the area's original residents returned, they found that other camp residents had taken up residence in their households. The recently returned Okinawans were therefore forced to live in pigsties next to their original family home at the direction of district leaders appointed by the U.S. military. This follows from the structure of settler colonialism, whether under Japanese rule or U.S. military occupation. As Wendy Matsumura writes, "Indigenous dispossession in one part of the empire facilitated the dispossession of other Indigenous people within and outside of its borders" (2023, 140). The displacement and dispossession of Indigenous Okinawans from the southern part of the island and their relocation to central Okinawa became entangled with other Okinawans displaced and dispossessed from the areas that constituted Camp Koza and later Koza City.

11. Yukitaka Shiroma, personal communication with author, September 2022.

12. In a slightly different context, Lisa Yoneyama notes that after the nuclear bombing of Hiroshima, the terms "akarui" (bright, sunny) and "kurai" (dark, sad, gloomy) in the growing peace movement reflected a shift in mainland Japan. Those associated with being kurai (nekura) were seen as at odds with those celebrating collective and joyous occasions because they chose to "criticize or raise questions" (1999, 181n29). While it would be difficult to make the case that Kishaba wrote with this awareness of akarui/kurai discourse in mainland Japan, the reception of those who are perceived as nekura adds another layer to understanding the story in the genre of protest writing. Its critique of the occupation counters discourses of progress and saviorism promoted by the U.S. military and its role in driving the economic boom in militarized towns like Koza, especially when considering the costs of this economic advancement were extracted from the labor and bodies of Okinawan women.

13. Miyazato-san, personal communication with author, September 2022.

14. Keiko Shiroma, personal communication with author, November 2022.

15. Dai Gushiken, personal communication with author, November 2022.

16. "Champuru" is an Okinawan term for "mix" used to refer both to foods (like stir fry) and to cultural mixes.

TIMOTHY HOUGE

"The Children Are Coming Home Singing Songs in Eskimo": Alaska Native Communities and the Pursuit of Indigenous Control over Native Education, 1969–1975

Abstract

The role of community control over education is an often-overlooked aspect of the history of Native American self-determination, sovereignty, and treaty rights movements, especially in Alaska Native history. Existing scholarship consistently implies that prior to the signing of the Indian Self-Determination and Education Assistance Act of 1975, Native Peoples had limited success in achieving sovereignty and control in any area, let alone in education. However, many Alaska Native communities successfully implemented community control over education well before 1975. Analysis of Alaska Native voices in newspapers, state and federal government documents, and the writings of educators and school administrators shows that not only did Alaska Native communities and leaders implement programs of community control over education, but also that education itself comprised a key component in the larger movement for political self-determination. Education thereby served as a primary mechanism by which Alaska Native communities resisted and reversed generations of erasure and cultural assimilation, achieving new levels of self-governance.

FIFTY YEARS AGO, on January 4, 1975, President Gerald Ford signed the Indian Self-Determination and Education Assistance Act (ISDEAA) into law.[1] The ISDEAA is still regarded by many Native Peoples to this day as a critical turning point in the federal recognition of tribal sovereignty and an empowering statute for tribes to facilitate their own communities' affairs.[2] Importantly, the 1975 Act authorized tribal governments to assume responsibility for programs and services that the Bureau of Indian Affairs (BIA) administered to them, along with a significant voice in the creation and implementation of federal services still operating within their communities.[3] In essence, Native Peoples finally received a commitment from Congress to support their right to self-government, as well as an acknowledgment that past federal practices hindered the "progress of Indian people and their communities."[4] This law fundamentally altered the relationship between Native Americans and the federal government, and ended generations of federal oversight, overreaching control, and assimilationist efforts that targeted Native people.

Some scholars have argued that the Richard Nixon administration laid the groundwork for Native American self-determination. In his 1970 Special Message to Congress on Indian Affairs, Nixon called for Native political self-determination without the paternalism of Termination legislation. Other scholars argue that Nixon's own upbringing in Southern California and his mentorship under a Native football coach played a critical role.[5] While there is some validity to these claims, Nixon's willingness to support self-determination "did not emanate from sudden federal enlightenment or largesse."[6] Rather, Nixon's support came from listening to the calls by Native peoples, from both within the federal government and outside government, for a return of control over their communities. Self-determination advocates also used the successes of programs funded by the 1964 Economic Opportunity Act (EOA), which provided funding for Indigenous self-determination through Community Action Programs, as evidence for the validity of their assertions of sovereignty. This is where education's role needs greater attention and clarity within the historical narrative. Native communities used EOA funds to administer Head Start programs, bilingual and bicultural pilot projects, and even schools such as the Rough Rock Demonstration School. These successes only served to increase calls for greater educational reform and control, a major component of the Native self-determination movement. As former Secretary of the Interior Deb Haaland (Laguna Pueblo) described the passage of the law, it was the product of "tireless Native activism that rallied against a centuries-long status quo."[7] This activism, which, from 1969 to 1975, consisted of the combined, yet oftentimes disconnected, efforts of grassroots Alaska Native groups, Alaskan Native organizations, educators, parents, and students, all focused on advocating for greater self-determination in Indigenous education to bring about an end to the centuries of paternalistic, assimilationist efforts by the federal government.

What then is Indigenous-controlled education, and what does the related educational activism and advocacy therefore look like in the context of the late 1960s and early 1970s, and particularly for the Native Self-Determination movement? Building momentum in the 1950s, Native communities advocated for educational reform, which included greater cultural pluralism. For Native communities in the 1960s and 1970s, this consisted of increased community participation in the schools, local control over the schools in the form of local school boards, bicultural curricula, and a greater percentage of Native teachers.[8] Therefore, historical (and, in some cases, contemporary) activism for Indigenous-controlled education refers to the combined efforts, undertaken consciously or unconsciously, by Native communities to create an educational system that protected their communities and preserved their languages and cultures all while increasing community control and participation in the schools themselves. These efforts included parents and community leaders meeting and engaging in dialogue with non-native school administrators regarding teachers, curriculum, and student engagement, petitioning the federal government to hire more Native teachers, advocating for more schools to be built in communities, and more. Indigenous-controlled education, then, is what resulted when the push for educational reform intersected with the larger movements for sovereignty and political self-determination.

The Indigenous advocacy for educational reform that began in the 1960s evolved dramatically throughout the 1960s and 1970s, becoming a full-scale movement for tribal control over community education. In essence, Native communities applied pressure, using their growing political force, to the federal government to gain recognition and support for their tribal sovereignty over education. Indigenous-controlled educational activism, then, entails the cumulative activism efforts of Native communities during the 1960s and 1970s to exercise their inherent right over all aspects of the education and schooling of their children. In other words, Indigenous-controlled educational activism was and is how Native communities actively engaged in "self-determination," exercising their inherent right of full control and say over the *implementation* of education and schooling policies among Native communities and control over *how* their communities used federal educational funding. Indigenous-controlled educational activism, and therefore, Native communities' control over education itself, followed no uniform path to reach full realization. It meant working towards increased numbers of higher-quality schools and better-trained educators, as well as greater focus on the curriculum and content that Alaska Native students learned in school.

In particular, the efforts of Alaska Native communities, leaders, and organizations, between 1969 and 1975 are significant, as these often at-odds groups engaged in activism to assert, maintain, and control their communities' own educational destinies. In this period before the ISDEAA became law, Alaska Natives' federal and state education entities attempted to implement policies in Alaska Native communities without meaningful contributions by the communities themselves. The role of educational activism as a mechanism by which Native communities throughout the United

States pursued self-determination claims has been an understudied aspect of this period. Even more so, scholars often fail to meaningfully include the vital histories and roles of Alaska Native communities in their narratives. In what follows, I revisit this critical period of Alaska Native history as well as of Indigenous education history. The history of activism for Indigenous-controlled education has significant implications for the study of Indigenous sovereignty during the twentieth century, particularly in relation to the rise of sovereignty, land rights, and treaty rights discourse in the second half of the twentieth century.

Indigenous-Controlled Education in Action for Alaska Natives, 1969–1975

From 1969 to 1975, Alaska Native villages experienced profound changes in their communities and in their relationship with the federal government. At the state level, a decade into statehood, the people and politics of Alaska encountered a moment that profoundly altered the course of the state: the oil boom. In early 1968, the Atlantic Richfield Company discovered the Prudhoe Bay oil field on Alaska's North Slope, a discovery of some 10 billion barrels of oil. This discovery and subsequent sale of land, followed by oil speculation, induced an increased interest among many Alaskan political leaders in the financial potential of oil; many believed that oil had the potential to stabilize the crests and peaks in the economic outlook of the state. The 1969 oil-lease sale was not the first major oil-lease sale to occur; in fact, it marked the twenty-third major sale since statehood a decade earlier, but this sale proved different because of the extreme quantity of money put up to bid for it, in excess of $900 million.[9] Conflicts between varying interest groups in the state erupted with the influx of new funds into the state's treasury, centered on how to spend the latest funds and potential future funds that came with new oil discoveries. The state's legislative body and the Office of the Governor of Alaska each contracted with research groups to plan how best to use this money. Both studies, one facilitated by the Brookings Institution and the other by the Stanford Research Institute, independently concluded that the money needed to be invested in Alaska's future by addressing the state's physical, economic, and social needs. Both studies also warned that if not used correctly and in the public interest, the money had the possibility of creating more issues than it solved. Importantly, both studies highlighted the need to address the inadequate educational system within the state.[10]

Meanwhile, the discovery of oil at Prudhoe Bay led to the greatest call for political organization and action among Alaska Native communities since the 1959 Statehood Act, in order to protect their land rights. The discovery opened the door to potential aggressive oil speculators looking to buy Alaska Native lands out from underneath communities' feet by circumventing the communities and dealing directly with the state and federal governments. With a long history of their land rights being ignored, Alaska Native leaders took immediate action. The Yup'ik communities living in Barrow, near the Prudhoe Bay oil discovery site, expressed concerns from the beginning about having their interests, land claims, and ways of life ignored by the oil companies. Fred Paul, a Tlingit attorney representing the "Arctic Slope Eskimos" organization, stated, "the oil companies are coming in and there is no way that we can stop them. No one cares that this is your homeland. These are bitter words, and I would be the first to say so, but unfortunately, they are the truth."[11] Alaska Native communities believed they had the ability to direct and decide for themselves how best to facilitate land development. In an editorial for the *Tundra Times,* one Alaska Native man, John Borbridge, stated that some politicians believed that the Alaskan Native land claims movement ". . . is impeding the economic development and progress of the state of Alaska." Rather, he argued that until Alaska Natives had the opportunity to no longer be restrained from their right to the lands, no one could safely say that Alaska Natives impeded development.[12] Speaking for Alaska Native villages, Borbridge believed that his people had the "sufficient leadership ability to direct the development of our lands and resources."[13] The tenor of Borbridge's editorial rested on a call for an organizational body to use its leadership experiences to exercise its rights to develop and facilitate their own lands and natural resources, a key component to the drive for self-determination.

Alaska Native leaders mobilized to organize themselves into a formal body that championed the land, cultural, and educational rights of their communities. Organization also meant the opportunity to pursue self-determination and Indigenous-controlled education through the various channels of the Economic Opportunity Act. In early 1969, the Alaskan Federation of Natives (AFN) lobbied and battled for, and represented at the state and national level, the various interests and pursuits of Alaska Native communities. The AFN, in particular, led the fight in advocating and facilitating the land claims settlements that persisted into the 1970s, thus serving as the unified body for all Alaska Native community corporations and interests.

When Nixon assumed office at the beginning of 1969, his political rhetoric brought about a new set of concerns regarding federal Indian policy. The Nixon administration pursued a withdrawal of federal power over states' use of federal funding in favour of state funding and policy. Still, it simultaneously increased the scope and oversight of federal administrations and legislation to offer increased protection and federal services that affected the American people. With the Nixon administration's push for New Federalism, power over policy and its implementation transitioned from a federally centered practice to one that emphasized a state's right to facilitate funds and policies to fit their own unique needs. This policy shift meant that Native Peoples not only had to maneuver the new federal policies created between 1969 and 1975, but also the novel approaches of the states as they tailored and implemented policies of their own. This new change in policy created a host of problems for Native Peoples, as they needed to navigate even more government bureaucracy, but also opened new avenues to pursue community control over education. Native American leaders and communities focused on policies that could be directly applied to their own communities and lobbied state and local officials to apply policy in more specific ways. As new laws were passed, such as the Indian Education Act (1972) and the Indian Education and Self-Determination Assistance Act (1975), state-specific applications of these laws created greater opportunities for the guarantee, and continuation of, self-determination and Indigenous-controlled education protected by legislation.

Between 1969 and 1975, significant breakthroughs in developing programs and opportunities for community control over education occurred and played a critical role in Alaska Natives' tribal sovereignty, pursuit of self-governance, and their advocacy for their land rights. The greater influence of Alaska Native political voices coincided with increased participation in, and concern with, the state of education policy for Alaska Native children and adults. Groups like the AFN and Alaska Native Brotherhood and Sisterhood (ANB and ANS, respectively) not only represented the Alaska Native people on the issue of land claims, but also on education and socioeconomic issues prevalent in their communities. Meanwhile, organizations like RurAL CAP, run primarily by Alaska Natives, wielded community action legislation from the Economic Opportunity Act and cultivated education programs for Alaska Native communities. Native-run school advisory boards gained greater authority and influence in the coordination and implementation of education policy for their schools. Alaska Native individuals and communities took steps to reverse generations of cultural assimilation and erasure facilitated by BIA and missionary schools, all while vocalizing their dissent or approval of federal and state education policy that affected their children and communities, especially in newspapers like the *Tundra Times*. As the decade closed, Alaska Native communities more vigorously pursued and implemented their visions and versions of Indigenous-controlled education and self-determination, sometimes in concert with the state and federal government, and sometimes against their policies.

In 1969, greater parental participation in the Alaska Native schools manifested increased opportunities and training for school board participation, thereby instituting greater checks over local schools and ensuring community involvement in school administration. For example, in late March 1969, the BIA hosted an education workshop in Brigham City, UT, where one member of the Fairbanks Native Association (FNA) participated in the programs, including training of school board operations, parental participation in school affairs, and the utilization of education advisory committees.[14] The growing political awareness developed into a potent tool for Native American leaders, and it also became a powerful asset for the leaders and members of Native communities.[15] As more Alaska Native community members created an increasingly sophisticated approach toward community control over education, advisory school boards took another powerful step toward educational self-determination. In late April 1969, the first pan-Alaskan Education Advisory Committee (EAC) was organized formally in response to a meeting between twenty-five Alaska Native leaders representing the Advisory School Boards and other political organizations throughout Alaska. In conjunction with the BIA's assistant area director of education, Warren Tiffany, and Dr. Clifford Hartman, Alaska's commissioner of education, the EAC explored the most problematic areas in Alaska Native education, including the state-operated school system, the regional high school concept, and the role of school boards and other advisory groups in education.[16] Through the EAC, Alaska Native leaders and community members created an agency that would enable them to more effectively advocate for improved educational services and greater control over education.

RurAL CAP: Alaska Native Community Action Programs and Education Control

While Alaska Native leaders and community members pursued greater involvement in the school boards and administration of their schools, community action program groups, particularly RurAL CAP, gained greater control over the implementation of village-centered educational programs. First organized in August 1965, and known then as the Alaska State Community Action Program (ASCAP), it primarily facilitated the contracts and administration of programs under the EOA, particularly the Head Start program and Adult Education program.[17] Yet, as the 1968 ASCAP application to the OEO stated in its Long Term Goals, the true motivation for ASCAP was facilitating and supporting self-determination and sovereignty throughout rural Alaska. RurAL CAP sought to develop programs created by the very people the CAP's involvement targeted, and to utilize education programs to "target area residents to cross over from the status of 'tax user' to 'tax payers.'"[18] In 1968, as in 1964, the federal push for antipoverty programs hinged on the success of expanded and improved educational opportunities, and RurAL CAP facilitated educational programs that centered on economic prosperity.

Between 1969 to 1970, RurAL CAP increased the amount of financial and logistical support for training programs for Head Start teachers in Alaska Native communities. The Head Start programs in Alaska, funded and operated by RurAL CAP, hired Alaska Natives primarily to serve as educators; by 1970, nearly 90 percent of all new teachers came from rural Alaska Native villages.[19] This Indigenous-centered educator movement had several key outcomes that helped to develop greater control over Indigenous education throughout Alaska Native communities. First, these Alaska Native advocates established and maintained cultural ties for many young Alaska Native students in the classroom who otherwise faced the prospect of being sent to boarding homes and schools. This meant that money earned by these teachers stayed in the villages, helping to boost local economies and providing opportunities for Alaska Natives to enact changes in their educational systems. Second, the teacher training courses served as opportunities for Alaska Native trainees to earn college credits toward teaching degrees and licenses, many of whom had neither a high school nor a college degree, thereby providing means for potential socioeconomic growth.[20] These educational opportunities fit directly into the EOA and OEO's agenda of mobilizing educational services for increased economic advantages within Native communities.

RurAL CAP also expanded the amount of financial support and investment in new and existing cultural and community education centers, as well as facilitated parental involvement in educational affairs during the 1970s. As critical a role as schools played in the growth of Indigenous-controlled education, cultural and community centers played an equally important role. As sites of dialogue, exchange, and celebration of Native American history and cultures, community and cultural centers nurtured not only children, but also adult members of the community. For example, on March 18, 1970, the Alaska Association for Continuing Community Education began to serve as the site for assisting in the development of programs and curriculum for adult education in Alaska.[21] A year earlier, the village of Klukwan began construction on their tribal house and community hall, creating a space that fostered cross-cultural growth and sanctuary for the Tlingit people. This Indigenous space, with RurAL CAP sponsoring its construction alongside the U.S. Department of Labor, existed as a center for "Indian dances, sale of Indian crafts, and for community cultural activities such as story-telling and traditional festivities."[22] Such spaces became integral parts of Alaska Native communities where community members rediscovered and strengthened their cultural ties to their pasts and their neighbors, and created opportunities for economic growth. In other instances, RurAL CAP's Norton Sound Regional Community Center in Nome hired Alaska Native women to teach and "revitalize the crafts and heritage of their people while stimulating a new economy at the same time."[23] In doing so, these cultural centers, in Alaska as well as in other parts of the U.S., invigorated and sustained efforts for self-determination and Indigenous-controlled education by resisting generations of assimilation while simultaneously melding Western and Indigenous socioeconomic practices.

Educational needs and cultural preservation continued to be intimately linked in the 1970s, as Alaska Native families and villages challenged previous generations of assimilationist policy. During the Fourth of July celebrations in the Athabascan village of Minto, northwest of Fairbanks, adults met to sing and dance to Athabascan songs and then taught children their traditional dances. As the *Tundra Times* wrote about the dances, "This example is one of the many which illustrates the determination of the native peoples of Alaska to keep alive the distinctive traditions of their cultures."[24] In fact, at the end of August, the first International Conference on Cross-Cultural Education in the North concluded that "Native children should begin their primary education in their mother-tongue instead of the language of the dominant culture," and that "people who live in the Artic and subartic regions of the world should be involved in planning and carrying out their own educational programs."[25] In 1969, educators and professionals outside of Alaska Native communities also advocated for Indigenous-controlled education and self-determination. In some instances, Alaska Native communities and individuals worked outside the purview of the AFN and RurAL CAP to pursue their own ideas for Indigenous-controlled education. For example, several Nenana mothers established their own preschool system for Nenana children to prepare them for entrance into the public-school system, because no adequate preschool program existed in their community.[26] The preschool flourished into the late 1970s, becoming the de facto community preschool that employed fifteen mothers from the community working with two certified teachers to prepare the young children for primary school.[27] By establishing their own preschool, these women showcased one of several different ways in which Alaska Native communities and individuals created their own solutions to educational problems but also subverted previous generations of assimilationist and erasure policies.

Alaska Native community investments in preserving and strengthening cultural bonds in classroom settings both encouraged greater parental participation in school advisory boards and helped slow, and in some cases reverse, the student dropout rate. For instance, RurAL CAP advocated for increased parental involvement in 1969, with Executive Director Byron Mallott stating that "one of the most critical needs in both the State of Alaska's and the Bureau of Indian Affairs Rural Education Program is parental and community involvement in the development of basic educational policy."[28] While parental advisory boards existed and Alaska Native parents served on these boards, they lacked meaningful authority to enact changes in policy, as Michael Cline stated in his memoir on his time as a teacher at the Tannik School in Anaktuvuk Pass.[29] Cline stated that the parents who served on the school boards held what they saw as largely symbolic positions. Cline also stated that he saw many parents as apathetic to what happened in the school (though the parents experienced exclusion and apathy from the former teachers prior to Cline). RurAL CAP attempted to, at an early stage of self-determination in Alaska, transform educational policy from a top-down directive to an active dialogue between Alaska Native communities and the state and federal governments.[30] In doing so, RurAL CAP planted the seeds of Indigenous-controlled education, both within rural Alaskan communities as well as in the state government, to achieve true, not performative, self-determination (i.e., moving beyond token efforts by the state and federal government for Alaska Native villages' inclusion in policy and administration toward actual and meaningful participation in educational policy development and implementation).

Though the inclusion of Alaska Natives in program and policy decisions in education remained fairly unique in the 1960s and 1970s, this collaboration did not always happen smoothly. While organizations like RurAL CAP exerted greater oversight and control over educational programs, the state's educational system—the Alaskan State Operated School System (SOSS)—did little at first to incorporate Alaska Native community input into the decision-making processes that significantly influenced the educational futures of Alaska Native children and communities. In fact, when SOSS officials visited Alaska Native communities throughout rural Alaska in the early 1960s to discuss the transfer of BIA schools to state control, they framed these discussions in a manner that dictated, rather than negotiated, the transfer, thereby further excluding the input of Alaska Native communities. John Eichman, the Area Public School Relations Specialist and member of the Alaskan Department of Education committee that planned the transfer of BIA schools, wrote in a memo that the committee had met with several villages to ". . . give the residents of the village an insight of knowledge of the State and [BIA] schools, to develop community readiness attitudes which could affect transfer."[31] The language of the memo does not insinuate that any negotiation took place, but rather, the transfers occurred without addressing Alaska Native concerns or ideas. These examples of unilateral policy implementation without Alaska Natives' input only contributed to the continuing concerns and hesitations within Alaska Native communities.

Alaska Native Communities and State-Operated Schools

By 1969, with the process of SOSS's takeover of BIA schools entering its seventh year, Alaska Native leaders and villages continued to protest the transfer of schools to the state, largely due to concerns about whether state schools delivered the same educational effectiveness as the BIA schools. One editorial in the *Tundra Times* expressed concerns that "the state pays its teachers less than the BIA pays its teachers. And, too, the state system will be subject to political influences."[32] Alaska Native individuals and communities continued to voice their dissent over the transition to state-controlled schools, expressing an ever-growing desire to have a choice and control over where their children attended school. The same editorial thus encapsulated the concerns of many Native Peoples, stating that the arbitrary process of transitioning schools and removing the option of the BIA schools "smacks of being undemocratic in the country that practices democracy."[33] The issue of control over educational choices and practices remained a central concern in the Alaska Native pursuit of community sovereignty over education and federal programs.

While SOSS made concerted efforts to address the BIA's problem of inadequate funding that led Alaska Native students to attend boarding schools, the state's inability to overcome logistical challenges meant the regional schools continued separating children from their families and villages, encouraging assimilation. For example, SOSS created a policy of sponsoring "boarding homes" for Alaska Native students in Alaskan cities. The program's intent was to have people in urban areas, such as Anchorage and Fairbanks, house Alaska Native students from rural areas, allowing them to attend larger high schools. While this program saw some initial academic successes among Indigenous students, it faced increasing resistance in Alaska Native communities, who recognized the program as a boarding school with a different name. Alaska Native communities continued to worry that their children kept losing their cultural and linguistic ties to their homes and might suffer further homesickness.[34] Many of the younger students again experienced homesickness while attending schools in Fairbanks, Anchorage, or Juneau. Parents and communities felt disconnected from their children and the experiences they had at the boarding homes and schools.[35] As a consequence, some Alaska Native communities protested the boarding home programs because they felt their communities had a sufficient student-aged population to warrant the creation of local schools, thereby removing the need to send their children to Alaskan cities.

In fact, in May 1971, four teenage girls and their families from Kivalina, Lucille and Stella Sage, Myra Hawley, and Dolly Hawley, sued the state of Alaska for failing in its constitutional duty to provide high school classes in their villages. According to the State of Alaska's revised 1968 edition of "An Overall Education Plan for Rural Alaska," Kivalina claimed fifty students and two total teachers, which, according to state law, meant that the state had to provide educational facilities so long as more than three elementary-age students or five secondary-age students at one grade level wished to remain home.[36] Initially, the four teenagers had returned home from the Mt. Edgecumbe and Fairbanks boarding school programs. They received tutoring from the village's grade school teacher, but the state soon transferred the teacher from the village school, citing that the tutoring program by village teachers did not apply to "out-of-school children." When their attorney introduced litigation against the state, the state responded by immediately resuming the tutoring program for those students, though this did not solve the boarding school issues.[37] The issue with boarding schools continued (and still does to this day). It remained an integral component to Alaska Natives' pursuit of village control over education because it meant having a choice in the educational opportunities open to them and their children.

While some students returned home due to their negative experiences at these boarding schools, the children who did not have that luxury created Alaska Native youth groups to connect with one another based on shared cultures and to alleviate their loneliness, frustrations, and dislocation. The boarding home program relocated Alaska Native students from rural areas without high school facilities to larger, completely unfamiliar urban areas, such as Anchorage and Fairbanks, to attend public high schools. At the behest of some teachers in the Anchorage Borough School District, the public school system rolled out a new program to try to ease the transition from rural to urban schooling, as well as introducing classes on Alaska Native history and culture in the schools.[38] However, many of these students, while finding the boarding home program more favorable than the alternative of living in dormitories at boarding schools, still struggled with the new social situations they had been thrust into, especially one in which white American culture dominated.[39] For example, in Fairbanks, when the schools did not provide adequate support for these students, they created a school club called the Alaska Native Youth Association (ANYA). ANYA provided the boarding home students, and anyone else who wished to join, a sense of community, and, as their counselor for boarding home students Irene Cleworth noted, "'It gives many of the students more of a feeling of self-identity.'" Alaska Native students attending the urban schools from a rural background showed remarkable maturity and tenacity with the creation of ANYA, using the club as a mechanism to "learn more of the arts and crafts of our people . . . instill a pride in our heritage . . . [and] promote better education opportunities of the Native Youth."[40] These students demonstrated that they knew the issues Alaska Native peoples and communities faced in the schools and assumed solutions of their own, and thereby resisted the assimilationist efforts of the boarding home program.

In the wake of litigation by Kivalina students, and as more Alaska Natives voiced concerns over the lack of educational opportunities in their communities, lawmakers advanced legislation for local schools in rural areas. In 1972, one legislator, Martin Moore (D-Emmonak) introduced House Bill 640, which called for the state of Alaska to uphold their constitutional duties to provide every Alaskan child with equal educational opportunities and build village high schools in rural communities. Moore cited several critical reasons why the state needed to provide these schools, including loss of parental guidance and family ties at a young and crucial age, as communities had seen their children, some fourteen hundred 14- to 19-year-olds, forced to attend boarding schools across the state and in the lower forty-eight. This legislation, supported by Alaska Statute 14.03.080, led to the creation of the contentious regional high school initiative.[41] The increasingly sophisticated political voice of Alaska Native villages and organizations encouraged legislators to fulfill their promises of equal educational and socio-economic opportunities for their communities. It demonstrated the tenacity of Alaska Natives in asserting their inherent rights to the education of their children.

Many Alaska Native organizations believed that BIA and SOSS initiatives moved too slowly and were unable to deal with these educational deficiencies. In 1971, the ANB of Sitka sent a resolution to Governor William Egan and the BIA demanding the immediate termination of BIA Assistant Area Director (Education) Warren Tiffany, for failing to address what they perceived as woefully inadequate educational opportunities available to Alaska Native children. In particular, the ANB argued "Warren Tiffany has repeatedly undercut or killed efforts by Native people themselves to develop and exercise an independent, meaningfully effective voice in how these BIA schools are run."[42] Furthermore, the ANB argued that Tiffany "has generally failed to demonstrate that he feels any real concern about [the] educational advancement of Alaska Native youth . . . [and] that the BIA immediately fire Warren Tiffany for gross incompetence . . ."[43] While Tiffany argued that the BIA had instituted several new programs to address Alaska Native educational needs, including greater provisions for teaching Alaska Native culture in schools, hiring more Alaska Native teachers and teachers' aides, and implementing bi-cultural/bi-lingual education in these schools, Alaska Native leaders argued these measures did not produce the promised results.[44] Tiffany also stated that "Native participation and involvement in the operation of the schools" had been addressed with the creation of Local School Boards. However, the ANB, as well as evidence provided by teachers like Michael Cline of the Tannik School in Anaktuvuk Pass, demonstrated that the Local School Boards simply did not have the power and ability to assert control within the schools effectively.[45] The policies implemented by the state and BIA did not go far enough to ensure Indigenous control over education. As Robert L. Thomas, Deputy Commissioner in the Alaskan Department of Education, stated, the state knew of the plans within the BIA to institute "a policy of greater self-determination for native peoples and is exploring the concept of . . . [Native Americans] . . . performing some education services on their own behalf, i.e., conceivably a community school now operated by the BIA would be turned over to village operation . . ."[46] While community schools gained popularity around the U.S., especially in Arizona with the Rough Rock Demonstration School and the Rock Point School, in Alaska, those promises fell short of reality.

Despite the Alaska Department of Education's efforts to address the larger structural concerns that Native parents and educators had with the SOSS system, the minutiae of the school system, which also needed regular updates, continually failed to be a focus of the SOSS administrators. For example, teachers and parents claimed that the SOSS was unable to respond to requests for more relevant and modern books in libraries to teach Alaska Native children how to read, as well as providing Alaska Native cultural materials for students to be used in concert with village participation, remodeled school facilities, materials for Indigenous crafts, and more. Friese and the SOSS board decided that the budget should not be used in these areas, especially for rural schools, drawing criticisms from organizations like the District One Education Association (DOEA), the AFN, and prominent leaders within Native education circles in Alaska, such as Clifford Hartman and Emil Notti. These critiques of Friese came to a head in 1972, as Alaska Native leaders like Hartman and Notti demanded the resignation of Superintendent Stephen Friese.[47] In particular, Alaska Native leaders criticized the slow pace of the Alaskan Rural Teaching Training Corps program (ARTIC) and the lack of teaching jobs, which had been promised to graduates of the program, all of whom were Alaska Natives.[48] Other Alaska Natives wrote to Governor Egan to express their concern that educational decisions continued to be made by bureaucrats in Anchorage, Juneau, and Washington D.C., not by the Native Peoples in the state.[49] Alaska Natives worried that the ARTIC program did not focus on their communities, asking Friese to "reorganize the plan to benefit the natives, as the program now operates the overall effort is oriented to please white team leaders, and is not to advance the teacher education of village ARTIC members"[50] These individuals believed the SOSS drifted away from ensuring the educational opportunities promised under law and expressed an adamant desire to exert greater Indigenous input and control over the educational system. While Friese did not resign in the wake of these criticisms, Alaska Natives continued to voice their concerns to the governors and legislators in Alaska whenever they perceived the SOSS failing in its responsibility to their children.

The Indian Education Act and Increased Alaska Native Involvement in Education

After Congress passed the IEA, which thereby authorized tribal communities to apply for federal funding to assess their own needs and develop culturally relevant teaching approaches, Alaska Native villages used the BIA's Alaska Native Needs Assessment in Education (Project ANNA) to directly voice their feedback on educational policy to the Juneau Area Office. In February 1973, the BIA surveyed Alaska Native students and parents, asking for their input and guidance on what they wanted to see happen with BIA schools. Project ANNA—created because of the unique nature of Native American education in Alaska—signaled a turning point for the BIA, serving as its most comprehensive and introspective look at the Bureau's role in Alaska Native education to date. To improve educational policies and support Alaska Native education, Project ANNA recommended to the state and federal governments, based on feedback collected from Alaska Native students and parents, that control over schools in Alaska be transitioned to the local school boards. Furthermore, the survey concluded that the BIA itself needed to transform into an agency focused on financial support for Alaska Native villages, not paternalistic controllers, reflective of the goals of Robert Bennett, Louis Bruce, and Morris Thompson.[51] Project ANNA first and foremost actively requested Alaska Native input to provide "assistance to decision-makers in a time of rapid change regarding the lives and education of Native peoples."[52] In doing so, Project ANNA highlighted that Alaska Native parents and community members wanted their childrens' education to create a foundation for their own Native culture, or in the non-Native culture, depending on which route students chose, and, to accomplish this goal, Alaska Native school boards needed genuine legal control of the village schools.[53] As the movement toward Indigenous community-controlled schools gained momentum throughout the rest of the U.S., serving as examples of the potential gains that Indigenous-controlled education provided for

Native American students, Alaska Natives took a more nuanced approach than other Native American communities. Instead of the complete removal of federal and state control, Alaska Native leaders sought to merge the competing factors of BIA and SOSS schools and community schools into one organization, where local school boards maintained the power to administer policy while the schools continued to have access to federal and state funding and support services.[54] The BIA proved agreeable to this approach because leadership within the BIA had slowly been transitioning toward tentative support of Indigenous-controlled education. Project ANNA then served as the mechanism for instituting self-determination and, in turn, Indigenous-controlled education in Alaska, providing information so that "Native peoples may use [it] to determine their own educational destinies."[55] Project ANNA and the IEA thus paved the way for greater implementation of Indigenous-controlled education in Alaska.

Meanwhile, Alaska Native villages further pressured the state Department of Education to implement facets of the Indian Education Act, advocating that authority over the administration of village schools be delegated to the rural local advisory school boards, for communities to develop and implement their own local Educational Plans directly.[56] The proposal also called for the creation of regional educational committees, which designated target communities based on educational needs, and the creation of six community-school coordinator positions, ideally staffed by members of Alaska Native communities from each region who were experienced in educational planning.[57] Most importantly, the 1972 Act and its implementation in Alaska allocated control of school affairs to local advisory school boards, a long-standing complaint of Alaska Native communities and educators.[58] Simultaneously, the IEA funded the creation of an Alaska Native advisory board for the SOSS, comprising members from various Alaska Native regional corporations and organizations. The advisory board then became the forum in which Alaska Natives communicated directly with SOSS administrators to express their concerns and desires for educational reform in their communities.[59] Ultimately, then, the state of Alaska acquiesced to the calls for Indigenous-controlled education.

Another product of the IEA's implementation in Alaska was that SOSS started collaborating with the Title I Advisory Board for Rural Education, an Alaska Native organization that advocated for communities to have greater control over school administration and curriculum development in the SOSS-operated schools. The board members consisted of Alaska Native representatives from throughout Alaska, as well as Stanley Friese, superintendent for SOSS.[60] In one of their first meetings, the board members voted on priorities via secret ballot for educational policies. The top-ten list emphasized, in order, better pre-school, bilingual language development, integration of culturally relevant materials, dropouts, and educating teachers to facilitate better community involvement.[61] The Advisory Board also became the site in which information regarding state and federal education-based programs and policies were heard and disseminated to Alaska Native communities. For example, the Phonolinguistic Program attempted to increase English literacy among Alaska Native students. The Board supported the program under the condition that the program did not discourage Alaska Native languages, and the three Board members actively participated in the success of the program.[62] In doing so, the Alaska Native members of the Board ensured that their people had a say in the direction of educational programs, while also ensuring continued community and government investment in Alaska Native futures.

Another critical piece of the IEA involved empowering Alaska Native organizations—both regional and statewide—to contract with the state and the BIA to administer their educational programs, which included Indigenous language and cultural lesson plans. These regional organizations, created to distribute funds gathered through the Alaska Native Claims Settlement Act (ANCSA), were thus further strengthened to implement self-determination via Indigenous-controlled education within their communities, outside the confines or in conjunction with the state Department of Education. For example, in 1972, the Tlingit-Haida Council, in Juneau, partnered with the ANB to create a cross-cultural education course that focused on the "folk history" of the Tlingit and Haida peoples. The basic premise of this course revolved around presenting Tlingit culture and history "through the eyes and terms of the Tlingit . . . [so that] cross-cultural understanding can come about."[63] For statewide organizations such as the AFN, education retained "the highest priority [in the] organization," and the AFN became the organization that took over various educational programs targeting Alaska Native children, such as Upward Bound, On Campus Special Services, and Talent Search. The AFN also became the first organization to combine these programs into one, while starting the Alaska Student Higher Education Service.[64] AFN's administration of these educational programs thereby demonstrates the critical role that advocates for Indigenous-controlled education had within the broader Indigenous self-determination movement.

Alaska Native communities found they needed to press the state Department of Education to apply for the grant monies supplied by Congress, as authorized by the IEA, to receive financial assistance for the development of educational programs designed to meet the needs of Alaska Native students. For example, while the IEA provided financial assistance to tribally controlled schools as well as "to local education agencies . . . federally supported schools for Indian children, and State education agencies," the law itself provided no mandate for state agencies to even apply for the grants, let alone use grant money to implement programs developed from community feedback effectively.[65] Therefore, the state Department of Education needed to reconceptualize how they received and implemented feedback from Alaska Native communities and organizations. But the state's Department of Education dragged its feet developing these new methods. Even with the IEA's passage in June 1972, and grant money available to apply for, it took the state Department of Education until late November 1973 to develop "procedures for implementing the Indian Education Act Program."[66]

In response to Alaska Native advocacy for increased local control over education, SOSS created "Regional Education Committee Meetings," whose purpose centered on studying regional education needs and prioritizing them with actionable recommendations, as well as serving as a regional advisory school board to the regional superintendent.[67] The Regional Education Committees provided statutory mechanisms to facilitate Alaska Native community input and control over education, and the financial means, via Congressional appropriations, to ensure that community members had the forum to participate. The SOSS's procedures for the IEA also implemented local control over educational program planning. The Local Advisory School Board served as the intermediaries between community members, parents, teachers, students, and the SOSS. The Local Advisory School Board's role focused on assessing the community's educational needs, creating goals and objectives to address those needs, providing activities, and evaluating procedures to regulate the program activities.[68] These programs needed to be designed to meet the "special educational needs of Indian children [and] must consider the inclusion of activities which build upon and support the heritage, traditions and lifestyle of the community being served."[69] These programs included bilingual education and cultural enrichment, alongside more traditional Westernized educational methods such as math and natural sciences. Alaska Native communities and leaders worked quickly to take advantage of the legal support for the programs and visions they had already been implementing throughout the state.

In particular, bilingual and bicultural education emerged as the central focus for Alaska Native communities in their advocacy for control over school curricula in the 1970s. In 1970, a pilot program for bilingual education started in the SOSS schools in Bethel, AK. Through a joint effort between the BIA, SOSS, and University of Alaska, Anchorage, first graders in the BIA schools at Napakiak, Nunapitchuk, and Akiachuk, as well as kindergarteners in the SOSS school at Bethel participated in the pilot program. The program aimed to preserve the Yup'ik language by teaching it to children, to accelerate their learning and prevent the loss of cultural connections that occurred when teachers used English as the primary language for instruction.[70] In May 1972, the Alaska legislature introduced four bills to provide funding to preserve Alaska Native languages through college courses and an Alaska Native language center at the University of Alaska. Alaska Native leaders and non-Native Dr. Michael Krauss, an expert linguist in Athapascan and Eyak languages, advocated to the state legislature for financial support to hire teachers fluent in Alaska Native languages to work in the bilingual education programs in the SOSS.[71] Alaska Native communities called on the state to increase financial support for bilingual programs because they knew that when their students learned in their Native language, they performed better in school. In fact, when studying the effectiveness of the bilingual programs throughout the state in 1974, the Northern Research and Education Institute found corroborating evidence mirroring other studies done in the lower forty-eight states, arguing that Alaska Native students who learned in a bilingual setting performed better academically, overall, than their peers in a monolingual system.[72] In their evaluation report of the first year of bilingual/bicultural programs in the Bristol Bay area, the Alaska Native Education Board found that 100 percent of "older" children and 96 percent of "younger" children enjoyed learning their native language in the classroom.[73] Specifically, the Bristol Bay Native Association began program planning and subsequent implementation of the bilingual/bicultural program in early 1973, and the preservation and enrichment of Indigenous languages and cultures took precedent in the development of Indigenous-controlled education.

Despite Alaska Native involvement in educational policymaking between 1969 and 1974, these communities continued to conflict with the Alaska Department of Education, particularly on the issue of quantity and quality of village schools. In October 1974, the village of Minto still did not have high school facilities, despite having sixteen high school–aged students who wished to attend school in their village. As previously noted, the Department of Education in Alaska had a legal duty to provide educational facilities to a village if a minimum of five high school students wanted to stay in their village for schooling.[74] The Tanana Chiefs Conference thus petitioned Governor Jay Hammond and the SOSS to rectify the situation. However, rather than requesting a building and staff for the school, the Tanana Chiefs made a more practical request for a certified instructor to live in the village and teach these students, hoping that a member of the village would become the teacher, therefore contributing both to the economic well-being of the community as well as fostering Indigenous-controlled education.[75] Alaska Native corporations, such as the Tanana Chiefs Conference, also petitioned on behalf of the villages they represented to provide adequate and equal education to Alaska Native students. For example, in the villages of Northway and Telida, when students were told to attend Mt. Edgecumbe for high school, the BIA and SOSS decided instead to provide ninth-grade classes in Northway, but nothing in Telida.[76] The Tanana leaders and other Alaska Native communities criticized the inefficiencies of the SOSS and asked for these issues to be addressed immediately. Alaska Native communities and organizations continued to pressure the state and federal government to uphold the promises of the new relationship and ensure that these government entities recognized and respected Indigenous voices in the process.

Alaska Native community members, as well as Native and non-Native teachers and administrators, expressed their frustrations with the SOSS to Governor William Egan. Between late March and early April 1973, Governor Egan's office received over seven dozen telegrams regarding the lackluster leadership of Stanley Friese and his continued actions that circumvented the local control and community input as protected by the IEA. One telegram from an Alaska Native from North Pole stated: "Why has Alaska continued to tolerate total upheaval in its education program caused and perpetuated by Stanley Friese." Another stated: "Remove Friese from SOS[;] Moral Extremely low due [to] his lack of understanding of educational needs." Others held a similar message of frustration in the lack of progress in Alaska education: "please fire Friese [,] in one and half years he has set back SOS 20 years." When Friese unilaterally removed Area Superintendent H. Edward Lilley in April 1973, the Aleut Village Council telegrammed Governor Egan stating: "The Aleut Village Council feels that the removal of Mr. Lilley as Area Superintendent [is] unfair as we were not contacted."[77] Egan and his successor, Jay Hammond, did not fire Friese in 1973 or 1974 as a result of the complaints made by Alaska Natives. Despite this, Alaska Native communities and organizations continued to advocate for control over their own educational destinies while simultaneously developing their own forms of Indigenous-controlled education.

In a significant political victory in 1975, Alaska Native communities—still advocating for increased local control over schools—lobbied for legislative action to abolish SOSS in favor of twenty-one regionally controlled school districts.[78] The rural school districts, dubbed Regional Educational Attendance Areas (REAA), meant Alaska Native communities no longer followed statewide, generalized policies regarding curriculum and administration of the schools, but instead designed "schooling policies and practices in ways that [were] appropriate for the particular region and for the cultural and linguistic group of people that it [served]."[79] In another victory, this time in the judicial system, Governor Jay Hammond signed a settlement agreement over the court case *Tobeluk v. Lind,* which argued that the state's inability to provide high school facilities for villages that desired them racially discriminated against Alaska Natives. The state promised in the settlement to establish a high school in each village in which an elementary school already operated.[80] Education-focused activism by Alaska Native communities succeeded in formalizing community control over education and continues to this day.

Conclusion

By the end of 1975, Alaska Natives and their persistent activism for community-controlled education—supported further with the passage of the ISDEAA, with the abolishment of the SOSS, and the judicial victory in *Tobeluk v. Lind* vindicating their continued efforts—finally attained state and federal recognition of their sovereign rights over their children's education. Congressional intent for the ISDEAA was, in part, a simple yet straightforward recognition of the actions already taken by Alaska Native communities for Indigenous-controlled education, while also serving as a renewed promise by the government to uphold its legal obligations to provide financial support to tribal education programs. For Alaska Native communities, their efforts to advocate for community oversight in education manifested between 1960 and 1975 as Community Action Programs, such as Head Start, and RurAL CAP's investments into Alaska Native community and education centers, as well as successful calls for increased input in the state educational system, and increased bilingual, bicultural curricula. These efforts not only led to new ways for Alaska Native villages to express their tribal sovereignty but also reshaped the political relationships between communities, the state, and the BIA. The twelve recently formed Alaska Native corporate organizations, established by provisions included in the ANCSA, served as the primary mechanism to facilitate educational funding, appropriated by Congress through the ISDEAA's regulations, as well as to administer their own educational programs and community centers. Since 1975, Alaska Natives have protected their right to control education in their communities against various changes in federal and state laws and other political assaults on their tribal sovereignty. Despite the challenges, Alaska Native communities never backed down in advocating for their right to control their educational destinies, upholding their rights, rather than merely fighting for recognition.

In April 2025, Native communities once again found themselves before Senate and House committee hearings justifying the continued existence of tribally controlled education, sovereignty, and self-determination, and further requesting that the federal government uphold its obligations to

Native education. Before the Senate Committee on Indian Affairs, Dr. Rosita K̲aaháni Worl, president of Sealaska Heritage Institute (SHI) in Juneau, listed the various ways in which Native education demonstrated tangible successes when federal dollars adequately reached community education systems. SHI used federal funding to "promote systematic changes with the integration of Native culture instruction into educational systems . . . [which] demonstrates academic progress."[81] In Alaska, as elsewhere in the country, Native leaders have continued to advocate on behalf of their communities for the federal government to uphold its obligations to Native education. At the same hearing, Jason Dropik, executive director of the National Indian Education Association, once again reminded the committee that the federal government had an obligation, through signed treaties with tribal nations, to ensure that Native education is maintained and that "Tribal sovereignty is respected at every stage."[82] While these witnesses requested that the federal government uphold its treaty obligations to Native education and listed the ways in which Indigenous-controlled education succeeds in the present, the tribal entities involved all implied that even without federal funding, Native communities would fight for their inherent rights over their children's education. This mentality stems from generations of advocacy, activism, and assertions of tribal sovereignty, traced back to the time of early Euro-American and Indigenous contact. However, it is also important to recognize how the contestations over tribal self-determination and self-governance today originated with the Indigenous-controlled education-based activism by Native communities in Alaska, as well as elsewhere throughout the country, during the 1960s and 1970s.

TIMOTHY HOUGE holds a PhD in History from Marquette University. His research, funded in part by the American Philosophical Society's Phillips Fund for Native American Research, examines the interconnected nature of Indigenous educational reform activism with the larger national movements for political self-determination in the 1960s and 1970s.

References

"4 Kivalina Teenagers Suing State Schools." *Tundra Times,* May 12, 1971.

Alaska Native Brotherhood, Sitka Camp #1, "Resolution." Record Group 01, Folder: Federal Government: BIA, Box 13, Office of the Governor, 1971, Education thru Federal Government, Alaska State Archives, Juneau, AK.

Alaska Native Education Board, Inc. "1973–1974 Final Evaluation Report: First Year of the Bilingual/Bicultural Program." Folder 9/11, Box 9, Bristol Bay Native Association, HMC-0075, Archives and Special Collections, University of Alaska, Anchorage, Anchorage, AK.

Alaska State-Operated School System. "Indian Education Act Proposal." Loose Booklet, Indian Education Program Files, 1973–1974, J27046-J27047, Box 22607, RG 163 SR1247. Alaska State Archives, Juneau, AK.

Alaska State-Operated School System. "Procedures for Implementing the Indian Education Act Program." November 23, 1973. Loose Booklet, Box VS 1671. Alaska State Archives, Juneau, AK.

AK Stat § 14.03.080 (2024), State of Alaska Legislature, https://www.akleg.gov/basis/statutes.asp.

Anders, Gary C. "Social and Economic Consequences of Federal Indian Policy: A Case Study of the Alaska Natives." Economic Development and Cultural Change. 37, no. 2 (January 1989): 285–303.

Anderson, Dianne. "Boarding Home Rural Students." *Tundra Times,* November 4, 1970.

"An Overall Education Plan for Rural Alaska." RG 75, Records of the Bureau of Indian Affairs, Office of Indian Education Programs, General Records Relating to Education, 1889–1972, Folder: An Overall Education Plan for Rural Alaska, Box 7, National Archives, Washington, D.C.

Barnhardt, Carol. "A History of Schooling For Alaska Native People." *Journal of American Indian Education.* 40, no. 1 (2001): 1–30.

Berg, Kaili. "50 Years of Self-Determination: How a Landmark Act Empowered Tribal Sovereignty and Transformed Federal-Tribal Relations." *Native News Online,* January 4, 2025. https://nativenewsonline.net/sovereignty/50-years-of-self-determination-how-a-landmark-act-empowered-tribal-sovereignty-and-transformed-federal-tribal-relations.

"BIA Forms Education Advisory." *Tundra Times,* May 16, 1969.

"BIA Plans Education Workshop in Utah." *Tundra Times,* January 17, 1969.

Brayboy, Bryan McKinley Jones, Susan C. Faircloth, Tiffany S. Lee, Margarent J. Maaka, and Troy A. Richardson. "Sovereignty and Education: An Overview of the Unique Nature of Indigenous Education." Journal of American Indian Education. 54, no. 1 (Spring 2015): 1–9.

Carpenter, Larry. "North Education While Retaining Culture Possible." *Tundra Times,* August 29, 1969.

Charlie, Melvin. "Letter to Stephen Friese, August 28, 1974." Folder: Education, Misc., Box 44, Office of the Governor, 1974, Economic Deveopment thru Federal Government, Location No. 4958, Alaska State Archives, Juneau, AK.

Clarkin, Thomas. *Federal Indian Policy in the Kennedy and Johnson Administrations, 1961-1969.* University of New Mexico Press, 2001.

Cobb, Daniel M., and Loretta Fowler, eds. *Beyond Red Power: American Indian Political Activism since 1900.* School for Advanced Research, 2007.

Cobb, Daniel M. *Native Activism in Cold War America: The Struggle for Sovereignty.* University Press of Kansas, 2008.

"Community Education Group Starts." *Tundra Times,* May 6, 1970.

Crawley, Cheryl K. *Native American Bilingual Education: An Ethnography of Powerful Forces.* Emerald Publishing Limited, 2020.

Davis, Julie L. *Survival Schools: The American Indian Movement and Community Education in the Twin Cities.* University of Minnesota Press, 2013.

Deyhle, Donna, and Karen Swisher. "Research in American Indian and Alaska Native Education: From Assimilation to Self-Determination." *Review of Research in Education.* 22, no. 1 (1997): 113–94.

DeJong, David. *Paternalism to Partnership: The Administration of Indian Affairs, 1786–2021.* University of Nebraska Press, 2022.

Deloria Jr., Vine and Daniel R. Wildcat. *Power and Place: Indian Education in America.* Fulcrum, 2001.

Dropik, Jason. "Written Testimony for 'Native American Education—Examining Federal Programs at the U.S. Department of Education.'' U.S. Senate Committee on Indian Affairs, April 2, 2025. https://www.indian.senate.gov/hearings/oversight-hearing-entitled-native-american-education-examining-federal-programs-at-the-u-s-department-of-education/.

"Editorial- Can Rural Schools Gain When State Takes Over?" *Tundra Times,* October 3, 1969.

"Friese Resignation Asked—Widening Rift Develops Between State Operated Schools Head, Teachers." *Tundra Times,* April 19, 1972.

Gilberston, Henry Collection, Series III, 1963–1975, University Archives and Special Collections, University of Alaska, Anchorage, Anchorage, AK.

Glasgow, Jacqueline. "Push on Bills 421-22-23-24: Bills Seek to Preseve Language heritages Through Native Center." *Tundra Times,* May 3, 1972.

Gray, Clyde Thomas. "Cultural Pluralism Increases in Southwestern Schools." *Journal of American Indian Education* 15, no. 1 (1975): 13–16

Grounds, Richard A., George E. Tinker, and David E. Wilkins, eds. *Native Voices: American Indian Identity and Resistance.* University Press of Kansas, 2003.

Haaland, Deb. "50 Years Later: Tribal Self-Determination is Flourishing." *Tribal Business News,* January 4, 2025. https://tribalbusinessnews.com/sections/opinion-op-ed/14943-50-years-later-tribal-self-determination-is-flourishing.

"Harry Carter on Education." *Tundra Times,* May 3, 1972.

Hirschfield, Martha. "The Alaska Native Claims Settlement Act: Tribal Sovereignty and the Corporate Form." *The Yale Law Journal* 101, no. 6 (April 1992): 1331–1355.

Hoover, Brant. "Bush Legislators Want High Schools—Rep. Moore Said State, BIA Negligent in Bush Education." *Tundra Times,* April 12, 1972.

"Hope They Don't Cry When Homesick." *Tundra Times,* April 28, 1967.

Jennings, Michael. *Alaska Native Political Leadership and Higher Education: One University, Two Universes.* AltaMira Press, 2004.

Johnson, Libet. "Nenana Mothers Start Wheels of Education For Head Start Tots." *Tundra Times,* October 21, 1970.

Juneau Area Office, BIA. "Alaska Native Needs Assessment in Education." Loose Booklet, Box VS1671, Alaska State Archives, Juneau AK.

"Klukwan's New Community Hall to Allow Tlingit Cultural Sharing." *Tundra Times,* May 9, 1969.

Lambert, Valerie. "Political Protest, Conflict, and Tribal Nationalism: The Oklahoma Choctaws and the Termination Crisis of 1959–1970." *American Indian Quarterly* 31, no. 2 (2007): 283–309.

———. *Native Agency: Indians in the Bureau of Indian Affairs.* University of Minnesota Press, 2023.

Lomawaima, K. Tsianina and Teresa L. McCarty. *"To Remain an Indian": Lessons in Democracy from a Century of Native American Education.* Teachers College Press, Columbia University, 2006.

"Long Term Goals." Education Program Decimal Files, Records of the Bureau of Indian Affairs Collection, 1793–1989, RG 75, National Archives, Seattle, WA.

McCoy, Meredith, and Matthew Villeneuve. "Reconceiving Schooling: Centering Indigenous Experimentation in Indian Education History." *History of Education Quarterly* 60, no. 4. (November 2020): 487–519.

Metcalfe, Peter. *A Dangerous Idea: The Alaska Native Brotherhood and the Struggle for Indigenous Rights.* University of Alaska Press, 2014.

"Minto Children Learn Culture." *Tundra Times,* July 11, 1969.

"Minutes of the Title 1 Advisory Board for Rural Schools, April 17–19th, 1972, Anchorage AK." Folder: Evaluation Report FY-72, Parent Advisory Board 72129–2, Box 4: Department of Education Administrative Services, Division, State Operated School Records, 1962; 1969–1976, RG 05/04, Location No. 4455, Series 36, Alaska State Archives, Juneau, AK.

"Minutes of the Title 1 Advisory Board for Rural Schools, April 17, 18, 19, 1972, Anchorage Alaska." Loose Booklet, Folder: Evaluation Report FY-72, Parent Advisory Board 72129–2, Box VS 1671, Alaska State Archives, Juneau, AK.

Naske, Claus-M and Herman Slotnick. *Alaska: A History.* 3rd ed. University of Oklahoma Press, 2011.

"Native Women Revitalize Crafts." *Tundra Times,* March 7, 1969.

"Parental Involvement Critical Education Need." *Tundra Times,* October 3, 1969.

"Pre-School for Tots Formed by Nenana Mothers." *Tundra Times,* January 2, 1970.

Philp, Kenneth R., ed. *Indian Self-Rule: First-Hand Accounts of Indian-White Relations from Roosevelt to Reagan.* Howe Brothers, 1986.

Pope, Mary L. "An Evaluation of the Current Bilingual Program in the Villages of Bristol Bay Area, March 1974." Folder 9.20, BBNA, Series 4. Box 9: Bristol Bay Native Assn., HMC-0075, University Archives and Special Collection, University of Alaska, Anchorage, Anchorage, AK.

Public Law 93–638, "Indian Self-Determination and Education Assistance Act, 1975." January 4, 1975. https://www.congress.gov/93/statute/STATUTE-88/STATUTE-88-Pg2203.pdf.

Reyhner, Jon, and Jeanne Eder. *American Indian Education: A History.* University of Oklahoma Press, 2004.

Rural Cap Records, HMC-0213. University Archives and Special Collections. University of Alaska, Anchorage, Anchorage, AK.

Sackett, John. "Oil Impact Stirs Eskimos: Barrowites Concerned About Land But Wish Part in Development." *Tundra Times,* January 17, 1969.

Shulman, Madelyn. "Solutions Sought—Unique Problems of Boarding Students." *Tundra Times,* April 7, 1971.

"Southwestern Alaska's Bilingual Program Now in Its 2nd Year." *Tundra Times,* May 10, 1972.

Szasz, Margaret Connell. *Education and the American Indian: The Road to Self-Determination, 1928–1975.* University of New Mexico Press, 1974.

Tanana Chiefs Conference Education Committee. “Board Resolution #74–75.” Folder: Education, Misc., Box 44, Office of the Governor, 1974, Economic Development thru Federal Government, Location No. 4958, Alaska State Archives, Juneau, AK.

Thomas, Robert L. “Letter to Governor William Egan.” Record Group 01, Folder: Federal Government: BIA, Box 13, Office of the Governor, 1971, Education thru Federal Government, Alaska State Archives, Juneau, AK.

Tiffany, Warren. “Memorandum: Resolution by Alaska Native Brotherhood.” Record Group 01, Folder: Federal Government: BIA, Box 13, Office of the Governor, 1971, Education thru Federal Government, Alaska State Archives, Juneau, AK.

“Tlingit Cross-Cultural Education Course to begin in Juneau.” *Tundra Times,* January 19, 1972.

Tobeluk v. Lind, C.A. No. 72–2450, Alaska Super. Ct., 3rd District. Approved October 27, 1976.

“Training of Head Start Teachers Begins: Being Conducted at Anchorage Community College.” *Tundra Times,* July 29, 1970.

U.S. Department of Education. “The Indian Education Act of 1972: Answers to Your Questions, 1981 Revised Edition.” U.S. Government Printing Office, February 2, 1981. https://eric.ed.gov/?id=ED103175.

“Various Loose Telegraphs.” Folder: Education 5–6, State Operated Schools I, Box 33, Location No, 4947, Office of the Governor, 1973, Education thru Environmental Conservation, Alaska State Archives, Juneau, AK.

Warren, Donald. “American Indian Histories as Education History.” *History of Education Quarterly* 54, no. 3 (August 2014): 255–85.

Wilkins, David E., and K. Tsianina Lomawaima. *Uneven Ground: American Indian Sovereignty and Federal Law.* University of Oklahoma Press, 2001.

Willoya, William. “Letter to Governor Egan.” Record Group 01, Folder: Education, Misc., Box 12, Location No. 4926, Office of the Governor, 1971, Commerce thru Education, Alaska State Archives, Juneau, AK.

Willoya, William and Carole. “Letter to Superintendent Stephen Friese, 1971.” Record Group 01, Folder: Education, Misc., Box 12, Location No. 4926, Office of the Governor, 1971, Commerce thru Education, Alaska State Archives, Juneau, AK.

Worl, Rosita K̲aaháni. “Written Testimony for ‘Native American Education—Examining Federal Programs at the U.S. Department of Education.” U.S. Senate Committee on Indian Affairs, April 2, 2025. https://www.indian.senate.gov/hearings/oversight-hearing-entitled-native-american-education-examining-federal-programs-at-the-u-s-department-of-education/.

“Youngsters From Villages—Problems of Boarding Students.” *Tundra Times,* February 10, 1971.

Notes

1. “Eskimo” is used in its historical context in the title, and is acknowledged to no longer be the appropriate name by which to refer to the Yup’ik and Central Yup’ik peoples of Alaska. Any reference to “Eskimo” is done so in

the historical context of the quote in which it is used in or which it has been paraphrased from. Also this article is a part of a larger dissertation project for a completed Ph.D. project with Marquette University, completed in May 2025. Special thanks to the American Philosophical Society for their funding through the Phillip's Fund for Native American Research, and Marquette University's Casper Dissertation Fellowship.

2. Kaili Berg, "50 Years of Self-Determination: How a Landmark Act Empowered Tribal Sovereignty and Transformed Federal-Tribal Relations," *Native News Online* (January 4, 2025). https://nativenewsonline.net/sovereignty/50-years-of-self-determination-how-a-landmark-act-empowered-tribal-sovereignty-and-transformed-federal-tribal-relations.

3. Public Law 93–638, Jan. 4, 1975; The Act's official wording said "to provide maximum Indian participation in the Government and education of the Indian people; to provide for the full participation of Indian tribes in programs and services conducted by the Federal Government for Indians and to encourage the development of human resources of the Indian People; to establish a program of assistance to upgrade Indian education; to support the right of Indian citizens to control their own educational activities; and for other purposes.

4. Public Law 93–638.

5. Berg, "50 Years of Self-Determination."

6. K. Tsianina Lomawaima and Teresa L. McCarty, *"To Remain an Indian,": Lessons in Democracy from a Century of Native American Education* (Teachers College Press, Columbia University, 2006), 117.

7. Deb Haaland, "50 Years Later: Tribal Self-Determination is Flourishing," *Tribal Business News*, January 4, 2025, https://tribalbusinessnews.com/sections/opinion-op-ed/14943-50-years-later-tribal-self-determination-is-flourishing.

8. Clyde Thomas Gray, "Cultural Pluralism Increases in Southwestern Schools," *Journal of American Indian Education*, 15, no. 1 (October 1975): 13–14.

9. Claus-M. Naske and Herman Slotnick, *Alaska: A History*, 3rd ed. (University of Oklahoma Press, 2011), 266.

10. Ibid, 266.

11. John Sackett, "Oil Impact Stirs Eskimos: Barrowites Concerned About Land But Wish Part in Development," *Tundra Times*, December 13, 1968, 1.

12. John Borbridge, "Then as Now," *Tundra Times*, January 17, 1969, 1–2.

13. Ibid, 2.

14. "BIA Plans Education Workshop in Utah," *Tundra Times*, January 17, 1969, 4.

15. Margaret Connell Szasz, *Education and the American Indian: The Road to Self-Determination, 1928–1973* (University of New Mexico Press, 1974), 158.

16. "BIA Forms Education Advisory," *Tundra Times*, May 16, 1969, 7.

17. "Minutes, August 26, 1965," Folder: ASCAP Board Meeting, 1965, Aug. 26–7, Juneau, AK, Box 1: Rural Cap Records, HMC-0213, Archives and Special Collections, University of Alaska, Anchorage, Anchorage, AK; Robert Bennett served as a member on the ASCAP until he was appointed Assistant Commissioner of Indian Affairs in early 1966.

18. “Long Term Goals,” 23–26, ASCAP, Folder: ASCAP Proposed Refunding Programs, January 1-December 31, 1968, Box 46: RG 75, Records of the Bureau of Indian Affairs [BIA] 1793–1989: Juneau Area Office, Education Program Decimal Files, SEAL-36, National Archives, Seattle, WA.

19. “Training of Head Start Teachers Begins: Being Conducted at Anchorage Community College,” *Tundra Times* (July 29, 1970), 4.

20. Ibid.

21. “Community Education Group Starts,” *Tundra Times*, May 6, 1970, 7.

22. “Klukwan’s New Community Hall to Allow Tlingit Cultural Sharing,” *Tundra Times,* May 9, 1969, 3.

23. “Native Women Revitalize Crafts,” *Tundra Times*, March 7, 1969, 2.

24. “Minto Children Learn Culture,” *Tundra Times*, July 11, 1969, 2.

25. Larry Carpenter, “North Education While Retaining Culture Possible,” *Tundra Times*, August 29, 1969, 1–2.

26. “Pre-School for Tots Formed by Nenana Mothers,” *Tundra Times*, January 2, 1970, 1.

27. Libet Johnson, “Nenana Mothers Start Wheels of Education For Head Start Tots,” *Tundra Times*, October 21, 1970, 8.

28. “Parental Involvement Critical Education Need,” *Tundra Times*, October 3, 1969, 4.

29. Michael S. Cline, *Tannik School: The Impact of Education on the Eskimos of Anaktuvuk Pass* (Alaska Methodist University Press, 1975), 199–200.

30. “Parental Involvement,” 4.

31. John Eichman, “Memorandum, For the Record,” 1, Folder: 1134, II: Misc. School Files, 1963–1965, Box 1: Henry Gilberston Collection, Series III, 1963–1975, Archives and Special Collections, University of Alaska, Anchorage, Anchorage, AK.

32. “Editorial- Can Rural Schools Gain When State Takes Over?” *Tundra Times*, October 10, 1969, 2.

33. Ibid, 2; Margaret Connell Szasz, *Education and the American Indian: The Road to Self-Determination, 1928–1973* (University of New Mexico Press, 1974), 126–27; the BIA sent several hundred Alaska Native students to school at Chilocco, Oklahoma alone, in the 1950s and 1960s.

34. “‘Hope They Don’t Cry When Homesick,” *Tundra Times*, April 28, 1967, 5.

35. Madelyn Shulman, “Solutions Sought—Unique Problems of Boarding Students,” *Tundra Times*, April 7, 1971, 5.

36. “An Overall Education Plan for Rural Alaska,” Revised, October 1, 1968, Folder: An Overall Education Plan for Rural Alaska, 1968, Box 7, RG 75 Records of the Bureau of Indian Affairs, Office of Indian Education Programs, General Records Relating to Education, 1889–1972, Entry 759B, NN3-075-95-039, National Archives, Washington, D.C; “4 Kivalina Teenagers Suing State Schools,” *Tundra Times*, May 12, 1971, 1, 5.

37. “4 Kivalina Teenagers . . .” 5.

38. Dianne Anderson, “Boarding Home Rural Students,” *Tundra Times*, November 4, 1970, 2, 6.

39. “Youngsters from Villages—Problems of Boarding Students,” *Tundra Times*, February 10, 1971, 5.

40. Ibid, 5.

41. Brant Hoover, "Bush Legislators Want High Schools—Rep. Moore Said State, BIA Negligent in Bush Education," *Tundra Times*, April 12, 1972, 4; Alaska Statute 14.03.080 states: "A child of school age is entitled to attend public school without payment of tuition during the school term in which he is a resident."

42. Alaska Native Brotherhood, Sitka Camp #1, "Resolution," 2. Folder: Federal Government: BIA, Box 13, Office of the Governor, 1971, Education thru Federal Government, Accession No. 88, Record Group 01, Location Np. 4927, Alaska State Archives, Juneau, AK.

43. Ibid, 3.

44. Warren Tiffany, "Memorandum: Resolution by Alaska Native Brotherhood," 1–2, Folder: Federal Government: BIA, Box 13, Office of the Governor, 1971, Education thru Federal Government, Accession No. 88, Record Group 01, Location Np. 4927, Alaska State Archives, Juneau, AK.

45. Ibid, 1; Cline, *Tannik School*, 155–59.

46. Robert L. Thomas, letter to Governor William Egan. Folder: Federal Government: BIA, Box 13, Office of the Governor, 1971, Education thru Federal Government, Accession No. 88, Record Group 01, Location Np. 4927, Alaska State Archives, Juneau, AK.

47. "Friese Resignation Asked—Widening Rift Develops Between State Operated Schools Head, Teachers," *Tundra Times*, April 19, 1972, 1, 6.

48. Ibid, 6.

49. William Willoya, Letter to Governor Egan, Folder: Education; Misc., Box 12, Location No. 4926, Office of the Governor, 1971, Commerce thru Education, Record Group 01, Series No. 88, Alaska State Archives, Juneau, AK.

50. William and Carole Willoya, Letter to Superintendent Stephen Friese," 1971, Folder: Education; Misc., Box 12, Location No. 4926, Office of the Governor, 1971, Commerce thru Education, Record Group 01, Series No. 88, Alaska State Archives, Juneau, AK.

51. Juneau Area Office, BIA, "Alaska Native Needs Assessment in Education," 5, Loose Booklet, Box VS1671, Alaska State Archives, Juneau, AK; David DeJong, *Paternalism to Partnership: The Administration of Indian Affairs, 1786–2021*, (University of Nebraska Press, 2022), 321, 328–330, 340–341.

52. "Alaska Native Needs Assessment in Education," 1.

53. Ibid, 5.

54. Lomawaima and McCarty, *"To Remain an Indian"*, 116–17; The desire to both assert control over curriculum and programs within the schools and maintain the relationship with the federal became a central component to the 1975 Indian Self-Determination and Education Assistance Act.

55. "Alaska Native Needs Assessment in Education," 15.

56. Alaska State Operated School System "Indian Education Act Proposal," 1. Loose Booklet, Box 22607, RG 163, SR1247, Indian Education Program Files, 1973–1974, J27046-J27047, Alaska State Archives, Juneau, AK; Alaska Native communities in particular drew inspiration from presidential candidate Senator George McGovern, who had initially proposed a bill supporting Native

American self-determination in 1966, and as presidential candidate, promised to accelerate and surpass the programs implemented by the Nixon administration. The process of local educational plans was a process already underway with projects such as the Bilingual Education program under Title I of the Act.

57. Ibid, 1.

58. Ibid, 9; Another critical component of the SOSS's proposal included directly empowering parents, as well as the local advisory school boards, to function as the "primary evaluators of the program . . . [to] determine the extent to which the program and student objectives are met." In doing so, the SOSS placed the power to be held accountable directly in the hands of Alaska Native parents and communities, a first for the state.

59. "Minutes of the Title 1 Advisory Board for Rural Schools, April 17—19th, 1972, Anchorage, AK," 1—3. Folder: Evaluation Report FY-72, Parent Advisory Board 72129—2, Box 4: Department of Education Administrative Services, Division, State Operated Schools Records, 1962; 1969—1976, RG 05/04, Location No. 4455, Series 36, Alaska State Archives, Juneau, AK.

60. "Minutes of the Title I Advisory Board for Rural Schools, April 17, 18, 19, 1972, Anchorage, Alaska," 6, Folder: Evaluation Report FY-72, Parent Advisory Board 72129—2, Box VS 1671, Alaska State Archives, Juneau, AK; The Alaska Native members included Ethel Adcox of the Cook Inlet Native Association; Susan Murphy of the Alaska village Council Presidents; Ida Angasan from the Bristol Bay Native Association; Harry Kaleak from the Artic Slope Native Association; Richard Mueller of the Tanana Chiefs; Walter Charley from the Copper River Native Association; and Al Nakak from the Bering Strait Native Association.

61. Ibid, 6.

62. Ibid, 7.

63. "Tlingit Cross-Cultural Education Course to begin in Juneau," *Tundra Times*, January 19, 1972, 7.

64. "Harry Carter on Education," *Tundra Times*, May 3, 1972, 1, 6.

65. U.S. Department of Education, "The Indian Education Act of 1972: Answers to Your Questions, 1981 Revised Edition," (Washington, D.C.: U.S. Government Printing Office, February 2, 1981), 1.

66. "Alaska State-Operated School System Procedures for Implementing the Indian Education Act Program, November 23, 1973," Box VS 1671, Alaska State Archives, Juneau, AK.

67. Ibid, 2.

68. Ibid, 5.

69. Ibid, 6.

70. "Southwestern Alaska's Bilingual Program Now in Its 2nd Year," *Tundra Times*, May 10, 1972, 13.

71. Jacqueline Glasgow, "Push on Bills 421-22-23-24: Bills Seek to Preserve Language Heritages Through Native Center," *Tundra Times* (May 3, 1972), 1, 6.

72. Mary L. Pope, Bilingual Programs Specialist, Northern Research and Education Institute, "An Evaluation of the Current Bilingual Program in the Villages of the Bristol Bay Area, March 1974," 12. Folder 9/20, BBNA, Series 4,

Box 9: Bristol Bay Native Assn., HMC-0075, Archives and Special Collections, University of Alaska, Anchorage, Anchorage, AK.

73. Alaska Native Education Board, Inc., "1973–1974 Final Evaluation Report: First Year of the Bilingual/Bicultural Program," 20. Folder 9/11, Box 9, Bristol Bay Native Association, HMC-0075, Archives and Special Collections, University of Alaska, Anchorage, Anchorage, AK.

74. Alaska Statute 14.03.080: "A child of school age is entitled to attend public school without payment of tuition during the school term in which he is a resident."

75. Tanana Chiefs Conference Education Committee, "Board Resolution #74–75," Folder: Education: Misc., Box 44, Office of the Governor, 1974, Economic Development thru Federal Government, RG 01, Series 88, Location No. 4958, Alaska State Archives, Juneau, AK.

76. Melvin Charlie, President of the Tanana Chiefs Conference, "Letter to Stephen Friese, August 28, 1974," Folder: Education: Misc., Box 44, Office of the Governor, 1974, Economic Development thru Federal Government, RG 01, Series 88, Location No. 4958, Alaska State Archives, Juneau, AK.

77. Various loose telegraphs, Folder: Education: 5–6, State Operated Schools I, Box 33, Location No. 4947, RG 01, Series No. 88, Office of the Governor, 1973, Education thru Environmental Conservation, Alaska State Archives, Juneau, AK; H. Edward Lilley wrote to Governor Egan himself after his firing to tell Egan that Friese's two years in power had caused extreme damage to the hopes of teachers, parents and administrators. Note: All telegram citations are taken verbatim, reflecting the original shorthand medium of telegrams.

78. Carol Barnhardt, "A History of Schooling for Alaska Native People," *Journal of American Indian Education* 40, no. 1 (2001): 21.

79. Ibid, 21.

80. Agreement of Settlement, *Tobeluk v. Lind,* C.A. No. 72–2450 (Alaska Super. Ct., 3rd District, approved October 27, 1976); Carol Barnhardt, "A History of Schooling For Alaska Native People," 40, No. 1 (2001): 21–22. This case is often referred to by the original plaintiff's name, Molly Hootch, the landmark court case that helped to reshape Alaska Native education by restricting the distance by which Alaska Native students could be sent away for school and ensuring state funding for schools within communities.

81. Rosita K̲aaháni Worl, "Written Testimony for 'Native American Education—Examining Federal Programs at the U.S. Department of Education," U.S. Senate Committee on Indian Affairs, April 2, 2025. https://www.indian.senate.gov/hearings/oversight-hearing-entitled-native-american-education-examining-federal-programs-at-the-u-s-department-of-education/.

82. Jason Dropik, "Written Testimony for 'Native American Education—Examining Federal Programs at the U.S. Department of Education," U.S. Senate Committee on Indian Affairs, April 2, 2025. https://www.indian.senate.gov/hearings/oversight-hearing-entitled-native-american-education-examining-federal-programs-at-the-u-s-department-of-education/.

NOTES FROM THE FIELD

TOMAS COLBENGTSON, HARALD GASKI, BRITT KRAMVIG, SCOTT MACKENZIE, *and* ANNA STENPORT

Arctic Indigenous Art: *Arctic Highways*, Capacity Building, Circulation, Contexts

Abstract

In the twenty-first century, Sámi artworks have increasingly extended their reach among global audiences. This article examines the international circulation of works tied to the land that situate the Indigenous Arctic as a site of meaning, activism, culture, politics, and dissent. In this understanding, in Sápmi, land and art are historically relational, a connection augmented by global circulation through specific Indigenous "Highways," as per the "Arctic Highway" concept first developed by Sámi writer and artist Nils-Aslak Valkeapää and further developed in the international *Arctic Highways* (2022–25) traveling exhibition. The case studies presented in this article employ mixed methodologies, examining the emergence of artist collectives in the 1970s and the current artistic practices of three contemporary Sámi artists in relation to land activism. These include a self-reflection by and study of the works of visual artist Tomas Colbengtson; contextualized first-person statements by video artist Marja Helander; and an analysis of the performance *Matriarchy* by Paulina Feodoroff, which convey messages of healing, renewal and land protection. These examples highlight the significance of ongoing artistic collaboration in relation to Sámi environmental stewardship and demonstrate how circulation through both nonprofit and commercial contexts showcased a growing number of practitioners and their multifaceted and interrelated activism.

IN THE TWENTY-FIRST CENTURY, a wide array of Sámi artworks circulate through global exhibitions.[1] We—both Sámi and white European and North American settler artists and academics—engage with these exhibitions and art practices to map two related constellations that at first glance may seem at odds: the international circulation of works tied to localized lands and their function as a means to globalize the Indigenous Arctic as a site of meaning, activism, culture, politics, and dissent. In Sápmi, as in other Indigenous territories, land and art are relational, embedded within one another in multiple and sometimes contrasting ways (see Allen 2012). Métis scholar Sherry Farrell Racette (2008) argues that Indigenous art mirrors the deep understanding of the land held by Indigenous communities. Therefore, as Liisa-Ravna Finbog proposes, art as well as *duodji*/handicraft may be considered as ways of practicing a Sámi epistemology of aesthetics and *muitalusat* [stories] centered within a system of relations expressed as bonds of kinship with the land (2023). This constellation of ideas and practices around art and land guides our examination of collaborative and collective circulation mechanisms such as the traveling transnational exhibition *Arctic Highways* (2021–2025) and the Sámi Pavilion at the Venice Biennale (2022). We also examine pieces by individual artists such as Nils-Aslak Valkeapää, Tomas Colbengtson, Marja Helander, and Paulina Feodoroff whose works are mobilized for a global audience through these exhibitions and have contributed to recent international recognition of pan-Arctic Indigenous artistic practice.

Our methodology foregrounds intersections of first-person and interview accounts of artists' practices to maintain heterogeneous voices within various Indigenous, especially Sámi, communities and positions, and to consider the ways in which circulation of these artists' works enhances a global presence of Arctic Indigenous artistic practice, capacity building, and recognition. This methodology serves to delineate both the circulation of these artists' works and to examine these in their global context, while integrating first-person expression as an important component of Sámi land-art activism.

Sámi Artist Collectives, Activism, and Land Determination

Over the last few years, the global circulation of Indigenous Arctic art and artistic practice has accelerated, spanning national museums, independent galleries, festivals, and virtual platforms (see MacKenzie and Stenport 2023, 2024). This follows a strong tradition of collaboration among Indigenous groups in the global circumpolar North, with international organizing around Indigenous rights in the 1970s representing an early starting point (e.g., The Arctic Peoples' Conference in Copenhagen in 1973 and the founding of the World Council of Indigenous Peoples in 1975). In 1978, the Sámi artist collective Mázejoavku (1978–1983) became one of the first Indigenous groups in the world to officially constitute itself as an art collective. Another

Sámi art collective called Dáiddadállu was established in Guovdageaidnu (Kautokeino) in 2014. It is a nonprofit collective with more than twenty artist partners working across media, from visual arts, film, and television production to choreography, dance, and theater, to music and vocal performance, especially yoik. These Sámi art collectives aim to facilitate artists' practices, make Sámi art visible in dominant societies and internationally, provide an open and supportive environment for Sámi artists, reflect how communities are embedded in Sámi knowledge traditions, and connect land to artistic practice (Danbolt et al. 2024).

One of the founders of the Mázejoavku collective, Synnøve Persen, confirms in an interview that the group's artistic activities arose in tandem with and in support of the political land activism of the Alta Dam protests of the late 1970s (indeed, the group is named after the Sámi village Máze, situated on the Alta River, upstream from the dam) but also that the collective struggled to sustain itself as it posed new questions to audiences about the connection between land and self-determination as mobilized through activist art practice: "We were always struggling economically. [. . .] There was no market for art, and no infrastructure. The odds were stacked against us, but we felt strong as a group. However, when an application for financial support from Norway's Regional Development Fund was rejected in 1983, we gave up. Little did we know at the time how much influence our efforts would have on the development of Sámi art in general. That only became obvious years later" (interview in Kuhn 2020, 49).

Persen's reflections confirm that art and political land activism in Sápmi has been a throughline of creative practice for many decades and that this connection remains strong. Indeed, many interviews in *Liberating Sápmi: Indigenous Resistance in Europe's Far North* (Kuhn 2020) feature evidence from a range of practitioners, from visual artist Anders Sunna to installation and recording artist Maxida Märak, about the ways in which Sámi land- and self-determination movements are tied to creative practice. Another example is the first-person writing of Sámi artists and activists in the collection *Samisk Vrede* ("Sámi Rage"; Grahn and Skåden 2016). *Samisk Vrede* shares a link to the action and tenets of the North American 1960s "Black Rage" movement, which ties creative practice to mental health advocacy and protests territorial political subjugation, and *Samisk Vrede* extends that stance of political and artistic activism to a Sápmi context. Interviews and first-person statements conducted and collected by Kuhn, Grahn, and Skåden also confirm how a current generation of Sámi artists continues to celebrate Elders as important knowledge holders for their art, and consider artistic inspiration as gifted from the land.

The Dáiddadállu collective, for example, describes itself as based on a Sámi epistemology that emphasizes collaboration and collective action to ensure "sustainability for nature, people, animals, our culture and our industries [. . . Where] our work contributes to developing and safeguarding a healthy and vibrant Sápmi. [. . .] with the goal of achieving fair, lasting and sustainable development" (Dáiddadállu). The collective focuses on strengthening Sápmi and Sámi art, while coordinating invitations coming from national and international institutions, to reclaim an artistic Indigenous sovereignty explicitly tied to sustainable land development while advancing land-determination political movements.

The rise of formal Sámi artist collectives such as Mázejoavku and Dáiddadállu are complemented by a proliferation of more loosely organized groups of artists and activists that call attention to, and protest, land infringement. These include Ellos Deatnu, Suohpan Terror, and Blodklubb (see Kuokkanen 2021; Røstvik 2023; and Danbolt et al. 2024) and the group of Sámi artists and reindeer herders who have joined forces through the art exhibition "Let the River Flow" and the film *The Sámi Have Rights* (*Sámiin Leat Rievttit*, Elle Márjá Eira and Mai-Lis Eira 2018). While artistic expression has been important in communicating Sámi sovereignty in these actions, art has also been central in bringing people together across differences (Danbolt et al. 2024). In addition, these examples of collective action in Sápmi cannot be disassociated from Indigenous political movements across the Arctic, which have brought attention to the importance of language and culture revitalization, self-determination, community and mental health, resource extraction, "green energy" infrastructure installations, and climate change. Land protest campaigns and Truth and Reconciliation Commissions (TRCs) in Canada, Greenland, Norway, and Finland (in Sweden, the process is called the Truth Commission) have emerged alongside enhanced exposure for and attention to Indigenous artistic practice in the Arctic, where many artists and political activists serve multiple, conjoining, and intersecting roles.

As we will explore in more detail shortly, there is a paradox at play here, represented by the international success of Sámi art versus the reluctance of national authorities to safeguard the land on which Indigenous art and artists depend and relate. For example, Norway's TRC was appointed in June 2018 and submitted its report to the Norwegian parliament in June 2023. At the same time as the TRC was underway, the grand chamber of the Norwegian Supreme Court found that the construction of the Fosen and Roa windmill park in Norwegian Sápmi violated United Nations Human Rights Article 27, which protects against interference in Indigenous Peoples' areas. Activists occupied the Norwegian Ministry of Petroleum and Energy in Oslove (Oslo), demanding that the government act upon the Supreme Court decision. This became the starting point for a recent wave of protests against the Norwegian government's appropriation of Sámi land, with strong parallels to the Alta dam protests of the late 1970s. Now, as then, artists were central to these protests. The work of the Swedish Truth Commission was put in jeopardy in 2024, when eight of the members had resigned, including the artist Britta Marakatt-Labba. Meanwhile, several legal issues pertaining to reindeer-herding rights, extractive resource generation, logging, and fishery access are pending judicial resolution; artists have documented these matters in ongoing efforts to raise public awareness and attention.

The Global Circulation of Indigenous Arctic Art in the Twenty-First Century

Contemporary Sámi artists play leading roles in the vital exchange of artistic work and in network and capacity building that have furthered the integration of Arctic Indigenous art into global market circulation, highlighting the connection and kinship between land and artistic practice. Though not necessarily explicitly political, these activities strengthen Indigenous networks of collaboration through which culture and artistic revitalization take on expanded societal roles, often with direct reference to land-use politics. The National Gallery of Canada's 2013 exhibition *Sakahán: International Indigenous Art* exemplified Arctic capacity-building and connectivity work, which subsequently generated significant collaborations between Indigenous artists globally. The contributions of Yukon-born curator Candice Hopkins (Carcross/Tagish First Nation) over the past two decades cannot be overestimated in this regard. Her internationally oriented focus advances networks of Indigenous practitioners and has contributed to the accelerated circulation of Sámi art by, for example, Keviselie/Hans Ragnar Mathiesen and Britta Marakatt-Labba, both represented at the international art show Documenta 14 in 2017, and both calling attention to colonialism and land use in Sápmi through their works and statements in that international context. For example, Marakatt-Labba's embroidery displayed at Documenta 14 includes what curators Carola Grahn and Maria Ragnestam describe as "a series of works addressing climate change," which calls attention to "the fact that nature is not an infinite resource. [Marakatt-Labba] depicts a landscape that is rebelling. Human desires have torn down the forest that used to provide shelter from the wind, such as the water out of the ground through its roots, and keep trees from falling" (Grahn and Ragnestam 2020, 62). Documenta 14 is generally seen as the starting point for the acceleration of mainstream attention to Arctic and Sámi art on the international circuit. Hopkins also brought the Igloolik-based Isuma collective to the Canadian

Pavilion at the Venice Biennale in 2017. In her role as artistic director of the Forge, Hopkins has featured work by Arctic Indigenous artists Sonya Kelliher-Combs (Iñupiaq and Athabascan), among others. Similarly, Taqralik Partridge's (Inuk) work over the past number of years has expanded Arctic-Indigenous curation at the Nordic Lab at the SAW Gallery in Ottawa, with several exhibitions featuring Arctic Indigenous artists. The global circulation of Arctic Indigenous art is indeed accelerating, with Tate Modern in London announcing in 2024 the creation of a special fund to purchase Inuit and Sámi art (Solomon 2024). Scandinavian art museums are increasingly featuring Arctic Indigenous artists. Examples include a major exhibition at Sven-Harrys Art Museum in Stockholm in 2020–21 called *Bakom hörnet vindens jojk* ['Around the Corner, the Wind's Yoik'], Marakatt-Labbas's *Moving the Needle* at the Norwegian National Art Museum 2024, and Jessie Kleeman's *Running Time* at Denmark's National Gallery in 2023. The Kleeman exhibition is the first time this Danish state institution has featured a Greenlandic Inuit artist in a solo show. In addition, Winnipeg Art Gallery-Qaumajuq hosted a major retrospective called *Inuit Sanaugangit: Art Across Time* that featured four hundred works in 2023–24.

In tandem with these efforts, several pan-Arctic collaborative curatorial efforts are underway or have recently been completed. Some of the better-known international group exhibitions include the Sámi Pavilion at the Venice Biennale (2022), the *Arctic Amazon* exhibition in Toronto (2022–23), and the *Arctic Highways* (2022–25) exhibition traveling across North America, Europe, South Africa, and Sápmi. These initiatives highlight the power of ongoing artistic collaboration, as well as the significance of public and private funding coming together to support the presentation of these works to a global audience. Further, they illustrate the ways in which circulation through both nonprofit and commercial contexts showcases a growing number of practitioners whose works are closely connected to ongoing land determination and land rights matters in Sápmi and beyond.

At the same time, Petra Laiti argues, a need remains to develop better Sámi cultural support systems to ensure that Sámi do not need to spend time explaining, translating, and legitimizing their work to majoritarian cultural agents and can instead spend time and energy to "think more deeply about what we want, not just what we absolutely need" (2024, 189). Given the de facto low institutional support structures for Sámi art in the Nordic nation states, community-organized festivals in Sápmi have been vital in sustaining, encouraging, and promoting artistic expression and experimentation (see MacKenzie and Stenport 2023). Sámi art and music festivals continue to be supportive venues for artistic works that address colonial dynamics in relation to land, and spaces for artists to collectively research artistic sovereignty and explore connections between artistic practice and self-determination movements (Danbolt et al. 2024). The importance of festivals such as the Easter Festival in Guovdageaidnu, and the summer festivals Riddu Riđđu in Manndalen and Márkomeannu in Skånland cannot be overstated, since these and other grassroots initiatives have, for decades, been some of the most important artistic, social, and economic infrastructures in the development of the transnational field of Sámi art (Danbolt et al. 2024).

Relevant locally and globally intersecting parallel developments in the film and media industry include the ImagineNative Indigenous Film Festival in Toronto/Tkaronto, the annual Skábmagovat film festival in Inari/Aanaar, the programs and conferences organized by the International Sámi Film Institute in Guovdageaidnu, the Sámi Film Festival organized by Scandinavia House in New York City, and the NATIVe film program at the Berlin International Film Festival. In the Sámi context, these efforts foreground ongoing exploration of Sámi ontologies, the importance of land, language revitalization, and Indigenous media.

One of the most salient examples in this vein is the Sámi Pavilion at the Venice Biennale in 2022, curated by Katya García-Antón, Sámi scholar Liisa-Rávná Finbog, and Sámi nature guardian Beaska Niillas. The immersive AR/VR new media installation Árran 360° (2022–), projected in a custom-built *lávvu* and circular screen, debuted at the Biennale. It has since traveled the world, featuring work by Ann Holmgren Aurebekk, Elle Márjá Eira, Marja Helander, Hans Pieski, Siljá Somby, and Liselotte Wajstedt. New works continue to be added. At Bodø2024 European Capital of Culture, ÁRRAN 360° entered a new phase, ÁRRAN 2.0, presenting five new 360-degree films: *Duiddo* by Siljá Somby, *In My Hand* by Marja Helander and Liselotte Wajstedt, *Máilmmittkus* by Hans Pieski and Arttu Nieminen, *OVIAS 2* by Ann Holmgren Aurebekk, and *PCA-TV 270* by Ken Are Bongo and Joar Nango.

These emergent modes of circulation have changed the way Sámi art is understood in a global context. In the remainder of this article, we trace the history behind the emergence of the "Arctic Highway" as a concept first developed by Sámi writer and artist Nils-Aslak Valkeapää. Then we turn, in the first person, to the writing and artistic practice of Sámi artist Tomas Colbengtson, with a focus on art and creative practice within the historiography of Sámi activism. We conclude with a reflection on examples of the land determination activism works by Sámi women visual artists whose works have circulated through these exhibitions, with a focus on Marja Helander and Paulina Feodoroff.

FIGURE 1. The opening of Árran 360° in Venice in 2022. Photo courtesy of the International Sámi Film Institute.

Nils-Aslak Valkeapää's Arctic Highway Concept

Examination of the multidisciplinary, multimodal art of Nils-Aslak Valkeapää (1943–2001) showcases how Northern circumpolar peoples have always exchanged ideas of culture and livelihood practices.[2] Valkeapää had just started working on a book project with a preliminary title "The Arctic Highway" when he passed away in November 2001. He had been entertaining the idea of the cultural highway for most of his career. Only late in life did he find the time to manifest his thoughts through writing, photography, and drawing.

The Arctic Highway concept runs through Valkeapää's poetry and accompanying artwork, where motives connect with one another. In form and theme, his poetry expresses and nurtures affinity with the Inuit in Greenland and the Native Americans of the North American prairie, as evident in the collections *Ruoktu Váimmus* (*Trekways of the Wind*, 1985) and *Eanni, eannážan* (*The Earth, My Mother*, 2001). At the time of his death, Valkeapää left behind one unfinished manuscript: "Eaidanas ealli" [The Withdrawn One, or the animal that keeps itself a bit away from the rest of the herd] and a brief note about his planned next project, "The Arctic Highway," a loosely designed conceptual work. The conjoining idea for both is the unity of the circumpolar region. "Eaidanas ealli" explains how Sámi viewed the world, building on Valkeapää's understanding of sources he had read as well as what he had reflected on based on his upbringing and conversations with Elders and knowledge-holders.

In related ways, "The Arctic Highway" was intended to highlight cultural connections across the circumpolar regions and to emphasize cross-geographical similarities in Indigenous rock art and carvings. These included photographs provided to Valkeapää by friends, one of whom had photographed carvings in the Peterborough area (125 km north of Toronto, Canada); another who gifted him two photographs taken by an American acquaintance, who had photographed circle-like figures carved into rocks in the coastal area of southern Alaska. The published work *Ruoktu vaimmus* includes examples of rock art symbols from Siberia as well as figures reminiscent of ancient rock drawings from the Southwestern regions of the United States. In a personal conversation with Harald Gaski, Valkeapää explained that he understood the drawings to be mental maps: showing what ancient peoples cared about and believed in, just as they functioned as means of communication between people and the powers they believed in. Therefore, he wanted to get to know the cultures that had traveled along what he conceptualized as an Arctic Highway. Unfortunately, when Valkeapää passed away in 2001, there were only a few sketches of the planned project, in addition to the idea being shared with his publisher and collaborators through conversations.

Valkeapää believed that these rock art representations and carvings demonstrated a common Northern Sámi symbolism, a theory he wanted to develop in "Arctic Highway." He saw many similarities across the circumpolar region, and his ideas focused on how nature forms beliefs and artistic practice, and how people manage, survive, and perceive the world. Even though there might not have been close connections between all the Northern peoples, at least the neighboring tribes knew one another and learned from one another. Ideas and thoughts had traveled and influenced ways of thinking, believing, and managing life. These sets of interchanges form the basis of Valkeapää's concept of the Arctic Highway. They also inform the ideas behind the travel exhibition *Arctic Highways*.

Sápmi Salasta and Arctic Highways

Sápmi Salasta (Sápmi Omfamnar/Sápmi Embraces) is an international residency program for Indigenous artists, started in 2018 at the initiative of Sámi artist Tomas Colbengtson and collaborators. Hosted by the Sámi

FIGURE 2. Founders of Sápmi Salasta. From left to right: Koji Yuki, Louise Fontain, Tomas Colbengtson, Britta Marakatt-Labba, Elisabeth Heilmann Blind, Matti Aikio, Lena Stenberg. Photo by Private.

cultural center Aejlies in Tärna/Dearna (Storuman) and funded by philanthropist Jan Wejdmar, the residency stems from an Indigenous Conference in 2017 and the Dellie Maa artist and film festival. Sápmi Salasta has hosted artists such as Colbengtson (Sámi), Julie Edel Hardenberg (Kalaaleq), and Sonya Kelliher-Combs (Inupiaq and Athabascan). One of the outcomes of this artist residency is the touring program *Arctic Highways*, which draws in part on the pan-Arctic conceptual frame imagined by Nils-Aslak Valkeapää.

Tomas Colbengtson on Sámi History and the Global Arctic Highways Exhibition

The Southern Sámi language is my mother tongue, which I partially lost during my schooling at the Skytteanska nomad school in Tärnaby due to a language ban. The Skytte school was the first nomadic school for Sámi children. It was established in Sweden in 1632. The purpose of the school was mainly to Christianize and transform the Sámi into Swedes.

Sámi Lars Hætta and Anders Bær wrote the book *Mui'talusat cáliiga* [Accounts of the conditions in Kautokeino before 1850] (2019) in captivity in Oslo in 1860. Both participated in the first organized rebellion against colonization in 1852 in Guovdageaidnu; the rebellion was crushed by Norway with the help of other Sámi. In the end, Hætta and Bær's writings had greater significance for the Sámi struggle than the rebellion itself. Since then, art and literature have become the Sámi's weapons and tools in the fight for their lost land and rights.

As Indigenous people, the general public too often expects individuals to be carriers of knowledge and to explain the entire history of their people in order to defend their existence and right to land. The Sámi people have been colonized for centuries. We lost much of our culture and land. For this reason, there is a knowledge gap in building Sámi cultural organizations, in addressing Sámi art today, and in understanding who the artists are. The Sámi artists' union *SDS Sámi Dáiddačehpiid searvi* (SDS) was founded in 1978 in Áillohaš' (Nils-Aslak Valkeapää] home in Finland. Today it is based in Kárášjohka/Karasjok, Norway, with union members living in Norway, Sweden and Finland. SDS has provided essential support for Sámi artists to develop their art.

A great deal of research has been done on the Sámi from non-Sámi perspectives, using Western academic methods. The Sámi were barred from higher education because the state policy held that Sámi people were primitive and wild (see Lantto 2012). Sámi were forced to relocate by state decree until 1937; the state dictated that reindeer herders were to live only in traditional huts. The common perception, circulated by the State Institute of Racial Biology (1922—1958), was that the Sámi did not create "art" but crafts. Therefore, for better or worse, Sámi visual art has been undervalued and has not been considered "real" art. At the same time, the artists and their art have raised awareness of Indigenous issues in Sweden and internationally.

Sweden, to date, lacks pure Sámi artists' associations. Some initiatives are in the initial phase, such as the Indigenous residence Sápmi Salasta. *Arctic Highways* is a branch of this initiative. The exhibition *Arctic Highways* was created because of the need to support Indigenous artists and to make visible Indigenous people in the Arctic region.[3] The artworks in *Arctic Highways* comment on and formulate the artists' vital questions about who we are, what we have left, what we may have lost, and our common future.[4] Our efforts to find funding for *Arctic Highways* and the Indigenous nomadic art residencies have included private and state support. Initially, we had a problem convincing the Swedish cultural bureaucracy that Sámi organizations could manage the financing and didn't need to be overseen by Swedish cultural organizations. After six decades of work, we have been able to inaugurate the Sámi culture center Aejlies [Holy and Wellbeing] in Dearna/Tärnaby, where Sápmi Salasta now resides.

An underlying principle is to avoid copying existing colonial structures in an Indigenous cultural center and, through this process, acquire knowledge of Sámi culture from a Sámi perspective. Touring *Arctic Highways* in the USA and Canada, meeting artists and audiences, helps us learn together.

The Sápmie Art of Tomas Colbengtson (2021)

Sápmie 2021 (2021) is a road sign installation by Tomas Colbengtson, which has been exhibited in numerous locations around Scandinavia, including in *Arctic Highways*, paralleling and defamiliarizing the defacement of Sámi-language town names on road signs in Sweden and Norway. The photo at the top left above shows the sign in front of Sweden's parliament building (Riksdagshuset); the one to the top right shows the sign in front of Stuhkie/ Stockholm City Hall (Stadshuset) with a Sápmi flag in the background. Four other pieces by the artist are also included in the *Arctic Highways* exhibition: *Giela dájva* (Language Landscape, 2021), *Residential School* (2021), *The Children of the Sun* (installation with a Sámi drum), and *Defaced* (2021). *Sápmie 2021* illustrates the political manifestation of Colbengtson's artwork, emphasizing the transnational, cross-border, and multilingual aspects of Sámi culture and society across the Nordic region, pointing to the absence of consistent recognition of the Sápmi region, Sámi history, and ongoing efforts at self-determination that are part of contemporary Sámi experience.

As displayed in the *Arctic Highways* exhibition, *Sápmie 2021* and *Defaced* (a similar road sign with Black Lives Matter written upon it) are, as the latter title demonstrates, "defaced," in this instance, with splatters of pink paint. This defacement suggests how colonial cultures erase and eradicate both the culture and lives of equity-seeking peoples, along with the solidarity that is needed to wipe away this defacement in a global context. As Colbengtson notes, the splatter effect is also a riposte to "Jackson Pollack's appropriation of Indigenous cultures, raising awareness about such practices and their implications" (Röder 2023, 210). Further, the use of road signs in a traveling exhibition accentuates the way in which dominant cultures set up their own routes, circulations, and highways that others need to follow. In contrast, both Valkeapää's concept of the Arctic Highway and the traveling exhibition *Arctic Highways* seek to trace new routes of knowledge, exchange, understanding, and solidarity.

The works *Residential School* (middle on the wall in the photo above), *Giela dájva* (Language Landscape, to the right on the wall) and *The Children of the Sun* (installation in the foreground) illustrate many of the points Colbengtson makes about his work. In the catalog's artist statement about these pieces, Colbengtson writes: "I, [. . .] suddenly saw, with complete clarity,

FIGURE 3. Photo montage about the *Sápmie 2021* project featuring the artist to the bottom right. Photos by Galleri Helle Knudsen, Tomas Colbengtson, and Dan Jåma.

the total destruction of Sámi lives caused by the relentless politics of the Swedish state. The authorities' policies have been so devastating that they almost beg the question of whether we are even deemed human. All of us in Sápmi carry with us similar wounds, and the role of art is to render visible the blind spots, and even vast islands of white in our collective consciousness" (Colbengtson, 2022, 20). The three works speak to Colbengtson's artistic manifesto, remediating colonial images through superimposition of Sámi

FIGURE 4. *Arctic Highways* at Scandinavia House in New York City, May 2023. Photo by Scott MacKenzie.

language and processes of defamiliarization. *The Children of the Sun* takes a different approach, remediating a Sámi drum with images of Sámi community and political leaders from the early 1920s. By placing a brass ring on the drum canvas and using an electric motor, the drum vibrates, conceptually bringing together the sounds of both Indigenous music and the voices of earlier Sámi activists that echo through history. In total, Colbengtson's pieces in the *Arctic Highways* exhibition signal the importance of artist collectives and of traveling Indigenous art shows for knowledge mobilization among Sámi as well as for foregrounding the connections among Indigenous circumpolar peoples and making those visible through the exhibition.

Reflections from Marja Helander in an Interview with Anna Stenport: Juxtapositions of Aesthetics and Environments

The work of Sámi visual artist, filmmaker, and photographer Marja Helander has been increasingly circulating in Arctic Indigenous exhibitions, including as a part of *Arctic Highways*; her short films have also been screened at ImagineNative, Sundance, and included in the *Arran 360* 1.0 and 2.0 iterations.

Helander has also had several solo exhibitions in Finland and the Nordic region and was featured in a major Sámi art exhibition at Sven-Harrys Konstmuseum in Stockholm in 2020–21. At Sven-Harrys, her work was described by the curators as "striking a delicate balance between unconventionally beautiful, enticing landscapes and political statements, [. . . where] postcolonial landscapes [. . . and . . .] the world of industry [. . . provoke] a darker, more destructive quality" (Grahn and Ragnestam 2020, 76). Her work is notable for its aesthetic and stylistic juxtapositions, derived perhaps in part from her background as a commercial photographer, working across portraiture, furniture design, fashion, and airline industries, while simultaneously deepening her creative inquiry and artistic practice. Quotidian household objects (a rubber glove; a children's trampoline); mainstream locations (a gas station; a shopping center); and practices that cut across Sámi and Nordic culture (an everyday get together over coffee or a refined ballet performance) are set against landscapes that may initially look "pristine," but are nearly always marked by industrialization, resource extraction, colonial or state presence, and the eradication of Sámi land-use and land-access.

In a recent interview with Anna Stenport, Helander discusses how her artistic practice has evolved from an early interest in rediscovery of her Sámi identity, evident in the photography series *Sukupolvet* (The Generations, 1991–94), toward single- and multichannel media art that leverages comedy and absurdism to intervene in contemporary political discourse: "I have always been fascinated by object incongruity. There should be a surprise moment and inspiration from everyday life. Ohcejohka/Utsjoki is my family home, but I keep driving here from Helsset/Helsinki. I want my work to address both a traditional Sámi way of life in contrast with the Nordic Majority society. I transitioned from mostly still photography in 2012 to performance video art to be able to tell a fuller story. And that I could be present, as an actor, in that story" (Stenport 2024). Her breakthrough video work *Trambo* (2014) provides an illustrative example of that "fuller story." Helander, dressed in Sámi *gákti,* pushes a suburban backyard trampoline, one seen in innumerable yards along the route from Helsinki to Utsjoki, across a snowy northern landscape marked by power lines, to convey a sense of imprisonment, by which, "perhaps also Sámi were constricted" (Stenport 2024) by such consumer objects. Similar juxtapositions guide the short film *Birds in the Earth* (*Eatnanvuloš lottit,* Finland, 2018), which screened at Sundance in 2019. In it, two young Sámi ballet dancers perform across Sápmi landscapes—whether an open mountain environment or by a wintry gas station—and in front of the parliament buildings in Helsinki, staging both a quiet protest and a powerful affirmation.

FIGURE 5. Marja Helander filming *Birds in the Earth* (*Eatnanvuloš lottit,* Finland, 2018). Framegrab from publicity video *Short Competition: Birds in the Earth* (2019) by the Sundance Institute, https://www.youtube.com/watch?v=chpO7hE8oXU.

FIGURE 6. *Birds in the Earth* (Marja Helander, *Eatnanvuloš lottit,* Finland, 2018).

A representative aspect of Helander's long career has involved extensive travel and visual documentation across Sápmi, from the Western Fjords to the Arctic Ocean, to the mining operations of Giron/Kiruna and the Guoládat/Kola Peninsula, as well as to modern Helsinki. As protests against public funding and support for mining operations in Aitik, Giron, and Gallok on the Swedish side of Sápmi have increased, Helander's recent suite of photography documenting the LKAB mine focuses on environmental degradation, while inserting a witnessing subject (the photographer, with back turned to the camera), who is observing the environmental destruction, perhaps suggesting both compliance and protest.

A correlate to that work is the landscape photography sequence shot around Russia's apatite mines on the Kola peninsula, documenting environmental degradation (see also Ollila 2024). Many of the images suggestively overlay examples of Helander's own collections of Kola peninsula herbs and flowers alongside reproductions of specimens from her own father's herbarium, collected while he attended school in Finland. These images, categorized by juxtapositions, present a different view of Sápmi—far from the pristine. They are also historical documents, given the current near impossibility of travel across the Russian border for Sámi (and others), and highlight the ongoing impact of superimposed national borders in eastern Sápmi, which separated the Skólt Sámi from their land during multiple relocations (see Lehtola 2000; Skolt 2018). In her characteristic style, Herlander's photographs are evocative, haunting, and layered, where artistic practice, aesthetics, and land interweave.

FIGURE 7. Marja Helander. *Hidden*. 2018. Kiruna, Sweden.

FIGURE 8. Marja Helander. *At the Heart of the Earth*. 2018. Kirovsk. Russia.

Helander's film *Dolastallat* (*To Have a Campfire*, 2016) is another example of juxtaposition, irony, and comedy, where land connections are paramount. It is shot in a derelict Stalin-era structure in Kirovsk, near Luyavvr/Lovozero, home of the largest Sámi community in Russia. Featuring Helander in *gákti* preparing a communal coffee event, she remarks on the image-theme juxtaposition: "I wanted to have a film with a bear. At the same time, having coffee is a very Sámi thing. The building, in ruins, was from the Stalin era, and it used to be the cultural palace. When Perestroika came, there was no money anymore to take care of the building. I wanted to show the beauty and degradation of the area, with the bear present as a reminder of the connection to Sámi myth" (Stenport 2024). Helander's works connect Sámi epistemology to geopolitics and the present political situation in Sápmi, while the highly aestheticized juxtaposition of contemporary and every day with landscape and tradition, open new opportunities for stories of global resonance. While contemporary environments connect to Sámi current culture and history, Helander's distinctive art is increasingly circulating internationally through *Arctic Highways,* the Venice Biennale, and other venues. "It is time now to work toward an independent exhibition," she confirms, "one that bridges my interest in telling Sámi stories to new audiences" (Stenport 2024).

The Sámi Pavilion at the Venice Biennale

The year 2022 was a pivotal period for the Nordic Pavilion in Venice due to its transformation into the Sámi Pavilion. The exhibition was curated by García-Antón, Finbog, and Beaska Niillas and coordinated by the Office for Contemporary Art Norway (OCA). The project represented a "sovereign call" (Finbog and García-Antón, 2022) for Sápmi by the invited artists Pauliina Feodoroff, Máret Ánne Sara, and Anders Sunna, and revolved around three elements: Sámi "transgenerational relations, holistic knowledge and learning, and spiritual perspectives" (Finbog et al. 2022). This was a significant moment for Sámi art as it took over the Nordic Pavilion, and for the Norwegian Truth and Reconciliation Commission's report, which documented how the Norwegian state's colonial assimilation policies exclude Sámi art and cultural expression from the public domain (Sannhets- og forsoningskommisjonen 2023). The institutional marginalization of Sámi art and culture has meant that the Sámi people "have not had the same opportunities to have life experiences, such as grief, pain, and experiences of loss acknowledged, articulated, [and] processed in public" (Sannhets- og forsoningskommisjonen 2023, 527; authors' translation). As the commission documents assert, Sámi art did not belong in mainstream Norwegian society and was thereby rendered invisible.

For Sámi society, the Venice Biennale was seen as a historical moment and a step toward making Sámi art present at all national art institutions and galleries (Sametinget 2022). Not only was Sámi art present through the Sámi pavilion: Sámi artists Britta Marakatt-Labba and Aage Gaup's art was curated in the general Biennale exhibition as part of the Biennale main program. In addition, *Aabaakwad*—the annual Indigenous-led conversation on Indigenous art founded and directed by Wanda Nanibush (Anishinaabe) for those who create, curate, and write—had its own venue and program through the week of the Sámi Pavilion's opening, showcasing a dynamic dialogue examining themes, materials, and experiences in Indigenous art practice globally.

Sámi artists and Elders, regarded as philosophers, played a central role at the Biennale. Helen Verran argues that art museums, galleries, and biennales can serve as institutions where philosophies are expressed. She suggests that the philosophies of institutions, shaped by different times and places, influence the creation of objects that ultimately appear in exhibitions. These objects, in turn, reflect the explicit philosophy of the art institution (Verran 2019). Verran's arguments raise important questions about what happens when Sámi philosophies of art—along with the processes behind the creation of art objects—are juxtaposed with the global art philosophies of the Biennale and how this interaction influences Sámi perspectives on the interconnectedness of land, traditional knowledge, memories, and resistance.

Paulina Feodoroff's Matriarchy (2022): Land, Trauma, Mimicry

The performance of Feodoroff's multimedia work *Matriarchy* was central to the Sámi exhibition at the Biennale. *Matriarchy* is a collective performance in three parts, which centers on matriarchal values of care, life as a gift, interconnection as a mode of existence, and healing as a return to a world of kinship between people, land, waters and spirits, as Feodoroff argues:

> Finland has treated the ancestral land we have lived in for centuries as their natural resource to exploit and sell piece by piece to any market that needs it. Sámi forests are logged for toilet paper. I have spent my life documenting all the losses on multiple levels, but now it's vital to focus on what we still have and how to make it stronger. When the earth is transforming, life needs havens and time to adapt. My work proposes ways to protect the last remaining old growth forests and let the logged areas have a time to heal. Our message is, please do not buy our land, buy our art instead. (OCA 2023)

In the first section, titled "First Contact," the performance contrasts colonized and Indigenous gesturality. Feodoroff highlights that Indigenous people and settlers never greeted each other with enough respect, care, and love. This generated epistemic violence that continues to be embedded in asymmetric relations. Part 2, "Auction," focuses on how the Sámi landscapes and all living memories, stories and nonhumans that are alive on and in that land are "auctioned off." Living landscapes, as human bodies, are violently transformed into commercial resources for sale. In Part 3, "Matriarchy," the effects of colonialism on the Indigenous female body are expressed as resistance and as a means of restoring sovereignty in Sápmi.

A startling moment for the audience in "First Contact" is the introduction of black birds that embody grief, fear, and rage, but also a sense of hope. The black crows embody isolation in the guise of a dancer clad in black, with outstretched wings and latex-covered high heels, who moves through the pavilion, evoking the trauma of colonialism and calling for healing. In the work, memory, violence, and trauma all coexist, and for many in the audience, it was embodied in the Sámi pavilion through "First Contact." Drawing on Homi Bhabha's concept of mimicry, Feodoroff exemplifies how Indigenous artists engage with mimicry of the world. In Bhabha's use, mimicry repeats rather than re-represents colonial mimicry, and within colonial discourse, mimicry is at once resemblance and menace (2019). This ambivalence contains the seeds of disruption of colonial authority.

The crow, both complex and contradictory, has also been used as a medium to mimic an essence of colonialism by other Sámi artists. It is a throughline in, for example, Marakatt-Labba's embroidery *The Garjját* (The Crows,1981) and in the massive tapestry *Historjá* (History, 2003–7; see also Røstvik 2023). The Garjá [crow] has become iconic not only for the Sámi but also for other Indigenous Peoples. "The picture came to me in Máze during the Áltá conflict," Marakatt-Labba (one of the members of the Máze collective) shared in an interview with Susanne Hætta (2022). This demonstrates the throughlines of artistic practice in Sápmi, which resonates with Persen's remarks earlier in this article. In Marakatt-Labba's depiction, the flying crows transform into police officers as they land, confronting and arresting Indigenous land protectors and their allies. Feodoroff's *Matriarchy* highlights that the crows continue to claim Indigenous land, challenging ongoing colonial authority and uniting us in the recognition of their presence and the resistance necessary for the survival of both the land and Sámi ways of knowing and caring for it.

The year following the Venice Biennale, the police (the garjját/crows) returned at night as a nemesis in the Sámi cultural imaginary to forcibly remove the Sámi demonstrators and their allies occupying the Norwegian Ministry of Petroleum and Energy in Oslo as part of the protests against the construction of the Fosen and Roa windmill park. Several activists refused to pay the fine and were called into court. In April 2024 the Oslo County Court ruled that the order to end their demonstration—that is, the police decision to physically carry demonstrators out of the ministry—and the subsequent imposed fine, violated their rights to demonstrate under the Norwegian constitution. For many Sámi, this development highlighted the long-standing connections between land and art (Danbolt et al., 2024). The prosecution, however, appealed the verdict all the way to the Supreme Court, where the protestors were finally acquitted.

Conclusion

Enhanced recognition of Greenlandic Inuit and Sámi art in the Nordic nation-states (Denmark, Finland, Norway, Sweden) has come only recently, after major international venues first took note of works by Indigenous artists from the circumpolar north. Curatorial efforts, however, often continue to remain confined within the traditional framework of art exhibitions, focusing on individual artists. However, increasingly, Sámi artists resist such a narrow view of how art, circulation, and exhibitions should converge, especially in relation to land activism. Notably, at the Venice Biennale, in addition to other venues featuring Sámi or Indigenous curators, the community and land from which their art emerges become more prominent. These are intentionally formulated to make the voice of nature appear stronger and convey the interests of many Sámi artists to listen to these voices and, through art, promote the safeguarding of land, and make that political stance more visible both to other Indigenous groups and to the majority society of the nation-state. In addition, in these Indigenous-led exhibitions and films, there is a growing tendency for Sámi collectives (and their allies) to be physically present, just as many celebrate Elders as Ofelaš/Pathfinders in Sámi artistic practices.

These exhibitions, hosted by major art institutions (some of them connected to a long history of colonial subjugation of Indigenous artistic practice), demonstrate the power of art to address societal change and to transform these exhibition spaces in the process. Moreover, the circulation and exhibition of global circumpolar Indigenous art points to the creation of new, independent highways, pathways and roots for creative expression, land activism, political resistance, and acts of Indigenous resurgence. These touring programs allow for new sites to be created that are distinct from spaces that simply mount individual works traveling through various art networks. The creation of Indigenous and Sámi spaces outside Sápmi creates new cartographies to understand politics and artistic practices related to the land. This demonstrates not only the specificity of Sámi art and politics but their intersection with global concerns about the relationship between Indigenous rights, land as a cultural (and not simply geographic) space, and new, shared, and contrasting highways of Indigenous knowledge.

TOMAS COLBENGTSON is a Sámi artist and curator. Tomas has an MFA in fine arts from Konstfack University College of Art Craft and Design. Besides his artistic work, Colbengtson has worked as a lecturer in Fine Printmaking at Konstfack between 2012 and 2020 and as artist in residence at KTH Royal institute of technology Stockholm, 1998–2008. Colbengtson has been working as Indigenous curator since 2016. In 2018 he initiated the art residence for Indigenous artists: *Sápmi salasta* and the 2020 Indigenous art exhibition *Arctic Highways*. Tomas has exhibited in twenty-three countries and is represented in the British Museum, the New National Museum Oslo, and the Norwegian Sámi Parliament, Norway. Colbengtson is the 2024 recipient of Queen Sonjas Print Award.

HARALD GASKI is professor in Sámi literature at Sámi allaskuvla / Sámi University of Applied Sciences in Norway. Gaski is also an author and editor. His research specializes in Sámi oral and written culture, traditional values, and aesthetics in addition to Indigenous critical studies.

BRITT KRAMVIG works as professor at UiT The Arctic University of Norway. She is an interdisciplinary scholar interested in Sámi landscapes, storytelling, archives, and memories. Britt is a descendant of the sea-Sámi in Orjješ-Ráisa /Sørreisa that suffered under colonialism, and a scholar who reclaims and recalls her Sámi heritage. Kramvig has engaged with the concept of landscape through storytelling throughout her academic career, including her work on Sámi art, land- and soundscape and (de) colonialism, as well as work on the Arctic sea- and soundscape, including collaboration with world-renowned sound artists and international academic networks. She recently coedited the volume *Searvedoaibma: Art and Social Communities in Sápmi* (with Mathias Danbolt and Christina Hætta), published by Sámi Allaskuvla in 2024. Her scholarship has been published in journals such as *Polar Record, Nytt Norsk Tidsskrift,* and *Environmental Research Letters.*

ANNA STENPORT holds a Ph.D. from the University of California, Berkeley, and is the University of Georgia Foundation Professor of Arts and Sciences, a professor of communication studies, and dean of the Franklin College of Arts and Sciences at the University of Georgia. She is coauthor of *New Arctic Cinemas: Media Sovereignty and the Climate Crisis* (2023; with Scott MacKenzie) and co-editor of *Nordic Film Cultures and Cinemas of Elsewhere* (2019; with Arne Lunde); *Arctic Cinemas and the Documentary Ethos* (2019; with Lilya Kaganovsky and Scott MacKenzie); and *Films on Ice: Cinemas of the Arctic* (2015; with Scott MacKenzie).

SCOTT MACKENZIE is professor in the Department of Film and Media, Queen's University, currently serving as Vice Dean of the Faculty of Arts and Science. His most recent books include: *Films on Ice: Cinemas of the Arctic* (2014; with Anna Stenport); *Arctic Environmental Modernities: From the Age of Polar Exploration to the Era of the Anthropocene* (2017; with Lill-Ann Körber and Anna Stenport); *Arctic Cinemas and the Documentary Ethos* (2019; with Lilya Kaganovsky and Anna Stenport); *Process Cinema: Handmade Film in the Digital Age* (2019; with Janine Marchessault); *Mapping the Rockumentary: Images of Sound and Fury* (2021; with Gunnar Iversen); and *New Arctic Cinemas: Media Sovereignty and the Climate Crisis* (2023; with Anna Stenport).

References

Allen, Chadwick. 2012. *Trans-indigenous: Methodologies for Global Native Literary Studies.* University of Minnesota Press.

Bhabha, Homi. 2019. "Of Mimicry and Man: The Ambivalence of Colonial Discourse." In *Tensions of Empire*, 152–60. University of California Press.

Colbengtson, Tomas. 2022. "*Dájvan*—The Home Landscape." In *Arctic Highways*, edited by Gunvor Guttorm and Yvonne Rock, 20. Bokförlaget Korpen.

Dáiddadállu. n.d. *Dáiddadállu.* https://www.daiddadallu.com/en. Accessed December 12, 2024.

Danbolt, Matthias, Britt Kramvig, and Christina Hætta. 2024. *Searvedoaibma: Art and Social Communities in Sápmi.* Sámi allaskuvla/Sámi University of Applied Sciences.

Farrell-Racette, Sherry. 2008. "My Grandmothers Loved to Trade: The Indigenization of European Trade Goods in Historic and Contemporary Canada." *Journal of Museum Ethnography* 20: 69–81.

Finbog, Liisa-Rávná, and Katya García-Antón eds. 2022. *Čatnosat: the Sámi Pavilion, Indigenous Art, Knowledge and Sovereignty.* Office for Contemporary Art Norway (OCA).

Finbog, Liisa-Rávná. 2023. *It Speaks to You: Making Kin of People, Duodji and Stories in Sámi Museums.* DIO Press.

Gaski, Harald. 2020. "The Arctic Highway—Some Congenial Thoughts on Nils-Aslak Valkeapää's Artwork and Endeavors." *Káataloga/Catalogue Nils-Aslak Valkeapää /Áillohaš.* Henie Onstad and Nordnorsk kunstmuseum. 71–78.

———. 2022. "Nils-Aslak Valkeapää and The Arctic Highways." In *Arctic Highways*, eds. Gunvor Guttorm and Yvonne Rock. Mötesplats Granö: Bokförlaget Korpen. 90–97.

Grahn, Carola, and Maria Ragnestam, eds. 2020. *Bakom Hörnet Vindens Joik.* Exhibition catalogue. Sven-Harrys Konstmuseum.

Grahn, Carola, and Sigbjørn Skåden, eds. 2016. *Samisk Vrede.* Special Issue of *Hjärnkontoret.*

Guttorm, Guvnor, and Yvonne Rock, eds. 2022. *Arctic Highways: Unbounded Indigenous People.* Bokförlaget Korpen.

Hætta, Lars, and Anders Bær. [1860] 2019. *Mui'talusat cáliiga.* Oslo: Orkana Akademisk.

Hætta, Susanne. 2022. "The Crows Take Everything." *Kunstkritikk/Nordic Art Review.* 4 November. https://kunstkritikk.com/the-crows-take-everything/.

Kuokkanen, Rauna. 2021. "Ellos Deatnu and Post-State Indigenous Feminist Sovereignty." In *Routledge Handbook of Critical Indigenous Studies,* edited by Brendan Hokowhitu, Aileen Moreton-Robinson, Linda Tuhiwai-Smith, Chris Andersen and Steve Larkin, 310–323. Routledge.

Kuhn, Gabriel. 2020. *Liberating Sápmi: Indigenous Resistance in Europe's Far North.* PM Press.

Laiti, Petra. 2024. "All the Things We Could Do." In *Searvedoaibma: Art and Social Communities in Sápmi*, edited by Mathias Danbolt, Britt Kramvig, and Christina Hætta, 186–91. Sámi Allaskuvla/Sámi University of Applied Sciences.

Lantto, Patrik. 2012. *Lappväsendet: tillämpningen av svensk samepolitik 1885–1971.* Umeå universitet Centrum för samisk forskning.

Last, John. 2023. "Finland's Debate over Indigenous Identity and Rights Turns Ugly." *Mongabay.* February 21. https://news.mongabay.com/2023/02/finlands-debate-over-indigenous-identity-and-rights-turns-ugly/.

Lehtola, Veli-Pekka. 2000. "The Idea of the Skolt Sámi Territory in the 1930s." In *Den komplexa kontinenten: staterna på Nordkalotten och samerna i ett historiskt perspektiv,* edited by Peter Sköld and Patrik Lantto, 209–215. Umeå Inst. för Historiska Studier.

———. 2018. "'The Soul Should Have Been Brought Along': The Settlement of Skolt Sami to Inari in 1945–1949." *Journal of Northern Studies* 12, no. 1: 53–72.

MacKenzie, Scott, and Anna Westerstahl Stenport. 2023. *New Arctic Cinemas: Media Sovereignty and the Climate Crisis.* University of California Press.

MacKenzie, Scott, and Anna Stenport. 2024. "Remediating Sápmi: Hypermediacy, the Global Indigenous Arctic, and *Samisk audiovisuell samling* (2018–2023)." *Screen* 65, no. 1: 106–15.

OCA [Office for Contemporary Art Norway]. 2023. "Pauliina Feodoroff" https://oca.no/thesamipavilion/thesamipavilion-pauliinafeodoroff#:~:text=%E2%80%9CIndigenous%20and%20non%2DIndigenous%20peoples,relations%20between%20these%20worlds%20today.

Olilla, Mirkka. 2024. "The Triangle of Extraction in the Kola Peninsula. *The Arctic Institute.* October 1. https://www.thearcticinstitute.org/triangle-extraction-kola-peninsula/.

Persen, Synnøve. 2000. "'White Mainstream Culture': Samisk-norsk, gjensidig påvirkning innen kunstområde?" *2000 pluss minus.* Nordnorsk Kunstnersenter og Nordnorsk Kunstmuseum.

Röder, Sara. 2023. *Tomas Colbengtson: As Told by Light and Shadow/Goh tjoevke kih soejvene soptseste.* Galleri Helle Knudsen.

Røstvik, Camilla Mørk. 2023. "Breaking the Dam: Sámi Art Histories." *Art History,* 46, no. 2: 394–401.

Solomon, Tessa. 2024. "Tate Modern Launches Acquisition Fund for Sámi and Inuit Art." *ARTnews.* April 16.

Sametinget. 2022. "Historisk begivenhet i Veneziabiennalen 2022." https://sametinget.no/aktuelt/historisk-begivenhet-i-veneziabiennalen-2022.20190.aspx.

Sannhets- og forsoningskommisjonen. 2023. *Sannhet og forsoning—grunnlag for et oppgjør med fornorskingspolitikk og urett mot samer, kvener/norskfinner og skogfinner. Rapport till Stortinget fra Sannhets- og Forsoningskommisjonen.* Oslo: Norway, 2023.

Stenport, Anna. 2024. Interview with Marja Helander. November 5.

Valkeapää, Nils-Aslak. 1985. *Ruoktu váimmus.* Guovdageaidnu: DAT.

———. 2001. *Eanni, eannážan.* Guovdageaidnu: DAT.

———. n.d. *Eaidanas ealli* (unpublished). Guovdageaidnu: DAT.

Verran, Helen. 2019. "Generative Ruptures and Moments of Confluence." *Journal of World Philosophies,* 4, no. 2: 55–60.

Notes

1. We thank the Academy of Finland for their generous funding of the Mediated Arctic Geographies project from September 2019 to August 2023 as well as the Finnish-American Research & Innovation Accelerator for their financial support of the Circumpolar Connections project from 2022 to 2024.

2. An earlier version of this sub-section was published in Guvnor Guttorm and Yvonne Rock, eds., *Arctic Highways: Unbounded Indigenous People* by Harald Gaski (2022). It has been revised for publication herein. Nils-Aslak

Valkeapää, was called Áillohaš (his "artist" name for a period), Áilu (the name his family and close friends used), and Nils-Aslak, in accordance with his given name.

3. *Arctic Highways* exhibition tour 2022–2025: House of Sweden, Washington DC, USA; Whitehorse, Yukon, Canada; American Swedish Museum, Chicago, USA; Scandinavian House, New York, USA; National Nordic Museum, Seattle, USA; American Swedish Institute, Minneapolis, USA; MoCNA, Santa Fe, USA; Swedish Institute, Paris, France; Saemien Sijte, Snåsa, Norway; Capetown, South Africa; Granö, Sweden.

4. *Arctic Highways* artists: Britta Marakatt-Labba, Sámi Sweden; Tomas Colbengtson, Sámi Sweden; Sonya Kelliher-Combs, Iñupiaq/Athabascan Alaska; Olof Marsja, Sámi Sweden; Meryl McMaster, Nêhiyaw/Plains Cree Canada; Maureen Gruben, Inuvialuk Canada; Dan Jåma, Sámi Sweden; Matti Aikio, Sámi Finland; Laila Susanne Kuhmunen, Sámi Sweden; Marja Helander; Sámi Finland; Máret Ánne Sara, Sámi Norway; Gunvor Guttorm, Sámi Norway.

NANCY STEVENS *and* ROSEMARY NAGY

Visioning Our Healing

Abstract

While there is an abundance of research on Indigenous healing in the context of residential schools and intergenerational trauma in Canada, very little has been written specifically about community-based sexual assault services providing Indigenous-specific supports for survivors of sexual assault. "Visioning our Healing" begins to remedy this gap through a research partnership with one of the few mainstream sexual assault centers (SAC) in northern Ontario that provides culturally specific supports to Indigenous women, men, and Two-Spirit people. Using photo voice and other forms of storying with Indigenous clients of the SAC, "Visioning our Healing" provides thematic analysis of Indigenous pathways to healing and discusses how the SAC might continue to develop its Indigenous support services. Our report identifies key strengths, promising practices, and organizational challenges in decolonizing community and social services and funding.

INDIGENOUS COMMUNITIES FACE disproportionate rates of sexual violence resulting from colonial policies such as residential schools. Students in residential schools were often subjected to sexual abuse, in many cases resulting in the intergenerational transmission of trauma. A robust, growing body of research exists on Indigenous healing in the context of residential schools and intergenerational trauma in Canada. Yet, very little has been written specifically about community-based sexual assault services providing Indigenous-specific supports for survivors of sexual assault. We redress this gap through "Visioning our Healing," a project and research partnership[1] with one of the few mainstream sexual assault centers (SAC) in northern Ontario, Canada that provides culturally-specific supports to Indigenous women, men, and Two-Spirit people. Using PhotoVoice, "Visioning our Healing" provides a thematic analysis of Indigenous pathways to healing and an exploration of gaps in service provision to suggest ways the SAC can grow its Indigenous support services.[2] We identify key strengths, promising practices, and organizational challenges in relation to decolonizing community and social services and funding. We hope that other organizations might be able to adapt this knowledge, with the guidance of local Indigenous communities, to support the growth of new Indigenous-specific supports.

Throughout this article, we use the term "Indigenous" to refer to individuals from more than one cultural group. Otherwise, we use First Nations' names for themselves (e.g. Anishinaabe). The catchment area of the SAC discussed in this research is rural and includes traditional Anishinaabe territory where several First Nations communities are located, with an off-reserve Indigenous population in various small towns. The individuals and communities in the region are closely connected. To protect the confidentiality of the participants, we withhold the name of the agency and use pseudonyms in this article.

The SAC provides services to individuals of all genders in a field that tends to focus on women. For many Indigenous people, starting particularly with residential school experiences, sexual violence is an experience that was not limited to female children but rather impacted children of all gender identities. In Ontario, the funding of SACs has primarily focused on female survivors, regardless of the reality of sexual violence in the lives of male survivors. Meeting the needs of all survivors, and doing so through a culturally appropriate lens, continues to be the priority of the SAC; addressing the needs of all survivors reflects the principles of balance that are integral to Indigenous cultures.

Over three decades, the SAC has evolved its programming to better meet the cultural needs of Indigenous Peoples in the region by recruiting Indigenous staff and Board members and building relationships with First Nations and off-reserve Indigenous communities. They offer individual and group counselling from an intersectional feminist and decolonizing lens. Indigenous ways of knowing, being, and doing are the basis for Indigenous-specific outreach and support. The SAC also offers a program for male-identified survivors following the Fireweed model,[3] which incorporates both Western and Indigenous healing methods. Ad hoc funding has enabled the SAC to offer several land-based healing events, and it continues to successfully find funding to create additional Indigenous-specific options for healing through various grant opportunities. However, these pockets of funding are for limited terms, with specific aims that often do not align with the organization's broader operational needs and mandate.

In this research, we worked with the women and Two-Spirit[4] clients of the sharing circle, which meets virtually three times a month. The sharing circle facilitator is an Anishinaabe Knowledge Keeper and staff member. Sometimes an Indigenous Elder also joins the circle. The circle was started online in the spring of 2020, not long after the COVID-19 pandemic lockdowns were initiated across Canada. Clients were provided with iPads if they did not have a computer. Due to its virtual format, the circle grew to include members living in Treaty 13, the Williams Treaties (Toronto), and the territory of the Council of Three Fires (Great Lakes area above and below the U.S.-Canada border). This is a particularly unique feature, reflecting the organization's commitment to recognizing Indigenous concepts of sovereignty, land, and home territories rather than following imposed colonial jurisdictions for service mandates.

To locate ourselves within this research, Nancy Stevens is of settler and Mohawk descent and worked as a counsellor in Indigenous mental health and Indigenous women's services for many years before becoming a university professor. This project builds on Nancy's prior relationship with SAC staff. Rosemary Nagy is a settler researcher who was previously co-director of the Northeastern Ontario Research Alliance on Human Trafficking.[5] We also acknowledge our research assistant, Morningstar Christianson, who assisted with transcripts and analysis. We are grateful to the Knowledge Keeper and Elder who assisted in our sharing circle, and we especially thank the five participants for their gift of personal stories and insights shared with us.

Supports for Indigenous Survivors of Sexual Violence—A Look at the (Lack of) Literature

The literature on systemic causes firmly identifies gender-based sexual violence as intrinsic to the broader project of colonialism (Hunt 2016; National Inquiry into MMIWG 2019). The protracted, multipronged attacks of colonialism have resulted in disproportionately higher rates of all forms of violence, poorer health outcomes, and earlier average mortality, along with other significant barriers to social, economic, and physical wellbeing for Indigenous people in Canada (Cotter and Savage 2019; Indigenous Services Canada 2023). The persistently high rate of sexual violence experienced by all genders is insidious in Indigenous communities (Heidinger 2021). Indigenous women and girls in particular face racialized stereotyping as being inherently available (Bourgeois 2015; Boyer and Kampouris 2014). Racist, sexist representations afford impunity to perpetrators and serve to blame victims/survivors for the sexual assaults they experience.

Very little has been written, in the academy or elsewhere, to address sexual assault services specifically for Indigenous survivors in Canada. A moderate body of work has emerged in response to human trafficking and Indigenous people. A much more substantial body addresses Indigenous child welfare, domestic or intimate partner violence, murdered and missing Indigenous women and girls, mental health, and the impacts of residential schools. These are all, of course, interconnected vis-à-vis colonialism, assimilation and genocide (Faller, Wuerch, Hampton, Barton, Fraelich, Juschka, Milford, Moffitt, Ursel and Zederayko 2021; Hrynyk 2018; Nagy 2015; Reeves and Stewart 2014). Writers in these different areas also generally address the need for culturally-based support to heal substance abuse disorders and intergenerational and colonial traumas (e.g., Boyer n.d.; Marsh, Coholic, Coté-Meek, and Najavits 2015; Gone 2013). They do not, however, address the specific context of sexual assault service provision.

While the residential school system has come to an end, colonialism persists. Colonialism continues to manifest in systems that maintain power imbalances, leaving Indigenous peoples bereft of lands, homes, cultures, languages and healthy relationships. Natalie Clark points out that in the mainstream discourse surrounding trauma, there is a clear pattern of maintaining the privilege of Western paradigms (2016). Yet, as Josie Nelson notes, sexual violence against Indigenous women requires "taking care of generations who have lived through trauma [which] is the responsible action to 'blood memory'" (2017, 16).[6] Nelson adds that supports must be grounded in cultural ways of healing so that anyone affected by violence can be included in the process (2017). In other words, where Western approaches would generally only address the needs of the victim, Indigenous people understand that the impacts of violence ripple out and impact others within the person's circle.

Incorporating Indigenous worldviews and approaches into their institutional design poses challenges for SACs. Government funding operates from a Western perspective, whether in outcomes or staff credentialing. Western systems get to define what is considered "best practice" and what evidence is considered valid, despite clear indications that the evidence is often well off the mark (Chandler and Lalonde 2013; Clark 2016). Below, the available literature is explored, connecting cultural perspectives and therapeutic practice needs.

Hospital-Based Sexual Assault Supports and Indigenous Survivors

Two documents focus on sexual assault services within the health system of Ontario. The first, Du Mont and Parnis (2002), is an overview of the sexual assault care available to any person across Ontario through hospitals. The authors point out that First Nations are among the hard-to-serve groups because they face a range of access barriers, including geographic barriers and inadequate funding. Several recommendations are presented, including learning how to better serve the needs of underserved populations such as Indigenous people (Du Mont and Parnis 2002).

In a second article, Du Mont, Kosa, Macdonald, Benoit and Forte (2017) examine how Indigenous and non-Indigenous survivors of sexual violence perceive their experiences with medically based sexual assault services. They state that Indigenous survivors are more likely to be younger, to show up at a medical centre because of sexual violence, and to have sustained more serious injuries or harm as a result of the assault than non-Indigenous survivors. The authors also connect the experience of sexual violence to colonial oppression for Indigenous survivors; as "one of the most pernicious form[s] of violence against women, sexual assault happens at a rate more than three times higher than non-Indigenous women (115 incidents per 1,000 vs. 35 per 1,000)" (Du Mont et al. 2017, 2). Additionally, the authors note that there have been calls to increase access to hospital-based treatment in forms that are sensitive to Indigenous peoples' experiences and needs. Although Indigenous survivors have expressed satisfaction with hospital service, they are also less likely to express high degrees of satisfaction (Du Mont et. al 2017).

Service Providers in Rural and Northern Regions

In a similar fashion, two articles look at the challenges of providing supports to victims of intimate partner violence in rural and northern regions across Canada. In the first, Catherine Carter-Snell et al. (2020) examine a two-year pilot project created to address the lack of comprehensive services for sexual violence survivors in rural areas of a western province. Through pilot funding, the communities involved in the project developed a locally based sexual assault response team intended to identify service gaps, and to implement and evaluate solutions, particularly in the form of medical supports. While not specifically focused on Indigenous survivors, the project required at least one region to have a sizeable Indigenous population. Although the project was successful overall, no factors were identified in the surveys that distinguish any unique facets for the Indigenous community's participation. As a result, it is difficult to determine how the project's success reflected the Indigenous community's experience in a more nuanced way.

In the second article, which focused on rural and northern service providers, Faller et al. (2021) note that the literature remains thin regarding intimate partner violence in the less populated areas of Canada. They also point out that there is very little in the way of literature on the service providers' experiences; all that was available highlighted that the paucity of resources—financial, human, and otherwise—had profound impacts on what supports were available to survivors. The authors include a section specifically noting Indigenous issues that emerged in rural and northern community services. Concerns include how racism and colonialism underpin many of the interactions Indigenous survivors have with services, such as police. They also point out how the geographic locations of many Indigenous communities contribute to the isolation of survivors, thus increasing risks, lowering response times of police, and making other support services harder to access.

Indigenous Helpers' Conceptions of Healing From Sexual Violence

Research into areas that are aligned closely with community sexual assault service provision for Indigenous survivors has touched on different elements. For example, Allison Reeves and Suzanne Stewart (2014) explore the Indigenous healing and Western service options provided through the mental health programs of Anishnawbe Health Toronto for survivors of sexual violence. Since 1984, Anishnawbe Health Toronto has provided health services that are rooted in Indigenous cultures, along with Western-oriented primary health and mental health services (Anishnawbe Health Toronto n.d.). The focus of their research is on the experiences of those who provide support to survivors, those who were identified as traditional healers or medicine people, and traditional counsellors or Elders. They cite a study done in British Columbia where the women survivors described the impacts of sexual violence as "a shattering of their psyches and souls . . . [the] dissociation was . . . not a symptom of PTSD, but rather as a spiritual phenomenon wherein the spirit left the body for a time in order for the victim . . . to survive the experience" (Reeves and Stewart 2014, 61). The healers and counsellors stress the relevance of culturally-informed and trauma-informed care for Indigenous survivors, emphasizing the importance of the spiritual aspect of healing. The authors emphasize that trauma-informed care must go beyond the conventional Western approach and understand that colonialism has profound impacts on the survivor.

In another vein, the option to blend Indigenous and Western approaches has been discussed in other related fields, such as Indigenous mental health. Arielle Dylan et al. (2008) explore how Indigenous survivors of sexual violence experience the criminal legal system. In their study, the authors uncover Indigenous survivors' thoughts on the "essential role played by therapists or advocates in their healing . . . Of the nine participants who sought professional help, each identified therapists and advocates as the professionals who provided the most support during their recovery" (Dylan et al. 2008, 689). Despite systemic issues, empathetic, supportive therapists and counsellors enable Indigenous survivors to focus on healing.

Other literature speaks to sexual violence and service provision indirectly. For example, Indigenous experiences of sexual violence in the context of university settings have raised concerns about the general lack of knowledge within these institutions (Brulé 2018; Hunt 2016). Sarah Hunt states, "Rape culture emerges from, and is fostered through, colonial ways of seeing the world which are expressed in the daily interpersonal actions, beliefs, and attitudes of all who make up the settler colonial nation of Canada" (2016, 2). Within this context and given the age range of a substantial portion of Indigenous survivors, Hunt points out that universities must fully understand the intersection of colonization, education, and the "widespread systematized sexual abuse experienced by students" (2016, 3).

Indigenous women, in related literature, offer thoughts on culturally-based ways to build prevention into communities and schools. Michelle Hrynyk (2018) explores what she calls "sexual assault resistance programs" that transmit skills, such as deescalation, empowerment, awareness and avoidance of risks, and emphasizes that such programs must be trauma-informed through an Indigenous lens. Kari Dawn Wuttunee et al. (2019) also discuss the concept of resisting colonial and gender-based violence by creating a ribbon skirt-making workshop that included women's teachings and that explored the connection of ribbon skirts to culture and identity for many women. They note that the reclamation of cultural practices and identities is a vital aspect of healing from colonial traumas.

In examining Indigenous women who experience intimate partner violence, Victoria Smye et al. make distinctions about Indigenous women survivors: "These experiences are differently shaped by the intersections of social inequities, ageism, sexism, classism, racism, ableism, and the differing historical, social, and political factors that influence women's lives" (2021, 1592). The authors point to relationships between state systems and Indigenous people, between land, community and Indigenous people, and the role and relationship of complex trauma, well-being and resistance for Indigenous people. Reclaiming traditional practices is intrinsic to well-being and healing from trauma, in asserting resistance to colonization, and revitalizing land and community relations.

Methodology

We received approval for this research through our ethics review board and the university's Indigenous community engagement plan review. This PhotoVoice project is a first step toward a larger endeavor to explore the history of this SAC's Indigenous-specific supports, to add to promising practices that can be shared with other community-based sexual assault services, and to understand where the key challenges lie for the SAC, such as securing adequate funding or addressing colonial concepts embedded within funding mandates.

We met with the executive director and the Indigenous Outreach Anti-Human Trafficking Worker to explore the need for and potential approaches to this research project. As details were solidified, an Elder was identified to provide additional support to any participants in the research. "Visioning Our Healing" was conceived as an opportunity for Indigenous clients of the SAC to share how they view their experiences with the culturally based supports offered by the organization. We invited the participants to take photographs to respond to three key questions:

1. What has your healing journey looked like? (Responses included up to three photos to share with the group.)
2. What has it meant for you to be able to access culturally-based services through the SAC? (Responses included one photo to share with the group.)
3. In what ways does the SAC need to grow its Indigenous-specific supports? Or what gaps need to be addressed? (Responses included one photo to share with the group.)

We met with the potential participants initially by videoconference to explain the research process and goals. The Indigenous Outreach Anti-Human Trafficking Worker and an Elder with whom they have frequently worked were present to provide support, if necessary, to the women during and after the information session. The potential participants were invited to contact the principal researcher to obtain more information and to have the consent form sent to them if they were interested in participating. A total of seven women expressed interest initially, although two were unable to finish the project.

The SAC organized a two-day retreat at a conservation area in their region. We were invited to attend in order to build relationships with the participants and to conduct a sharing circle with them. An Elder and the Indigenous Outreach Anti-Human Trafficking Worker were present for the entire retreat. The Elder also sat in on the sharing circle to be immediately available to the participants if needed, and to offer smudging (an Anishinaabe cleansing ceremony that burns sacred medicines like sage and sweetgrass) and guidance throughout. Sharing circles are an "open-structured conversational style methodology that respects story sharing within a Tribal protocol context" (Tachine et al. 2016, 278; see also Kovach 2021). Rooted in Indigenous epistemologies, sharing circles start with ceremony, and participants hold a talking stick or other sacred object while they share their stories without interruption. In our case, the participants shared the meaning of their photos and their experiences in healing from mid-morning to mid-afternoon, with a break for a shared meal. By wrapping the sharing circle into a full weekend, relationality and reciprocity were strongly embedded in the research process.[7] We audio-recorded the sharing circle. Two additional conversations were conducted and recorded via videoconferencing to include the two participants unable to travel to the retreat. The online experience was shorter in duration and less emotionally intense, but we still felt able to establish rapport and connection with the two online participants.

A research assistant was engaged after the interviews were completed, who then worked on transcribing each recording. Each participant received an electronic copy of their interview to review and provide any comments or edits, if they wished to. The research team then individually reviewed the transcripts and the available photos for themes. These were then compared for commonalities and compiled to develop into a report for the SAC. The themes that emerged from the interviews and the photographs were analysed to reflect on the critical ideas and concepts that were common in the participants' contributions. All the participants identified as Indigenous, with some participants also identifying as having European ancestry and one person identifying as being African and Indigenous in their lineage. Four of the participants identified as cis-women, while one identified as Two-Spirit.

Findings: Photo Voice and Sharing Circle

The participants who gathered were all survivors of various forms of sexual assaults and other forms of sexual, physical, and psychological violence. Speaking of the impact of repeated sexual and physical assaults in her early teens, Tina described how it "split me in all different pieces," leading to drug use and bad relationships. Eventually, this way of living became too much, and Tina found herself "just screaming" to Creator in all her nakedness and vulnerability. "Either it was for help or to take me out of this world" (see figure 1).[8] Importantly, however, all of the participants talked about the intersecting harms they have experienced under colonialism in "a country that just doesn't see me, doesn't see me as value [*sic*]" (Marie). All the participants pointed out family-of-origin traumas, which can be directly connected to colonial impacts on Indigenous peoples (and the enslavement of African peoples). Two participants discussed some of the difficulties they experienced as women of mixed race (African-Indigenous, European-Indigenous). Another raised critical issues of being Two-Spirit. Two spoke about financial

FIGURE 1. Tina describes this photo as her "just screaming" to Creator in all her nakedness and vulnerability: "Either it was for help or to take me out of this world."

stress and the challenges of parenting, demonstrating that supports needed by participants extend beyond "mere" sexual assault therapies to encompass the broad harms of colonial violence.

All participants spoke of the struggle to balance physical, mental, emotional, and spiritual health throughout their lives as they attempt to heal. The concept of balance and wholism/holism is seen directly and implicitly in the sharing of the participants and is a concept that is often not understood in non-Indigenous services. For the most part, participants perceived a lack of support available through formal Western helping systems. The participants talked about racism in their urban communities and in institutions (health, child welfare) where staff did not believe them or denigrated them. Marie's photograph of a maple leaf in figure 2 signifies her anger and alienation from Canada: "I have a lot of anger towards Canada . . . [this leaf reminds] me of a country that just doesn't see me . . . And doesn't want to protect me, doesn't want to protect women like me." We found that the participants engaged in healing work on their own, as well as relying on supports provided by the SAC. Most of them started using the SAC supports after being connected by the Indigenous Outreach Anti-Human Trafficking Worker, who is a Knowledge Keeper with active involvement in community.

FIGURE 2. "I have a lot of anger towards Canada . . . [this leaf reminds] me of a country that just doesn't see me . . . And doesn't want to protect me, doesn't want to protect women like me."

Our analysis of the photos and shared stories identifies several themes reflected in the participants' explanations of their healing journeys. These are:

1. struggles to understand one's identity and the development of self-confidence that participants experience through learning about their respective cultures;
2. the deep importance that the land and nature hold in the participants' sense of relationality in Creation;
3. the act of becoming/being a community helper (whether in a formal role or not) as part of the ongoing healing process;
4. the role of creativity in healing; and
5. the sense of wonder and pride in individual and collective acts of survival/survivance, resilience and resistance.

The struggle to understand one's identity is deeply related to disconnection from one's culture as well as from feelings of social and cultural isolation that result from living in hostile communities or from spending time in institutions. Many articulated or implied feelings of not being seen or not being heard in a racist society. As one informant stated, "I didn't think anybody was paying any attention to what was happening to me. And I never thought . . . my screams . . . I thought they fell on deaf ears" (Taylor). Not being believed was also a key theme amongst participants, who referred to denial or disinterest from white staff in colonial institutions and to unresponsive families who may have felt the abuse was deserved.

Being externally validated and believed was key to the participants' healing journeys because it confirmed that they were "worth doing the work" (Tina). The SAC's sharing circle especially provides validation, support, and a sense of belonging:

> When I joined these circles, I no longer felt alone . . . I finally had that community I didn't have growing up. My native sisters that could hear my stories and see themselves within parts of it. And that, you know, would just make space for me to heal." (Marie)

The SAC's nonjudgmental environment created a sense of relief at not having to prove anything (e.g., financial need) and a sense of safety and acceptance that enabled the participants to share thoughts that they may not have been able to share in non-Indigenous settings. As one participant noted, the sharing circle provided a space where "I can be 100% my authentic self and talk about anything and not be judged" (Taylor).

Many of the survivors had to learn, and continue to learn, about Indigenous cultures, values, and spirituality. They worked towards this on their own and through the sharing circle. Nature or Creation, regarded as a place of nurturing and "home," repeatedly arose as a theme and gestured to the importance of sharing time with family and community and learning/practicing traditional knowledge e.g., making medicines, full moon ceremonies (see figure 3), sacred fires (figure 4), smudging, cedar baths, etc. There was also a deep understanding among all the participants of the vital importance of (re)claiming healthy, nurturing family relationships with both human and more-than-human beings (e.g., plants, animals, spirit-beings). This understanding was modeled, for example, as the participants introduced themselves in the sharing circle and included their clan (if known) and home territory. All the participants shared experiences within their families of origin that underscore the harms of past and ongoing colonialism, particularly with the dynamics of family relationships and the impacts on homelands. In sharing their experiences with healing, they shared stories of learning about what it means to be part of a family that is constituted by more than just human-centered relationships, and the teachings they gained from those healing moments.

FIGURE 3. Full Moon ceremony: culture as healing.

FIGURE 4. "I go to that fire pit often and I'll take the ashes that are remaining. And I use it in prayer to protect myself. Protect me from memories of that night." (Marie)

FIGURE 5. Magnolia Tree: "I made you the way I wanted you and . . . you are beautiful."

The survivors shared how they draw validation, nonjudgment, and connection from their relationship with Creator, ancestors, land, water, and nature. One participant pointed to nature as a model of acceptance: "bears don't criticize other bears" (Laurie). Taylor, a Two-Spirit participant, drew strength and support from the trees in their city. Explaining their relationship with the magnolia tree, pictured in figure 5, they stated:

> You know how people treat other people of different genders [or] of different races, and I thought if you look at every single one of these trees, every single one is beautiful. And they don't talk to each other and say, because I have pink flowers, I'm better than you. Each has its own contribution. And it was much like, I was really frustrated because, you know, there's always an incident if I use a public restroom a lot of times, and I'm feeling really humiliated. (Taylor)

Mental, emotional, physical, and spiritual connection with land and nature is a source of love, healing, and self-worth. One participant noted her experience of her growing awareness of Grandmother Moon, and how that has benefited her as she learned about plant medicines. Other participants talked about different aspects of nature, including the importance of animals. As Laurie stated,

> Culture and the land, the trees, the rocks, the air, the rain, all of that totally saved me . . . when you're sitting out there, they hear you . . . And we forget that we're loved because of our trauma. We forget and we feel unworthy, undeserving, but those trees, those rocks, those animals, the eagles and the rain and thunderstorms and the snow—they love us unequivocally.

Plants in particular are referred to by all the participants as invaluable teachers and role models for healthy relationships. Plants are integral in the reclamation of traditional practices and ancestral connections for the participants. One participant shared a dream where plant medicine connected her with her grandmother and ancestral beliefs:

> I was braiding my grandmother's hair. And all you could see is sweet grass like floating. And you could smell it and I'm braiding my grandmother's hair. And that's when I realized my hair was my strong connection. (Rachel)

Another participant, Marie, explains how wasps on the brick outside her house protect her and her home from hostile family members and neighbors. The wasps do this "because they love me so much," and in return she plants bee balm, which is a wasp's favourite flower, pictured in figure 6. "Just in my working with the medicines, I just know now how beneficial the wasps are to my healing journey" (Marie). For another, "The sun is a reminder of how bright I can be, and how beautiful I can be. As long as . . . I have more of that love within myself. And nature reminds me about that love all the time" (Rachel).

FIGURE 6. Bee Balm. "The colour of it is just a pale, pale pink, and when the sun hits it, it just warms it up and the colour will warm up as well. But wasps love it."

Trees, specifically, emerged in the sharing by four of the participants as a connective force that represents rootedness, standing as guardians and as caregivers to their human kin, and trees are keepers of deep knowledge that the survivors connect to ancestral knowledge and teachings. In many

Indigenous cultures, trees have prominence and often have important roles in ceremonies (e.g., sweat lodge, sun dance). They were featured exclusively in Taylor's photos and story, including photos they shot and edited with various filters. They shared that they felt deeply drawn to trees since childhood, and that the trees were integral to their life; the trees are, in essence, reparenting them, teaching them about how to be a whole human being. "So now when I struggle, I go to the trees and I don't feel alone anymore . . . I can walk up and sit by a tree and know that tree knows exactly what's going on" (Taylor). Another participant, Rachel, shared her experience of some inner child work that connected directly with a tree:

> And the little girl [Rachel] was sitting like this by a tree and it was dark. But then the sun came out and shone so brightly on little [Rachel]. And that tree helped me release because I was stuck in trauma. And then I released it. And I know that those trees in that sun brought out somewhat of that happiness within that little girl because all I do [is] smile.

The work of healing is, in large part, a task of "breaking free" and "letting go." For Tina, figure 7 speaks to breaking free of the constraints of the past and of the vitality of claiming identity, cultural practices, and knowledge. Notions of breaking free and letting go also raise the vulnerability that comes with healing and the need to allow that vulnerability to emerge. For some participants, letting go is both a literal and figurative process of "getting clean." In the photo of the naked woman on the rock (figure 1), she is kneeling in a cleansing rain that is "washing it off of me . . . that dirtiness

FIGURE 7. Breaking Free of the Chains that Bind. "I was able to break free a little bit. So the rest of the chains is clearly the work."

that I feel" (Tina). Another participant, Rachel, connected the medicine of cedar with water in the form of cedar baths, which are used to cleanse the body and spirit, and are a cultural practice for Anishinaabe for different occasions, including healing work.

In a literal example of "getting clean," Taylor told of their experience of being directed by a spirit to clean up garbage around the trees in their city:

> And I picked stuff up, I put it in [in the bag] and it stunk. And it was heavy. And I kept telling Spirit, I'm gonna [*sic*] put it down. It's too heavy. I still got miles to walk. He kept telling me no, not yet. No, not yet. So I continue. And I continue, and I continue. And then it was like something came over me and said, Okay, now you can throw it away. And the lesson learned from that is that walking around carrying other people's trash. Stop. That is not mine to carry. It's heavy. And it makes me sick.

Laurie addressed the need to clear out unhealthy relationships: "When you start healing, you realize that you have to leave those people who are unhealthy behind if you want a new life." Rachel recalled the pain of losing three children, one because her mother and boyfriend made her get an abortion, another due to abortion after being raped, and the third due to miscarriage. The Elders told her to do ceremony by the river to release the grief and loss of those abortions. "I had to get a bottle of milk, and a baby blanket, and some socks. And I had to put it on a blanket. And I put it on that blanket. And I let it go down the river" (Rachel). She refers to this as "womb work" and later notes that she also does "inner child work" to no longer be "stuck" in trauma. This clearing out of old patterns of thinking and behaving can be long and difficult and needs the support found through the sharing of experiences.

An important part of the healing journey for the participants is the opportunity to share about themselves with others. The participants in this research seem to be giving out the care that they lacked growing up by caring for other humans, for nature, and for the trees. In some cases, this is the medicine knowledge acquired over time, such as with Marie, or the ability to facilitate workshops for Laurie. In Tina's case, her life experiences led her to become a community helper, in addition to helping create space for African-Indigenous artisans to share their creations. Tina notes that she clearly sees the intergenerational cycles of trauma in her mother and grandmother, all of which led to her own struggles with substance use, identity and disconnection. These are experiences that motivate her to help others.

> Since I was able to, you know, go to treatment three times, I put that in there . . . my journey walking the red road is to connect. And that's what I do now. I facilitate circles, healing circles, sobriety circles . . . I assist, I bridge, I communicate, I blend, I do it, I do it, anything that I can to help you get

> through whatever it is that you have gone through. I wish that I could prevent. I can't prevent. But I'd like to be on the other side for when you need somebody. (Tina)

Marie creates medicines, some of which she shared her knowledge about during the sharing circle, and some of which she shared as teas with those at the lodge.

> I learned to harvest them myself, I learned how to make medicine out of them myself. It's helped me help other people in my healing journey. (Marie)

For others, the act of caretaking comes through in different ways, such as cleaning up their surroundings, sharing their art, and more.

Taking part in different forms of activism, such as those pictured in Figure 8, is also an important part of sharing and giving back to the community and the land. For the participants, this can take on a protector role, such as Marie and Tina do with land and people respectively, or by raising the public visibility of Indigenous issues, such as a memorial for murdered and missing Indigenous women.

Throughout the stories shared by the participants, there was a strong sense that creativity plays an important role in making space for healing. Some remarked on this in the context of creating the photos shared through this process and how that allowed them to think about their healing journeys. Others shared things that they have been working at:

> I utilized my voice . . . and [have] been able to share my poetry and been able to open up my creative voice and my creative writing and just be able to explore with not feeling like I'm not able to talk, like I have a lump in my throat. (Rachel)

In a related vein, Tina shares that it was through an art therapy program (before her relationship with the SAC) that she was finally able to start connecting to her emotions.

> They broke me through art about things. I was like, really? [laughter] They would talk to me, they would stop me and I'd be upset because I'm trying to tell [them] my story. And they're like, 'Oh, gee, you know, how are you feeling?' I'm fine. [laughter] So, they couldn't get me that way. But they got me through art therapy. (Tina)

An additional theme that emerged was profound wonder and pride felt about the individual and collective acts of healing, resilience, survivance, and resistance that the participants experienced. This was also connected to how people saw the land and their more-than-human relations, a perspective they struggled with until they were working through their healing. The sense of community and acceptance experienced by the participants was pivotal to continuing to work through their trauma.

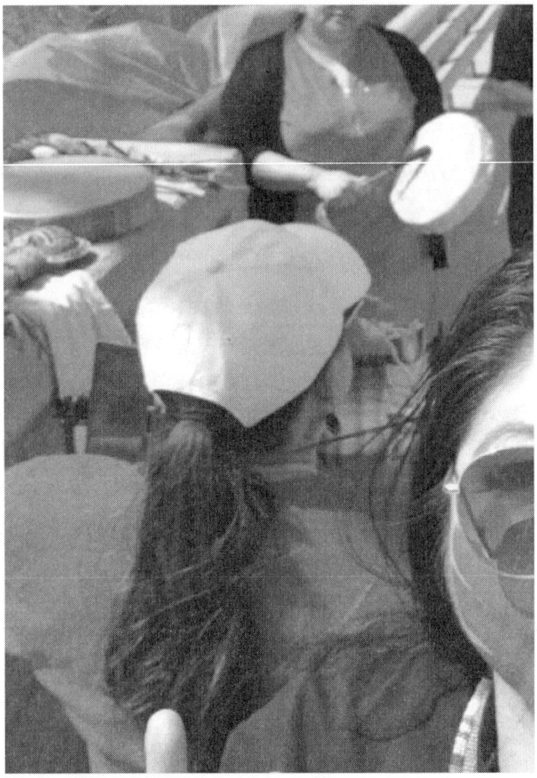

FIGURE 8. My existence is my resistance.

FIGURE 9. Creativity is a necessary part of healing.

> When I joined these circles, I no longer felt alone . . . my mom's non-Indigenous, my sister is non-Indigenous, and my husband's family. I finally had that community I didn't have growing up. (Marie)

> [T]this group has been able to help me tell my story in a good way . . . I have a community of women to teach me how to play that role of being a woman of learning to respect myself with certain medicines. (Rachel)

Two participants specifically referenced how the natural world provides teachings on acceptance.

> As human beings as people, as two legged, we cast this shame on each other, and judgment and ridiculing and criticisms. When in nature, other bears don't criticize other bears, or bears accept the buffalo for buffalo has medicine. (Laurie)

This acceptance is crucial to the participants' sense of connection with themselves, as they learn to navigate through their many experiences, and with each other as they support and learn from the members of the circle. They take their cues from each other and from the natural world, (re)claiming Indigenous values and beliefs. "There's beauty in life everywhere. Look at these pictures, it's [*sic*] full of life" (Taylor).

FIGURE 10. The Healing of Creation. "Whether through storms or the medicine of trees, Creation has more ability to heal than humans do, despite our best efforts."

Discussion

The participants noted how the Indigenous-specific services through the SAC were vital to their evolving well-being. The explanations given by participants for not sharing in non-Indigenous settings range widely. They indicated they had experienced everything from a therapist's lack of basic knowledge about colonialism, to a benign disinterest in hearing what the participant needed to share, to overt racism from the health care or clinical service provider. One participant also noted her experience of being harmed by non-Indigenous service providers who failed to understand that, despite being white-passing, the participant identified deeply as Indigenous. Another participant talked of being challenged by other service providers on her truthfulness when asking for help regarding financial challenges.

> And that's what [the SAC] brang [*sic*] me is no judgment, no criticism. They believe you. You don't ever have to prove your case. You don't have to prove that you're broke. (Laurie)

The complex identities of the participants (e.g. Two-Spirit and LGBTQ, mixed-race identities, individuals with histories of substance use) are compounded by the parameters of various services. They noted that too few services accept people as they are, and fail to meet clients where they are at, addressing client needs with the receptivity to support as the client is experiencing in that moment.

> I've been refused places because I wasn't drowning . . . And that's when I said, you know what? Something needs to be done for the people like myself. We're not just coming out of jail, who've got some clean time, who's got some healing. What about us? (Tina)

The need for lifelong supports is clear, particularly in the context of intergenerational trauma and the collective trauma of colonialism.

As often as possible, the SAC offers opportunities to spend time in natural surroundings to Indigenous clients, augmenting the sharing circles and the time spent with Elders. The participants have already done a substantial amount of their own healing and have taken on helping roles within their communities. Yet there have been times when they need to be the ones receiving help to avoid things such as compassion fatigue and burnout. Therapeutic modalities that focus more on creativity and the natural world are much needed for their holistic/wholistic approaches to healing. Culturally based practices, such as the sharing circles and ceremonies, help each participant feel safe enough to be authentically themselves and to be grounded in their Indigeneity.

Promising Practices

This research was initiated in the hopes of articulating the beginnings of promising practices, to affirm the strengths of the SAC in the ways it structures its programs, and to shed light on areas that need attention. The sharing circle and the individual interviews make several points that respond to these aims.

First, culturally based and culturally safe services are vital to ensure the well-being of clients, to create spaces where clients feel safe enough to share their deepest hurts, and where the mutual support of peers and formal helpers, of Elders and knowledge carriers become crucial to the (re)claiming of well-being. The holistic/wholistic approach to supporting clients also suggests that room must be made to acknowledge that Indigenous clients are not engaging with services solely as survivors of sexual violence. Indigenous clients experience collective, historic and intergenerational trauma that may be expressed as a range of concerns and must be responded to holistically/wholistically. This may mean that the SAC refers clients to partner organizations to help gain more support for specific issues. However, not all partner organizations have the capacity to work with Indigenous clients in ways that meet their needs. This leads to clients dropping out of services and can make it increasingly difficult for them to engage in any services that appear Western in orientation. This SAC has been proactive in creating a culturally safe and culturally based space for clients, but simultaneously has been hampered by the lack of sustainable funding.

Second, land-based programs are integral to offering supports and services that are fully grounded in cultural paradigms. Indigenous cultures, despite the ravages of colonialism, retain deeply rooted connections to their territories, values, and worldviews. Further, these relationships are not constrained by the nation-state boundaries that now divide Turtle Island into Canada, the United States, and Mexico. Nor do provincial, territorial, or state boundaries have any meaning within the context of traditional Indigenous territories. The colonial construction of municipal, provincial, and nation-state boundaries impacts Indigenous Peoples, and affects how they connect to resources, the land (Mother Earth), and each other. This is particularly relevant in urban locations where there are few spaces Indigenous Peoples can use to hold ceremonies, gatherings, or to simply exist peacefully.

Third, the SAC has actively created space to engage with clients on the clients' own terms, rather than imposing expectations for access to services. This cannot be overstated in its importance for client well-being. Being able to show clients that they are respected for who they are, as human beings, is crucial in creating a trusting relationship; this goes to the heart of effective therapeutic practice, regardless of cultural context (Baskin 2016). The field of social work is rife with examples of a deserving versus undeserving ideology. Nowhere is this more visible than in times of financial strain, as noted in the stories shared by some of the participants. When participants experience unconditional positive regard, however, they feel empowered to work through the many challenges they face. They then take up the responsibility of helpers and role models with their peers, family members, and beyond. This is part of a larger cycle of reciprocity in relationships, of reclaiming roles and responsibilities within cultural and community contexts, and of supporting positive self-worth.

Further Research

Some aspects of this research raise questions for future consideration. This was a small group, so generalizing these findings broadly to all Indigenous clients may not resonate. We cannot ascertain whether this work is consistent for Indigenous male-identifying survivors. In a field that has historically been dominated by female-identifying individuals, both as service providers and as clients, the lack of research for male-identifying survivors accessing community-based supports is a glaring gap.

Operational elements were raised as areas to explore further. One issue we noted during our analysis is the challenge of a single person carrying the responsibility for a full program and how to address this without unduly impacting clients. Other questions emerging from the research are: In what areas might the SAC grow its support options? What partnerships might be viable to enhance this effort? Where can organizations secure funding to support this work? Lastly, how does technology as an operational facet mediate clients' access to supports?

Conclusion

This research marks an initial step in understanding the promising practices that support Indigenous clients in a community-based sexual assault center. Our findings confirm the importance of culturally based healing for various colonial harms, while highlighting the specific needs and experiences of survivors of sexual assault. Through this PhotoVoice research, we have been able to see and hear the stories of the participants, as they identified what has been important to them in their healing journeys, what has been helpful through the SAC, and where the organization could expand. The participants in this project shared deeply moving stories, as well as meaningful insights that they have gained as a result of participating in the sharing circles at the

SAC. The pandemic made participation possible for some due to the rapid expansion of computer technologies that enabled people to connect virtually while remaining socially distanced.

The next step in our process will be to examine the organization's operational history in greater detail. We hope to understand some of the factors that enabled the SAC to develop such a strong commitment to culturally based supports in an era of inconsistent government funding for any type of Indigenous-specific programs and services, and an ever-decreasing base of funding for sexual assault services despite their ever-increasing need.

NANCY STEVENS is associate professor and chair of the First Nations Studies department at the University of Northern British Columbia in Prince George, BC, and the unceded territory of the Lheidli T'enneh. She has worked in the field of Indigenous mental health and wellness as a counselor and coordinator largely in northern Ontario and in the Yukon Territory. She also worked in Indigenous women's service (violence against women supports) as a counselor and program director in southeastern Ontario. Nancy is a mother of four and grandmother of two. Nancy is an adoptee, with European and Mohawk ancestry, and has been slowly gathering an understanding of her family connections. She has lived mostly in northern areas, and so her learning has been mainly from Anishinaabe lenses through the education, work, and personal relationships she has developed over the years.

ROSEMARY NAGY is a settler Canadian who lives and works in the territory of the Anishinabek Nation, Nipissing First Nation, on lands protected by the Robinson-Huron Treaty of 1850. As a professor at Nipissing University, Rosemary has conducted research on residential schools, the Truth and Reconciliation Commission, MMIWG2S, and human trafficking and sex work in Northeastern Ontario. She has published in journals such as *International Journal of Transitional Justice, Human Rights Review, Feminist Studies,* and *First Peoples Child and Family Review.* Rosemary is mother to two sons and enjoys swimming and gardening in her spare time.

References

Anishnawbe Health Toronto. n.d. "Our History." https://aht.ca/who-we-are/our-history/.

Assembly of First Nations. 2023. "Progress on Realizing the Truth and Reconciliation Commission's Calls to Action—June 2023." Halifax, Nova Scotia: Assembly of First Nations. https://afn.bynder.com/m/72ac245d0dc83e8a/original/2023-TRC-Report-Card.pdf.

Backhouse, Constance B. 1985. "Nineteenth-Century Canadian Prostitution Law: Reflection of a Discriminatory Society." *Histoire Sociale/Social History* 18, no. 36: 387–423.

Baskin, Cyndy. 2016. *Strong Helpers' Teachings, 2nd Edition.* Canadian Scholars Press.

Blair, Peggy J. 2005. "Fact Sheet: Rights of Aboriginal Women On- and Off-Reserve." The Scow Institute. https://web.archive.org/web/20131101203800/http://www.scowinstitute.ca/library/documents/RPRightsofWomen.pdf.

Boucher, Lisa. 2021. "Making Change on Gender-based Violence: Assessing Shifting Political Opportunities in Canada." *Journal of International Women's Studies* 22, no. 9: 222–35.

Bourgeault, Ron. 1989. "Race, Class and Gender: Colonial Domination of Indian Women." *Socialist Studies* 5: 87–105.

Bourgeois, Robyn. 2015. "Colonial Exploitation: The Canadian State and the Trafficking of Indigenous Women and Girls in Canada." *UCLA Law Review* 62, no. 6: 1426–63.

Boyer, Yvonne, and Peggy Kampouris. 2014. "Trafficking of Aboriginal Women and Girls." Ottawa: Public Safety Canada (Canada). https://publications.gc.ca/site/eng/9.699327/publication.html.

Boyer, Yvonne M. n.d. "Guidebook Supporting the Use of Natural Medicines in Culturally-Based Healing Practices for NNADAP/NYSAP Counsellors." Thunderbird Partnership Foundation. https://thunderbirdpf.org/wp-content/uploads/2019/01/SUPPORTING_NATURAL_MEDICINES_WEB.pdf.

Brulé, Elizabeth. 2018. "The REDress Project: Casting an Indigenous Feminist Worldview on Sexual Violence Prevention and Education Programs in Ontario's Universities." *Studies in Social Justice* 12, no. 2: 337–44.

Carter-Snell, Catherine, Sonya Jakubec, and Barbara Hagen. 2020. "Collaboration with Rural and Remote Communities to Improve Sexual Assault Services." *Journal of Community Health* 45, no. 2: 377–87.

CBC News. 2023. "A Report Card on the MMIWG Inquiry's Calls for Justice." *CBC News,* June 5. https://www.cbc.ca/newsinteractives/features/cfj-report-cards#:~:text=It's%20been%20four%20years%20since,including%20education%2C%20justice%20and%20health.

Chandler, Michael J., and Christopher E. Lalonde. 2013. "Transferring Whose Knowledge? Exchanging Whose Best Practices? On Knowing about Indigenous Knowledge and Aboriginal Suicide." In *Setting the Agenda for Change,* edited by Jerry Patrick White, Paul S. Maxim and Daniel J. K. Beavon, 111–23. Thompson Educational Publishing Inc.

Choate, Peter W., Natalie St-Denis, and Bruce MacLaurin. 2022. "At the Beginning of the Curve: Social Work Education and Indigenous Content." *Journal of Social Work Education* 58, no. 1: 96–110.

Clark, Natalie. 2016. "Shock and Awe: Trauma as the New Colonial Frontier." *Humanities* 5, no. 1: 1–16.

Collin-Vézina, Delphine, Jacinthe Dion, and Nico Trocmé. 2009. "Sexual Abuse in Canadian Aboriginal Communities: A Broad Review of Conflicting Evidence." *Pimatisiwin A Journal of Aboriginal and Indigenous Community Health* 7, no. 1: 27–47.

Cotter, Adam, and Laura Savage. 2019. "Gender-based Violence and Unwanted Sexual Behaviour in Canada, 2018: Initial Findings from the Survey of Safety in Public and Private Spaces." Statistics Canada. https://www150.statcan.gc.ca/n1/pub/85-002-x/2019001/article/00017-eng.pdf.

Daschuk, James. 2019. *Clearing the Plains: Disease, Politics of Starvation, and the Loss of Indigenous Life.* University of Regina Press.

Du Mont, Janice, and Deborah Parnis. 2002. "An Overview of the Sexual Assault Care and Treatment Centres of Ontario (revised and expanded) for the World Health Organization." Toronto: Ontario Network of Sexual Assault Care and Treatment Centres.

Du Mont, Janice, Daisy Kosa, Sheila Macdonald, Anita Benoit, and Tonia Forte. 2017. "A Comparison of Indigenous and Non-Indigenous Survivors of Sexual Assault and Their Receipt of and Satisfaction with Specialized Health Care Services." *PLoS ONE* 12, no. 11: 1–15.

Duran, Eduardo, and Bonnie Duran. 1995. *Native American Postcolonial Psychology.* SUNY Press.

Dylan, Arielle, Cheryl Regehr, and Ramona Alaggia. 2008. "And Justice for All? Aboriginal Victims of Sexual Violence." *Violence Against Women* 14, no. 6: 678–96.

Faller, Y. Nichole, Melissa Anne Wuerch, Mary Rucklos Hampton, Sylvia Barton, Cheryl Fraehlich, Darlene Juschka, Krista Milford, Pertice Moffitt, Jane Ursel, and Alexis Zederayko. 2021. "A Web of Disheartenment with Hope on the Horizon: Intimate Partner Violence in Rural and Northern Communities." *Journal of Interpersonal Violence* 36, no. 9–10: 4058–83.

Farley, Melissa, and Jacqueline Lynne. 2005. "Prostitution of Indigenous Women: Sex Inequality and the Colonization of Canada's First Nations Women." Vancouver Rape Relief and Women's Shelter. https://rapereliefshelter.bc.ca/prostitution-of-indigenous-women-sex-inequality-and-the-colonization-of-canadas-first-nations-women/.

Frideres, James S. 2020. *Indigenous Peoples in the Twenty-first Century, 3rd edition.* Oxford University Press.

Gone, Joseph P. 2013. "Redressing First Nations Historical Trauma: Theorizing Mechanisms for Indigenous Culture as Mental Health Treatment." *Transcultural Psychiatry* 50, no. 5: 683–706. https://doi.org/10.1177/1363461513487669.

Green, Joyce. 2006. "From Stonechild to Social Cohesion: Anti-Racist Challenges for Saskatchewan." *Canadian Journal of Political Science* 39, no. 3: 507–27.

Hanson, Erin. 2010. "Marginalization of Aboriginal Women: A Brief History of the Marginalization of Aboriginal Women in Canada." UBC. https://indigenousfoundations.arts.ubc.ca/marginalization_of_aboriginal_women/.

Hargreaves, Allison. 2017. "Violence against Indigenous Women: Representation and Resistance." In *Violence Against Indigenous Women: Literature, Activism, Resistance,* by Allison Hargreaves, 1–28. Wilfred Laurier University Press.

Heidinger, Loanna. 2021. "Intimate Partner Violence: Experiences of First Nations, Métis and Inuit Women in Canada, 2018." Statistics Canada.

Holmes, Leilani. 2000. "Heart Knowledge, Blood Memory, and the Voice of the Land: Implications of Research among Hawaiian Elders." In *Indigenous Knowledges in Global Contexts: Multiple Readings of Our World*, edited by George J. Sefa Dei, Dorothy Goldin-Rosenberg and Budd L. Hall, 37–53. University of Toronto Press.

Hrynyk, Michelle M. 2018. "Towards the Development of a Culturally Sensitive, Empowerment-based Sexual Assault Resistance Model for Anishinaabe Women." Master's thesis, Laurentian University.

Hunt, Sarah. 2016. "Decolonizing the Roots of Rape Culture: Reflections on Consent, Sexual Violence and University Campuses." In *The Power of Our Collective Voices: Changing the Conversation on Sexual Violence at Post-Secondary Institutions*, 1–13. University of British Columbia. https://icclr.org/publications/the-power-of-our-collective-voices-changing-the-conversation-on-sexual-violence-at-post-secondary-institutions-summary-report/.

Indigenous Services Canada. 2023. "An Update on the Socio-economic Gaps between Indigenous Peoples and the Non-Indigenous Population in Canada: Highlights from the 2021 Census." https://www.sac-isc.gc.ca/eng/1690909773300/1690909797208.

Jewell, Eva, and Ian Mosby. 2023. *Calls to Action Accountability: A 2023 Status Update on Reconciliation*. Yellowhead Institute.

Joseph, Bob. 2018. *21 Things You May Not Know about the Indian Act: Helping Canadians Make Reconciliation with Indigenous People a Reality*. Indigenous Relations Press.

Journal of Obstetrics and Gynaecology Canada. 2013. "First Nations, Inuit, and Métis women's sexual and reproductive health." *Journal of Obstetrics and Gynaecology Canada* 35, no. 6: S28-S32.

Kovach, Margaret. 2021. *Indigenous Methodologies: Characteristics, Conversations, and Contexts, Second Edition*. University of Toronto Press.

Mahrabadi, Azar, Kevin J. P. Craib, Katharina Patterson, Warner Adam, Akm Moniruzzaman, Barbara Ward-Burkitt, Martin T. Schechter, and Patricia M. Spittal. 2008. "The Cedar Project: A comparison of HIV-related vulnerabilities amongst young Aboriginal women surviving drug use and sex work in two Canadian cities." *International Journal of Drug Policy* 19, no. 2: 159–68.

Marsh, Teresa. N., Diana Coholic, Sheila Cote-Meek, and Lisa M. Najavits. 2015. "Blending Aboriginal and Western Healing Methods to Treat Intergenerational Trauma with Substance Use Disorder in Aboriginal Peoples Who Live in Northeastern Ontario, Canada." *Harm Reduction Journal* 12, no. 1: 14. https://doi.org/10.1186/s12954-015-0046-1.

Nagy, Rosemary. 2015. "Combatting Violence Against Indigenous Women." In *Rape Justice: Beyond the Criminal Law*, edited by Nicola Henry, Anastasia Powell, and Asher Flynn, 182–99. Palgrave Macmillan UK.

National Inquiry into Missing and Murdered Indigenous Women and Girls. 2019. *Reclaiming Power and Place: The Final Report of the National Inquiry into Missing and Murdered Indigenous Women and Girls (vol 1b)*. National Inquiry into Missing and Murdered Indigenous Women and Girls.

Nelson, Josie. 2017. "Storying Gendered Violence: Indigenous Understandings of the Interconnectedness of Violence." Master's thesis, Wilfred Laurier University.

Ontario Coalition of Rape Crisis Centres. 2023. "About the OCRCC." https://sexualassaultsupport.ca/about-ocrcc/.

Ontario Coalition of Rape Crisis Centres. 2022. "Sexual Violence in Ontario: Trends in Survivors Seeking Support." Toronto, May 2. https://sexualassaultsupport.ca/sexual-violence-in-ontario-trends-in-survivors-seeking-support/.

Ontario Native Women's Association. 2017. "Fact sheet: Violence against Indigenous women and girls." Fort William First Nation: Ontario Native Women's Association, September 8.

Ontario Network of Sexual Assault/Domestic Violence Treatment Centres. 2021. "The Network." https://www.sadvtreatmentcentres.ca/about-the-network.html.

Papps, Elaine, and Irihapeti Ramsden. 1996. "Cultural Safety in Nursing: The New Zealand Experience." *International Journal for Quality in Health Care* 8, no. 5: 491–97.

Piapot, Ntawnis. 2021. "Being Called a 'Sq—w' Is an Attack on What It Means to Be Indigenous and Female." *CBC News Saskatchewan—First Person.* July 8. https://www.cbc.ca/news/canada/saskatchewan/indigenous-women-slur-ntawnis-piapot-1.5973697.

Razack, Sherene. 2014. "'It Happened More Than Once': Freezing Deaths in Saskatchewan." *Canadian Journal of Women and the Law* 26, no. 1: 51–80.

Reeves, Allison, and Suzanne Stewart. 2014. "Exploring the Integration of Indigenous Healing and Western Psychotherapy for Sexual Trauma Survivors Who Use Mental Health Services at Anishnawbe Health Toronto." *Canadian Journal of Counselling and Psychotherapy* 48, no. 4: 57–78.

Ross, Rupert. 2014. *Indigenous Healing: Exploring Traditional Paths.* Penguin Random House Canada.

Shenoy, Rupa. 2020. "A Racial Slur Remains in Hundreds of Place Names Throughout North America." *The World.* September 17. https://theworld.org/stories/2020/09/17/there-s-new-push-eliminate-squaw-place-names.

Smye, Victoria, Colleen Varcoe, Annette J. Browne, Madeleine Dion Stout, Viviane Josewski, Marilyn Ford-Gilboe, and Barbara Keith. 2021. "Violence at the Intersections of Women's Lives in an Urban Context: Indigenous Women's Experiences of Leaving and/or staying with an abusive partner." *Violence Against Women* 27, no. 10: 1586–1607.

Tachine, Amanda R., Eliza Yellow Bird, and Nolan L. Cabrera. 2016. "Sharing Circles: An Indigenous Methodological Approach for Researching with Groups of Indigenous Peoples." *International Review of Qualitative Research* 9, no. 3: 277–295. https://doi.org/10.1525/irqr.2016.9.3.277.

Truth and Reconciliation Commission of Canada. 2015. *Truth and Reconciliation Commission of Canada: Calls to Action.* Truth and Reconciliation Commission of Canada.

Vowel, Chelsea. 2016. *Indigenous Writes: A Guide to First Nations, Métis and Inuit Issues in Canada.* Highwater Press.

Wesley-Esquimaux, Cynthia, and Magdalena Smolewski. 2004. *Historic Trauma and Aboriginal Healing.* Aboriginal Healing Foundation.

Wuttunee, Kari Dawn, Jennifer Altenberg, and Sarah Flicker. 2019. "Red Ribbon Skirts and Cultural Resurgence." *Girlhood Studies* 12, no. 3: 63–79.

Yellow Horse Brave Heart, Maria, and Lemyra M. DeBruyn. 1998. "The American Indian Holocaust: Healing Historical Unresolved Grief." *American Indian and Alaska Native Mental Health Research* 8, no. 2: 60–82.

Notes

1. This project is supported by an internal research grant from Nipissing University.

2. Photo voice is a research method where participants are asked to take photographs in response to research questions or themes. The participants are then asked to share the meaning of these photographs.

3. The Fireweed model program is one that blends Indigenous and Western approaches to healing from sexual violence in a group format. This is a model that was developed specifically for male-identifying survivors of sexual violence at any age. Survivors share only to the degree that they are comfortable sharing, and the content of the sessions is adapted to the group's needs.

4. Two-Spirit is a modern term coined to convey Indigenous conceptions of the multiple genders present in many different Indigenous cultures. It should be noted that it does not necessarily equate to a physical gender identity but rather is more of a deeper reflection of the individual's spirit. Thus, a person may identify as Two-Spirit but not as LGBTQ++.

5. See https://noraht.nipissingu.ca.

6. Blood memory is a term used to express the idea that we carry our ancestors' memories within us. Blood memory is a similar concept to epigenetic transmission but is more expansive in its conception (Holmes).

7. Reciprocal and responsible research relationships are key when conducting research with Indigenous Peoples. We have tried to give back to our participants by inviting them to a one-day conference on sexual assault supports that we organized and by setting up a display of their photos with captions, which is now located at the SAC.

8. Tina started her healing journey with sobriety supports and connected to the SAC much later in life.

PHILIP J. DELORIA

Old, Indigenous, Continuous, American Continent: A Critical Review Essay

Indigenous Continent: The Epic Contest for North America
by Pekka Hämäläinen
Liveright, 2022

The Rediscovery of America: Native Peoples and the Unmaking of U.S. History
by Ned Blackhawk
Yale University Press, 2023

Native Nations: A Millennium in North America
by Kathleen DuVal
Random House Press, 2024

WITH THE 2025 Bancroft and Pulitzer Prizes in History both going to Kathleen DuVal for *Native Nations: A Millennium in North America*, practitioners of Native American and Indigenous studies might find the time is right to take a step back and ask, "Whoa! What just happened?" Beginning in 2022, the field has seen three doorstop-sized, publicly facing works, landing one after the other like incoming jets stacked up at O'Hare or LaGuardia. The three offered distinct interpretive lenses, were pitched at discrete registers on the academic-to-trade publisher gradient, and were crafted by historians with disparate pathways into and engagements with the field of Native American and Indigenous studies. What should we make of the nearly simultaneous arrival of 1,466 pages of synthesis, sprung from ambitious books making bold arguments that seek to structure Native American and Indigenous history for popular readers and field specialists alike?

Are the books a sign that the field has (following similar proclamations over many decades) finally "arrived," legitimated at long last in an American intellectual conversation—and thus garnering the respect of New York publishers, a collection of major reviews, and important prize recognitions—not only DuVal's but also Ned Blackhawk's 2024 National Book Award for *The Rediscovery of America*? Or perhaps the reverse: Is it that Native American studies was experiencing something of an analytical and theoretical crisis, such that three different authors felt the need to step forward with new organizing principles? Are the books simply the idiosyncratic statements of three individual authors, coincidentally timed to appear in succeeding years and so reflecting absolutely nothing of a field zeitgeist? Or are they all historical correctives, part of a long-standing common project that aims, more than anything else, to destroy American nationalist mythmaking? Should we look for their origins and overlaps in the 2019 publication of *The 1619 Project*, and see in them a shared effort to flip American history in a parallel, Indigenous way? Or do they flow more directly from the earlier works and particular analytical inclinations of the authors? The answer, one suspects, is "all of the above."

Whether the authors appreciate it or not, the three of them are likely to be lumped together as a trio from this point forward, caught up, as they are, in a tangle of mutual disagreement. When Ned Blackhawk critically reviewed Pekka Hämäläinen's *Indigenous Continent: The Epic Contest for North America* for the *Washington Post*, everyone knew that his own rival book was arriving shortly, and that it would bring a very different interpretation. The same held true in turn as Kathleen DuVal reviewed Blackhawk's *The Rediscovery of America* for the *Wall Street Journal*. (We are only missing a Hämäläinen review of DuVal to close the circle.) The disagreements might simply be inherent to the effort. Because a work of synthesis aims both to deconstruct existing master narratives and to supplant them, each author is structurally cast in a position of critique when it comes to the arguments of the others. The stakes are heightened, and thus the pointed disagreements and damning with faint praise. For the rest of us, however, the challenge is whether we will choose one camp or another and seek to defend it—or decide instead to sift and sort, integrate and synthesize for ourselves across the three works. I recommend the latter course.

Pekka Hämäläinen's *Indigenous Continent: The Epic Contest for North America* arrived first (though one should note that it followed in the footsteps of other recent synthetic works, including the first of Jeff Ostler's planned two-volume survey, *Surviving Genocide: Native Nations and the*

United States from the American Revolution to Bleeding Kansas, published in 2019, David Treuer's *Heartbeat of Wounded Knee*, published that same year, and Roxanne Dunbar Ortiz's 2014 standard, *An Indigenous People's History of the United States*). Hämäläinen aims to decenter a classic American narrative conceit, that the continent was *always already* colonial property, waiting only for inevitable settlement. He wants instead to flip the script: North America, in Hämäläinen's telling, stayed Indigenous for centuries, with colonists making slow inroads in the face of prolonged resistances that faded only in the late nineteenth century. In the years between, he suggests, Indian people often manhandled white settlers in battle and dominated them in diplomatic negotiations. It is an agency argument pumped up on steroids, and several reviewers have suggested that, in his zeal for a new American story, Hämäläinen has overclaimed the extent of Native power. "When war did come," he writes, "Indians won as often as not" (xiii). One would like the assertion to be true, perhaps—but is it really?

The book periodizes four centuries of history, loosely tracing the arrival of the classic European empires, the familiar moments of middle grounds, shatter zones, and religious rebellions, eighteenth century colonial geopolitics, the American Revolution, and in a final section, the nineteenth century, centered in Hämäläinen's previous work on Comanche and Lakota equestrian power. Hämäläinen concludes with a few paragraphs pointing to the twentieth century and beyond, cast in the agentic, *longue durée* terms that shape his argument: "It was only 130 years ago, a brief span when compared to the long pre-contact history of Indigenous America, that the United States could claim to have subjugated a critical mass of Native Americans . . . On an Indigenous timescale, the United States is a mere speck" (462).

That may be true, but it seems beside the point. It is an assertation that, as is characteristic of the book, zooms across temporal scale in a way that sometimes confuses the terrains of power, violence, and survival. Too often, Hämäläinen's Native people lose the violent battle but somehow win the war for power (or they win the battle *and* win the war too). Persistent resistance and the sheer fact of survival overwrite episodes of military defeat and are read as long-term Indigenous wins.

Native studies scholars have long critiqued the all-too-common narrative gesture to the 1890 Wounded Knee massacre as marking the end for Indian people. For Hämäläinen, the opposite is true. Wounded Knee was, instead, "a sign of American weakness and fear," evidence of a nation exhausted by its interminable Indian wars (458). It's hard to juxtapose that claim with the sensibility of the United States in, say, 1893, a year that saw the military-backed American coup that overthrew Liliuokalani and the Hawaiian kingdom, the exuberant nationalism of the Columbian Exposition, and Frederick

Jackson Turner's enunciation of the Frontier Thesis. Within a few years, those supposedly exhausted and weakened Americans would move quickly toward the new violence of a modern blue-water imperialism.

In the enthusiasm of these narrative inversions, *Indigenous Continent* evinces a logical genealogy to Hämäläinen's earlier scholarship. His first book, *Comanche Empire,* made the bold argument captured in the title—that for all intents and purposes, the Comanche functioned like an empire relative to Spanish, later Mexican, and then American colonial settlement. He used the term in uncompromising ways. I recall, shortly after the book's publication, a visit by Hämäläinen to a small Native studies faculty seminar at the University of Michigan. For two hours, we questioned him on how and why he was so committed to framing Comanche history in terms of empire. He answered every objection adroitly and confidently, and he won our respect and appreciation—if not necessarily our full agreement. One might have imagined a parallel conversation surrounding his second book, *Lakota America: A New History of Indigenous Power,* which described Oceti Ŝakowiŋ history in similar terms, charting a century from 1776 to 1876 and the rise of an Indigenous power in conflict with the settler United States. Readers have always appreciated Hämäläinen's willingness to take Indigenous power seriously, while noting, often vehemently, that even these two substantial power centers—Comanche and Lakota—were perhaps not as equivalent as he might have wished. In these books, and in *Indigenous Continent,* then, he is sometimes left alone with empire, caught up in a game-board sense of *Risk* geopolitics.

It is in one of Hämäläinen's shorter pieces, the 2014 essay "The Shapes of Power: Indians, Europeans, and North American Worlds from the Seventeenth to the Nineteenth Century" that one finds an agenda for both the large-scale comparative ambitions of his European Research Council–funded *Kinetic Empires* project and the synthetic argument found in *Indigenous Continent.* In the essay, Hämäläinen offered what he hoped would be a field-defining agenda. Early American studies, he suggested, was in danger of fragmentation, in large part because a brilliant scholarship of particulars lacked the synthetic organizing principles that would make trees visible as forests. His solution to this problem was a consideration of *power,* which he framed in strokes broad enough to encompass both military violence and the governmental and social mechanisms of cultural consent. And yet "power," even in its most Foucauldian abstraction, has a way of being easily translated into violence and force, and such is often the case with *Indigenous Continent,* which arranges itself rather effortlessly as military history. As Kathleen DuVal observed, Hämäläinen's book is devoid of much social-historical content—women's history, for instance, so important in the field over the last decades—and turns frequently into a litany of great men fighting other great men.[1]

As important, Hämäläinen's emphasis on centuries of violent conflict and Indigenous power displaces also what has been the most dominant synthetic tradition in the field over the past two decades: settler colonialism. As he observes, "There were many types of colonialism—settler, imperial, missionary, extractive, commercial, and legal—and they emerge cumulatively as the story told here progresses" (xiii). Part of settler colonial argument has rested on a clear differentiation between it and those other forms of colonialism. Though of course these colonial modes might overlap, settler colonialism's claim to theoretical uniqueness—as a growing body of rules, aphorisms, and debates—has elevated it as an explanatory force. For all that *Indigenous Continent* takes aim at the American mythic structures of manifest destiny and vanishing Indians, then, it also works to minimize the conceptual work of settler colonial theory, which has attempted to frame violence and power within its own grand narrative scaffold, seeking to unite land, violence, politics, law, and ideology under the concept of "elimination." Since Patrick Wolfe's earliest writings (and in particular his 2006 article, "Settler Colonialism and the Elimination of the Native"), Native American and Indigenous studies has been trying to account for settler colonialism's persuasive explanatory power and its simultaneous tendency to obscure Indigenous agency and complication behind a veil of seemingly inevitable settler "structure." It is here, perhaps, that the differences between "history" per se, and the distinctive interdisciplinary inclinations of Native American and Indigenous studies become visible. Settler colonialism may have been more useful in the latter context than the former.

Indeed, one might wonder if this particular body of theory does not now find itself at a curious moment. On the one hand, our colleagues outside NAIS have been increasingly willing to pick it up as a tool that offers wide, integrative access to Native histories. You hear it uttered in the same breath as "racial capitalism," for instance, or "racial slavery" or "Atlantic world." It has become a synthetic strategy in American history writ large. Ironically, that broad uptake arrived at the same moment that at least some scholars in Indigenous studies seemed to have grown tired of it, or perhaps a little wary, or flat-out critical. But there's a double irony here as well: As settler colonialism becomes a point of critique from those attacking the intellectual interests and directions of contemporary universities, even the skeptic might find themselves defending the concept.

In that sense, Hämäläinen's writing prods scholars to think again about how we may or may not be using settler colonialism these days. DuVal invokes the term almost immediately but does not take it as a central analytic; for

Blackhawk, it is more thoroughly threaded, both implicitly and explicitly, even earning a spot in a chapter title. Like other historical fields, Native American and Indigenous studies confronted calls, in the 1990s and early 2000s, for more capacious and innovative narrative structures able to generate new questions and assert field coherence. When settler colonialism appeared on the scene, it seemed to fit the bill. But, alas, no paradigm lasts forever.

Indigenous Continent thus raises relevant questions for all three books: How does a work of paradigmatic synthesis work? How does it succeed or fail? What are its elements? Does it emanate from a theoretical position, or does it work inductively to produce its own theoretical and argumentative claim? In this sense, all three books entertain a core set of shared argumentative moves—call these the structure of the synthetic work. Each book aims to *refute* other narratives, primarily those tired things we consider "mythic" or "ideological" in an American context. Each seeks to *reorient* the contemporary, to shift current understandings of the past to gain analytical leverage on the present, and to do so in the interests of contemporary Indigenous Peoples. And each work hopes to *re-paradigm,* to establish new structures for a next generation of scholarship and storytelling. These are grand ambitions, and not for the faint of heart.

To craft a synthetic narrative, one must make hard decisions: a bounded timeframe, to be sure, but even more challenging, a selection of cases, threads, and events that take on, in these books, the impossible task of unifying a continent-wide, centuries-long story. "To synthesize," argues Ned Blackhawk, "is to omit."[2] Omission is an existential condition of historical writing: We cannot include everything, nor would we want to, and so are always frustrated by those things left on the cutting room floor. But omission also carries a methodological imperative, for we cannot deliberately exclude evidence that contradicts—or even complicates—our argument. To do so is to invite the critique of colleagues and perhaps even the dismissal of the work itself.

Omission and inclusion are both choices. Both require justification. And while, in a monograph such explications may be modest and manageable, in a grand work of synthesis, how can they be anything other than inevitable and necessarily crucial (if deliberately un[der]acknowledged)? Because a grand synthesis must gesture to an impossible completeness, it will inevitably fail. Because the historian's mantra, "it's complicated" is not in and of itself an argument, the synthesizer will be forced to articulate a less-complicated claim: In Hämäläinen's case, it's that Indians won those military encounters more often than we might think. In Ned Blackhawk's case, it's a reorientation of the familiar structures of U.S. history, achieved "by redressing the absences of American Indians within it" (8).

Blackhawk's *The Rediscovery of America* is a second book project, long in gestation following his multi-prizewinning 2006 effort, *Violence Over the Land.* As is the case with Hämäläinen, it is not difficult to see an analytical genealogy between the first monograph and his later work of synthesis. In *Violence Over the Land,* Blackhawk lingered on the idea of "the Indigenous body in pain," emphasizing the devastating violence borne on the bodies of Great Basin peoples in the vortex of Spanish colonialism. The book had an element of rejoinder to James Brooks's *Captives and Cousins,* which Blackhawk had argued was insufficiently attentive to the violence and the literal pain of the slave raids and markets characteristic of the New Mexico settlements and their joined hinterlands.[3] Blackhawk aimed to uncover complexities and strained forms of commensurability in colonial situations defined by power relations that always included the threat and practice of violence.

Violence Over the Land was both an investigation and a responsive intervention, and so too is *The Rediscovery of America.* Blackhawk delves deeply into settler colonial encounters to make sense of the American Revolution, and the nation founded in its wake. In that sense, it is very much a response. Especially in its introductory framing, *The Rediscovery of America* serves as a direct rebuttal to Jill Lepore's *These Truths,* yet another a work of synthesis that, in the view of several critics, rather famously *omitted* any sense of the significance of North American Native history.[4]

Lepore's book engages thoroughly with the conflicted, contradictory, hypocritical utopian dreams of American democracy, captured best in the Declaration of Independence, the Constitution, and particularly the Fourteenth Amendment. Blackhawk responds with a synthetic framework deeply attentive to Indigenous presence in American political history, including these same touchstones. The book's most compelling chapters offer stunning and detailed accounts of the vagaries of the American Revolution; they deconstruct the old stories and force readers to confront the centrality of Native lands, peoples, and conflicts in the forming of a new postsettler colonial nation. This is not the old argument about Haudenosaunee influence on the idea of a confederation but of the many ways that Native resistance and diplomacy shaped the course of discussions commonly thought to emerge out of European philosophy and the mechanics of colonial state formation and governance. When, in a stunning discussion, Blackhawk situates western Pennsylvania rebel "Black Boy" James Smith—a man who had attacked British troops as early as 1765—as a delegate to the 1776 state constitutional convention in Philadelphia, one can see painfully how backcountry Indian hating functioned as something more than racial formation. It literally produced a powerful species of American political thought and practice that took concrete form in governing documents (172).

If Hämäläinen is at heart a military historian, narrating geopolitical power over time, Blackhawk is an early Americanist, spending a full half of the book taking readers through the three standard empires and the origins of the U.S. Constitution. The other half will be devoted to a somewhat quicker tour—not unsatisfying, exactly, but brisk—through the nineteenth and twentieth centuries. The pace quickens as the book reaches its end, which surprisingly, simply stops in time, eschewing any summary notes or statement of argument. It is a curious way to end a book so rich with argument. In that sense, the omissions at the heart of *Rediscovery* are both argumentative—where's the conclusion?—and historical: How to reconcile the disproportion between eighteenth, nineteenth, and twentieth centuries? Or does that even matter?

Jill Lepore was not the only scholar taken down a notch in the flurry of reviews surrounding these books. They evidence a critical intertextuality and remind us of the politics of those who would aspire to big-story synthesis. Blackhawk, for instance, dismissed Hämäläinen as "an important historian of the early American West, who studies equestrianism as well as anybody." That came in a *New York Times* article that emphasized—as many others have done—that Hämäläinen is Finnish. There is an identity politics at play here, of course, and one pauses to wonder just what is being signified by the label. Is it just the unanticipated nature of a Finnish historian writing about Native America? Only to a *Times* headline writer, one guesses, for others might be aware of names like Markku Henriksson, Sami Lakomäki, Janne Lahti, and Rani-Henrik Andersson, among others, and the long-standing pipeline of American scholars, including John Wunder, Willard Rollings, Daniel Cobb, and Susan Gray, who have been part of the Eagle and Maple Leaf conferences or who have held the Fulbright North America chair at the University of Helsinki.

Are "Finnish" and "Oxford" meant to convey a geographical chauvinism, as if one needs to be in and of North America to write Native histories? Or is it a rejection of the "big tent" theory of NAIS, in which all are supposed to be welcome? Or—as is sometimes the case—is the assumption that while we expect everyone else to *read* our stuff, others may or may not be welcome to write it? Or is it about the methodological distance of work not more directly engaged with community members, a critique that has dogged Hämäläinen (and which may not be wholly fair when it comes to a large-scale work of synthesis). Is it then unusual that Ned Blackhawk—the only Native writer among the three—ends up with a text that most thoroughly addresses United States history, as refracted through Native history? What is right and proper, and who gets to decide? These are unresolved—and perhaps unresolvable—tensions within Native American and Indigenous studies.

In his own more thorough *Washington Post* review of *Indigenous Continent,* Blackhawk dissected Hämäläinen point by point. So intent on inverting the story of Native helplessness, Blackhawk claimed, Hämäläinen misread Indigenous military power, ignored disease losses and settler incursions, and completely missed the political and legal maneuverings that would power his own book, *The Rediscovery of America.* DuVal took her own shot at *both* writers, her critical but fair review of Hämäläinen perhaps gaining a bit of bite from memories of his not entirely laudatory review of her first book, *The Native Ground.* Indeed, revisiting that review, one is caught up in a moment of supreme irony. Hämäläinen observed in 2007 that *The Native Ground* suffered from "a discrepancy between argument and analysis," specifically criticizing a broad, bold claim ("In the eighteenth-century mid-continent, Osage, not European sovereignty was dominant") that might easily have appeared in *Indigenous Continent.*[5]

Lurking in the background of this intermural tussle, one cannot but see traces of Richard White's three-decade-old work *The Middle Ground,* which continues to have relevance. DuVal's title—*The Native Ground*—made it clear that she intended to argue, in the case of the Arkansas river valley, for something other than White's zone of balanced power and cultural creativity (or, for that matter, the "inverted colonialism" found in Hämäläinen's *Comanche Empire).* DuVal focused on Native power, not overstated in its sweep and reach but not compromised either, contested primarily with other Native nations and seeking to incorporate Europeans into Indigenous geopolitics, which were primary.

Much as Hämäläinen and Blackhawk carried arguments forward from their first books, so too with DuVal, whose title—*Native Nations*—emphasizes the continuities of Indigenous political autonomy not only in place but across time and draws upon her previous writing: the Quapaw, for instance, so important to *The Native Ground,* serve as one of seven tribal cases that DuVal will track from early days up to the present. *Native Nations* concerns itself with both Native nationhood and politics. Unlike Ned Blackhawk, however, who centers much of his story on a focused chronology defined by American political history, DuVal extends Native nationhood into the temporality of deep history and the spatiality of world history.

Indeed, her most striking argument incorporates both. Keying in on the climatic changes of the Medieval Warm Period—predictable weather, warmer temperatures, longer growing seasons—DuVal recounts a global burst of city construction, characterized by flows of agricultural surplus, long-distance trade networks, and monumental buildings and edifices. Cahokia, Chaco, Casa Grande, Moundville—the urban infrastructures of Native North America often required (as cities tend to do) social hierarchies, classes of dominating, perhaps hereditary, elites and of the worker bees: farmer, soldiers, the toters of baskets of earth.

As climate giveth, DuVal reminds us, so it taketh away. In the thirteenth century, around the globe, weather first became less predictable, and then cooled significantly, around 1250, into what we've named the Little Ice Age. How were the great cities to cope? As DuVal observes, the stories that descend from those moments are not ones of decline and decay, but of *origin*—for a new set of societies. Native peoples "developed a deep distrust of centralization, hierarchy, and inequality. The former residents of North America's great cities reversed course, turning away from urbanization and political and economic centralization to build new ways of living" (43). DuVal wants to avoid environmental determinism—these were human decisions, she insists, and they played out differently in time and place. Were those decisions deliberate and intentional? That's the sense one gets, though of course evidence for such intentionality does not readily leap from the archeological record, and reading it out of the accounts of ancient times embedded in oral traditions requires a certain interpretive boldness.

Arguably—and it is one of the book's central arguments—the decisions to turn to a small-scale, more egalitarian social and political life defined the colonial interactions to come. For in other parts of the world—Europe—societies did not choose to shrink and decentralize, but instead doubled down on hierarchical social relations—monarchy, feudalism, papacy, and large-scale warfare. These quite different decisions would produce the social and epistemological chasms apparent in the middle grounds, Native grounds and contact zones that would crisscross the continent. Indeed, DuVal is not the only advocate of this view of a decentralized, kin-based political philosophy. Blackhawk, too, surveys the diversity of Indigenous political formations, while Hämäläinen reminds readers that "North American Indians had experimented with ranked societies and all-powerful spiritual leaders and had found them deficient and dangerous. They had opted for more horizontal, participatory, and egalitarian ways of being in the world" (24). In this sense, DuVal offers readers an actual historical origin for the epistemological distinctiveness so often invoked theoretically in narratives of cultural contact and political difference. At the same time, one wonders about societies that developed along other lines. The Pacific Northwest, which is not mentioned in the book, might have complicated the question still further.

But DuVal does more than pull readers back to a deep time that vitalizes Juliana Barr's admonition that "there is no such thing as prehistory."[6] She constantly knits together past and present, leaping, with substantial rhetorical skill, from the fourteenth century to oral traditions and written accounts recorded over the last 150 years, to the thoughts and deeds of contemporary Native people. If Hämäläinen's narrative stops in the late nineteenth century, and Blackhawk's follows chronology into the twenty-first, while maintaining a broad angle of view, DuVal traces both large chronology and specific tribal history, with frequent skips to the present day. The book features a judicious use of the "I," as DuVal situates herself as proxy for contemporary readers who might find themselves climbing Monks' Mound, visiting the National Museum of the American Indian, or otherwise meeting up with Indian Country today. She takes pains to elevate and cite Native scholars. In the fifteen pages of the introduction, for instance, she quotes or cites fifteen Native scholars or tribal leaders—and that is while also taking down epidemic disease theory, American mythmaking, and standard U.S. history textbooks and introducing concepts including genocide, settler colonialism, survivance, enslavement, sovereignty, world history, terminology, and even "power." The conclusion offers a whirlwind tour of scholars and friends, a rich chorus of Native thinkers who help her frame the book's arguments and consequences.

In one way of thinking, these three books—and their authors—must end up in conflict with one another, pointing out the inevitable omissions and simplifications, the insufficient invocations of complexity, the missed opportunities, the overclaiming of a thesis or two, the failure to adequately balance persistent resistance and survival with genocide, violence, and the sufferings of history: the seemingly careless neglect of things that some other writer might care more deeply about. But in a different way of thinking, we might admit the structural impossibility of an adequate synthesis and refuse to become too invested in our critique. We might instead work to extract the important lessons, and then thank our colleagues for having the boldness, courage, and scholarly chops to craft long, complex books such as these. At a moment that seems to fetishize the ungenerous and to be constantly on the attack, this feels to me like the better course. What if we tried to synthesize the syntheses?

These works would spur us to remember that Native North America is old—a lot older than scholars once allowed—and that it has had a rising and falling of classical civilizations to rival that of anywhere else on the planet. In one of those moments of transformation, many Indigenous North Americans chose to respond to climate change by going small and getting decentralized when it came to their social and political organization. They built economies based on sustainable subsistence, kin-based networks, and significant trade systems. Philosophies, practices, and epistemologies followed suit.

When Europeans came for North America, they often stalled out in the face of Native resistance. Rather than sweeping across the continent, they spent centuries trying to figure out how to plant and maintain colonies and bring Native people to heel. Even in the nineteenth century, that moment of rapid American expansion, the continent remained highly contested. Europeans and, later, Americans invented stories about Indian vanishings and savagery to cover their tracks and claim new settler identities.

And while the American narratives seem to capture a kind of final military domination, located in the late nineteenth century, in fact the twentieth century has seen a powerful resurgence of Indian populations and political, economic, and cultural capacities. Indeed, the continuing existence of Native America demands a rethinking of the crucial origin moments of the national history of the United States. This story—so often seen in terms of liberal political theory, economic growth, and the binarism of the Black-white relations powered by enslavement—is transformed when one embeds it within Native history (or, at the very least, when we embed Native history within it!). Resistant and resilient Native nations have continuities that stretch far back into history but also connections that shape the present and will continue to mold the future.

These arguments are familiar, especially to practitioners of Native American and Indigenous studies. But these works also offer the chance for something unique: an amalgamation of argument and story, of big claims mixed with characters, settings, and events, a scholarship that seeks to speak to the average citizen in ways that both honors their intelligence and shakes their foundations. If Jill Lepore took 960 pages to synthesize a history of the United States, then these historians have collectively responded (if not to Lepore specifically then to American history as a whole) with 1,466 pages of Native history. They arrive at a moment of danger, of course. And in that sense, these books are timelier than Ned Blackhawk, Kathleen Duval, and Pekka Hämäläinen could have ever anticipated.

PHILIP J. DELORIA (Dakota descent) is the Leverett Saltonstall Professor of History at Harvard University.

Notes

1. Kathleen DuVal, "'Indigenous Continent' Review: The Not-So-New World," *Wall Street Journal*, September 16, 2022, https://www.wsj.com/articles/indigenous-continent-book-review-america-the-not-so-new-world-11663342792.

2. Ned Blackhawk, "The Iron Cage of Erasure: American Indian Sovereignty in Jill Lepore's These Truths," *American Historical Review* 125, no. 5 (December 2020): 1752.

3. See, for example, Blackhawk's review of James Brooks' *Captives and Cousins in American Indian Culture and Research Journal* 28 no. 1 (2004): 85—90.

4. Christine DeLucia, "The Vanishing Indians of These Truths," *Los Angeles Review of Books,* January 10, 2019, https://lareviewofbooks.org/article/the-vanishing-indians-of-these-truths/; Blackhawk, "The Iron Cage of Erasure: American Indian Sovereignty in Jill Lepore's These Truths," *American Historical Review* 125, no. 5 (December 2020): 1752.

5. Pekka Hämäläinen, "Review of The Native Ground: Indians and Colonists in the Heart of the Continent," *Western Historical Quarterly* 38 no. 3 (Autumn 2007): 388–89.

6. Juliana Barr, "There's No Such Thing as 'Prehistory': What the Longue Duree of Caddo and Pueblo History Tells Us about Colonial America," *William and Mary Quarterly* 74, no. 2 (April 2017, 3rd Series): 203–40.

K. TSIANINA LOMAWAIMA

Memoirs of Indian Boarding Schools, Residential Schools, and Other Carceral Institutions

Brown Tom's Schooldays
by Enos T. Montour, edited and with an introduction by
Mary Jane Logan McCallum
University of Manitoba Press, [1985] 2024

Indian School Days
by Basil H. Johnston
University of Oklahoma Press, 1988

The Middle Five: Indian Schoolboys of the Omaha Tribe
by Francis La Flesche
University of Nebraska Press, [1900] 1963

While the Locust Slept
by Peter Razor
Minnesota Historical Society Press, Native Voices Series, 2001

Where Courage Is Like a Wild Horse: The World of an Indian Orphanage
by Sharon Skolnick and Manny Skolnick
University of Nebraska Press, 1997

THIS REVIEW ESSAY was inspired by the 2024 reissue of Enos T. Montour's memoir about the five years (1910–15) he spent at Mount Elgin Residential School—the "Mush Hole"—in Ontario, Canada. Montour's account resonates with others—of boarding/residential schools and institutions that separated Indigenous children from families and communities. Like Francis La Flesche ([1900] 1963), in his account of a Presbyterian school adjacent to his Omaha village in the 1860s, and Basil Johnston (Ojibway) in his 1988 book about a Jesuit residential school in Ontario in the 1940s, Montour wrote for a broad audience, using humor to educate. None of these three authors dwell on the violence inherent in childhood separation or the violence that permeates carceral institutions, but all three describe oppressive discipline, a dearth of affection for children or respect for Indigenous Peoples, and students' daily companions: hunger, homesickness, boredom, camaraderie, and creative resistance. Those themes, and more explicit accounts of violence, are shared in *While the Locust Slept* (2001), Peter Razor's (Fond du Lac Ojibwe) memoir about seventeen years at the State School in Owatonna, Minnesota and *Where Courage is Like a Wild Horse* by Sharon Skolnick (Fort Sill Apache), a memoir about the year—1953—when she and her sister lived at Murrow Indian Orphanage in Muskogee, Oklahoma. All these authors vividly recreate worlds viewed through a child's eye, and taken together, their memoirs hold important lessons about authorship, trauma, and survival.

Centuries of Indigenous experiences with schooling have been documented and archived in both oral and written forms and by settler and Indigenous authors. The *Jesuit Relations,* for example, or New England missionary John Eliot's *Indian Dialogues,* can easily be read "against the grain" of the missionary authors' intentions, revealing sophisticated Indigenous critiques of proselytizing pedagogies and curricula (Bowden and Ronda 1980). Native-authored documents reflecting school life run the gamut: from *The Letters of Eleazar Wheelock's Indians* who attended Moor's Charity School in Connecticut in the 1700s (Finley and Townsend 2022; McCallum 1932) through archived Native student artwork of the nineteenth and twentieth centuries (Lentis 2017) to the poetry of Diné student Henry Tinhorn at the Intermountain Indian School in Utah in the 1960s (Taylor and Wride 2020). These rich archives are a treasure trove, but they represent a genre distinct from the Native autobiographical memoirs at the heart of this essay. Memoirs constitute a precious, intentionally composed and published repository of diverse Native voices, full of nuance, contradiction, and emotional impact.

Brown Tom's Schooldays

Enos T. Montour (1899–1984) was Delaware, from Six Nations of the Grand River reserve, and a United Church minister. His memoir was self-published in 1985; the 2024 publication is enriched by a foreword by Elizabeth Graham and an introduction by Mary Jane Logan McCallum. Graham, a non-Native researcher and author of a scholarly book on Mount Elgin, was introduced to Dr. Montour in 1982; she helped Montour transcribe and edit his memoir and wrote the preface to the first edition. McCallum, Canada Research Chair in Indigenous People, History and Archives at the University of Winnipeg, contextualizes Montour's life within the genre of "Ontario Indian" literature as well as residential school scholarship and the personal narratives recorded by the Truth and Reconciliation Commission (TRC).

Montour attended Mount Elgin from 1910 to 1915, a period for which we have few first-hand Native accounts. He was an accomplished writer, journalist, and historian; Appendix 2 provides a bibliography of his published and unpublished works. According to Graham, Montour "did not wish to write a diatribe against the church" but produced vivid descriptions of positive and negative elements "that characterized Residential schools" (Graham and McCallum [1985] 2024, xv). Both Graham and McCallum note Montour's love of language and writing: "*Brown Tom* is firmly rooted in Canada's classical (British) curriculum" (McCallum and Graham [1985] 2024, 7). The title *Brown Tom's Schooldays* is a play on *Tom Brown's School Days,* written by British social reformer and politician Thomas Hughes (1822–1896) about the Victorian-era Rugby School.[1] Appendix 1 of *Brown Tom,* a "Glossary of Idioms and References" compiled by McCallum, is extremely useful for readers not steeped in biblical allusions or references to late nineteenth-century British literature.

Despite its pervasive Christian ethos and British literary influences, *Brown Tom* is no apologia for the residential school system. Hunger lurks behind every page of Montour's memoir, and his conclusion employs a clever rhetorical strategy, imagining doubts that might have assailed the school *staff* at the 1915 graduation ceremonies:

> Had all this been a mistake? Had these gifts not only served to unfit them [students] for the old Reserve life without being able to promise them very much out in the great big Anglo-Saxon world? Had it been for better or worse? ([1985] 2024, 152)

Through a Child's Eyes

All the memoirs reviewed in this essay were written by adults well after their institutionalized experiences. Nonetheless, their vivid narratives immerse the reader in the mysteries, challenges, and occasional delights—especially the friendship of other inmates—of a world experienced by children. Skolnick, for example, draws her readers immediately into the sights, sounds, and smells of the Indian orphanage.

> To begin at the beginning. A line of girls in a long gray corridor. It may be a trick of the light, but each, dressed only in a slip or frayed undershirt, appears thin. The light streams in, golden, through the high, small window above and behind the vast oak cabinet. Our closet is framed in the fire of sunrise; it seems that the door opens into a brilliant tunnel. A crisp, bracing smell of soaps and cleansers issues from the cabinet. (Skolnick and Skolnick 1997, 3)

Johnston, like many boarding/residential school survivors, vividly recalls events of the first day:

> With fear and misgiving I followed the priest to the third floor, where he ordered me to shed my clothing. He handed me a bar of carbolic soap and shoved me into a shower. "Scrub. Scrub hard." The shower hissed and then stopped . . . When I emerged from this purge, Father Buck gave me a small green bag with my uniform inside and a pair of work boots. After I had dressed, my guide led me to the dormitory where he assigned me a bed in the junior section. It smelled of piss. "You are number forty-three," he informed me. (Johnston 1988, 22–23)

La Flesche learned quickly about the disjuncture between social norms of home and mission school:

> Before schools . . . were known among the Omahas, Indian parents warned their boys and girls against a free association with the children of persons who did not bear a good character . . . At the school we were all thrown together and left to form our own associates. The sons of chiefs and of prominent men went with the sons of the common people, regardless of social standing and character. The only distinction made was against cowardice; the boy who could not fight found it difficult . . . [I was told] "You must fight." (La Flesche 1900 [1963], 11)

The boys' gangs worked out their rankings through "fair fights" while boys and girls found ways to communicate across the strictly enforced divide of gender-segregated school space, as Montour describes:

> That evening the miracle took place. It was at milking time when [Brown Tom] was detailed to keep the cows quiet. The Girls did the milking while a Senior Boy stood by saying soothing things to the cow . . . Florence Wawanesa was the girl whom he was protecting. As she finished milking, Florence stepped lightly away from the cow and thanked him. In a halting Iroquois accent she said: "Thank you, Tom. I was so scairt. I did not know what I was going to do" . . . The combined impact on Brown Tom was most upsetting. It struck him like the breath of Spring come to the frozen prairie. He almost rocked on his feet. (Montour [1985] 2024, 126–27)

All five authors vividly describe their uncertainty, anxiety, or fear as they entered their respective institutions and were—often harshly—introduced to its rules and regimentation. Some accounts are more explicit than others about the traumas and terrors that, in Razor's words, "haunted" their lives (2001, 200).

Authorship

How and why did these survivors decide to write about their experiences? We have some clues in the case of La Flesche, while other authors speak straightforwardly about the challenges of remembering and of writing. La Flesche dedicated *The Middle Five* "To The Universal Boy" (1963, frontispiece), aiming "to reveal the true nature and character of the Indian boy" to early twentieth-century readers ([1900] 1963, xv). As an accomplished ethnographer employed by the Bureau of American Ethnology, La Flesche understood that "Indians" were marked by "savagery" in the American mind and found it "difficult to lay claim to a share in common human nature" ([1900] 1963, xv). He wrote to assert that claim to humanity. Montour, also an accomplished professional, began to write about the "Mush Hole" years before the Canadian residential school lawsuits and Truth & Reconciliation Commission hearings. He believed that non-Native Canadians needed to be educated about the residential schools and that humor and resilience go hand in hand. Montour documents hunger, bullying, and homesickness for the "warmth and freedom" of life on the Reserve (2024, 107).

Johnston dedicated *Indian School Days* to "all the boys who preceded us and bequeathed their maroon sweaters to us, to all of my colleagues with whom I endured the hurts and shared the laughter, to those who inherited our maroon sweaters . . . and to all the prefects and priests and teachers who tried to instruct us" (1988, 11). While acknowledging that Spanish was "the worst possible experience" (1988, 12) Johnston—like Montour—uses humor to educate and engage his readers. In his foreword to *Magic Weapons,* Johnston wrote that the "modest aim" of the 1988 book was "to recount and relive some of the few cheerful moments in an otherwise dismal existence, a memorial to the disposition of my people, the Anishinaubaek, to find or create levity even in the darkest of moments" (2007, viii). Only later, in the context of TRC investigations, did he reveal the abuse he suffered at the hands of the prefects, priests, and teachers.

Razor recalls his daughter asking him about relatives one day and how hard it was for him "to resurrect those old memories" (2001, 197). Encouraged by his children to write, he assembled "flashes" of memory, "like a lantern blinking in the night" (18). The State School had closed in 1945 and been turned into a museum; he dove into school records, visited archives, and reconnected with an old school chum. Skolnick paints a similar picture of fitting together fragments of "intensely personal and subjective" memories from before and during Murrow (Skolnick and Skolnick 1997, xi). Both Razor and Skolnick comment on the lack of photographs that anchor many of our memories of family and childhood, and neither kept in touch with other institutional alums. Johnston, on the other hand, had many opportunities to rehash "old memories" (2007, vii), working with a cadre of schoolmates after graduation; socializing with Spanish alums while working in Toronto; and then back home at Cape Croker talking about Spanish with former classmates "but not to our children" (2001, viii). We know little about La Flesche's processes of remembering and writing, but he does detail his intensive training in Omaha social protocol, correct grammatical use of the language, and respect for elders. I believe he also may well have benefited from the intensive training in accurate memory recall that was so integral to Indigenous societies of his day.

Trauma

Being separated from family and community is traumatic. Growing up in an institution is traumatic. Institutions designed to remake Indigenous people, fueled by settler colonial prejudice and the compulsion to eliminate the Native, compounded the trauma, but even "mainstream" institutions were no cakewalk. In *The Middle Five,* an impoverished Omaha grandmother brings her beloved grandson to the mission school because the Omaha social "safety net" had crumbled under settler colonial pressures. Skolnick chronicles the chaos of a life orchestrated by state child welfare agencies, a life she describes as like an "expanding graveyard of one-time acquaintances from whom I'd become separated forever" (1997, 55). Johnston and Razor, the former in an Indian residential school and the latter in a public State School, endured devastating physical and sexual assaults.

It was not until 2007, nineteen years after the publication of *Indian School Days,* that Johnston wrote about the sexual abuse he and others endured at the residential school they called Spanish. "Terror," he wrote, "terror at night, terror of dying and going to hell, dogged me for years . . . How I was damaged I cannot say. If I've healed I cannot say. But I do bruise" (2007, xi). Johnston's understatement is devastating. It reeks of the abusive power wielded by settler society and its appointed authorities—priests and nuns, teachers, matrons, disciplinarians, doctors, social workers, reservation/reserve agents and superintendents, and more. Some carceral institutions—asylums, boarding/residential schools, outing programs, and the like—were designed to house, "rehabilitate," "civilize," and remake Indigenous people. Similar institutions—orphanages, reformatories, and the like—were designed to remake non-Indigenous people, and they shared similar abusive power relations and disciplinary structures, as attested by Razor.

Razor's memoir documents his commitment in 1930, at seventeen months of age, to the State Public School in Owatonna, Minnesota. He spent most of seventeen years at Owatonna, where he recalls being targeted by some staff for being Native but where he also chronicles the abuses heaped on non-Native youth. Similar institutions share similar strategies, and like the Outing Program in U.S. Indian boarding schools, the State School placed students with farm families. Many families seeking placements were more interested in access to cheap (or free) labor than in fostering children. Razor's first placement was horrific: He was bullied, kept out of school, overworked and underfed, and was never paid the wages he was owed. After running away, he endured more abuse at the school until a supportive foster family gifted him with a more optimistic view of life.

Razor's experiences resonate with those of Skolnick in her memoir about Murrow Indian Orphanage, where she and her sister, as the only Apache students, were—even among other Natives

> the distrusted and despised daughters of a tribe that inspired fear even in this outpost of Indian country. . . . savages in a savage land. Everything in my brutalized childhood had prepared me to play that part, and I did play it—with effect and relish—from the moment I was ushered into my bare single room. (Skolnick and Skolnick 1997, xii)

Skolnick survived Murrow, was adopted by a loving family, and found her identity as a painter. The theme of survival, like trauma, is addressed more explicitly by some authors than others, but all the memoirs stand as testaments to survival.

Survival

How did these authors survive? Razor credits his last foster family with showing "me a different life" where he "learned at last what it meant to be a boy, without fear of abuse" (2001, 199). As an adult, he returned to his Ojibwe culture, learning to make traditional garments and musical instruments. He raised three children, and he writes: "My children have been my joy, and they have saved me" (2001, 200). Skolnick also found a stable life in an adoptive family; her considerable artistic talent led her to the Institute of American Indian Arts in Santa Fe, New Mexico, where she "learned that being American Indian was a prideful thing" and she found relatives who connected her to her Apache family (1997, 148). La Flesche, Montour, and Johnston—in different eras—achieved professional success in mainstream society while maintaining their connections to home, family, and community. Johnston wrote in 2007:

> On reflection today, I believe that I escaped crippling damage by putting into application a lesson that I learned from the boys on the playgrounds of the residential school itself. "When knocked down, get up!" (xi)

Over time he realized he could put his fists down, and then he found love with his wife: "With Lucie's love began the restoration of my sense of worth.

I didn't know it then, but my service with Native organizations in and around Toronto contributed to the recovery of my sense of worth, as well" (xii).

Indigenous art, music, social life, and language; familial and marital love; friendships with fellow survivors; professional accomplishment within and outside of Indigenous communities—all contributed to the ability of these remarkable individuals to survive, chronicle, and share their experiences. All these survivors found a life shaped in some way, in Montour's words, by books.

I began this essay by noting the treasure trove of sources—many, I believe, yet to be discovered or explored—held within Indigenous and non-Indigenous archives, including the precious archives of living memories and inherited stories of survivors. The memoirs considered here are part of a distinctive genre, quite intentionally composed and equally intentionally published for dissemination to a broad audience. For ease of reference, I'll call all these narratives "boarding school stories." I grew up with the boarding school stories told by my dad, Curtis Thorpe Carr (1918–2012), about his childhood (from 1927 to 1935) at Chilocco Indian Agricultural School, a federal off-reservation boarding school in Oklahoma.

Based on personal, familial, and professional experience, I strongly believe that preservation of and access to boarding school stories is critical to the healing and well-being of all the Indigenous people and nations affected by these institutions. Based on my experiences as an educator, communicating boarding school stories to the public and the press, I am also seriously concerned about how our boarding school stories—particularly those of trauma and terror—can be misused to reinforce a settler colonial agenda committed to seeing Natives as victims and reluctant to recognize—let alone valorize—Indigenous resilience and survivance. Let me try to explain my concern.

"Indians" as Victims

Over time, settler imagination has mostly doomed Native Peoples to extinction. If you've attended a state or county fair, you've likely seen the ubiquitous image of the sculpture *End of the Trail* engraved on belt buckles, cast in pottery, painted on black velvet, or—most weirdly—emblazoned on the Confederate flag. The self-serving myth of Indigenous extinction was buttressed early on by "An Essay on Man," published by English poet Alexander Pope between 1732 and 1734. The stanza that begins "Lo, the poor Indian! whose untutor'd mind; Sees God in clouds, or hears him in the wind" was so widely familiar that in the 1800s to early 1900s a newspaper editor could title an article "Poor Lo"—or just "Lo"—and every reader would know it was about American Indians. So, the settler conception of Indians as inevitable victims doomed to extinction (or at least poverty and dysfunction) has a deep history.

The extinction myth had some basis in reality. By the 1920s, centuries of disease, warfare, dispossession, removal, malnutrition or starvation, and mundane settler violence had decimated Native populations. Despite the devastation, Native Peoples did not disappear, which left settler society and policymakers wrangling with what they called "the Indian problem." The "problem" was all about justifying settler claims to Native lands and waters. The U.S. Supreme Court's 1832 dicta in the case *Cherokee Nation v. Georgia* presented an elegant judicial solution to "the Indian problem." The Court interpreted the U.S. Constitution to say the Cherokee Nation had no legal standing to bring the case forward; created the status "domestic dependent nation" to characterize Native nations; and noted the "resemblance" of Native Peoples to "wards" of a federal "guardian."

The guardian/ward relationship was immensely convenient and became enshrined as dogma in federal Indian law and policy almost overnight. Native adults, as wards, were consigned to the legal status of minor children and incompetent adults, and thus had no enforceable rights to vote, file lawsuits, manage their own financial affairs, self-govern, manage resources on their lands, or raise or educate their own children, a responsibility appropriated by mission and federal Indian school systems, child welfare agencies, and other state institutions.

The guardian/ward relationship also proved useful to settler land claims. When claims to title have proved murky—or nonexistent—the relationship could juridically and morally validate a kind of inheritance from ward to guardian. To demonstrate that lands and waters have been justly transferred to capable heirs—the United States and its fully en*title*d citizens—"Indians" have to persist as incompetent wards and incapable tribes, which goes a long way to explaining the federally engineered poverty that has haunted many Native nations over time.

We cannot underestimate the degree to which settler society has justified its claims to nation and territory by the representation of Native Peoples as incompetent, dysfunctional, perpetually damaged goods—that is, victims. I believe the "Indian as victim" narrative continues to power public and media interest in boarding school stories of trauma and dysfunction, and their disinterest in—or active denial of—boarding school stories of resilience, resistance, survival, and optimism. That reality calls for care and caution in archiving, determining access to, and disseminating boarding school stories. We must always consider who our audience is, and what their needs and agendas might be, as carefully as we consider the content and impact of our stories. In the fraught landscape of Indigenous-settler relations, Native memoirs are critically important to counter settler narratives that conflate "Indigenous" with "victim."

Memoirs chronicle abuse and trauma, but they speak to resilience and survival as well. Within Indigenous families and communities, we must honor those who survived childhood separation and those who did not, those whose stories we cherish and those whose stories remain forever beyond our reach. All the stories, archives, and memories build critically important histories, impart lessons for the present, and guide us into the future. They may also contain the building blocks for healing individuals, families, and communities scarred by institutional separation.

K. TSIANINA LOMAWAIMA (Muscogee/German Mennonite descent), one of the six co-founders of NAISA, is retired from the faculty of the University of Arizona and Arizona State University.

References

Bowden, Henry W., and James P. Ronda, eds. 1980. *John Eliot's Indian Dialogues: A Study in Cultural Interaction.* Contributions in American History 88. Greenwood Press.

Finley, Chris, and Camilla Townsend. 2022. "'All He Had Told Them Was True': Native American History and the Witnessing of Abuse in the Archive." *NAIS* 9, no. 2: 95–123.

Hughes, Thomas. [1857] 2013. *Tom Brown's School Days.* HarperCollins.

Johnston, Basil H. 2007. "Foreword." In *Magic Weapons: Aboriginal Writers Remaking Community after Residential School,* by Sam McKegney, vii–xv. University of Manitoba Press.

McCallum, James Dow. 1932. *The Letters of Eleazar Wheelock's Students.* Dartmouth College Publications.

Taylor, Michael P., and Terence Wride. 2020. "'Indian Kids Can't Write Sonnets': Re-membering the Poetry of Henry Tinhorn from the Intermountain Indian School." *American Quarterly* 72, no. 1: 25–53.

Note

1. Hughes's account was first published in 1857 and has been almost continually in print since; it was most recently reprinted by Collins Classics in 2013.

PHIL HENDERSON *and* SHIRI PASTERNAK

The Political Economies of Ongoing Settler Colonialism

Carbon Sovereignty: Coal, Development and Energy Transition in the Navajo Nation
by Andrew Curley
University of Arizona Press, 2023

Refracted Economies: Diamond Mining and Social Reproduction in the North
by Rebecca Jane Hall
University of Toronto Press, 2022

Plundering the North: A History of Settler Colonialism, Corporate Welfare and Food Insecurity
by Kristen Burnett and Travis Hay
University of Manitoba Press, 2023

ASSESSING THE STATE OF Indigenous studies literature, Anishinaabek scholar John Carlson has recently argued that "the reality and implications of money, commodities, and wage-labour for both Indigenous resurgence and the organization of struggle," have been marginal within the field and aligned scholarly/activist research (2023, 9). This, in spite of the fact that Indigenous Peoples and nations "continu[e] to depend on them in practice," even in the most militant of anticolonial struggles. Though these tactics do not always seek to consciously politicize the political economy of colonial society, nor intend to show how that conditions the possibilities of anticolonial struggle (26). This lingering absence within the field is a compelling reason to read—and welcome—the three texts under review here, as each represents a significant contribution to overcoming the relative dearth of political economy scholarship within Indigenous studies.

Andrew Curley's *Carbon Sovereignty* (2023), Rebecca Hall's *Refracted Economies* (2022), and Kristin Burnett and Travis Hay's *Plundering the*

North (2023), all offer distinct and compelling investigations of political economy. Each considers in some detail how Indigenous Peoples respond to, engage with, or plan around the ways in which the market—be it in the form of coal power plants, diamond mines, or big retailers—conditions the scope of possibility for exercising autonomous political authority. In the case of *Carbon Sovereignty* and *Refracted Economies,* both books share an approach that foregrounds careful yet unsparing ethnography of the profound social and political complexities driving Indigenous decision-making regarding resource extraction. *Plundering the North,* by contrast, delves into the archives of the Hudson's Bay Company (HBC) and it's successor, the North West Company (NWC), in order to show the deliberate role played by both firms in perpetuating food crises in the North in order to secure new rounds of state-backed profitability models that made the hunger of Indigenous northerners a bankable commodity for southern capital.

In Navajo territory, Curley shows how carbon economies introduced a complex history of colonial capitalism to Diné relationships with the land, both enabling and restricting the nation's self-determination over time. Curley expands on the critique of the "resource curse" developed in Timothy Mitchell's *Carbon Democracy*. Mitchell argues that resource dependency has been falsely conflated with underdevelopment; instead, he argues, it has also provided opportunities for modern state formation. *Carbon Sovereignty* is structured along successive waves of extraction, through which Curley demonstrates both the racial logics that have configured the conditions of possibility for Diné sovereignty within American law but also the way Diné subjectivity has been shaped through labor relations and revenues derived from coal, oil, hydro, and green energy economies. These economies, he argues, invested Diné people in reproducing particular forms of tribal sovereignty. This insight opens space for Curley to avoid rigid binaries of state versus Indigenous sovereignty, or of Indigenous/environmentalist alliances. Instead, he writes, "What 'carbon sovereignty' advances here is the metabolic connection of raw resources and consumption within abstract notions of political economy that influence what tribal actors do with their sovereignty and what is made possible" (19). For Curley, "Carbon sovereignty" is a category of Indigenous agency that manages to take all this into account, since it is rooted in material realities.

Carbon Sovereignty is extremely well researched and benefits from Curley's firsthand experience attending meetings and reporting on issues at the center of the book: for instance, why Navajo workers, with the nation's support, fought to keep coal plants running on the Arizona reservation despite its deleterious effects on human and environmental health. Despite the local focus of his scholarship, his analysis of political economy has profound implications for understanding the relationship between capitalism and colonialism in North America as it has developed through violent underpinnings of early settlement, through the high modernization period, and into our contemporary moment. He writes, "Settler colonialism explains the utility of land theft but not land devaluations. The currents of modern capitalism made reservations into spaces of poverty redeemable through development in the form of extraction, or carbon sovereignty" (59). Internal decolonization processes, he notes, must not only reckon with dispossession but also with the way these lands become property through their market value in extractive industries.

Similarly, Hall shows how several Yellowknives Dene communities have maintained a "mixed economy" within the diamond mining industry of the North West territories. Focusing on women's reproductive capacities as central to both Indigenous resistance and exploitation, Hall provides a fascinating in-depth study of how the Fly-in-Fly-Out (FIFO) system arose as an accommodation in response to workers' demands that there be less separation from their families. This new work model, adopted by the mining industry, has created new kinds of exploitation and hardship for women's reproductive labor within Indigenous subsistence economies. Hall argues that FIFO "is a spatial articulation of the capitalist separation of production-for-surplus from social reproduction" (13); in short, FIFO creates conditions of work in which the mine worker becomes almost entirely disconnected from the conditions of their one material reproduction (i.e. from the typically—and, within FIFO contexts, increasingly—feminized labor of cooking, cleaning, child/Elder care, emotional labor, etc.).

Drawing on Indigenous and antiracist feminists and feminist political economy, Hall argues that the distinction between subsistence production and social reproduction is less salient and categorical in land-based/traditional economies, "in that both are forms of labour directed toward the social needs of the community" (28). Yet within capitalist economies, these forms of labor are both minimized and integral to the wage labor system—as they mediate workers' reliance on and demands for expansions to the wage package. In practical terms, if socially necessary goods are secured through subsistence production (e.g., hunted/fished/trapped game meat) and if the reproduction of the worker is secured through the unwaged labor of another (e.g., through the domestic labor of their partner), this means workers will not need to demand as much from their employers in the form of growing wages/benefits. Therefore, she argues, "social reproduction sits as a site of tension between subsistence and capitalist production" (28). Through this theorization and her interviews with women in Dettah, N'dilo, and Behchoko, Hall deepens the vocabulary for mixed economies to include the keystone role of social reproduction in both sustaining and challenging capitalist accumulation in the diamond mines. Through her ethnographic approach, Hall shows that her interlocutors are extremely aware of the contradictions—limitations and possibilities—of the diamond industry, as it has enabled newfound levels of material security for some while severely exacerbating forms of exploitation and precarity for others. Consequently, she makes a powerful case for recognizing social reproduction as a vibrant and vital site of struggle, one that necessarily conditions anticolonial possibilities generally.

In *Plundering the North,* Burnett and Hay track the long historical arc through which the HBC and the NWC colluded with successive state authorities to produce conditions—throughout vast swaths of the North—wherein they would hold a functional monopoly over market-based food distribution. Beginning with a history explaining how colonial processes of dispossession and extractive economies have seriously disrupted the capacities of Indigenous communities to engage in land-based subsistence production, the authors then show the predatory ways these retailers seek to ensure that communities remain dependent upon their distribution network for basic essentials. As a consequence, today the NWC exercises considerable power within many northern communities, extracting super-profits while often silently shaping the very conditions of social life within these communities. Moreover, Burnett and Hay (63) track how, since the rise of the modern state-welfare regime, this profit-seeking collusion between state and capital has been rhetorically obscured behind an ever-shifting language of paternalism that purports to benefit Indigenous communities by "disciplining . . . [them] to the foodways and domesticities of settlers," even as it has regularized and dramatically expanded corporate profits. In many ways, the present era of "corporate social responsibility" rhetoric finds its progenitor in this mask for mere profit-seeking in Indigenous communities.

Departing from Curley and Hall's ethnographic approaches, Burnett and Hay instead offer an extensive engagement with archival materials from the Government of Canada, HBC, and NWC. While the authors clearly worked in close collaboration with northern communities impacted by the HBC/NWC, the research focuses on understanding the linkages between corporation and state, so as to develop a more thorough appreciation of how each provides the enabling conditions for the other. *Plundering the North* peers into modes of accumulation that depend upon an indirect corporate seizure of the social wage through the extraction of super-profits from communities undergoing forms of organized state abandonment. As the authors detail, in many instances, forms of state support that for most Canadians would be issued as cash are transformed into de facto NWC scrip in communities where the company is the primary financial actor and major retail outlet (121). This, in function, uses some of the most marginalized communities in the country as a pass-through to transfer public monies into private hands. Whereas the other two books offer us compelling accounts of how labor exploitation (in both waged and unwaged sectors) is central to the reproduction of colonial capitalism, the analysis offered here echoes powerfully with Ruth Wilson Gilmore's observations in *Golden Gulag* (2007): that *surplussed* populations are often made into crucial sites of profit extraction through state and corporate collusion that facilitates the capture and further privatization of even the most meagre allotments of the social wage.

Taken together, these texts show that colonialism and capitalism are coconstitutive modes of social organization, which must be confronted and challenged as such. Importantly, though, this is achieved without reducing their accounts of colonial capitalism to some sort of caricature or malevolent external force. Rather, these texts offer profound insight into colonial capitalism as a mode of relationality—albeit one that is particularly undesirable for most of its subjects. They show us how "participation" in colonial capitalism is at once compelled as a consequence of dispossession (Carlson 2023, 23; Mau 2023), while also showing how Indigenous people and communities struggle to produce more favorable terms by which to actualize self-determination within these prevailing conditions. By understanding colonial capitalism as a social relation that exists not external to but through the interactions of its subjects—actions that while free, are nevertheless conditioned in their range of possibilities—texts like these dispense with tired structure-versus-agency dichotomies. Instead, they show that structures emerge as a consequence of agential activity, even as such activity is simultaneously enabled, conditioned, and limited by social structures. Likewise, the approach common across these texts also challenges accounts of relationality that skew toward romanticization. If colonial capitalism is a mode of relating—to one another, to our social environment, and to the more-than-human world—then embracing mere relationality is not a sufficiently robust political agenda by which to pursue *good* relations (for a powerful elaboration of this point see Starblanket and Stark 2018).

In Curley's account, the coal industry has been a fundamental enabling condition for the present form of Diné sovereignty, even as it has simultaneously transformed or even undermined many vital national mores that offer alternative visions of what that sovereignty might mean. Likewise, as Hall shows, Indigenous women experience profound transformations in their social conditions as a consequence of the wages available through work in diamond mining (either through their own direct involvement or, more often, through that of a partner), but this has also evidently redefined the nature of the household—increasingly nuclearizing the family unit and accelerating the exploitation of feminized reproductive labor. Finally, in Burnett and Hay's account, the very condition of abandonment that many northern communities face as a consequence of colonial and racist indifference, has become a structuring logic by which private super-profits are extracted. The private monopoly of the NWC is enabled through indirect, but fully anticipated, appropriation of public monies. Liberal commentators might suggest that these lessons evidence the necessity of a *nuanced* account of colonial capitalism—one that implicitly wouldn't throw the capitalist baby out with the colonial bathwater. However, the real strength of these texts is their attention to *contradiction*. That is, their recognition that the practical activities of social relations are not characterized by neatly fitted particularities that merely need to be accounted for, recognized, and accommodated, but rather by constitutive antagonisms that actually drive modes of social struggle.

Taken together, these texts show that the strategic and politicized repression of the capitalist compulsion toward market activity is the practical condition for the flourishing of anticolonial politics rooted in Indigenous sovereignties that are autonomous, not only from the colonial state but from the coercive force of capital and the market as well. The emergence of these texts in close succession to one another, and the vast range of their national and theoretical engagement with political economy in relation to Indigenous Peoples, portends an important and timely development within the field. While much remains to be sorted out in terms of theoretical/methodological particularities, this upsurge of political economy promises crucial innovations for Indigenous studies writ large.

PHIL HENDERSON is a settler scholar and Banting Postdoctoral Fellow at York University's Global Labour Research Centre.

SHIRI PASTERNAK is an associate professor in criminology at Toronto Metropolitan University.

References

Burnett, Kristin, and Travis Hay. 2023. *Plundering the North: A History of Settler Colonialism, Corporate Welfare, and Food Insecurity.* University of Manitoba Press.

Carlson, John. 2023. "Empowering Indigenous Self-Determination In-Against-and-Beyond Capitalism: A Theory of Dual Dispossession." PhD diss., Carleton University.

Curley, Andrew. 2023. *Carbon Sovereignty: Coal, Development, and Energy Transition in the Navajo Nation.* University of Arizona Press.

Gilmore, Ruth Wilson. 2007. *Golden Gulag: Prisons, Surplus, Crisis, and Opposition in Globalizing California.* University of California Press.

Mau, Søren. 2023. *Mute Compulsion: A Marxist Theory of the Economic Power of Capital.* Verso Books.

Starblanket, Gina, and Heidi Kiiwetinepinesiik Stark. 2018. "Towards a Relational Paradigm—Four Points for Consideration: Knowledge, Gender, Land, and Modernity." In *Resurgence and Reconciliation: Indigenous-Settler Relations and Earth Teachings.* Edited by Michael Asch, John Borrows, and James Tully. University of Toronto Press, 175–208.

PAUL M WORLEY

New English Translations of Zoque and Zapotec Poetry

How to Be a Good Savage and Other Poems
by Mikeas Sánchez, translated by Wendy Call and Shook
Milkweed Editions, 2024

Nostalgia Doesn't Flow Away Like Riverwater
by Irma Pineda, translated by Wendy Call
Deep Vellum, 2024

Stolen Flower
by Irma Pineda, translated by Wendy Call
Yale University Press, 2025

In the Belly of the Night and Other Poems
by Irma Pineda, translated by Wendy Call
Pluralia Ediciones, 2022

IT IS COMMONPLACE to state that literature in translation tends to be all but invisible in the U.S. literary market, with poets and translators alike noting that poetry in translation especially lags well behind even prose translations in both opportunities for publication and sales. And yet, despite what may seem like an uphill battle, the past several years have seen a surge in the translation of poetry by Indigenous people from throughout Latin America. Recent publications such as Michael Bazzett's translation of the K'iche' poet Humberto Ak'abal, *If Today Were Tomorrow,* Seth Michaelson's translations of the Mapuche poet and essayist Liliana Ancalao, *Women of the Big Sky* and *The Sun of Always,* and Clare Sullivan's translation of the Zapotec poet Natalia Toledo, *Carapace Dancer,* clearly showcase the depth and breadth of Indigenous literary movements throughout the hemisphere as they bring a variety of experiences and voices to an English-speaking audience. While many Indigenous poets and authors from Latin America are excited to have their works circulate in English, in conversations about different translation projects, many have told me directly that their primary aim is to create and sustain conversations with Indigenous communities in the U.S. and Canada, however indirectly these may occur through the medium of translation. My hope is that this review essay of works by the Zoque poet Mikeas Sánchez, translated by Wendy Call and Shook, and the Zapotec poet Irma Pineda, translated by Wendy Call, will introduce readers to these important works if they are not already familiar with them, and forward such dialogues in some way, no matter how small.

As suggested by its very title, Sánchez's *How to Be a Good Savage and Other Poems* is a volume loaded with ironic wit and humor, at turns devastating, hopeful, defiant, and resilient. Echoing a text like Frantz Fanon's *Black Skin, White Masks,* the title poem takes up the image of a grandfather who, in the words of the poetic voice, "wanted to be a good savage." Rather than being a poem of condemnation or mockery, the poetic voice traces the contradictions inherent in trying to assimilate into dominant culture, as the grandfather learns Spanish and the saints' names, while also being "a poet/who healed with words." It continues: "The Nhkirawa's electric lamps impressed him," and yet the grandfather "was a powerful shaman/ who spoke the gods' language." Concluding that, "He wanted to be a good savage,/ but he never quite learned how" (135), the speaker in the poem offers the reader a searing and open-ended critique of colonialism and its effects: is the grandfather's "never quite" learning an act of rebellion running just below the surface of his apparent desire? Does it mean that members of the dominant culture never quite accept him? Does it mean that the grandfather's actions of assimilation are never more than caricatures of the dominant culture? Perhaps all of these?

Although the poem appears toward the end of the volume, I begin with it because it offers readers unfamiliar with Sánchez a powerful segue into her work. Diné poet Jake Skeets's excellent and thoughtful introduction to the work exemplifies the kind of dialogue that many Indigenous writers in Latin America seek to have with their counterparts in the U.S. and Canada, with the cowritten translators' note providing the reader with a thorough background to the poet, her work as a writer and activist, and the challenges faced by languages such as Zoque in México. In general, Sanchez's poems linger on the complexities of Zoque life, with the volume inviting the reader in while eschewing the impulse to provide easy direction or explanation. Indeed, one of the threads found throughout the works under consideration here is that they undo outsiders' perceptions and perspectives on the world we all share. For example, while a Mexican scholar famously declared (not so long ago) that the country's Indigenous people cease to be Indigenous when they change their so-called tradition dress for ballcaps and blue jeans, the poem "Mokaya," begins with an epigraph from none other than Walt Whitman. Across pages 28 and 29, it appears as,

> Wanjampatzi te' sis' teserike te sutku'y
> [. . .] tese' mumu'tiyä, mumu tzyi'ä'tyampä tiyä' äj nepa'
> tä' komiste tzyäki.
> Creo en la carne y en los apetitos,
> [. . .] y cada parte, cada pizca de mí
> es un milagro
> I believe in the flesh and the appetites,
> [. . .] and each part and tag of me
> is a miracle

One could do a lot with this inclusion of this passage in the poem from a critical point of view, but many English language readers will be shocked to find mention of Whitman in a work by an Indigenous poet from México and surprised to see his words translated into Zoque. In other words, here and elsewhere, the poet makes a powerful statement about the fact that we all share the same world, and that Whitman is subject to translation into languages like Zoque just as much as Sánchez is subject to translation into English.

As Call and Shook point out in their introduction, Sánchez consciously subverts readers' expectations of what Indigenous literature is or should be through what she refers to as her "non-Indigenous poems" set in Barcelona and/or New York (xviii). For example, her poem "Aisha," about a young female who immigrates from Morocco to Spain, connects powerfully with themes that run throughout Sánchez's work, from navigating patriarchal structures to female sexuality and feminine knowledges. Here, the young woman, having defied the conventions of a culture bent on controlling the female body, "will anoint her wedding dress/ with the scent of hashish and cinnamon/ so that her groom does not discover/ the scent of other men that lingers on her skin" (85). The complexity of these four verses weaves these themes together in such a way that it gestures toward a kind of solidarity that transcends national, linguistic, and cultural boundaries, participating in global discussions on gender and sexuality.

Coincidentally, the author of the other three books reviewed here, Irma Pineda, served on the United Nations Permanent Forum on Indigenous Issues from 2020 to 2022. The first of these analyzed here, *Nostalgia Doesn't Flow Away Like Riverwater,* is a series of persona poems dealing with immigration to the United States from the perspectives of a man who goes to America and the wife he leaves behind. The collection's three sections, "My Heart in

Two," "On the Path," and "The Day Will Come" each mark different phases of the immigrant's journey, moving us through the painful decision to leave, the difficult road north, and the creation of separate but interconnected lives in the U.S. and México. The work is not simply one of defeat or frustration, however, as elements from the first section are threaded throughout the second and third, suggesting not only the instance on return found in the first poem found in the line, "You must return to your lifeline's home" (3), but that, in the words of the speaker in the final poem, "I insist/ that day will come . . ." (153). That is, while the volume's protagonists unflinchingly detail the heartache and difficulties of immigration, they yet maintain that these are not the sum total of immigration's impact and that the future remains to be written.

The first section dwells on the emotional trauma of leaving one's loved ones and hometown in search of a way to support those very entities. As the poem "Two Paths" makes clear, the speaker feels caught between two impossible options:

> If I stay   if I go
> both paths lead toward pain
>
> but hunger hurts us, too
>   sickness
>   poverty's dark night
> hurts more   (31)

Here and elsewhere, the collection thus humanizes the immigration experience by insisting on the impossibility of the immigrant's choices for an English-speaking audience whose popular media tends to ignore or even deny the realities that drive people to consider immigration in the first place. Quite hopefully, the section's final poem ends with the verse, "I will someday return."

The second section traces the immigrant's experience of the journey north while recognizing that the journey for the immigrant and their loved ones does not end once they have reached their final destination. The first poem opens with a meditation on the poetic voice that has been left behind, stating, "and I've found nothing to ease this pain/ hatcheted in my brain. . . . / But my pain's blade won't kill our hope" (53). While they anxiously await word from the immigrant, this voice reflects further on immigration and the larger context that has produced large-scale immigration to the United States. Describing the ecological collapse that currently wracks the planet, they describe having "left cornfields plowed and parched/ one ox thin and one dead" while saying the sea:

. . . long ago stopped giving us fish
and now vomits rusted cans
[and] no longer hears our pleas
when we pray
. . .
The sea went deaf and tossed us
into the desert's arms
The sea went deaf and hurled us
onto someone else's path (65)

The sense that the world is upside down and misordered (". . . the sky/ rains down endless stars/ ferocious lights in metal towers") (89) only continues once the immigrant has arrived in their destination, and underscores the notion that the immigrant's choice to leave is symptomatic of the social upheaval of a planetary society that has lost its way.

Although the third and final section does not bring the kind of resolution the English-language literary market tends to expect, it nonetheless anticipates a different, if not hopeful, future. The speaker who was left behind harbors anguish that has become a sea that endeavors "to go unnoticed, to go unseen/ because it now knows/ not everyone loves the sea" (103). At the same time, the immigrant ponders how, exactly, they will return carrying the burden of those who have not and will never do so, asking, "What can I say to their people/ What can I do so these deaths/ don't hurt" (106). Despite the magnitude of these trials, in one of Pineda's most discussed poems the speaker who has remained powerfully proclaims,

and you will not see me die
because we will stay strong
we will always survive
. . .
and we will be many hearts
anchored to the core of the Binnizá. (125)

And it is precisely the notion of this steadfast anchoring that enables both voices to envision a future in which the immigrant, despite the odds, returns.

Stolen Flower similarly holds a mirror to the contemporary reality of the consequences of the global, increasingly militarized world we all share. As Call lays out in the "Translator's Introduction,"

> In February 2007, a group of Mexican soldiers raped a seventy-three-year-old Indigenous Nahua woman, Ernestina Ascensio Rosario, and left her for dead . . . When journalists began to investigate the case, they learned that

> girls as young as twelve in Soledad Atzompa (in Veracruz, México) were mothers. According to the girls' families, they had also been raped by soldiers stationed nearby. (v)

According to Call, Pineda, whose own father, Victor "Yodo" Pineda, was a victim of state violence, told her that the situation in Soledad Atzompa "reminded [her] of other situations during [her] life when the military was in conflict with [Indigenous] communities" (v). Even within México, the volume itself represents a gesture of trans-Indigenous solidarity insofar as Pineda, who is Zapotec, crafts this series of persona poems based on the lived experiences of Nahua women, understanding what happened to them as being all too common in their communities' relationship with the Mexican state. In turn, the volume resonates with calls to recognize Missing and Murdered Indigenous Women in the U.S. and Canada, with the volume's translation into English marking an important moment bringing attention to the hemispheric nature and legacy of this ongoing violence.

In the translation of Pineda's *Guie' Ni Zinebe/ La flor que se llevó,* which was first published by Pluralia, Yale University Press made the excellent decision to follow Pluralia's lead and include documentary-style photographs along with the poems, as the volume expresses the fear, anger, and resilience of these women as state-militarization upends their everyday lives. In a poem printed above a photo of a squad of troops walking alongside a column of Humvees, one poetic voice tells the soldiers to "Stop following my footsteps," before railing against the fact that the soldiers pursue the women as though they were animals and laying bare the impact that such violence has on the perpetrator, stating,

> We are your mirror
> See yourself in us and
> know we are not your enemy. (16)

In a more hemispheric context, the photograph expands the context of the "you," as the United States' ongoing arms shipments to militaries in places like México, represented by the Humvee, implicates readers as being passive participants in facilitating and supporting México's militarization and the subsequent violence there.

Many of the poems strike a tone of open defiance, with one of the main threads running throughout the volume being the notions that violence dehumanizes both perpetrator and victim, as well as the fact that in a country like México, many soldiers themselves are from Indigenous communities and therefore potentially also members of the collection's collective "we." For example, late in the volume one of the speakers states, "My voice will weigh on you/ like a rope hanging from your neck," before ending the poem, "you clawed the light/ from our ancestors' eyes" (76). Committing an act of violence against this woman becomes a "rope" weighing the soldier down, while, if we understand the "our" more expansively, by participating in these atrocities, he has harmed his own ancestors as well.

Stolen Flower ends with a picture of a young woman carrying a toddler on her back, which in any other publication may be read as simply a tender moment between mother and child. In the final poem that precedes it, however, a poetic voice speaks directly to her rapist and ends by saying,

> And I would tell him:
> though he is the hand of evil
> he too
> is my brother (94)

The intersection between image and poem is inescapable, lends itself to multiple, even conflicting readings, and encourages readers to sit with the juxtapositions of word and image throughout the rest of the volume. It is a devastating way to conclude such a powerful and challenging work.

In the Belly of the Night and Other Poems is a rare trilingual (Zapotec-Spanish-English) book published by the Mexican publishing house Pluralia that includes the translation and re-edition of Pineda's first book as well as additional poems. First published in 2005, the *Ndaani' gueela' ne xhupa diidxaguie'/En el vientre de la noche,* the book from which the volume takes its name, marks an important milestone in both the trajectory of Latin American Indigenous literatures and the poet's own poetic evolution, as it was Pineda's first book. In many ways, it is one of the texts whose publication helped initiate Mexico's current boom in bilingual Indigenous literatures. Thematically, the collection's emphasis on topics ranging from femininity and motherhood to migration breaks with the tendencies in Mexican Indigenous literatures that began emerging in the 1980s that, for many scholars, critics, and even authors, privilege male perspectives and an uncritical approach to traditions. As such, the publication of the collection twenty years ago immediately positioned Pineda as an important, iconoclastic voice in Indigenous literatures.

Beginning with an insightful note to the poet from Mexican sociologist, poet, and activist Elisa Ramírez Castañeda and a translator's note by Call, the collection itself is divided into six sections: "In the Belly of Night," which draws on this original volume; "Old Poems"; "Nostalgia of the Sea"; "To Heal a Soul"; "Cord House"; and "From the Cord House to the Nine Handspans." One of the most striking things about the first section is the juxtapositions that the poet was already adept at creating early on in her career. For example, her treatment of the motif of the city in a poem like "I was given this day" resonates powerfully with her representation of the burial of her son's umbilical cord in "Guest" two poems later. In the first of these, while the poetic voice does not necessarily despair at being in an urban environment, the city is notable for what it does not hold as much as for what it does. The day has the "songs of silent birds" and "the small of wet earth in the balconies' flowerpots" while hummingbirds are "absent" and iguanas present only insofar as they are "embroidered on my son's shirt" (42). As, perhaps, a response to this earlier poem, in "Guest" the speaker invokes the practice of burying a newborn's umbilical cord in an act that places them in a relationship of reciprocity with the land, saying,

> . . . I'll bury it under a large shade tree
> so you will never forget the land
> that holds your soul. (47)

Potent reminders to remain grounded despite one's circumstances can be found in the eponymous "In the Belly of the Night" and throughout the rest of the book.

In comparison with the more somber tone of the other poems, "It Happens Sometimes" takes up female sexuality in a delightfully unexpected way, beginning with the speaker's falling in love with a tree, stating,

> It also happens, sometimes,
> that the tree you love
> turns into a man,
> and you love his ideas,
> his lips,
> his heart,
> his arms
> or his sex
> (because trees have sex). (66)

Referring to him as the "sun-tree-man" (67) in the penultimate line, the poem's speaker blurs the line between the human and nonhuman, with the poem's final line in which the speaker looks at him "until going blind," suggesting everything from sexual climax to a deeper understanding of creation that exceeds reason and one's senses. The entire volume is filled with such unexpected moments and epiphanies, particularly the final section, "From the Cord House to the Nine Handspans," which outlines a human life cycle from birth to death.

Finally, all four books evoke nonalphabetic, Indigenous forms of recording knowledge and human interaction through their form and, to some extent, share a kinship with many of the bilingual (Indigenous languages/Spanish) books produced by the Mexican press Pluralia through their stunning use of different-colored fonts and illustrations. *Stolen Flower*'s juxtaposition of words and images evokes the relationships created between these in Mesoamerican codices, while both *In the Belly of Night and Other Poems* and *How to Be a Good Savage and Other Poems* make strategic use of red and black throughout. In the case of the former, the titles and occasionally the first lines of poems appear in a soft, purplish red that conjures the use of cochinilla dye in Pineda's home state of Oaxaca, providing a striking contrast with the black of the main text. In the case of the latter, the Zoque-language text of Sánchez's poems appears in bright red on the left pages of the volume, across from their gray-black versions in Spanish and English on the right side. While these are certainly striking aesthetic choices, they also evoke the Aztec scriptorial tradition in which red and black symbolize writing and wisdom (respectively) (Anzaldúa 1999, 91).[1] Both books also employ what seem to be woodblock prints of jaguars on the covers, with *In the Belly of the Night,* appropriately enough, a Pluralia publication, making creative use of that and additional illustrations by Natalia Gurovich throughout the text. The large cat depicted on the cover and inside of *How to Be a Good Savage* is even based on a Zoque glyph. Along those lines, the cover of *Nostalgia Doesn't Flow Away Like Riverwater* employs a similar interplay among the colors of its fonts (light purple, black, and aquamarine) while incorporating a close-up from a beaded wall hanging by Natividad Amador that is evocative of the designs on an embroidered blouse, or huipil. The scholarship on understanding textiles as text is ample, and growing, and the inclusion of these bright purple flowers in a hue that matches the colors of the fonts of the names of both poet and translator serves as a powerful reminder that words in alphabetic script are not the only form of writing: The poetic traditions upon which this body of literature draws precede and exceed colonization.

Readers and scholars alike will be delighted to pick up these works, whether for the first or five-hundredth time. Call and Shook's collaborative translations of Sánchez are truly wonderful, while Call's solo translations of Pineda further underscore her role as one of the most important translator activists working in the field. Particularly as they are available in these trilingual formats, Sánchez's and Pineda's works are timely contributions to Indigenous literatures on a hemispheric level, as well as an invitation to continue such broader, hemispheric dialogues.

PAUL M WORLEY is professor of Spanish at Appalachian State University.

Note

1. Gloria Anzaldúa, *Borderlands/La Frontera: The New Mestiza* (Aunt Lute Books, 1999).

REVIEWS

JOHN BLANCO

Bundok: A Hinterland History of Filipino America
by Adrian De Leon
University of North Carolina Press, 2023

"WHO COUNTS AS A FILIPINO?" This question, which Adrian de Leon poses in the conclusion to his recent work, captures the author's larger stake in exploring the politics of national culture and identity, both within the Philippines and the U.S.; and the anomalous designation of the Ilocos region and Ilocanos as part of both. The nebulousness of the question intends to provoke further questions: What does it mean "to count?" Are there different, even contradictory ways of counting? Are there those who don't count for nefarious or ideological reasons? (210—24). Finally, are the ones who (do) "count" the beneficiaries of an unearned privilege? The author proposes that many of these questions will have been answered in the course of his study. While answering some, de Leon also opens other questions, which he ultimately can't answer. Both kinds of questions provide material for reigniting and reorienting cultural debates that either bring together or drive apart Filipinos and their diasporic, cross-Pacific, brethren. For this reason alone, *Bundok* deserves to be read and discussed.

De Leon's investigation into the intersection between the cultural politics of Filipino identity in the U.S. and the complex engagement of Philippine nationalism with Indigenous pasts and Filipino emigration in the present references and echoes the classic work by Benedict Anderson, *Imagined Communities*. Both highlight the artificial or constructed character of (Filipino) national identity. Yet the author's return to Anderson's thesis also represents a development; for, rather than focusing on vernacular or popular expressions of cultural identity in print culture, as Anderson does, De Leon exposes the overdetermination of "(the) Filipino identity" by agricultural capitalism as well as statistics and technologies of U.S. empire such as photography and ethnology. In doing so, the author calls attention to the pre- or overdetermined contours of cultural identity, which (in de Leon's account) owe themselves more to Spanish and U.S. colonialism than to Filipino writers and intellectuals themselves. The acknowledgment of these disavowed roots, de Leon argues, decenters the triumphant ethno-nationalism promoted by a putatively "Tagalog bourgeois world," which claims to represent the ninety-five major ethnolinguistic groups throughout the archipelago while suppressing the participation of those groups in the national project. By critiquing the national pretensions of a regional ethnic minority, *Bundok* anticipates the possibility of imagining a global Indigenous epistemology of Ilocanos that survives, untainted, by the official nationalism decried by Anderson and others. The book promises a more nuanced retelling of the nation's origins: with a closer attention to regional identities like that of Ilocos as representative of "the Amianan" or the North (i.e., Northern Luzon); population displacements and proletarianization; forms of cultural marginalization; and diaspora, particularly to the United States.

De Leon's argument is bookended by two prominent authors who both hail from the northern provinces of Luzon: Isabelo de los Reyes (Ilocos Sur) and Carlos Bulosan (Pangasinan). Each, in their own separate ways, have been celebrated as precursors of cultural nationalism (in the case of Reyes) or U.S. Asian American identity politics (Bulosan). As *Bundok* persuasively argues, in elevating each writer, both Philippine nationalism and Asian American cultural politics obscure or erase the affirmation of Reyes and Bulosan's own broadly regional attachments. De Leon takes this cultural amnesia to task. Behind the critical contribution of this gesture, however, lies an open question: Can such disparate instances of historical suppression, separated by half a century and the Pacific Ocean, nevertheless propose a hinterland history in which Ilokano-speaking peoples remember, retell, and prioritize *their own* regional history, regardless and even in defiance of their insertion into a national narrative about Philippine history and culture? Could such a hinterland history frame the inclusion or exclusion of Indigenous Peoples from the national narrative differently than from the "bourgeois Tagalogs"?

Over the course of several chapters, de Leon pursues the outlines of what such a history might entail: highlighting the multiple ways in which the Philippines became integrated into the world economy and the way(s) Filipinos became marked by that integration. The continuous thread that the author pulls through the episodes of this integration is the role of racialization and racial hierarchies in mobilizing and organizing the colonial and commonwealth labor regimes in the Philippines (7). Chapter 1, for example, shows how the creation of the state tobacco monopoly in northern Luzon necessitated the racialization of Chinese merchants, Ilokano *indio* peasants, and highland *infieles* or non-Christian "tribes" (39). The resulting concept of what De Leon calls a *racial economy,* in turn, frames the two main subsections of *Bundok,* which deal with the role of ethnology and photography in configuring the imagination of the Philippine northern highlands (chapters 2–4); and the rhetorics and tropes of Ilokano diaspora throughout the U.S. (chapters 5 and 6).

Both sections examine the interpellative role of colonial sciences, technologies, and discourses in conjuring an image of "the Filipino," which De Leon juxtaposes with the redemptive rhetorics of Filipino identity promoted by (presumably) Manila-based academics and statesmen. These same interpellations of the Filipino, however, also facilitate expressions of cultural agency and self-assertion: whether these concern the practice of dog-eating among the highland "Igorot" tribes who performed their rituals and customs before an American audience at the U.S. world exhibitions (chapter 3) or the self-justification of economic exile and diaspora throughout the U.S. (chapter 6). These arenas of accommodation and negotiation reinforce an argument familiar to many readers today: Systems of cultural subjection and control inevitably generate emergent forms of social dissidence and resistance. In *Bundok,* this system is given the name of the "ethno-racial archive," which distributes its effects according to differential racial categorizations while also contributing to the U.S. corporate and imperialist imaginings of "the Filipino" in general (19). Yet, to the degree that such systems depend (however partially) on the will and agency of individuals and communities who are coopted by capital, these individuals and communities can also conserve, reproduce, and even reinvent their own histories from their own perspective(s) and in alignment with their own values.

De Leon's book shares with a recent work by Mark Dizon (*Reciprocal Mobilities*) the decentering of Philippine histories that privilege the Spanish Empire's colonial capital Intramuros (Manila) and its environs as the primary point of reference. By reorienting Philippine history around northern Luzon, the author of *Bundok* also invites us to consider the genealogy that divides "Christian" Filipinos from "non-Christian" ones: a dichotomy that in turn informs the distinction between "native" Filipinos and "indigenous" ones. As the author quips in the introduction, "while all Indigenous people from the Philippines (Igorot, Lumad, and Aeta, among others) are native, so to speak, not all native people are Indigenous" (21). Both native and Indigenous Filipinos, in any case, share a common subjection to a larger history of agricultural capitalism, proletarianization, and commodification: elements of the social history perspective advanced by Alfred McCoy and Edilberto de Jesus a generation ago, yet expanded to encompass contemporary debates on critical regionalism and Filipino diaspora in the U.S.

One cannot but appreciate the theoretical sophistication with which the author has framed compelling readings and interpretations of cultural texts that include works of ethnography, photographic collections, autobiographies and memoirs. Yet de Leon's dependence on the lowland vs. highland, coastland vs. hinterland categorizations that the work as a whole sets out to critique, render certain aspects of De Leon's thesis unexplained, if not inexplicable. Take, for example, the anomalous designation of the Ilocos region, which occupies the center of De Leon's "hinterland" history of the Amianan or North but does not *itself* belong to the so-called hinterland. Much of the region, which lies on the western coast of Luzon, was colonized by Spain during the first century of conquest precisely *because* it comprises a geographically accessible plain that blends with that of central Luzon: it represents, in other words, the lowlands. Yet, in a book where Ilokano proletarianization, diaspora, and the racialization of the *sakadas* (Filipino migrant workers on the Hawai'i plantations) lead to stereotypes of highland savagery, the mischaracterization of Ilocos would also lead one to ask: Would Ilokanos identify themselves as Indigenous people similar to the Ifugaos, Aetas, or Ilongots in the mountainous provinces? Would they identify their own region as a "hinterland"? The politicization of lowland and hinterland histories, while convenient, nevertheless relies on a distinction that remains quite nebulous itself. Consciously or unconsciously, De Leon's book borrows from regionalists like Aurelio Agcaoili, who identify northern Luzon as "the Amianan," with the implication that the geographical proximity between Native and Indigenous groups fosters a kind of pan-Indigenous ethnic sensibility. Theoretically, such a sensibility might ultimately lead one to (mis)identify Ilokanos as an Indigenous people, which would certainly qualify their contribution to the global Indigenous epistemology that *Bundok* anticipates. At the very least, Philippine historiography could finally dismiss the clumsy articulations of Philippine ethnonationalism promoted by a putatively Tagalog-speaking cultural elite. To what degree, however, would such a global Indigenous framework be any *less* imaginary than any other ethnonationalism: Whether or not it comes from Manila?

De Leon's entanglement with regional polemics extends to what seems to be an unnecessary and misguided characterization of "Tagalog ethnonationalism," which appears sprinkled throughout the chapters without ever receiving a sustained analysis. In the opening pages, the author contrasts the proto-regionalist, Ilokano-speaking Don Isabelo de los Reyes, with national martyr Dr. José Rizal, whom the author portrays as a "Tagalog mestizo intellectual" who "regards people from the hinterlands as unruly and less civilized than their southern native counterparts" (3). Leaving aside my earlier observation regarding the Ilocos region as a questionable hinterland, nothing about this statement regarding De Los Reyes and Rizal is true. In fact, and paradoxically enough, in the only significant debate between the two writers (who later came to publicly support one another's efforts), Rizal argued that native Filipinos were in fact *more* civilized than their Spanish counterparts at the time of the conquest. And in response to Rizal's contention, Reyes mused that Rizal was too blinded by his excessive patriotism to see the *primitivity* of preconquest Native society and culture, *particularly in Ilocos.* The mischaracterization of this debate in *Bundok* would not be so egregious, if it did not engender other misconceptions later in the book: such as the author's speculation that Rizal "fear(ed) the preponderance of Northern Luzon in the making of a modern Filipino" (201). Beyond the libelous character of such a contention, one wonders how necessary these and other statements are to support an otherwise plausible argument on the constructed nature of Filipino-Ilocano identity.

The mischaracterization of Rizal here adumbrates a contention that has arisen in U.S. based scholarship in recent decades; that is, the conflation of a Manila-centric, Chinese mestizo, *ilustrado* [educated] elite at the turn of the century with a kind of Tagalog-based ethnonationalism. Without pretending to give the last word on this misunderstanding here, anecdotal evidence suggests the two representations of the Philippine intelligentsia remain separate. For example, two of the most prominent members of Rizal's circle of *ilustrado* propagandists were the Luna brothers (Juan and Antonio), whose families came from Ilocos Norte and La Union in Pangasinan. Bishop Gregorio Aglipay, former military vicar general during the Philippine Revolution and later head of the first Filipino-centric Christian denomination (the *Iglesia Filipina Independiente*), also hailed from Ilocos Norte. Perhaps the only major figure of the Philippine Revolution to speak of the Tagalog people [*Katagalugan*] as an ethnic synecdoche for the Philippines as a whole, Andres Bonifacio, was himself an uneducated warehouse worker who had dabbled in popular theater—hardly a model of the bourgeois intellectual. A generation later, the two arguably most important politicians of the U.S. Commonwealth era and founders of the Liberal and Nationalist parties, Elipidio Quirino and Manuel Quezon, hailed from provinces outside Manila: Vigan, Ilocos Sur and Baler, Aurora, respectively. Quirino's *kabayan*, Jorge Bocobo, whom we credit for promoting Philippine arts and culture throughout the archipelago and the world as president of the University of the Philippines, came from Tarlac, Pangasinan—again, the Ilocos region. Clearly, these pioneers of Philippine nationalism do not fit De Leon's characterization of an "elite minority, who, by and large, had nearly zero linguistic contact with the majority of the colonial population" (8). Who exactly, one wonders, would these elites even be?

The fuzzy indigenization of Ilokanos and concomitant counter-racialization of "Tagalogs" stand out as notable shortcomings in *Bundok*.

Neither issue, however, should dim an otherwise enthusiastic appreciation of the book as a foray into testing arguments made by critical regionalisms on a hitherto largely theoretical and speculative level. This foray yields some original insights into the articulations and calibrations of race/racialization, monopoly capitalism, the rise of ethnology, and the commodification of images through photography and World Fair exhibitions. De Leon's exploration of the "Kodak Zone" in the photographing and documentation of "non-Christian tribes" by Dean Worcester and others, for instance, provides a provocative model of the ethno-racial archive concept in miniature. To bring the Philippines into the "Kodak Zone," De Leon remarks at one point, means "entangling the visual commodification of bodies as human resources into a larger context of the commodification of land agriculture and mineral resources in the Cordilleras" (82). By examining various cultural artifacts and exhibits, ethnological portraits, and corporate documents, *Bundok* outlines a process in which the proletarianization of Ilocanos, the criminalization of Ilongots, and the conditional inclusion of Ifugaos as subjects of rehabilitation, all configured the possible ways in which Filipinos could be conceived as Filipinos. This, in turn, influenced the paths and horizons of agency within the label. Whether De Leon's constructivist critique of national identity politics succeeds as a hinterland history, of course, ultimately depends on how one judges the prospects of an "insurgent ethnology" capable of overcoming the prejudices and stereotypes upon which the field of ethnology is built. Bringing to mind poet Audre Lorde's fateful pronouncement that "the master's tools will never dismantle the master's house," it may be that even insurgent ethnologies produce racial stereotypes.

JOHN BLANCO is professor of comparative literature, Spanish and cultural studies at the University of California San Diego.

NICOLAS G. ROSENTHAL

Indigenous Chicago
directed by Rose Miron, Meredith McCoy, Analú María López, and Blaire Morseau
Includes exhibition, digital resources, digital mapping, curriculum, oral history, and contextual programming. https://indigenous-chicago.org/

CITIES HAVE ALWAYS BEEN Indigenous places. This is something well understood by Native people throughout what is now the United States. Over the past twenty-five years, the long-standing relationships between Indigenous Peoples and cities have received considerable attention in history, literature, sociology, and other disciplines that make up Native American and Indigenous studies. Based on collaborations between the Newberry Library and Native communities throughout the region, the *Indigenous Chicago* project now stands as one of the first public history projects of its kind to explore the concept of cities as Indigenous places, with a focus on Chicago.

The different components of *Indigenous Chicago* provide valuable resources for community members, educators, scholars, students, and a public interested in reading the city's history through a Native lens. An exhibition, which ran from September 2024 to January 2025, is documented by video and audio tours telling the story of Chicago as an Indigenous crossroads that continues to be a Native place over centuries of European and American colonialism. Drawing on items from the Newberry's substantial collections, it explored topics ranging from Native peoples' encounters with Europeans in the seventeenth century to the late twentieth century activism of Chicago's Native American community. It also featured new works by contemporary Native artists to engage in conversation with this history. A good overview of the exhibition and how it came about is discussed in a podcast episode of *Curious Chicago*, produced by a local affiliate of the Public Broadcasting Service (PBS) and posted to the website.[1] It reveals that *Indigenous Chicago* was rooted in the need to go beyond the practice of land acknowledgments and to validate and explore Native presence in more meaningful and complex ways.

The most in-depth, detailed information about Native experiences throughout Chicago's history is in the Digital Resources Story Map section, split into two main areas, each of which creatively combines interactive maps with images, primary sources, narrative text, and links. Specifically, five "story maps" develop the themes "Chicago is a Native Place," "Early Contact and Travel to Chicago," "Increased Settlement and the Transformation of the Great Lakes," "Removal and Erasure," and "Indigenous Chicago, Present and Future," while nine interactive digital maps visualize and expand upon topics such as Native place names throughout the region (featured in seven languages), the areas from which Native peoples traveled to participate in the Bureau of Indian Affairs Relocation Program, and Native-centered urban walking tours. Many digital resources are integrated into the "Curriculum" section, which is designed for high school educators and organized around four modules on engaging themes. The "Programming" section is a record of presentations and workshops by the *Indigenous Chicago* project team, community members, and scholars, some of which are available for viewing. Finally, the Oral Histories section is the result of an ongoing effort to interview members of Chicago's Native community and provide the recordings and transcripts to the public.

Indigenous Chicago's intention to tell the city's history while "centering Indigenous voices, laying bare stories of settler-colonial harm, and gesturing towards Indigenous futures" frames each of its parts. In doing so, *Indigenous Chicago* follows from the scholarship of the past decades, which has demonstrated that settler colonialism depends on erasing the evidence and ongoing reality of Indigenous people in cities, while Indigenous survivance includes persistence within urban centers, the active Indigenizing of urban spaces, and telling histories that affirm urban Indigeneity. One surprising aspect of *Indigenous Chicago* is how few references there are to this scholarship, especially since Chicago has been central to it since the pathbreaking 2002 publication of *Native Chicago* by the Chicago-based Native American Educational Services College, the first higher education institution established to serve an urban Native population. Nonetheless, *Indigenous Chicago* stands as exemplary of an ongoing, collaborative, community-engaged public history project. It also demonstrates the rich possibilities for narrating the past, present, and future of cities like Chicago as Indigenous places.

NICOLAS G. ROSENTHAL is chair and professor of history at Loyola Marymount University.

Note

1. https://www.wbez.org/curious-city/2024/11/21/indigenous-chicago-project-shows-the-city-has-always-been-a-native-place.

MONIQUE MOJICA

Retreating to Re-Treat: A Performance Encounter at the 'Edge of the Woods'
by The Collective Encounter, with Jill Carter
Plawrights Canada Press, 2024

THIS BOOK is a provocative documentation of a performance intervention rooted in Indigenous resistance and "survivance." It is an archive of a dramatic process that Anishinaabe/Ashkenazi theater artist and scholar Jill Carter undertook with diverse University of Toronto students and community members in 2019. It models one possible path to respond to the ninety-four "Calls to Action" that resulted from Canada's Truth and Reconciliation Commission. As of 2024, only eleven of those calls were complete. In particular it was Call 45—one that is designated by the government of Canada as "not started" that drove the inquiry of this project. As the lead artist, Dr. Carter, says: "It was Call 45 that I wished to address with this project—a project I envisioned as a collectively devised address of this imagined future. Such an address, I anticipated, would carry its participants into spaces in which they were compelled to see, remember and respond to a tangled history of settlement, to long-suppressed histories, to buried waterways, to silenced voices and to ravished earth. This was a project that would require willing bodies, open hearts, and an absolute commitment to the task at hand" (9).

This work is a valuable text for scholars of performance studies, Indigenous studies, Indigenous performance theory and theater. It uses an innovative format, beginning with theory and reflections on artistic process following the 2019 premiere and includes the full production script of the play, *Encounters at the 'Edge of the Woods.'*

The title of the book, *Retreating to Re-Treat,* is a further invitation for readers to examine how Indigenous Peoples and settlers might come together to create new treaties through re-negotiating the ongoing challenges of being in a treaty *relationship.* This premise also introduces what Métis curator David Garneau terms "irreconcilable spaces," described by Carter as "those spaces in which to repair the split mind and from which we might re-encounter each other and the biotas that sustain us with generative action powered by good intention." This meant that during the creative process it was imperative to include safety constructs for when the two groups needed to be apart, this was nonnegotiable. It is important to note that this project did not aim for an immediate dismantling of that which is irreconcilable but honored the uncomfortable moments.

The subtitle, *A Performative Encounter at the 'Edge of the Woods'* is a reference borrowed from the cultural protocols of many Indigenous Peoples from the Haudenosaunee to the Plains Cree and from north to south in this hemisphere. "Calling Out from the Edge of the Woods" refers to when one is about to enter another group's territory, recognizing there are certain protocols and activations to follow. It requires a calling out of a greeting of peace, identification of who one is—what one's lineage is and from what lands—to state one's intentions upon entering another group's lands and to ask permission to do so.

This calling out and the response it elicits provide the structure for both the narrative for the process of how the piece was developed and for the script itself. Call and response weaves throughout this volume as a challenge to reveal and an invitation to repair. In the production script, the artists/scholars/devisers wove their personal stories together in this way using the traditions of ensemble performance and devised theater. The result is poignant, moving, angry and at times absurd. It is an uplifting example of what can happen when the vehicle of theater is courageously activated with the intent to encounter and heal in order to tell hard and uncomfortable truths.

MONIQUE MOJICA (Guna and Rappahannock) is an actor, playwright, dramaturg and writer of Indigenous performance theory.

JULIANA HU PEGUES

Settler Attachments and Asian Diasporic Film
by Beenash Jafri
University of Minnesota Press, 2025

BEENASH JAFRI'S *Settler Attachments and Asian Diasporic Film* focuses on cultural production to theorize Asian North American ontologies and epistemologies within settler colonial structures and in relation to Indigenous lands, bodies, and peoples. Rather than simply ask whether Asian immigrants and their descendants participate or collaborate within settler structures, Jafri compellingly questions how and why settler colonial desires are persistently expressed by Asian diasporic artists and activists. Building from work on Asian-Indigenous relationalities by scholars such as Iyko Day, Manu Karuka, and Quynh Nhu Le, *Settler Attachments* places film and visual culture at the center of its analysis. The book elucidates how the construction of race and national identity in North America coincided with the emergence of filmic technology and aesthetics. What has been left understudied is how film as a medium both reflects and reiterates discourses of settler colonialism, specifically related to Indigenous dispossession. Rather than reading for stereotype and representation, however, Jafri provides a structural methodology for reading film, specifically the structural differences of diaspora and Indigeneity within settler colonialism, and the incommensurate impasse that results.

Settler Attachments and Asian Diasporic Film makes a major theoretical contribution in its attention to the analytical framing of attachment, specifically the psychic and affective diasporan investment in settler colonialism. Affective analysis has been central to scholarship in critical race studies and queer and feminist theorizing but is less often applied to studies of settler colonialism. With its resonance with Indigenous feminist scholarship, such as Tanana Athabascan scholar Dian Million's theorization of "felt theory," *Settler Attachments* convincingly argues that registers of feeling, emotion, and affect within Asian diasporic film and media exhibit a stubborn and abiding attachment to settler structures. The first chapter of the book analyzes settler attachment through the figure of the Asian cowboy in two independent films from the 1990s. Pivoting from the oft-discussed idea of "playing Indian" to "playing cowboy," Jafri underscores how such settler cosplay potentially undoes whiteness, but never colonialism, and melancholic loss is registered through both ambivalent assimilation and Indigenous erasure. Jafri extends her study of settler attachment in chapter 2, looking to the early 1990s experimental films of Shani Mootoo and a 2021 photo essay by Vivek Shraya. Here Jafri underscores a startling contradiction, that even as these queer and trans South Asian diasporic artists have expressed political commitments to Indigenous sovereignty, their artistic works validate attachments to settler colonial landscapes and aesthetics. *Settler Attachments* robustly demonstrates that ideological transformation alone is insufficient to shift diasporan attachments to settler coloniality.

Herein lies the power of an affective reading. Not only does it strengthen understandings of settler complicity among non-Native oppressed peoples, but a focus on attachment allows for potentialities within and through the impasse. The book's second half does just that, shifting to attachment's fleeting and intangible realms to position decolonization as an active and aspirational process, and the possibilities afforded by Asian-Indigenous radical friendships and queer relations. Chapter 3 examines the decades-long friendship between South Asian diasporan filmmaker Ali Kazimi and Onondaga photographer Jeffrey Thomas, within the context of Indigenous resurgence and South Asian diasporic activism connected to the artists' collaborative and respective works. The book's final chapter focuses on two recent feature-length films directed by Asian diasporic filmmakers. Catherine Hernandez's *Scarborough* tells the entwined story of three children—Filipino, Mi'kmaq, and white—in a working-class and immigrant neighborhood of a Canadian suburb while V.T. Nayani's *This Place* is set in Toronto and chronicles the romantic relationship between two young women, one Tamil and the other Kanien'kehá:ka and Iranian. Queer studies critique finds its strongest engagement in this chapter, and Jafri posits a concept of queer of color ephemerality to apprehend what might be missed in didactic understandings but witnessed within the quotidian intimacies and kinships of those who live, love, and work together. The second half of the book also underscores the importance of Jafri's structural analysis, especially in her attention to the productions of these films, such as V.T. Nayani's coauthorship of the screenplay for *This Place* with Mohawk actress Kawennáhere Devery Jacobs (who also plays one of the film's leads) and Iranian artist Golshan Abdmoulaie.

This book offers singular and vital contributions to settler colonial studies, Indigenous studies, Asian American studies, film studies, critical ethnic studies, and feminist and queer studies. Scholars and teachers working in these areas will find much to study and learn from. *Settler Attachments and Asian Diasporic Film* is a richly theorized and deeply ethical text that I expect will change and shape scholarly and political conversations in profoundly meaningful ways.

JULIANA HU PEGUES is associate professor at Cornell University in the Department of Literatures in English.

MARK MINCH-DE LEON

Earth Diplomacy: Indigenous American Art, Ecological Crisis, and the Cold War
by Jessica L. Horton
Duke University Press, 2024

JESSICA HORTON'S *Earth Diplomacy* positions itself between two ambiguities. The first: how white anthropologists and art patrons turned Native American art into a resource for developing a uniquely American aesthetic, producing the dilemma: Art or culture? This tired question is haunted by the second ambiguity: Western humanist conquest and the expulsion of Indigenous Peoples' worlds and nonhuman kin from politics led to the question—are Native relational forms political? Horton responds to this dual dilemma (art or culture/politics or culture) by arguing that Native American art is diplomacy and analyzes Native cosmological thought in international contexts.

Horton focuses on a United States Information Agency (USIA) project to enlist Native artists in Cold War propaganda tours. In 1953, embattled by Soviet propaganda that correctly identified the U.S. as a brutal settler colonial (and anti-Black) regime, the U.S. government began a campaign to counter these narratives, enlisting artists as cultural ambassadors. Horton discusses the artwork of Fritz Scholder (La Jolla Band of Luiseño Indians), Fred Stevens (Diné), Bertha Stevens (Diné), Darryl Blackman (Blackfeet), and Oscar Howe (Yanktonai Dakota) in this context, emphasizing the relational forms, spatial practices, and materiality of their work. Essentially a psyop and soft power counterinsurgency (following a wave of decolonial, revolutionary uprisings), the USIA tours presented a reconciled relationship between the U.S. and Native people to promote U.S. exceptionalism, individualism, and a capitalist economy.

The USIA project was also a reaction to the Bandung Conference (1955) of twenty-nine African and Asian nations, which explicitly excluded the U.S. This is a compelling juxtaposition that Horton fails to address. Importantly the USIA anticommunist tours ran parallel to termination policies, due to Native reservations being "hothouses for communism," a suggestive contradiction that undergirds the material and ideological formation of these tours (4).

Which "international" are these Native artists engaged in? Native American art history, as Horton observes, has reinforced the naturalization of the settler state, containing Native American art (23–24). Horton seeks to subvert this containment by appealing to the international. In fact, Horton claims the USIA tours laid the groundwork for international Indigenous justice movements, placing Indigenous internationalism squarely in the Western-dominated framework of international humanist relations. Though "broken," this framework, according to Horton, is merely in need of rejuvenation (5). Numerous Native American and Indigenous studies scholars have critiqued recourse to this international as reproducing imperial and colonial formations. Further, Bandung claimed to be anticolonial and excluded Western nations due to their "racialism." The lack of reference to existing anticolonial versions of the international indicates that, for Horton, the U.S. is ultimately the horizon, the modernist, leaky container in which Native diplomacy operates.

Such Indigenous modernisms come at the expense of Native antagonism to the U.S. settler project. Horton writes, "My account appreciates the fraught nature of artists' positions vis-à-vis the federal government without reinforcing a limited political choice 'for' or 'against' the settler colonial nation" (13). This lack of oppositionality informs her analysis of Cold War deterrence, framed as a foil but one in which Native relations to U.S. settler capitalism are treated with nuance while Soviet communism remains a monolith. This ignores the relations that Native American resistance groups have had to revolutionary communism. The internationalism that Horton is interested in, through her concept of earth diplomacy, as a neutral, nonviolent third way, is grounded in a Western liberal perceptual tradition. It is one more akin to recognition-based human rights frameworks than decolonial and revolutionary notions of an internationalism of the people, hence the emphasis on diplomacy.

While the stories, artwork, and contexts that Horton addresses are important (and many of her readings are exceptional), the book suffers from a lack of material and power analysis. The contradiction between U.S. termination policy and the promotion of Native art abroad, for instance, is never analyzed but noted as an historical fact. This disconnect between propaganda and material reality is a basic contradiction, turning the uprooted art into ideology: reconciliation. Horton, however, brackets critiques of U.S. hegemony, and the radically unequal power relations it creates between colonized and colonizer, in the name of "mutual legibility and exchange" (250). She claims that the Native artists she discusses undermined the U.S. propaganda project by rejuvenating a failed international diplomacy, injecting it with Indigenous cosmological thought. But does this cohere with reality? If not, what are the effects of making this argument?

The main effect is not a rejuvenation of international diplomacy but of art history as an ideological state apparatus, a field defined by a white fantasy of participation in Native authenticity. It is the oldest of settler desires, challenged only by the desire to replace. Are the aesthetic elasticity and political flexibility of Indigenous modernisms and earth diplomacy a new turn in this desire?

MARK MINCH-DE LEON is associate professor of English and co-director of the California Center for Native Nations at the University of California, Riverside.

DAVID MEDINA

Inscribing Sovereignties: Writing Community in Native North America
by Phillip H. Round
University of North Carolina Press, 2024

PHILLIP ROUND'S NEW MONOGRAPH, *Inscribing Sovereignties: Writing Community in Native North America,* centers Indigenous *graphogenesis,* or the creation of graphic systems for languages whose speakers had not previously needed or desired them. Round reminds us that from the Wabanaki of the eastern woodlands to the Wakashan of the Pacific Northwest, Indigenous Peoples across North America have historically utilized complex forms of media alongside oral traditions. Indeed, of the more than five hundred federally recognized nations connected to lands appropriated by the settler-colonial project known as the United States, not a single group has relied solely on oral tradition. Despite this, the myth persists that Indigenous groups were solely oral and later "converted" to alphabetic literacy by abandoning traditional modes of communication. Round's work shows how Indigenous Peoples translated their spoken languages, oral traditions, and material culture into Western alphabetic forms and, crucially, back out of them in ways that resisted assimilation and cultural erasure. By developing vernacular scripts or adopting orthographies from other Indigenous groups, Round demonstrates how Native authors sought both visibility in the settler public sphere and control over how their histories and futures were represented. Building on earlier work such as *Removable Type* (2010), Round offers a more nuanced account of how Indigenous Peoples used alphabeticism not to replace traditional practices but to supplement them—strategically engaging settler print culture to assert cultural sovereignty.

Following an introductory chapter that traces the arrival of alphabeticism in Indian Country, Round offers a series of compelling case studies centered on the creation or adoption of Indigenous writing, often in the vernacular. Focusing on three distinct language families—Iroquoian, Siouan, and Central Algonquian—each chapter explores "the myriad possibilities vernacular alphabetic literacy offered to Native communities suffering from diaspora, disenfranchisement, and dispossession" (80). While one might critique Round's decision to group together such linguistically and culturally diverse nations—each facing its own historical and political challenges—the work ultimately presents a persuasive picture of the shared strategies through which Indigenous Peoples used alphabetic and visual systems to sustain what Round calls "interlocutive communities" (34). Each chapter is grounded by this robust theoretical framework and rethinks the social, cultural, and political contexts surrounding the invention and adaptation of Indigenous scripts.

The first two chapters situate vernacular writing not as a break with tradition but as part of a broader continuum of Indigenous graphic representation. Haudenosaunee wampum belts, Ojibwe birch bark scrolls, and Lakota *waniyetu iyawapi* (winter counts), he argues, were dynamically supplemented by alphabetic writing—not replaced. The comparative framework allows Round to recast nineteenth-century Indigenous writing as both a progressive engagement with new communicative technologies and a conservative gesture aimed at preserving core social and religious practices (81). Round also presents readers with an impressive range of Indigenous material texts. The sheer diversity of these texts and bibliographic objects is perhaps the work's greatest strength. The result is a necessary reorientation of Indigenous script, one that emphasizes sovereignty not only as a political status but also as material, intellectual, and semiotic acts.

In chapter 2, Round explores how Haudenosaunee communities incorporated alphabetic script into their existing media systems and ceremonial protocols, including the condolence ceremony. Rather than displacing traditional practices, Round shows how Indigenous script was deployed as a supplement. Here and in each chapter that follows, Round makes clear that the uptake of writing was never wholesale adoption, but a situated and strategic act of cultural persistence.

One of the most compelling illustrations of how Indigenous script sustains interlocutive communities appears in the analysis of Lakota visionary Black Elk's engagement with alphabetic literacy. In a letter expressing sincere happiness at encountering Lakota rendered in alphabetic form, Black Elk becomes, for Round, a case study in strategic adaptation in a time of upheaval (134). This chapter succinctly demonstrates how hybrid systems of communication—oral, visual, and alphabetic—were mobilized to stabilize Lakota social order during periods of profound colonial disruption.

The following chapter turns to the Anishinaabe Waki peoples of the Great Lakes region, with a focus on how language itself is often best understood as "an organic outgrowth of Indigenous homelands" (220). Through a case study on the creation of the Great Lakes syllabary—used by groups such as the Ho-Chunk—Round further demonstrates that Indigenous scripts were not merely mnemonic tools or salvaged ethnographic artifacts. Rather, they functioned as living technologies that enabled dynamic forms of cultural continuity. A compelling case is made in this chapter that writing in vernacular script can function as a means of fostering social practices that not only bridge spatial and temporal divides but also sustain intergenerational knowledge transfer.

Concise, conscientious, and well-researched, *Inscribing Sovereignties* will interest scholars of Indigenous literature and culture, nineteenth-century book history, and Indigenous mediascapes. In tracing how Native communities adopted, adapted, and invented scripts to meet their evolving social, political, and ceremonial needs, Round's work offers a vital framework for future comparative studies of Indigenous graphic traditions across the Americas and beyond.

DAVID MEDINA is assistant professor of U.S. Indigenous studies and early American literature at Florida Atlantic University.

NICK ESTES

My Grandfathers Alter: Five Generations of Lakota Holy Men
by Richard Moves Camp, edited by Simon J. Joseph
University of Nebraska Press, 2024

AS-TOLD-TO BIOGRAPHIES of medicine men have become a subgenre defined and proliferated mainly by white interlocutors. The most famous of these is *Black Elk Speaks.* Subsequent studies have cast a critical eye on these accounts, questioning the genre's authenticity. Richard Moves Camp's *My Grandfather's Alter: Five Generations of Lakota Holy Men,* edited by religious studies scholar Simon J. Joseph, offers a different approach, perhaps sidestepping the genre's conventions entirely. Moves Camp fills the pages as the primary narrator; Joseph's guiding hand in the project is detailed in a brief introduction and lengthy footnotes describing his positionality. The book, as memoir and biography, provides a profoundly intimate and human portrayal of a prominent family of Lakota medicine men—their faults, trials, powers, and, most importantly, the life lessons Moves Camp hopes to impart to a younger generation.

"We were invisible people in the last century," Moves Camp asserts as he describes Lakota spiritual life (7). His narrative encompasses the transition to the reservation period in the late nineteenth century, which forced Lakota ceremonies underground, to the rebirth of Lakota spirituality in the latter half of the twentieth century, which revived public practices such as the sun dance. Central to his telling is the power of Wóptuȟ'a, the holy man who provided Crazy Horse with his protection medicines and Moves Camp's great-great-grandfather. His great-grandfathers James Tȟahúŋska Moves Camp and Horn Chips kept alive Lakota ceremonies in the early reservation years while also adding new dimensions to the tradition. Moves Camp credits Tȟahúŋska as "the original founder" of the powerful Yuwípi healing ceremony, which he learned from Holy Arrow and later taught to his brother Horn Chips (80). Even at a time when Lakota ceremonies were outlawed, punishable by imprisonment or withholding rations, Moves Camp shows that spiritual life continued to evolve and grow, taking on new practices and altering old ones, and, in some cases, under the burden of Christianization, doing away with some old ways entirely. Despite the weight of colonialism, Lakota holy men kept alive that connection to the spiritual realm.

The figure central to Moves Camp's spiritual journey was his grandfather, Hóchoka Tópa, known as Samuel Chips Moves Camp, from whom he received his ceremonial altar. "I don't know if there's [*sic*] any other people in this world that have that connection [to the spiritual realm] like my grandpa," Moves Camp concludes (178). Grandpa Sam becomes an archetype of a great generation of Lakota holy men. Despite the suffering on the Pine Ridge reservation and the suppression of Lakota spirituality and culture during the first half of the twentieth century, Moves Camp holds up this period as the reservation's spiritual halcyon days. He recalls that even white ranchers from surrounding communities participated in Lakota ceremonies, some learning the Lakota language. The book's final chapter deals with the increasing disruption of Lakota spiritual life through drugs, alcohol, and Christianity in the latter half of the twentieth century.

The stories throughout the book weave back and forth in time, centering the lives of Moves Camp's ancestors while offering rare perspectives on Lakota views of the spiritual cosmos. This knowledge system extends beyond this plane of existence. It includes other-than-human characters, such as spiritual helpers who assist medicine men in performing healing ceremonies and the pantheon of spiritual beings, from human ghosts to those who have never walked this plane of existence. These are multilayered modes of existence where life and death are not absolutes, and the distinctions between humans and animals are blurred.

The book is written in a way that captures the power of Moves Camp as a skilled orator. It is conversational, translating the esoteric spiritual world of the Lakota language into the imperfect medium of English and the written word. His recollections are earnest and, at times, humorous and humbling. Yet, at the heart of his narrative is a human story of tragedy, sacrifice, and humility in the face of losing the world we once lived in as Lakotas. This world lives on through the lives of our revered spiritual leaders who safeguarded those relations with our ancestors and the other worlds. Moves Camp is clear that this book is for young Lakota people interested in the spiritual traditions of our medicine people (he only briefly mentions women's roles). There is also a rich Lakota vernacular of concepts, places, people, practices, and experiences, the nuances of which may be lost on some readers. Moves Camp's outstanding achievement, however, is showing the universal power of Lakota spirituality while maintaining an abiding respect and reverence for the particularities and uniqueness of its practice among its gifted interpreters and practitioners.

NICK ESTES (Lower Brule Sioux Tribe) is associate professor of American Indian studies at the University of Minnesota.

JEFFREY P. SHEPHERD

What Side Are You On? A Tohono O'odham Life Across Borders
by Michael Steven Wilson and José Antonio Lucero

WHEN I FIRST MET Mike Wilson nearly two decades ago, I thought he was a fascinating and inspiring individual, mainly for his humanitarian work providing water for migrants crossing the border in the Sonoran Desert. We occasionally talked over email, and I brought him to speak at my university, which is situated along the U.S.—Mexico border and serves a community impacted by many of the issues covered in this innovative book. Over the years I watched him help migrants, struggle with the border patrol, and navigate the politics of the Tohono O'odham Nation as the Nation itself grappled with immense geopolitical pressures. I had long thought that Mike needed to write an autobiography, so I was excited to read this creative collaboration between Wilson and José Antonio Lucero. The result is a wonderful book that teaches us a lot about borders, Indigeneity, identity, faith, sovereignty, and humanity.

There is a long history of "as told to stories" that reflect unequal power relations between Indigenous "informants" and scholars, but *What Side Are You On?* offers a remarkable model for cross-cultural collaboration and knowledge production. José Antonio Lucero, himself a *fronterizo* and professor of border studies, Indigenous studies, and global politics at the University of Washington, collaborated with Mike Wilson for over a decade to create what he and Wilson term a "hybrid form of testimonio" (5). Wilson and Lucero state that the "work represents a dialogue of different forms of knowledge," which is based in a methodology drawing upon oral history, Indigenous studies, transnational histories, autobiography, and critical self-reflection (6). This decolonizing approach yields an engaging account of Wilson's impressive life, which provides a window onto the transformation of the borderlands over the past four decades. Wilson and Lucero offer us an analysis of multiple forms of Indigeneity as they interact with several complex, sometimes contradictory borders and borderlands. As discussed in the book, the Tohono O'odham Nation runs along a large section of the U.S.-Mexico border, due to the intrusion of the boundary through their homelands, which extended deep into Sonora. Its southern border is also the international border, and this has created a series of interlocking conflicts between the U.S., Mexico, and the O'odham peoples because their homelands have been drawn into transnational debates about immigration, drug and human trafficking, and neoliberal reforms and boundary policies.

This micro and macro approach informs the entire book, which follows Wilson from his upbringing on the reservation and across southern Arizona, to his time in college, seminary, two decades in the Special Forces as an advisor in Central America, and ultimately to his transformation as a lay preacher who decides to place water in the desert for migrants as they enter the United States. In between chapters where Wilson narrates his life story, Lucero offers what he terms "interludes," which are analytical contributions that contextualize and expand on the issues Wilson covers in his chapters. Whereas Wilson walks us through his "non-traditional Tohono O'odham life," which includes much of the Western Hemisphere, Lucero interrogates the global, transnational, ideological, and even religious dimensions of the stories that Wilson shares. The balance between the granular detail of growing up in rural communities on the reservation and in Mexico, to the global analyses of neo-liberal economics, U.S. policy in Central America, and border militarization, generates a wonderfully rich collaboration of ideas and perspectives.

This book is unlike most collaborative projects I have encountered. Wilson has lived an amazingly complex, rich, and eventful life and his chapters lead readers across the borders and boundaries of nation-states, identities, and cultures. We are left with the distinct impression of a person who is deeply dedicated to human rights and the self-determination of his people, the O'odham, who have lived in the Sonoran Desert for millennia. Similarly, Lucero's insights as both a *fronterizo* and an intellectual help us grapple with the complex collision of U.S. imperialism, border policy, neoliberal reforms, and Indigenous sovereignty. He is truly committed to an equitable and ethical collaboration with Wilson, perhaps because he sees the inherent value of Wilson's impressive life story. Considering the inspiring story told in *What Side Are You On?* this book will be of tremendous interest to undergraduate and graduate students but also to a general public hoping to learn more about the struggles of Indigenous Peoples and border crossers everywhere.

JEFFREY P. SHEPHERD is professor of history at the University of Texas at El Paso.

KASEY KEELER

Michigan's Company K: Anishinaabe Soldiers, Citizenship, and the Civil War
by Michelle K. Cassidy

IN *MICHIGAN'S COMPANY K: Anishinaabe Soldiers, Citizenship, and the Civil War,* scholar Michelle K. Cassidy reframes a story of the Civil War, moving Anishinaabe peoples—Ojibwe, Ottawa, and Boodewaadamii—and their communities from the periphery to the center of the historical narrative. In doing so, Cassidy extends her analysis beyond military service to tell a more nuanced version of nineteenth-century history.

Central to Cassidy's detailed history of Anishinaabe participation in the Civil War are recurring themes of diplomacy, citizenship, land, and religion in the decades prior to and following the Civil War. While entangled with each other, these themes appear early in the monograph and are woven throughout, as Cassidy provides substantial context for Anishinaabe military participation, a decision that does not come easily for American Indians.

From beginning to end, Cassidy points to the ways diverse Anishinaabe tribal nations worked to navigate an ever-changing political and settler landscape and shifting relationships with multiple colonial powers—the French, the British, and, eventually, a young United States. While the monograph is focused on the political moment of the Civil War, Cassidy tells us how Anishinaabe in Michigan fought to protect and retain their land, again: prior to, during, and after the war leveraging military service.

Throughout *Michigan's Company K,* Cassidy consistently reminds the reader that before the Civil War unfolded, and in its aftermath, tribal nations across the United States faced profound land loss: first through treaties and then through allotment and processes like the Homestead Act. It was Anishinaabe people's deep relationship with the land that shaped the ways they viewed citizenship, both at the state and federal levels. During the nineteenth century, U.S. citizenship was murky for all American Indians, generally hinging on levels of perceived assimilation. As Cassidy unpacks the complexity of U.S. citizenship for American Indians, she provides important commentary on what was at stake for tribal members. When state and federal officials began recruiting and enlisting American Indians, it was not clear whether military service was dependent on U.S. citizenship or whether U.S. citizenship would follow military service. Despite this, Anishinaabe soldiers used their military service as a mechanism to advance conversations around not only citizenship but access to and protection of land. Yet, as Cassidy points out, there was no clear line between military service and citizenship and no clear line between military service and property ownership. Rather, the lines became even blurrier.

While Cassidy details the complexity of citizenship, she simultaneously narrates a story of Anishinaabe land. This is particularly poignant because, during the Civil War era, as American Indian people enlisted and served, they faced a constant threat of dispossession. Here, Cassidy powerfully speaks to how American Indian soldiers had to negotiate military service at the same time they faced removal, reservations, and assimilation. Anishinaabe who considered military service weighed citizenship alongside the ability to politically influence treaty making and the potential to enter into new treaties to protect and preserve land. Once the war ended, the attack on Indian land only became more powerful with dual policies of the Homestead Act and the Dawes General Allotment Act. In the war's aftermath, American Indian veterans continued to negotiate their identities as tribal members alongside their service to the United States, a nation-state that continued to racialize them.

Michelle K. Cassidy's *Michigan's Company K: Anishinaabe Soldiers, Citizenship, and the Civil War* brings together Native American and Indigenous studies and Civil War studies in a way that respects the difficult terrain tribal nations and individual tribal members were forced to navigate during the mid-nineteenth century in the Upper Great Lakes. This book tackles complex topics—like citizenship and Christianity—and presents them in an accessible way, providing a useful resource for teaching. At the same time, Cassidy highlights the importance of the land and the unwavering commitment of Anishinaabe to protect their land even in the face of assimilation and the violence of war.

KASEY KEELER (Tuolumne Me-Wuk/Citizen of the Potawatomi Nation) is associate professor in the School of Human Ecology and American Indian & Indigenous Studies at the University of Wisconsin, Madison.

CLIFFORD E. TRAFZER

Where We Belong: Chemehuevi and Caxcan Preservation of Sacred Mountains
by Daisy Ocampo

AT THE TIME OF ORIGINS, creators placed the Indigenous Peoples of the Native Universe in specific places, then gifted the First Peoples with their holy lands. Creators instructed the people to take care of the land and nurture the soil, waters, plants, and animals. The people enjoyed a spiritual bond with their landscapes and everything within their environments. In return, the land—and all encompassed within—cared for the people. This sacred bond was meant to last forever, but years of foreign invasions, wars, and colonialism created barriers between the people and their homelands. Colonial disruptions posed challenges and threats to spiritual relationships between Indigenous people and their homelands, but colonialism could not break the sovereign spiritual bond and cultural continuum. This is the essence of Ocampo's significant work, *Where We Belong,* which focuses on the desecration of the place of her people's creation and the preservation of a Chemehuevi landscape.

Ocampo offers a compelling historical narrative through a Native American lens and theory. She compares the modern treatment of Tlachialoyantepec, the place of creation for her Caxcan people of southern Zacatecas, Mexico, with Mamapukaib of the East Mojave Desert, a sacred mountain of the Nuwuvi or Chemehuevi people. The comparison offers dramatic differences and ancient similarities. In recent years, Instituto Nacional de Antropología e Historia (INAH) of Mexico has invaded, stolen, and desecrated Tlachialoyantepec, arrogantly preventing Caxcan people from visiting, nurturing, and interpreting their relationships with this place of creation: the mountain. In comparison, in 1998 a coalition of Native and non-Native people formed the Native American Land Conservancy and began a journey leading to the purchase of Mamapukaib, also known as the Old Woman Mountains. The NALC uses the range as a healing and learning landscape. Rather than excluding Indigenous people, the conservancy offers ceremonial and educational programs to teach people to tenderly nurture the fragile desert environment.

Ocampo, a professor history at California State University, San Bernardino, draws on the work of Native American writers and other scholars to offer new pathways into public history. She draws on community-based methods, content, and research that privileges Indigenous ways of knowing. She spent many hours recording, listening to, and learning from Caxcan and Chemehuevi people, which informs her book. Caxcan and Chemehuevi people often shared the shortcomings of governmental stewardship of Indigenous lands. Representatives of INAH have silenced, misrepresented, and dismissed Caxcan villagers, making them invisible. The Caxcan refuse to have their relationships with the land denied. As Ocampo makes clear, the people continue their ancient relationship with their place of creation, visiting the mountains and utilizing its resources. Similarly, Chemehuevi cultural leaders, including the Mike and Hanks-Leivas families, have led the preservation of their cultural landscapes along the Colorado River and the deserts beyond.

The Indigenous landscapes presented in *Where We Belong* offer many sites of prayer, ceremony, and reflection. The people continue their cultural relationship with their landscapes by showing respect for places and continuing songs, dances, and ceremonies. Places within their respective environments offer ways of knowing many elements of their cultures, especially the relationship of humans to seen and unseen elements of the earth, air, sky, sites, and spaces. Ocampo often refers to the *Xúchitl* Dance or flower dance of her Caxcan people. The dance pays homage to Xochipilli who was resurrected and returned to Caxcan people, a symbol of life represented by moisture, flora, especially flowers, and an abundance of fauna. Natural elements of the Caxcan landscape supports the health, wellness, and identity of the people.

In similar fashion, Ocampo explains Nuwuvi *Asi Haviavi* or Salt Songs, that the Wolf and Coyote placed in a cave called *Ting-i-ai* along the Bill Williams River. After *Hutsipamamau'u* or Ocean Woman used her body to create the earth, the first people lived and died at the Nuwuvi creation mountain of *Nivaganti* (Snow Having), where clouds gather, create moisture, and support life. Wolf and Coyote created *Nuva Kiav,* a pathway for deceased Nuwuvi to travel into the Milky Way. Nuwuvi sing Salt Songs at *Yaagaps* or wakes, sending souls across an expansive landscape to the stairway and on to the Milky Way. Ocampo uses the *Xúchitl* Dance and *Asi Haviavi* as her literary devices to address ancient but living landscapes. Caxcan and Chemehuevi conduct ceremonies as sovereign acts of cultural continuum. Government agencies are disconnected from the spirit and instead tell their own stories, denying Indigenous Peoples' deep relationships with their place. Ocampo's book privileges Caxcan and Chemehuevi people who inform readers and interpret their sacred landscapes.

CLIFFORD E. TRAFZER is distinguished professor of history at the University of California, Riverside.

ELLEN CUSHMAN

People of Kituwah: The Old Ways of the Eastern Cherokees
by John D. Loftin and Benjamin E. Frey
University of California Press, 2024

PEOPLE OF THE KITUWAH: *The Old Ways of the Eastern Cherokees* offers insights into the rich legacy of thought and lifeways that animate contemporary settings in and among the Eastern Cherokee. Coauthors John D. Loftin and Benjamin E. Frey locate themselves in relation to the Eastern Cherokees. Loftin is a historian of religions and a lawyer in North Carolina, and Benjamin E. Frey, a sociolinguist and enrolled citizen of the Eastern Band of Cherokee Indians, is assistant professor of Cherokee Language and Culture at the University of North Carolina, Asheville. The book illustrates the ways in which Eastern Cherokee actions adhere to the spiritual roots of the Kituwah people, which imbue every aspect of contemporary culture, history, language, ceremony, and relationship to land. The authors' professional and personal experiences enliven these pages, as does their judicious and well-illustrated use of the Cherokee language. Benjamin E. Frey, a well-regarded Cherokee sociolinguist, explains the Cherokee language as it's used in the book. The authors draw primarily on secondary sources to inform the argument. They add interesting experiences, stories, and examples of the Cherokee language to illustrate key points in the opening and closing chapters.

The book is organized into two parts, featuring ideas, stories, and insights into Kituwah ways before contact and after contact, covering a period from 1540 to the early twentieth century. "Part One. Before Contact" includes four chapters that focus on foundational concepts and practices as written in the Cherokee language. Chapter one features Eastern Cherokee Creation and Subsistence Narratives. Chapter two draws on Kituwah notions of community, clan, family, and death. Chapter 3 includes ceremonial rituals and practices that motivate Kituwah lifeways. Chapter 4 focuses on medicines, particularly drawing on Mooney's work with Swimmer, a prominent Eastern Cherokee healer. These chapters present, in broad strokes, several elemental structures of thought in early Cherokee cosmologies to set the scene for postcontact Cherokee life.

The chapters appearing in "Part Two. After Contact" provide a rough chronology of challenges Eastern Cherokees faced as they encountered economic, cultural, religious, and governmental impacts of colonialism. The chapters succinctly synthesize key sources as they trace settler colonial history and its impact among the Eastern Cherokee. Moving quickly from the "The Contact Era: 1540–1760" (chapter 5) to "Contact, Colonialism, and Christianity: 1725–1799" (chapter 6) then from "Christian Missions and the Ghost Dance: 1799–1815" (chapter 7) to "Missionaries and Medicine Men: 1815–1828" (chapter 8), the book follows Kituwah lifeways as they persisted and changed throughout key historical moments between 1540 and 1828.

In chapters 9 through 12, the authors consider Christianity's impact among the Kituwah, suggesting that Eastern Cherokee conversion to Christianity always remained consistent with Cherokee cosmologies. Chapter 9, "Cherokees, Christianity, and Myth: 1818–1830," revisits anthropological studies, census data, and stories from the *Cherokee Phoenix* to suggest that "the Cherokee nation in 1830 still consisted largely of traditionalists" and that "the synthesis of Christianity with Cherokee religion was tenuous at best" (154). Stories of Eastern Cherokee people's persistence offer grounded illustrations. The story of Tsali's life and death, told in chapter 10 ("Christianity and Cherokee Removal: 1831–1838"), "connects Cherokees to their traditional roots and values" and imparts a sacred story that occurs "in the undeniable context of American colonialism and conquest" (164). Chapter 11, "Cherokee Isolation, the Civil War, and Traditional Religion: 1839–1900," returns to the ethnographic record of Cherokees during the Civil War between 1839 and 1900. The authors note that "most of the archival material on the Cherokees was written by Europeans and Americans with a less than sympathetic eye toward Cherokee traditional religion and culture" (172). Moving into the Civil War years, the chapter ends with reference to census data from 1900, showing the number of men and women who could read in Cherokee to suggest how, despite centuries of forced contact, Cherokees still remained a separate people (178).

Chapter 12, "Cherokee Traditions in the Twentieth Century," and the epilogue offer insights into current language practices that illustrate Cherokee lifeways, drawing on the sociolinguistic expertise of Benjamin Frey as well as literature surveys of fieldwork with Cherokees. The Cherokee language examples offered in this chapter, as well as references to key Cherokee thinkers and scholars, offer contemporary insights into the ways that Eastern Cherokee maintain Kituwah lifeways.

People of the Kituwah offers a readable survey of secondary sources on the Eastern Cherokee and offers several starting points for further study. The authors measured their claims against Cherokee lifeways they experience and practice among the Eastern Cherokee. An approachable work for scholars interested in the history of the Eastern Cherokee, *People of Kituwah* provides many paths and resources to consider for further study.

ELLEN CUSHMAN (Citizen of Cherokee Nation) is Dean's Professor of Civic Sustainability and professor of English at Northeastern University.

AVERY VELEZ

One Man's Journey: The Mi'kmaw Revival in Ktaqmkuk
by Calvin White
Memorial University Press, 2023

THE HISTORY OF MI'KMAQ in Ktaqmkuk (Newfoundland) is as long as it is complex, interwoven with colonial mythologies and racist denials of our ancestral and ongoing presence on the island that have been falsely presented as fact for over two centuries (White 2023). This history needs to be unpacked, teased apart, and opened up to both academic scrutiny and community fact-checking. *One Man's Journey* is one of Calvin's many contributions to this much-needed work. The book recounts Calvin's memories of growing up in Flat Bay, learning to live off the land, and joining the movement of Mi'kmaw political advocacy in the early 1970s. Calvin shares his account of the evolutions of this advocacy, from early consultations with Mi'kmaw leaders in Nova Scotia to building the Federation of Newfoundland Indians (FNI) and finally to government negotiations that led to the development of the Qalipu First Nation, which was formed out of the amalgamation of various distinct bands, as an Indian Act band. Throughout his book, Calvin centers his lifelong relationships with the land and his community alongside his growing awareness of the impacts of Newfoundland and Labrador entering confederation in 1949.

In the early drafts of the 1949 Terms of Union, there were several references to Indigenous Peoples in the province that were "pencilled out" and excluded from the final version (Tompkins 1988; White 2023). *One Man's Journey* describes Calvin's efforts alongside many others to address this exclusion, working with anthropologists, genealogists, and communities across the island and elsewhere in Mi'kma'ki to understand and share the true story of Mi'kmaq in Ktaqmkuk. Calvin writes about exchanges with governments, persistence through fractures and divisions, and eventually, the development of a document called the 2002 Regime. Appended to *One Man's Journey* in full, the 2002 Regime was a proposal to the federal government developed by the FNI for the recognition of Mi'kmaw communities in Ktaqmkuk (White 2023). It proposed that a tribal council be created to empower the ten communities that were part of the FNI at the time; it had membership criteria, governance structures, and funding requests designed to preserve autonomy, invest in the longevity of Mi'kmaw communities in Ktaqmkuk, and respect relationships across Mi'kma'ki (White 2023, 147–61). It is difficult to tell what happened after the Regime was developed because as negotiations ramped up in the early 2000s, Calvin was no longer on the board of directors of the FNI (White 2023). Somehow, when the Agreement in Principle that created the Qalipu First Nation as a band was finalized in 2007, the 2002 Regime had been replaced with an agreement to create an amalgamated Indian Act band with dozens of communities organized under a ward system with no access to lands and resources and a fatally flawed membership registration process (Federation of Newfoundland Indians 2007; White 2023). This is the structure that many Mi'kmaq in Ktaqmkuk are living within—or excluded from—today.

One Man's Journey provides readers with the context and documentation needed to understand how Mi'kmaq in Ktaqmkuk got to where we are and, perhaps even more importantly, reminds us that this was not the only possible outcome. A "landless" band with chaotic membership requirements and relationships strained to the breaking point was not the inevitable outcome. We lived through over 450 years of colonialism from first contact to confederation. And although Calvin and the movement builders he worked alongside made great strides in achieving recognition for our people in the years since then, it will take more than one lifetime to fully understand and begin to address the impacts of settler colonialism. Calvin finishes his bout of storytelling with a reminder that if we are sincere and honest, if we focus on self-reflection and community empowerment, and if we receive and share stories in a good way, then Mi'kmaq in Ktaqmkuk can "continue to reclaim [our] roots in the land that [we have] called home for generations" (White 2023, 118). Calvin reminds us that this is not only a possibility but also our responsibility. This review has been part of my ongoing effort to honor and enact this responsibility.

AVERY VELEZ (mixed Mi'kmaw and Portuguese) is a PhD student at Memorial University of Newfoundland, Grenfell Campus.

References

Federation of Newfoundland Indians. 2007. *Agreement for the Recognition of the Qalipu Mi'kmaq Band.* Qalipu Mi'kmaq First Nation. https://qalipu.ca/qalipu/wp-content/uploads/2016/02/2011sept-Agreement-In-Principle.pdf.

Tompkins, Edward. 1988. *Pencilled Out: Newfoundland and Labrador's Native People and Canadian Confederation, 1947–1954.* House of Commons.

White, Calvin. 2023. *One Man's Journey: The Mi'kmaw Revival in Ktaqmkuk.* Memorial University Press.

NEW FROM UNC PRESS

SPIRITS OF EMPIRE
How Settler Colonialism Made American Religion
Tisa Wenger

"Wenger's lively study has the potential to recharge and reorient American religious history. This book gives a rich documentary account of the entanglements between secularism and settler colonialism."
—**Tracy Fessenden**, Arizona State University
368 pages $34.95

THE ANCIENT HOUSE
Constructing Community in the Seventeenth-Century New York Borderlands
Erin B. Kramer

"A welcoming and interesting look into the Mohawk, Iroquois, and Dutch histories of the region of upstate New York."
—**Eugene Tesdahl**, University of Wisconsin, Plattsville
224 pages $27.95 paper

HISTORIES IN COMMON
Native American Literatures, Extra Archives, and the Indigenous Transpacific
Alyssa A. Hunziker

"A timely contribution to the growing body of scholarship attendant to the intimacies, contestations, and affinities between Pacific and Turtle Island peoples who continue to live under US occupation. The richness of Hunziker's scholarship is balanced with prose that is crisp and eminently readable."
—**Kathryn Walkiewicz** (Cherokee Nation), UC San Diego
232 pages $39.95 paper

PERILOUS WATERS
Settlers, Swamps, and the State, 1775–1920
Anthony E. Carlson

"A particularly prescient history of wetlands, swamps, and other watery landscapes in early America as historians and the public grapple with the intertwined questions of environmental justice, Indigenous dispossession, and settler colonial capitalism in the era of human-induced climate threats."
—**John William Nelson**, author of *Muddy Ground*
288 pages $29.95 paper

WAGING SOVEREIGNTY
Native Americans and the Transformation of Work in the Twentieth Century
Colleen O'Neill

"O'Neill skillfully demonstrates how tribes and Native workers turned away from the language of rights-based liberalism, instead embracing tribal sovereignty to protect their interests as workers and managers."
—**Kevin Whalen**, author of *Native Students at Work*
240 pages $29.95 paper

THE POWER TO HARM AND HEAL
Intercultural Medicine in Modern Mexico
Joshua Mentanko

"A novel and compelling history of traditional medicine in Mexico that centers and critically evaluates Indigenous agency in histories of development, science and medicine, and the Global South."
—**Sarah Foss**, Oklahoma State University
256 pages $37.50 paper

IRRECONCILABLE
Indigeneity and the Violence of Colonial Erasure in Contemporary Canada
Joseph Weiss

"A powerful study that reveals the anti-Indigenous violence of reconciliation politics in Canada. Sparkles with theoretical acuity and clarity."
—**Audra Simpson**, author of *Mohawk Interruptus: Political Life Across the Borders of Settler States*
240 pages $29.95 paper

THE AGE OF THE BORDERLANDS
Indians, Slaves, and the Limits of Manifest Destiny, 1790–1850
Andrew C. Isenberg

"With talent and insight, Isenberg tells surprising new stories of cultural encounters and western settlement. As a result of this important and compelling book, readers will see the West in new ways."
—**Alan Taylor**, author of *American Civil Wars*
296 pages $35.00

N|C THE UNIVERSITY OF NORTH CAROLINA PRESS
at bookstores or 800-848-6224 • uncpress.org • uncpressblog.com